10/98

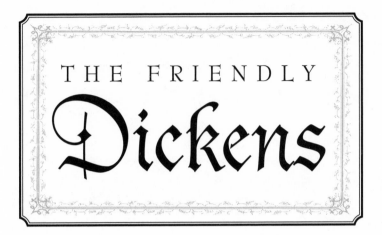

THE FRIENDLY

Dickens

Also by Norrie Epstein

The Friendly Shakespeare

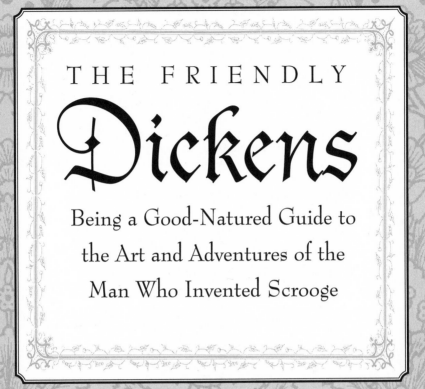

THE FRIENDLY

Dickens

Being a Good-Natured Guide to
the Art and Adventures of the
Man Who Invented Scrooge

❧ *Norrie Epstein* ❧

A WINOKUR/BOATES BOOK
VIKING

VIKING
Published by the Penguin Group
Penguin Putnam Inc., 375 Hudson Street,
New York, New York 10014, U.S.A.
Penguin Books Ltd, 27 Wrights Lane,
London W8 5TZ, England
Penguin Books Australia Ltd, Ringwood,
Victoria, Australia
Penguin Books Canada Ltd, 10 Alcorn Avenue,
Toronto, Ontario, Canada M4V 3B2
Penguin Books (N.Z.) Ltd, 182-190 Wairau Road,
Auckland 10, New Zealand
Penguin India, 210 Chiranjiv Tower, 43 Nehru Place,
New Delhi 11009, India

Penguin Books Ltd, Registered Offices:
Harmondsworth, Middlesex, England

First published in 1998 by Viking Penguin,
a member of Penguin Putnam Inc.

1 3 5 7 9 10 8 6 4 2

A Winokur/Boates Book

Illustration credits appear on page 428.

LIBRARY OF CONGRESS CATALOGING IN PUBLICATION DATA
Epstein, Norrie.
The friendly Dickens : being a good-natured guide to the art and adventures
of the man who invented Scrooge / Norrie Epstein.
p. cm.
Includes bibliographical references and index.
Filmography: p.
ISBN 0–670–83943–4 (alk. paper)
1. Dickens, Charles, 1812–1870. 2. Novelists, English—19th century—Biography. I. Title.
PR4581.E67 1998
823'.8—dc21   98–21320
[B]

This book is printed on acid-free paper.

∞

Printed in the United States of America
Set in Century Old Style
Designed by Jessica Shatan

In memory of my teacher,
George H. Ford

No one thinks first of Mr. Dickens as a writer.
He is at once, through his books, a friend.
—GEORGE ORWELL

If you could make the public understand that my father was not a
jolly, jocose gentleman walking about the earth with a plum
pudding and a bowl of punch you would greatly oblige me.
—KATE DICKENS PERUGINI,
in a letter to George Bernard Shaw

Acknowledgments

I n writing this book I've accumulated an almost Dickensian list of obligations. My greatest obligation is to generations of biographers and scholars whose work made mine possible. I am deeply grateful to my interview subjects for their time and enthusiasm, and to all those people—practically strangers—who loved Dickens enough to send me assorted clippings, articles, and photographs. I also had expert help from great Dickensians: the late biographer Edgar Johnson and his son Larry, Cedric Dickens, William Palmer, Alan S. Watts of the Dickens Fellowship, Andrew Xavier and David Parker of the Dickens House Museum, and the members of the Philadelphia branch of the Dickens Fellowship, especially Martha Rosso, editor of the *Buzfuz Bulletin*.

I would also like to thank those scholars and friends who have helped in ways too numerous to mention: Tony Church, Dave Donovan, Judith Green, Cyrus Hoy, Barbara and Henry Epstein, Norman Kiell, Alisa Kramer, Tom Kavanagh, Cate Olson, John Mcintyre, Stan Osher, Martha, Joel, Katharine, Caroline, Meredith, and Mariana Pierce, Nash Robbins, Judy Rousuck, and Elinor Winokur. I am especially indebted to Pam Dorman, Beena Kamlani, and Kristine Puopolo at Viking for their help in preparing the manuscript, Gillian Speeth, whose ingenuity helped me get the right pictures for the book, and Stephen Wigler who remains "ever the best of friends."

Finally, I'd like to thank the two people who made this book possible: Reid Boates, who belies all the horror stories one hears about agents, and Jon Winokur, whose wisdom, kindness, and good sense carried me through this daunting project.

Contents

🐾 EARLY LIFE 🐾

🐾 INTERREGNUM 🐾

❧ MIDDLE YEARS ❧

🍀 FINAL YEARS 🍀

Introduction

·永·

My earliest impression of the nature of reading, to paraphrase David Copperfield, was of a long row of maroon books with gilded letters stamped on their spines. Later, as I learned to read, I pieced out the words: *The Pickwick Papers, Dombey and Son, Bleak House, Hard Times, Great Expectations,* and my favorite, *Our Mutual Friend.*

Like messages from another world, they meant nothing, yet somehow evoked everything, and they made me want to know what was inside them. From an early age, my pleasure in reading was linked with the name Charles Dickens. Our family's set had originally belonged to my great-great-grandfather, making me part of a tradition that I came to think of as "Discovering Dickens." *The Complete Dickens* was once a household fixture, alongside the Bible and Shakespeare—the former for edification, the latter for culture. But Dickens was simply for fun. Sometimes I think my generation is the last to have grown up with Dickens, the last who will wonder at those evocative titles.

At the centennial celebration of *Pickwick* in 1936, the chairman of the Dickens Fellowship lamented that there was no one left who remembered Dickens alive. As we enter the second millennium, are we in danger of forgetting him completely? As his world recedes further into the past, will his vocabulary, humor, and characters seem as archaic as Shakespeare's?

Yet whether we've read him or not, we still feel we know him. There's the Dickens of *Oliver!, Nicholas Nickleby,* and *A Christmas Carol.* His name alone summons a cluster of rich images and unforgettable catchphrases:

Christmas, orphans, clerks, Tiny Tim, "God bless us, everyone," "Something will turn up," and "It is a far, far better thing . . ." We readily apply the adjective *Dickensian* to anything outmoded, gnarled, queer, or impoverished. Of all the great writers, Dickens is the most beloved. We feel comfortable with him in a way we never can with, say, Proust, or Tolstoy, or Henry James. His genius speaks *to* us, not *at* us. If we don't like Milton or Shakespeare, we blame ourselves; if we don't like Dickens, we blame him.

In short, Dickens is our mutual friend. Despite his association with all things English, our friendship transcends time and place and crosses racial, cultural, social, and political barriers. The best-selling novelist in Russia is neither Tolstoy nor Dostoyevsky, but Dickens. Several African-American novelists have acknowledged their debt to Dickens as a compassionate voice for those who have none. And although Dickens savaged the English, their institutions and customs, his countrymen embrace his vitriol as if it were praise.

The idea of making Dickens user-friendly must seem like another instance of "dumbing down," for if any novelist is approachable, it's Dickens. Witness the extraordinary popularity of *Oliver!, Nicholas Nickleby,* and the annual frolic of *Carol*s. Yet such accessibility can be misleading. There are many Dickenses, layers upon layers of them, and most of us have taken the surface one for the only truth.

There is no monolithic interpretation of Dickens. Just as we neatly divide his fourteen and a half novels into "early" and "late," so we bifurcate his personality into the dark and the light. Is he tormented genius or benevolent moralist? Both? Neither? Throughout this century our view of him has changed as revelations about his character—his liaison with his mistress Ellen Ternan, his treatment of his wife, his indifference to fatherhood, and his hunger for applause—have emerged. The uproar that greets each disclosure reflects the public's need to see Charles Dickens as a Dickens character, the Good Man, much like his own Mr. Cheeryble, rather than the complex, fully rounded character he was.

In this post-Freudian age, traits and activities that the Victorians would have unhesitatingly accepted are subject to intense scrutiny. Without examining the larger historical context, scholars probe Dickens's fascination with prostitutes and with the death of children, and his secrecy about his own childhood misery. Today we tend to look less toward the psyche and more to brain chemistry: Dickens is now diagnosed as manic-depressive or, to use the even more fashionable term, bipolar.

Naturally, this changes the way we read the novels. I am not interested in biographical criticism, nor do I care to turn the sunny Mr. Pickwick into an anguished idealist like Dostoyevsky's Prince Myshkin. *Pickwick* is still a literary idyll, and *Nicholas Nickleby* remains one of the funniest novels in the language. But knowing the man behind the words does change their significance. Of course Dickens's novels are all examples of terrific storytelling; but they are also more profound, enlightening, and at times unsettling than many of us have been led to believe.

Ultimately Dickens and his novels evade definition: labels, diagnoses, and theories rein in a man of almost radioactive intensity, transforming him into a disease or a bundle of motives and responses. The difficulty in defining Dickens lies in his own singularity—his self-appointed epithet "The Inimitable" is not hyperbole. There is simply no one who could possibly compare with him today. His death in 1870 left a void that has never been filled.

The Friendly Dickens is not a pathobiography that will disclose the "real" man behind the mask of Father Christmas but an attempt to reveal some of the contradictions and nuances of the man and the novels. Hence its title, which refers not only to our feelings for Dickens—and his toward us—but to my desire to make a complex figure more understandable and, yes, friendly.

All quotations from Dickens's novels are from the Penguin Classics editions.

—N. E.
September 1998

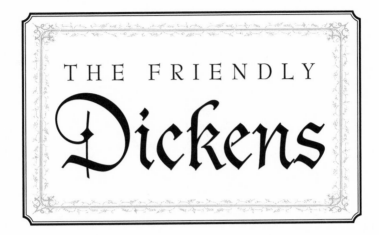

THE FRIENDLY

Dickens

On Dickens

*T*here is everything in Dickens.
—JULES VERNE

*I*n literary matters my dividing line is: Do you like Dickens or do you not?
If you do not, I am sorry for you and that is an end of the matter.
—STANLEY BALDWIN, speech, *Spectator* Centenary, October 30, 1928

*T*he operation of flogging a dead horse is always popular and is
very congenial in Rhetoricians. Dickens was careful to
castigate abuses that were being reformed.
—W. R. INGE, *The End of an Age*

*D*ickens was not the first or the last to find virtue
more difficult to portray than the wish for it.
—V. S. PRITCHETT, *Books in General*

It has often been said of Charles Dickens (not quite accurately, by the way) that though he created scores of immortal characters, there was not a gentleman among the lot.
—ALEXANDER WOOLLCOTT, *While Rome Burns*

*Charles Dickens
Could find nothing to say to chickens,
But gossiping with rabbits
Became one of his habits.*
—W. H. AUDEN, "Academic Graffiti"

How true to nature, even to their most trivial details, almost every character and every incident in the works of the great novelist . . . really were. . . . But none, except medical men, can judge of the rare fidelity with which he followed the great Mother through the devious paths of disease and death. In reading Oliver Twist *and* Dombey and Son, *or* The Chimes, *or even* No Throughfare, *the physician often felt tempted to say, "What a gain it would have been to physic if one so keen to observe and so facile to describe had devoted his powers to the medical art."*
—British Medical Journal

Dickens's achievement was to create serious literary art out of pop material. . . . He also worked in a climate of Christian evangelism that allowed big unqualified moral gestures. Language and morality add dimensions to his cartoons and turn them into literature. We lack enthusiasm and are embarrassed by moral fervour and grandiloquence alike. That is why our attitude to Dickens is ambivalent—nostalgia mixed with distaste, nausée in the presence of the spreading chestnut tree.
—ANTHONY BURGESS, *Urgent Copy*

Dickens' people are nearly all flat. . . . Nearly everyone can be summed up in a sentence, and yet there is this wonderful feeling of human depth. . . . It is a conjuring trick; at any moment we may look at Mr Pickwick edgeways and find him no thicker than a gramophone record. But we never get the sideways view. . . . Those who dislike Dickens have an excellent case. He ought to be bad. He is actually one of our big writers, and his immense success with types suggests that there may be more in flatness than the severer critics admit.
—E. M. FORSTER, *Aspects of the Novel*

While reading him I have the impression that I am contemplating one of Fra Angelico's Last Judgements *where you have the redeemed, the damned and the indeterminate (not too numerous!) over whom angel and demon struggle. The balance that weighs them all, as in an Egyptian bas-relief, reckons only the positive or negative quality of their virtue. Heaven for the just: for the wicked, Hell. Herein Dickens is true to the opinion of his countrymen and of his time.*
—ANDRÉ GIDE, *Dostoyevsky*

He violated every rule of art
Except the feeling mind and the thinking heart.
—JOHN MACY, *Couplets in Criticism*

[He is] deeper than all, if one has the eye to see deep enough, dark, fateful, silent elements, tragical to look upon, and hiding amid dazzling radiances as of the sun, the elements of death itself.
—THOMAS CARLYLE

Charles Dickens, whose books, though classed as novels and duly hampered with absurd plots which nobody ever remembers, are really extraordinarily vivid parables. All the political futility which has forced men of the calibre of Mussolini, Kemal, and Hitler to assume dictatorship might have been saved if people had only believed what Dickens told them in Little Dorrit.
—GEORGE BERNARD SHAW, *Introduction to Collected Prefaces*

If it were possible I would like to devote the fifty minutes of every class meeting to mute meditation, concentration, and admiration of Dickens.
—VLADIMIR NABOKOV

The enchanter-quality, the ability to keep people wanting more, it's not something which can be taught, and often it is associated with what critics call a "bad literary style," but it is irresistible. Dickens had it. Nobody praises Dickens's style, but who can resist his enchantment? Only professors, and only some of those.
—ROBERTSON DAVIES

Dickens was a "special correspondent for posterity."
—WALTER BAGEHOT

My mother read secondarily for information; she sank as a hedonist into novels. She read Dickens in the spirit in which she would have eloped with him.
—EUDORA WELTY

How to Read Dickens

❦ Take a Zen approach: the destination doesn't matter, it's the journey that counts. Savor each word; don't rush. And don't try to think logically! You are entering a different universe, where people are the same and yet not the same. And remember that truth is not always literal. (To paraphrase a Zen proverb: Before you read Dickens, a bowl is a bowl and tea is tea. While you are reading Dickens, a bowl is no longer a bowl and tea is no longer tea. After you've read Dickens, nothing is ever the same again.)

❦ Read like a child, i.e., allow yourself to slip into Dickens's world completely. Let go of the desire to "find out what happens." The plots are the least interesting parts of Dickens—the real pleasure is in the reading itself.

❦ If tempted to skip something that looks boring, and it's either skip it or not finish the book, skip it.

❦ Expect the author to make mistakes. He's not an impersonal god perfected by dozens of editors at a vast publishing empire. He wrote fast. He wrote to entertain.

❦ Expect inconsistency, and it won't exasperate you. For instance, don't bother about the fact that Dickens makes fun of Pecksniff's pious oracular apostrophes and then does the same thing himself when extolling Tom Pinch.

❦ Read out loud! Dickens spoke his characters' lines as he wrote.

❖ If one Dickens novel is not to your taste, try another. *A Tale of Two Cities,* often the only one we've read, is the least Dickensian of them all. Try *David Copperfield,* or if you want a shorter book, *Great Expectations.*

❖ If you've read a late Dickens novel (anything after *David Copperfield* or 1850) and hated it, try an earlier one. It's almost as if the two groups were written by different authors.

The First Time:
Memories of Dickens

🟊

or generations, reading Dickens was a rite of passage, something everyone did before they could consider themselves literate. With Shakespeare and the Bible, a complete set of Dickens
was a household fixture, and children grew up with intriguing
titles like *The Pickwick Papers, Great Expectations,* and *A Christmas Carol,*
which beckoned to be explored. Early memories of Dickens can evoke a
nostalgia associated with home itself.

For many, reading Dickens is still a transforming experience: fantastic situations and characters are revealed, opening a world that beggars the imagination. Suddenly one sees through a Dickensian lens, and everything appears
different, distorted, yet oddly the same. For some, the shock of a Dickens
novel can turn a life around: George Bernard Shaw claimed that *Little Dorrit*
made him a socialist; John Irving attributes his desire to write novels to *Great
Expectations.*

For imaginative, dreamy children, Dickens provides access to a world
unlike any other, doing for young writers what the great authors of the past
did for him. He shelters them from the mundane world, provides a model for
how to tell a story, and gives them friends for life; characters like David Copperfield, Pip, Oliver Twist, and Scrooge become lifelong frames of reference.

For others, the name Charles Dickens evokes memories of required reading and tests—textbooks, not novels. "Required Dickens" sounds almost
redundant; indeed, many contemporary students are surprised to discover
that people actually read Dickens for fun.

To potential young Dickensians, reading Dickens in school can elicit a

WHAT ADVICE WOULD YOU GIVE SOMEONE JUST STARTING TO READ DICKENS?

—⁓—

I'd certainly read *Great Expectations* rather than *A Tale of Two Cities,* which is always given to kids at the beginning. That's useless on a lot of levels, except for that common quote. The best story ever written is *A Christmas Carol.* And if we are talking about children who want to start loving Dickens, I can't imagine a better way. It's one of the cleverest stories, as well as one of the most moving ones. I would have liked to play with how many layers of meaning there are in this story.
—ROGER ROSENBLATT

—◆·◆·◆—

I think I'd probably suggest *Great Expectations.* It's short, it's accessible, and it's very very good all the way through.
—DAVID LODGE

—◆·◆·◆—

vague sense of loss, a feeling that they're missing out on something wonderful and funny. Like a joke that requires explanation, the explicated Dickens loses much of its charm. Dickens himself, of course, would be appalled at the idea of his novels being forcibly ladled down the throats of schoolchildren like Mrs. Squeers's castor oil.

But Dickens, of course, is not just for children, and there is no right age to read him. Indeed, reading him as a child and as an adult are distinct experiences: he seems magically to write to all ages, so one can reread him and always discover something new.

*M*y *own first exposure to Dickens was having* David Copperfield *read to me by my mother when I was seven or eight. That single reading planted the book so firmly in my memory that I was able to pass university exams about it and discuss it in college seminars without ever perusing it again until I was thirty-six. . . . All the details remained absolutely as I had remembered them: Peggotty's red face, Little Em'ly's blue eyes, Steerforth's handsome good looks. Mr. Micawber's syntactical convolutions, and so on. But what I only saw for the first time during this adult reading was the way the novel is actually constructed around the idea of an adult re-encountering childhood memory. It was quite a disconcerting experience.*
—WENDY LESSER

—◆·◆·◆—

I was supposed to be delicate when I was a child, and I enjoyed and exaggerated my illnesses, with the special food and added attention. My mother used to read aloud to me. Scott rather bored me, and I was horribly embarrassed by the passages which she rendered in a rather good Scottish accent. But Dickens I loved. We would be both quite overcome with emotion in the sentimental scenes, and by the time we had killed Dora or Sydney Carton we would both be choking and "too full of woe to speak!"
—JOHN GIELGUD

I can remember a Sunday School prize . . . when I was about 11 years old. I won a copy of David Copperfield. *Up to that time I'd read the Bobbsey Twins and then Tom Swift and the Rover Boys and Tarzan, but since I got this as a prize, I decided I should read it. I found a world that was realer than the world I lived in, unlike these Tarzan and other books. This was a whole other world, and it was a world of art. I couldn't have defined it as that, but, one thing, I knew David Copperfield better than anybody I knew in the real world, including myself. I said, "My God," to myself, "this is a whole world." I didn't then read Dickens or start becoming a serious reader until three or four years later, but I remember vividly having that reaction to that book* David Copperfield. *I think most writers probably have that experience.*
—SHELBY FOOTE

For a writer, the first experience with Dickens is a dazzling entry into Novels with a capital N, a transition between short, limited children's stories and the longer works of adult fiction. People who read usually love Dickens simply because the magic of reading him captures all the old pleasures of childhood reading. For one thing, he gives us a story—all too rare today, and for anyone who loves words, his books are a linguistic banquet. When I first read Oliver Twist, *in my own childhood, I did not know that Sikes's lover Nancy was a prostitute; and it is safe to bet that Queen Victoria, enthusiastically following the novel as it appeared in serial numbers, did not realize that Fagin was a pederast.*
—GARRY WILLS

The first thing I remember my mother reading to me deeply influenced my life. It was Bleak House *by Charles Dickens, a tremendous book about a terrible law case and the people involved in it. My father was a Chancery Lawyer, and I don't know whether my mother realized it, but the reading of it to me made one thing quite sure: I would never become a lawyer.*
—RICHARD CROSSMAN, British government minister

Being taught by the Christian Brothers can be, and I speak from experience, something of an education. When I was about four, my parents had emigrated to Cape Town and there, on the side of the hill, rose the handsome brick college where I was to be educated.

It was not inappropriate that I should be there during the war years of 1939–45. More than one of the Brothers was prone to unexpected attacks of violence. Ear- and hair-pulling, rapping the knuckles or buffeting the head suddenly from behind, were methods used frequently to emphasise points, while the "strap," a sinister black weapon in layered leather, was employed for punishment. We were beaten fairly regularly and fairly savagely. It was, in retrospect, something of a Dickensian world. Hardly surprising, then, that when benign old Brother Enright, with his silver hair and gold-rimmed spectacles, hitched his left buttock on to the corner of his desk and began to read Great Expectations *to us, we relaxed for once and listened to what he was saying. The gloomy Victorian landscape which Dickens had painted, with its forbidding marshes, gibbets, village blacksmiths and crowded churchyards, was unfamiliar territory, though, of course, we were sympathetic to Mrs. Joe's assertion that Pip had been brought up "by hand," for indeed so had we, the Brothers being, like her, all too frequently "on the Rampage."*

What a world it was, though, to which the saintly Brother Enright introduced me. Mr. Wemmick, Mr. Wopsle, Uncle Pumblechook, Old Orlick, cobwebbed Miss Havisham in her yellowing shroud of a wedding dress and everyone nodding away like mad at the Aged P. I was hooked.

Bleak House *was next, then* David Copperfield, A Tale of Two Cities, Nicholas Nickleby. *I was off on a marathon. I even read on the bus to and from school. "Serve you damn well right!" said my dad when I told him I'd have to wear glasses in the future, but I didn't care. This was my magic world and into it I could retreat. God bless you, gentle Brother Enright, for so elegantly pointing the way. And God bless you, dear old Pip, old chap.*

—NIGEL HAWTHORNE

WHY READ THE VICTORIAN NOVEL?
INTERVIEW WITH PHYLLIS ROSE

—⟋⟍—

NE: *Why should we read the nineteenth-century novel today?*

PR: I still think that the models of society constructed in the nineteenth-century novel are the most complete, the most convincing, and the most absorbing. In the last hundred years the novel has gotten narrower and narrower, and it's a very rare novel now that tries to construct a model as complicated as the Victorian novel. In the nineteenth-century novel there is a community; you know the backgrounds of its people, and you know everyone's status, you know what they wear and what they have in their houses. And that kind of complicated re-production of reality is very unusual today. I want to get away from my own life and yet read about a situation that illuminates my own. It's satisfying to live in another community for a while, whether in space, as in California, or in time, as in nineteenth-century England. It almost doesn't matter.

NE: *How would you define the "Dickensian" novel?*

PR: It's a novel that aims at a picture of society rather than of a small family, or one or two people. It generally means that the author deals with character types rather than fully realized characters. And they tend to be funny, almost carica-tures. The book works through caricature rather than characterization. And again, I don't think you can say it too many times, this is not a limitation; it's just a different type of fiction, and it's a way we have lost. We don't understand it anymore. To praise a novel today, you have to say that the characters are deep. That is so limiting.

EARLY
Life

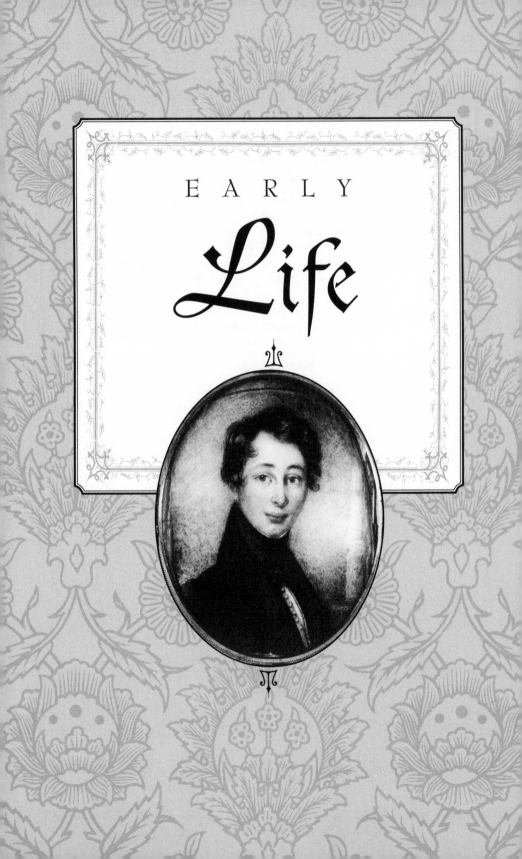

John and Elizabeth Dickens

❧

🍩 On the night of February 6, 1812, Elizabeth Dickens (née Barrow) went dancing. Which would not be remarkable, except that a few hours after she returned home, she gave birth to a son, christened Charles John Huffam Dickens. Even impending childbirth could not stop Elizabeth from pleasure-seeking. As her son would discover, she took her maternal duties lightly.

Since 1805 the author's father, John Dickens, had been a clerk in the Navy Pay Office in Somerset House, London, where his job was to allocate money for sea voyages. He met the sixteen-year-old Elizabeth through her brother, Thomas Culliford Barrow, a fellow employee at the pay office. Their father was Charles Barrow, a former music teacher who had rapidly risen from clerk in the same office to chief inspector of monies in the town, a position that entailed sending large sums of money under armed guard to various seaports.

Elizabeth's background was genteel: she was well educated—rare for a young woman of the time—and her father, a trusted civil servant and a member of the gentry, earned more than 350 pounds a year—the modern equivalent of about $80,000. Her fiancé was marrying up; his clerk's position was only a short step from that of his parents, both of whom were in service on the estate of Lord Crewe, who probably used his influence to get the young man a clerkship in the pay office. Both Dickenses would later claim kinship with the ancient Dickens family of Staffordshire, and Charles would spuriously assert the right to use the family coat of arms, which he casually referred to as "my father's crest: a lion couchant, bearing in its dexter paw, a Maltese cross."

Pretty, amusing, and intelligent, Elizabeth Barrow was a catch. Against her father's wishes, she and John were married on June 13, 1809. In January 1810 Charles Barrow was accused of embezzling 5,000 pounds. He confessed, fled to the Isle of Man, and was never seen in England again. Any great expectations John Dickens might have entertained of the old man were shattered. The name of John and Elizabeth's eldest son, Charles, was a reminder of their lost hopes.

Charles Dickens's paternal grandmother, a widow who lived at Crewe Hall, resided in a world that was still feudal. Proud to be in service, she regaled Charles with stories from history and her own past. She adored her grandson but couldn't abide his father, whom she referred to as "that lazy fellow John, who used to come hanging about the house," adding, "Many a sound cuff on the ear I've given him." She had saved a substantial sum of money over the years, and while she delivered blows, she also dispensed handouts.

According to the strict class divisions in early-nineteenth-century England, the Dickens family would have been considered "upper lower-middle" class. In other words, they hovered between gentility and poverty. After a pay raise and a move to better lodgings, they fancied themselves "almost gentry." Then came a pay cut, and down they slid once more. As they struggled to put food on the table, they labored to keep up appearances. Reading, music, and theater were almost as important to them as food and shelter. As creditors banged at the door, John Dickens's unmistakable voice could be heard spouting imprecations.

What pulled John Dickens downward after so promising a beginning? At least one scholar has suggested that his pecuniary difficulties began with his father-in-law's defection. Given John's imprudent generosity, it is likely that he sent Charles Barrow money through the years. But even that would not account for his financial ruin. Rather, his downfall was bred in the bone. John Dickens was convivial and easygoing. If he had seven pounds, he spent eight. Born around 1786, he was less the earnest Victorian than the Regency buck, attached to elegant attire and locutions. Although the son of a housekeeper and a steward, he had been raised on a large estate and fancied himself well-connected.

The elder Dickens's high-flown emotionality, his penchant for florid oratory, his love of reading, and his get-rich schemes came from a theatrical temperament that his son inherited—and would put to better use. As a character in fiction, John Dickens would have been an appealing eccentric; as a father he was an unmitigated disaster. With the ebb and flow of his fortune, the family moved more than twenty times in eighteen years. In bad times, they kept just ahead of debt collectors. As money grew scarce and household expenses mounted, John and Elizabeth grew more careless and haphazard, living  only for the moment. As so often happens to a child with childish parents, Charles Dickens developed a precocious sense of responsibility. He became a son who was indeed father to the man.

John Forster, Dickens's best friend and biographer, writes that Dickens did not "owe much to his parents." But one could say he owed them everything. His entire life was a reaction against them and his childhood: as a boy he was a passive witness to his parents' follies; as a man, he was compulsively controlling. Their prodigality made him worship labor and frugality. In his novels, every abandoned waif was a version of himself; his negligent, silly mothers were caricatures of Elizabeth; his wastrel, selfish fathers were all John.

Childhood and Other Sorrows

※

Many people have had worse childhoods than Charles Dickens; few have profited as much by them. To paraphrase the poet Philip Larkin, childhood misery was for Dickens what daffodils were for Wordsworth. Perhaps because he had once known moments of familial closeness and happiness, his parents' subsequent lack of concern for his well-being was all the more painful. Because we tend to accept uncritically Dickens's assessment of his past, it's hard to know how much of it he dramatized. (In his autobiographical fragment, he claims he exaggerated nothing.) While evidence suggests that in his own feckless, narcissistic way John Dickens, and to a lesser extent Elizabeth, loved their eldest son, they exploited him, treating him as an equal rather than a child. As a result, the adult Dickens fiercely championed every child's right to an innocent childhood free from adult burdens.

His own childhood ended at age twelve, his first dozen years an overture containing the motifs that would resound throughout his life and work. His childhood falls rather neatly into two distinct parts: the deep joy of Chatham, and the blank misery of London.

HE IS BORN

Charles John Huffam Dickens was born at 387 Mile End Terrace in Landsport, Portsmouth, on February 7, 1812. Huffam, misspelled Huffham in the baptismal register, was a hopeful offering to his wealthy godfather, Christopher Huffam, a naval rigger from whom the family perhaps entertained great expectations. Dickens detested the name Huffam, blamed his parents for it, and never used it.

When Charles was born, the family consisted of John and Elizabeth and their two-year-old daughter Fanny, Charles's favorite sibling and his childhood companion. (Ebenezer Scrooge and Little Dorrit have sisters named Fanny; and the real Fanny's son is the model for the saintly Paul Dombey.) Dickens's love and yearning for his sister are commemorated in the numerous brother-and-sister "marriages" in his novels (such as that of Tom and Ruth Pinch in *Martin Chuzzlewit;* John and Harriet Carker and Florence and Paul Dombey in *Dombey and Son;* and Louisa and Tom Gradgrind in *Hard Times,* to name a few).

For three years the family lived in Portsmouth (with at least three local moves). Its fortunes took a downward turn when John was forced to accept a pay cut and transferred to London, where the family moved to smaller quarters in seedy Camden Town. This period lasted only two years, from 1815 to 1817, and is important in at least one respect: it was then that Elizabeth Dickens taught her eldest son the alphabet (thus somewhat countering his later contention that she was a neglectful mother). His memories of early lessons, which must have begun when he was two, suggest a happy time: "What fat black letters to begin with!" Dickens further recalled:

"A was an archer, who shot at a frog." Of course he was. He was an apple-pie also, and there he is! He was a good many things in his time, was A. And so were most of his friends except X, who had so little versatility that I never knew him to get beyond Xerxes or Xantippe—like Y, who was always confined to a Yacht or a Yew Tree; and Z condemned for ever to be a Zebra or a Zany.

(Even when he was an adult, sounds, words, and letters had personalities for Dickens, a vestige perhaps of this early introduction to the alphabet.) Obviously, with fewer worries and children, Elizabeth Dickens could afford the luxury of being an attentive mother.

1817–1822: CHATHAM AND BEYOND

*I*n January 1817 John Dickens was transferred to Chatham, just outside the cathedral city of Rochester, the dreamlike setting for Dickens's last novel, *Edwin Drood.* Although it lasted only five years, this was one of the most important periods in Dickens's life. It was in Chatham that his most vivid memories were formed, and where, like Pip, he began to develop a sense of himself. As his friend John Forster noted, Dickens's memory stretched back to the dark reaches of infancy, and in later life he recalled the Chatham years in rich detail. Though he could not have been older than five, he remembered that he lived next door to a heavenly "peach-faced creature in a blue sash" whose life seemed to consist entirely of birthdays, sweet wine, and presents. He also remembered the childish experience of going to bed every night and crying, "either with the remorseful consciousness of having kicked Somebody else, or because still Somebody else had hurt my feelings in the course of the day."

When he was five or six, his father would take him to the local tavern, lift him on the counter, and prompt him to sing comic songs for the regulars, who marveled at this infant phenomenon. Basking in his father's pride and the enthusiastic applause, Dickens developed what biographer Fred Kaplan calls a "performance personality," an intense need for approbation and applause.

He was happy in Chatham but would only realize it later, as people do when looking back after a period of misery. His father earned a steady income from the navy and lived within his means, and more important, Charles was sent to school and discovered books and the theater.

For Elizabeth and John, stability was a relative term: in 1816, 1820, and 1822 Letitia Mary, Frederick William, and Alfred Lamert Dickens were born (two other children died in infancy) and there were at least three more moves within Chatham itself. One, near the dockyard, afforded the romantic vista of ships leaving for far-flung places; Charles would watch for hours, fixated on a convict hulk that he called a "wicked Noah's ark," which seemed to be "ironed like the prisoners themselves."

In addition to the books and the dockyard, he also loved the stage. An uncle, Dr. Matthew Lamert, regularly took him to the Theatre Royal in Chatham, and when Dr. Lambert moved away his son, James Lamert, completed the boy's initiation into the mysteries of stagecraft. Dickens recalled a performance of *Macbeth* in which he marveled at the witches, who terrified him, and noted that King Duncan "couldn't rest in his grave, but was continually coming out of it and calling himself something else."

The adult Dickens described his child-self as "little and sickly," and although he didn't enjoy sports, he was "fond of observing others at play." He suffered from mysterious aches and kidney spasms, which would recur in adulthood when he was under stress. The spasms set him apart and allowed him certain indulgences, one of which was the solitude to explore inner gifts. He preferred observing to doing, and this would serve him well. He liked companionship—he always would—but a part of him always remained detached, silently watching. A keen eye is not simply a gift, and whether he knew it or not, young Dickens was training his inner eye while his schoolmates developed their bodies.

Dickens's brief childhood, cordoned off from the cares of his later life, ended in 1822, when the family left Chatham for London—a city that would become a realm of adult experience and terrible knowledge.

He was a terrible boy to read.
—MARY WELLER, the family maid

The family owned a modest number of books, which they referred to with typical exaggeration as the Library (it would eventually be carried off, volume by volume, to the pawnshop). Charles was encouraged to read anything he liked. His favorites were adventure tales of voyages, fairy stories, *The Arabian Nights,* and the great eighteenth-century novels *Roderick Random, The Vicar of Wakefield, Robinson Crusoe,* and *Tom Jones*—all tales of men who must

make their way in the world. Like David Copperfield, Charles envisioned himself as his favorite characters. Fielding's lusty hero was beyond even Charles's imagination, and so he was, as he put it, a "child's Tom Jones, a harmless creature." In a sense, Charles's version of Tom Jones was the prototype for his early heroes: what else is Nicholas Nickleby but a "harmless," i.e., desexed, Tom Jones? Charles was never an intellectual; most of his important reading was completed by the time he was twelve. (George Henry Lewes, consort to George Eliot and one of the leading intellectuals of the age, was surprised to find such a pedestrian assortment of books in Dickens's library.) He was a child reader because the neat, methodical world of the novel was a sanctuary when the disarray of his parents' affairs threatened to overwhelm him.

Fiction fueled an imagination that was already turning ripe and strange. When the family maid took him to visit a friend whose children had died, he closely noted that the "deceased young people lay, side by side, on a clean cloth on a chest of drawers, like pigs' feet as they are usually displayed at a neat tripe shop." The grisly and inventive image shows how any child's, and particularly a young genius's, mind works when faced with something threatening or unknown: he domesticates it by comparing it to something familiar and safe. Yet Dickens's childish imagery reveals a startling turn of mind, both morbid and highly suggestive. To him, the world was always new and curious, and he had an astonishing gift for pairing the most unlikely objects: Scrooge's door knocker is like a "bad lobster in a dark cellar"; Krook's face with its white whiskers is like "a root in snow."

"CAPTAIN MURDERER" AND OTHER TALES

After he became famous, Dickens was often asked to name his earliest literary influence. Very often he cited Mary Weller, the family's gin-soused

As My Father Would Say

———ᴍ———

Dickens would often jokingly preface a statement with "As my father would say," followed by a burst of swollen verbiage in such convoluted syntax that the sentences seemed to bend over onto themselves. John Dickens was as prodigal with words as he was with money. Like Mr. Micawber, he was fond of writing letters with rhetorical flourishes, a style often in marked contrast to the contents, as in this missive to officials at the Royal Academy of Music explaining why his daughter's tuition was past due:

A circumstance of great moment to me will be decided in the coming term, which I confidently hope will place me in comparative affluence, and by which I shall be ready to redeem the order before the period of Christmas Day.

thirteen-year-old maid. Although she was more often found asleep by the fire than cleaning, she happened to be a histrionic virtuoso who specialized in heart-stopping tales of terror. Such were the five-year-old Charles's bedtime stories. A poor man's Scheherazade, Mary enthralled the terrified boy each night with tales of devilish pacts and cannibalism. His favorite was the Bluebeardish story "Captain Murderer," and every night he begged to hear it again.

Stories heard and remembered at an impressionable age become an unconscious frame of reference, and it's worth noting that Dickens probably heard "Captain Murderer" at least a hundred times. Perhaps Dickens was simply being disingenuous when he cited Mary as his influence, but some critics, such as Eliot Engel, take him at his word. If the stories novelists love at an early age influence the ones they tell as adults, then Mary's bedtime tales were the template for Dickens's adult narratives.

For Mary Weller, as for Dickens, accuracy was not synonymous with realism, and the truth about human nature was contained in tales that transcend belief. Krook's spontaneous combustion in *Bleak House* is no less sensational than Captain Murderer's "auto-explosion." Mary was a devotee of the macabre, and she had a tendency to take a small truth and magnify it to outrageous dimensions. The crude grotesques who populate her tales would reemerge, transformed by artistry, as Krook, Pa Smallweed, Gaffer Hexam, and Magwitch. Dickens expressed his gratitude to Mary through her namesake, Sam Weller, Mr. Pickwick's inexhaustibly inventive servant.

EARLY INFLUENCES

*D*ickens's early life permeates his novels: As a boy he possessed a visual concentration and a sharp eye for detail. Tics, gestures, facial expressions, odd features, and mannerisms fascinated him. He loved to watch people at church, in the market, at school. Even the pawnshop owner who bought the family's goods came under young Dickens's observation.

When describing a character, Dickens tends to focus on one telling detail, a trait, a gesture, a feature—and usually one that only a very small child looking up at an ugly adult face would notice. (Dickens once confessed to Forster that he often did not even listen to people as they talked to him, he was so beguiled by the play of the speaker's features, "which would acquire a sudden ludicrous life of their own.")

Dickens's evil adults are pockmarked and pimpled, their faces dotted with moles, warts, and eruptions. Cruel women are hirsute, with a fringe on the upper lip or eyebrows that meet in the middle. His childlike way of observing people, his adult irony, and what George Orwell called his "generous anger" created the unique Dickens style. Dickens's influences, unlike those of other writers, are neither intellectual nor literary but personal. The man is his style. With Shakespeare and a handful of others, he is one of literature's true originals.

Annus Horribilis

ife for the young Dickenses must have been an emotional roller coaster. There were highs: a pay raise, a larger house, a new financial venture, an unexpected windfall, and the sigh of relief when a debt was paid or postponed. And there were lows: demotions, salary cuts, a move to smaller lodgings, another baby. They finally reached a trough that seemed permanent: Charles was sent to work at Warren's Blacking Warehouse, and his father was imprisoned for debt at the Marshalsea. Charles was twelve years old. The year was 1824, his *annus horribilis.*

"THE SECRET AGONY OF MY SOUL"

Unexpectedly, in an "evil hour," his cousin James Lamert (the one who had made him the toy theater), knowing the family circumstances and thinking he was being helpful, used his influence to get Charles a job at Warren's Blacking Warehouse. To Charles's astonishment, his parents didn't object: "My father and mother were quite satisfied. They could hardly have been more so, if I had been twenty years of age, distinguished at a grammar-school, and going to Cambridge." (In light of this, one can see why Dickens was so moved when his son Henry informed him that he had won a scholarship to Cambridge.)

Charles's work address was 30 Hungerford Stairs, Strand, a place name

Old Hungerford Stairs, the site of the blacking warehouse where the twelve-year-old Dickens worked labeling pots of boot blacking. Years later he wrote: "Until old Hungerford-market was pulled down, until old Hungerford-stairs were destroyed, and the very nature of the ground changed, I never had the courage to go back to the place where my servitude began. I never saw it. I could not endure to go near it."

that's positively Dickensian. The warehouse no longer exists—it was torn down during Dickens's lifetime—but Dickens's detailed memory paints a more graphic picture than any vintage photograph:

> The blacking warehouse was the last house on the left-hand side of the way, at old Hungerford Stairs. It was a crazy, tumble-down, old house, abutting of course on the river, and literally run down with rats. Its wainscotted rooms, and its rotten floors and staircase, and the old grey rats swarming down in the cellars, and the sound of their squeaking and scuffling coming up the stairs at all times, and the dirt and decay of the place, rise up visibly before me as if I were there again.

His job was to "cover the pots of paste-blacking; first with a piece of oil paper, and then with a bit of blue paper; to tie them round with a string; and then to clip the paper close and neat, all round." He was to do this over and over from morning until night—for six shillings a week.

Due to the Lamert connection, he was promised preferential treatment. He ate his midday meal upstairs, apart from the other workers, and he was referred to as "the young gentleman" or "Master Dickens." Most important, he was assured that Lamert would tutor him in his spare time. But any attempts at tutoring were eventually abandoned: he was slowly becoming part of the element he worked in, his life a blur of pots, blacking, labels, glue, and string. And his special privileges ultimately did more harm than good: smaller and younger than the others (by his own account he looked young for his age), Master Dickens was ripe for teasing—and worse. An older boy, resentful of the "young gentleman's" status, picked a fight, but another rose to his defense. His defender, Bob Fagin, grew attached to the frail boy, bringing him hot water bottles for what were called "kidney spasms" (an old childhood complaint) and escorting him home at night. The adult Dickens discharged this debt of kindness in strange coin, giving Fagin's name to one of his worst villains (see page 91).

Adding to his humiliation, his sister Fanny had received a generous scholarship to study piano at the Royal Academy of Music, so while his fingers were grimy with blacking, hers were curled over ivory. He never forgot watching her play for the royal family: "The tears ran down my face. I prayed, when I went to bed that night, to be lifted out of the humiliation and neglect in which I was."

To say that the ordeal at Warren's was torture understates its effect. For a sensitive boy with great expectations, it must have seemed that life, which once had stretched out so promisingly, had trapped him in an existence meant for someone else. Dickens could never recall how long he was at Warren's. Scholars have estimated the time at between four months and a year. To Dickens it felt like a lifetime.

THE SUN SETS

*E*leven days after Charles started work, on February 20, John Dickens was arrested for debt. (To complete the family's despair, Dickens's godfather, the wealthy Huffam, upon whom their hopes rested, was declared bankrupt.) All the family goods—including the shirt Charles wore to work—were appraised, and John was sent to the "sponging house," a temporary detention center, before entering prison.

Charles became the family's go-between, running from the sponging house to the outside world, relaying messages to friends and relations, frantically trying to raise money to secure his father's release. Three days after his arrest, John Dickens entered the Marshalsea, the famous debtor's prison that was finally shut down in 1842. Since the prison didn't supply dining implements, Charles was sent upstairs to borrow a fork from a "Captain Porter." Even in his misery he used this errand as an opportunity to investigate and observe the other prisoners: "There was a very dirty lady in [Captain

Porter's] room," he recalled, "and two wan girls, his daughters, with shock heads of hair. I thought I should not have liked to borrow Captain Porter's comb." He instinctively knew that the two girls were the Captain's "natural" (i.e., illegitimate) daughters, "and that the dirty lady was not married to Captain P." He obtained the knife and fork and hurried back to his father, who despite his grief managed to tuck away a hearty meal with the borrowed implements. Nevertheless, before the iron doors closed on him that night, he announced that the sun had set on him forever. Father and son clutched each other and cried. Dickens wrote: "I really believed at the time that they had broken my heart."

As was common practice, the rest of the family, which now included four other children, moved in with John Dickens at the Marshalsea, while Charles lived alone, first in lodgings in Camden Town and later near the prison. The prison lodgings were surprisingly comfortable, and they even had a servant, dubbed the "Marchioness." (It is a feature of Victorian life that even the poorest families always kept one servant, who worked in exchange for lodging and food.)

Charles's life was not quite as genial. He describes his desolation in his unfinished autobiography: "No advice, no counsel, no encouragement, no consolation, no support, from any one that I can call to mind, so help me God." Although his father paid his rent, his weekly wage of six shillings was insufficient, and he often went hungry: "I was so young and childish, and so little qualified . . . to undertake the whole charge of my own existence, that in going to Hungerford Stairs of a morning, I could not resist the stale pastry put out at half-price on trays at the confectioners' . . . and I often spent in that, the money I should have kept for my dinner." In this fragment Dickens insists that he neither exaggerates nor dramatizes his past, but his tone is a curious mix of compassion for a child and maudlin pity for himself.

That April John Dickens's mother died, leaving her son a small legacy. What in a Dickens novel might have been a fairy-tale conclusion to the nightmare was in fact merely ironic: the money was tied up in probate and was useless to secure his release, and later it was swallowed up by creditors. Nonetheless, on May 28 John Dickens was released under the Insolvent Debtor's Act, which enabled him to reach an accommodation with his creditors. His son, expecting his own imminent release, continued his daily grind at Warren's.

Warren's moved to Chandos Street, to a new and larger warehouse with windows. For the sake of the light, Dickens and Bob Fagin worked at the front window, amusing passersby with their dexterity. One day John Dickens caught sight of his son in the window, and perhaps he was moved. ("I saw my father coming in at the door one day when we were very busy, and I wondered how he could bear it.") Soon thereafter John Dickens argued with James Lamert and, summoning all his dignity, took his child home with him. At last John Dickens assumed his proper role as a father. The day Charles left the warehouse for good, he felt "relief so strange it was like oppression."

Thus began one of those decisive moments that determine a child's disposition—and his fate. After neglecting his son's education, John suddenly insisted that Charles be sent to school; Elizabeth, however, wanted him to return to the warehouse. With great bitterness Dickens recalled, "I never afterwards forgot, I never shall forget, I never can forget, that my mother was warm for my being sent back." The repetition—the sound of the words themselves—is stern with unforgotten anger. But John Dickens prevailed, and Charles was sent to Wellington House Academy. To all outward appearances the sordid episode was closed; his parents never mentioned it again. Dickens wrote,

> ## FINANCIAL ADVICE FROM JOHN DICKENS
>
> —⁓—
>
> In his autobiographical fragment, Dickens recalls: "Once my father was waiting for me in the lodge, and we went up to his room . . . and cried very much. And he told me, I remember, to take warning by the Marshalsea, and to observe that if a man had twenty pounds a year, and spent nineteen shillings and sixpence, he would be happy; but that a shilling spent the other way would make him wretched." This immortal advice would be repeated, almost verbatim, some thirty years later by Mr. Micawber in *David Copperfield*.

From that hour until this at which I write, no word of that part of my childhood . . . has passed my lips. . . . I have no idea how long it lasted; whether for a year, or much more, or less. From that hour, until this, my father and mother have been stricken dumb upon it. I have never heard the least allusion to it, however far off and remote, from either of them. I have never, until I now impart it to this paper, in any burst of confidence with anyone, my own wife not excepted, raised the curtain I then dropped, thank God.

Dropped, yes, but lifted again and again—in oblique allusions in his novels, in his autobiographical fragment, and of course, disguised, in *David Copperfield* and *Great Expectations*. The episode stained his feelings about his parents just as the boot blacking had soiled his fingers.

Even after he became a world-famous novelist, Dickens could not walk by the site of Warren's without weeping. A whiff of glue was a perverse madeleine that sent him back to a past he did not want to recapture. As he himself declared in his autobiographical fragment, his unhappy childhood experiences were the signature events that made him Charles Dickens: "I do not write resentfully or angrily for I know how all these things have 'worked together to make me what I am.'"

❖ Allusions to bootblack, blacking pots, and even Warren's itself are sprinkled throughout Dickens's novels. They are a verbal private joke and a proud reminder to himself of how far he had come. In *Nicholas Nickleby,* a novel many consider autobiographical, Nicholas works in an office where there is always a bootblack bottle containing not blacking but a flower. The image suggests that even in the bleakest circumstances, some things still bloom.

❉Biographers, critics, and readers of Dickens customarily regard the months he worked at the warehouse as the seminal experience of his life, as if his entire personality emanated from that one period. That's probably an overstatement, and it's difficult to assess just how much one event makes a man. But Dickens's early vulnerability and his rage against his parents was to be redirected against all authority figures, bureaucracies, officials, and parental figures, who passively sit by in the face of suffering.

SCHOOL DAYS

*F*rom warehouse to schoolhouse in two days must have been a dizzying leap. After a four-year hiatus in his schooling, Charles took his place among the other boys at Wellington House Academy as if his life had never been interrupted. He must have felt like an impostor among the sons of aspiring, prosperous tradesmen.

Wellington House Academy, as Dickens describes it, sounds like a typical Victorian school: brutal headmasters, stupid teachers, and a grueling regime. The headmaster, a "thrasher" by the name of Jones, was, according to Dickens, "by far the most ignorant man I have ever had the pleasure to know." Nevertheless, Dickens was happy at last to be educated, for although he would never be a gentleman, education was a mark of refinement that would ensure that he would never do menial work again.

These were easier years for the Dickenses. Having retired from the Navy Pay Office, John Dickens was receiving a handsome pension. (Despite his reputation, he was not indolent, and was soon looking around for a new profession.) Most important, school life allowed Charles to be a child again, albeit briefly. Like the other boys, he kept live mice in his desk and read penny weeklies.

Dickens probably had less formal education than any other great man of letters. Although his classmates remembered him as sharp-witted rather than intellectual, he conducted himself honorably, surprising everyone by graduating with a prize in Latin—odd for a man known for his lack of classical knowledge.

About three years after Dickens started school, his father suffered another financial decline, and Dickens had to drop out. Once more he was sent to work, but at the ripe age of fifteen and with some education behind him, this time he could choose his profession.

Interregnum

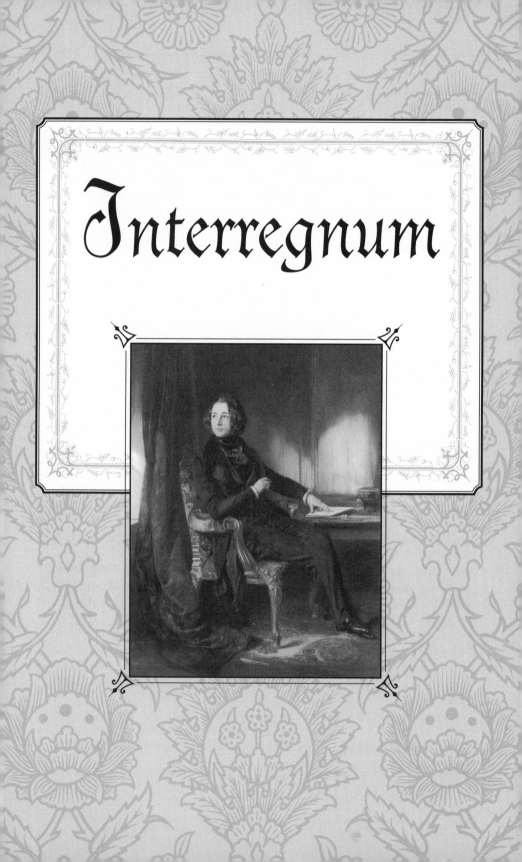

Journalism:
Biding Time

> *Politicians have their uses: their dullness*
> *may have driven Dickens to original composition.*
> —CLIFTON FADIMAN, "Pickwick and Dickens"

In 1827 the Dickens family was evicted for nonpayment of rent; Augustus "Moses" Dickens, John and Elizabeth's last child, was born; and their eldest son, Charles, now fifteen, left school to work as an office boy (*not* as a clerk, as he was quick to point out) for the law firm of Ellis and Blackmore. The firm's building still stands, and tourists walk through the doorway that Dickens used every day for the eighteen months he worked there. For his labors he received 15 shillings, 1 pence a week, roughly equivalent to $1.20 (a little more than Bob Cratchit's salary). Dickens might have hated the law, but he came to love the leafy, almost pastoral quietude of the Inns of Court, the law "schools" and offices where law students, barristers, and legal personnel lived, studied, and practiced.

As an office boy he ran errands through arteries of hallways filled with offices bearing such names as "Pronotaries," "Sixpenny Receivers," and "Exigenters." At Doctors' Commons he watched

A portrait of the novelist at age eighteen. The artist—Dickens's aunt by marriage—has captured a look of surprised comicality.

⤥⤦

blissful or diffident couples register for marriage licenses, and miserable ones plead for divorce; he saw wills drawn up and relatives contest them. No doubt he was quick to note any fanciful names that might appear on these documents.

He quickly sensed that he didn't have the stomach or the temperament for the law. It was stodgy and slow, with ponderous proceedings that often dragged on for months, if not years, without resolution. His mercurial, ambitious nature craved drama and excitement, and he needed a career that would give him room for movement. He needed to be noticed. Everything he did cried out, "Look at me!" Both journalism and acting appealed to him as professions that would put him in the public eye. For the next two years, however, he remained an obscure office boy while he decided what to do with the rest of his life.

During this time he resumed his childhood habit of walking for hours throughout London's boroughs. He was particularly drawn to the seamier, raffish sections where the indigent, the depraved, and the wicked lived. He never returned empty-handed: each visit would yield some human quirk or oddity, an inflection or a gesture that he would put to future use. A fellow clerk recalled, "I thought I knew something of the town, but after a little talk with Dickens I found that I knew nothing. He knew it all, from Bow to Brenford. . . . He could imitate, in a manner I never saw equalled, the low population of the streets of London in all their varieties."

He also spent as many evenings as possible at the theater, favoring burlesque and melodrama. There he imbibed the hackneyed devices that he would put to better use in his own fiction: the lost heir, the misplaced will, the foundling, the parent united with the child, and the usual assortment of virile villains and fluttering maidens.

When he wasn't at the theater, he was improving himself, reading at the British Museum, history's central meeting point, where Newton and Marx both studied. Mixing the fanciful with the practical, he laboriously taught himself Gurney's shorthand—a skill that would be essential to his success as a reporter and journalist. A maddening system of chicken scratches and curls, it took him a year to master; but the experience taught him the importance of diligence—which, he later maintained, was more important than genius in life. By 1831 he was good enough to become a freelance court reporter. As he sat on the bench waiting for a case, he had ample time to watch the human species in extremis, and the futility of a legal system that failed to help them.

All this time, Dickens had been flirting with the idea of going onstage. A theatrical career was not considered respectable, particularly for a young man who hoped to marry one day into a conventional family, but he felt drawn to the stage's flamboyance and yearned, as he put it, to make a "great splash." Since childhood he had amused friends and family with his droll turns and imitations. He modeled himself on a popular comedian named George Matthews, who specialized in imitations and monologues, which he called "monopolyogues," sketches in which he meets an assortment of colorful characters, all played by himself. Dickens practiced Matthews's technique and style in front of a mirror for hours. In the fall of 1831 he wrote to Matthews's manager requesting an audition, and much to his surprise was granted one. In his letter he described himself as having "a strong perception

Gurney's shorthand often defeated the most determined student. "The changes that were rung upon dots, which in such a position meant such a thing, and in such another position meant something else entirely different; the wonderful vagaries that were played by circles; the unaccountable consequences that resulted from marks like flies' legs . . ." By methodically applying himself, Dickens mastered the arcane symbols in record time and became the fastest shorthand reporter in the country. Perhaps in homage to its most illustrious practitioner, several of Dickens's novels have been translated into shorthand.

of character and oddity, and a natural power of reproducing" what he saw. Even at twenty-two, Dickens had a vivid sense of his own innate abilities. A bad head cold forced him to cancel the audition, and he never scheduled another, having already been hired by a newspaper. For the sake of a good anecdote, there are some who maintain that it was a head cold that gave us Charles Dickens, novelist, instead of Charles Dickens, comedian. In a sense he became both, for he ended up doing on paper what he wanted to do on-stage, and in his later years he finally fulfilled his theatrical ambitions.

Meanwhile, he had been hired as a general reporter for a new paper called the *True Sun*. In less than four months the paper folded, causing Dickens to write to a friend, "The Sun is so obscured that I intend living under this planet no longer." He was next hired by the *Mirror of Parliament* as a Parliamentary reporter and subeditor. By this time his reputation for speed and accuracy had spread, and Lord Stanley specifically requested the services of the only person who had reported his speech accurately. (Stanley was shocked to find that his reporter looked like a mere boy.)

Transcribing the verbiage spewed in the House of Commons was exhausting and frustrating, with debates and speeches sometimes dragging on until the wee hours of the morning. It was also physically demanding: "I have worn my knees by writing on them in the old back row of the old House of Commons, and I have worn my feet by standing to write in a preposterous pen in the old House of Lords where we used to be huddled together like so many sheep," Dickens wrote. As Dickens's fictional double David Copperfield said, "I wallow in words. Britannia, that unfortunate female, is always before me, like a trussed fowl. . . . I am sufficiently behind the scenes to know the worth of political life. I am quite an Infidel about it, and shall never be converted." Indeed, Dickens was never awed or cowed by authority. The House of Commons was a sideshow, "particularly strong in clowns":

Night after night they twist and tumble about, til two, three and four o'clock in the morning; playing the strangest antics, and giving each other the funniest slaps on the face that can possibly be imagined, without evincing the smallest tokens of fatigue. The strangest noises, the confusion, the shouting and roaring, amid which all this is done, would put to shame the most turbulent sixpenny gallery that ever yelled through a boxing night.

As a journalist he watched the show with detached amusement, but as a man he was enraged by the spectacle. First as legal office boy, then as journalist and court reporter, Dickens's beats were mainly Parliament and the courts of law, and this familiarity bred contempt. Dickens had little interest in politics and even less in law, but he was fascinated by the human drama behind these abstractions—the shifty, double-talking lawyers, the lazy politicians, and the naive souls caught in the grinding cogs of bureaucracy. His miserable childhood had made him acutely sensitive to neglect of all kinds. The law was the father who abandoned his children. But Dickens should have been grateful to politicians and lawyers for at least one thing: they furnished him with a lifetime's worth of material.

Luckily, Dickens's editor recognized his reporter's untapped gifts and encouraged him to write stories or vignettes of city life. He wrote a short story called "Dinner at Poplar Walk," a slight but amusing tale. "One evening at twilight," as Dickens described it, "with fear and trembling," he stealthily dropped the story into a "dark letter-box, in a dark office up a dark court in Fleet Street." The letterbox was that of the *Monthly Magazine,* and so Dickens submitted his first work of fiction.

In December 1833, about a month later, he nervously entered a book shop and asked for the latest edition of the *Monthly Magazine;* for the first time Charles Dickens saw his own words "in all the glory of print." Years later he recalled the moment: "My eyes so dimmed with pride and joy that they could not bear the street, and were not fit to be seen." The occasion was also portentous in another way. The salesman who sold him his copy was John Hall, the man who three years later would offer him the chance to write *The Pickwick Papers,* the novel that would launch both their careers—and a new era in book publishing.

As a journalist, he had to write fast and meet deadlines—ideal training for a man who would soon be churning out fiction by the month. His scope of activity expanded to the provinces, and he traveled throughout England and Scotland covering elections, debates, and official dinners. He usually stayed up all night, first recording every word and then racing back to London to meet his deadline, "galloping through a wild country, and through the dead of night,

When a young writer at Dickens's journal, *Household Words,* seemed careless of his literary talents, Dickens took the time to write an admonitory letter that contains the Dickensian work ethic in a nutshell. His advice may also explain how he managed to accomplish the work of ten men in one lifetime:

> But frequently it appears to me that you do not render justice to your many high powers, by thinking too slightingly of what you have in hand, instead of doing it, for the time being, as if there were nothing else to be done in the world—the only likely way I know of, of doing anything.

—October 31, 1852

at the then surprising rate of fifteen miles an hour." Sometimes he dashed off his pieces en route to London as the coach rattled beneath him.

He observed human behavior at its most artificial and self-inflated. Official ceremonies, elections, courtroom procedure, and parliamentary debates—such bewigged pomposity was refracted through the Dickensian lens and represented, often with a subtle twist. He managed to inject some Dickensian wryness into his account of a dinner in honor of Earl Grey, the retiring prime minister:

The Honoree did not arrive on time and the guests began to grow impatient and hungry.

One eyeing the cold fowls, roast beef, lobster, and other tempting delicacies (for the dinner was a cold one), appeared to think that the best thing he could posssibly do, would be to eat his dinner, while there was anything to eat. He accordingly laid about him with right good-will, the example was contagious, and the clatter of knives and forks became general. Hereupon, several gentlemen, who were not hungry, cried out "Shame!" and looked very indignant; and several gentlemen who were hungry cried "Shame!" too, eating, nevertheless, all the while, as fast as they possibly could. In this dilemma, one of the stewards mounted a bench and feelingly represented to the delinquents the enormity of their conduct, imploring them for decency's sake, to defer the process of mastication until the arrival of Earl Grey. This address was loudly cheered, but totally unheeded; and this is, perhaps, one of the few instances on record of a dinner having been virtually concluded before it began.

This account could appear almost verbatim in one of his novels. Dickens refused to be invisible or anonymous in his writing; he put his mark on everything he did—even dry accounts of elections or speeches. Of a halting speech by Lord Lincoln, he wrote, "Lord Lincoln broke down, and sat down."

Meanwhile Dickens continued to write sketches of urban life; after the third or fourth, he adopted the nom de plume "Boz" in honor of his youngest brother, Augustus (see page 39). As brief as comic skits and as detailed as fine miniatures, the sketches began to catch the public's attention. Soon readers were wondering about this Boz, who wrote with such accurate intimacy about London. At twenty-one, Dickens was thus beginning to make a name for himself. But those who think success came early to him forget that he had already been working for a full six years.

Dickens in Love

t the age of eighteen, Charles Dickens fell passionately in love. The object of his affections was a "pocket Venus" named Maria Beadnell, the flirtatious twenty-year-old daughter of a City banker. Dickens was probably introduced to the family by a mutual friend, Henry Kolle, who was engaged to Maria's elder sister, and he soon became part of the young woman's charmed circle of admirers, who gathered at her house on Lombard Street. Her keepsake album (a Victorian version of an autograph book, an accessory no proper young lady was without) from the period is filled with versified professions of love from stricken men, all of whom she apparently kept dangling. Dickens's first entry is a strained acrostic on her name, which begins:

My life may chequered be with scenes of misery and pain,
* And it may be my fate to struggle with adversity in vain . . .*

In honor of a dinner party given by the Beadnells toward the end of 1831, Dickens composed a bit of doggerel entitled "A Bill of Fare," in which each guest is described as an item on the menu. Of himself he wrote:

And Charles Dickens, who in our Feast plays a part
* Is a young Summer Cabbage, without any heart;*
Not that he's heartless, but because, as folks say,
* He lost his a twelve month ago, from last May.*

*M*aria Beadnell, the coquette who broke Dickens's heart, would be immortalized as the fetching Dora in *David Copperfield* and less kindly as the middle-aged Flora Finching in *Little Dorrit.*

He had already fallen in love with Maria by May 1830, almost immediately after they met. The chronology and vicissitudes of his relationship with Maria are hazy; the relationship lasted between three and four years, but precisely how they met and the exact nature of their spats and separations are unknown. Although she denied it after he became famous, Maria never took Dickens seriously.

What is certain is the intensity of Dickens's ardor. To say he fell in love doesn't do justice to the emotion that "filled every crevice and chink" of his mind and "excluded every other idea." Unable to do or feel anything lightly, Dickens's adolescent infatuation became a magnificent obsession.

At first his visits to Lombard Street were, if not encouraged, then at least accepted. He had, after all, a talent to amuse that could enliven a dull evening. Yet the stolidly middle-class Beadnells could hardly have been pleased to see John Dickens's name listed in the *London Gazette* as an insolvent debtor. (Dickens could always count on some member of his family to embarrass him.) Although he was rising in his career and beginning to write the droll accounts of urban life he called "sketches," the Beadnells saw him merely as a political reporter without prospects.

And when they became alarmed by his unabashed devotion to their daughter, they began subtly to discourage his attentions. From the perspective of middle age, Dickens recalled how once he unexpectedly met Maria and her mother while they were shopping; after he escorted them to their destination, Mrs. Beadnell, afraid he might decide to accompany them into the dress shop, turned to the young man and declared, "And now, Mr. Dickin, we'll wish *you* good morning."

Maria had the conventional good looks of the age; petite, with blond curls, she had an engagingly coquettish manner and the ability to play the harp, giggle, and look charming. But she was also flighty, pettish, and willful: when she refuses to accept a pair of gloves Dickens had presented her, he writes in desperation:

Surely, surely you will not refuse so trivial a present: a mere common place trifle; a common present even among the merest "friends." Do not misunderstand me: I am not desirous by making presents or by doing any other act to influence your thoughts, wishes, or feelings in the slightest degree.—I do not think I do:—I cannot hope I ever shall: but let me entreat of you do not refuse so slight a token of regard from me.

Written more than 160 years ago, this touching plea still evokes the timeless ache of unrequited love. Dickens ends with an appeal to let him see her—a striking contrast to the stern letters he would write his fiancée, Catherine Hogarth.

Dickens's biographers claim that during the winter of 1831–32, the Beadnells, determined to separate the two lovers, sent Maria to finishing school in Paris. But in *Dickens and Women,* Michael Slater asserts that the twenty-one-year-old Maria would have been too old for school, and that she finished her education in 1830, a year before meeting Dickens. Besides, there was never any danger of the shallow, passionless, self-indulgent young woman actually falling for Dickens.

The early months of 1833 marked a crisis in their relationship. Up to that point, Maria had always been affectionate if coquettish—although Dickens read more into her friendliness than she intended. For some reason—perhaps a perverse desire to stir things up—Maria suddenly turned cold and indifferent, plunging Dickens into despair. Thereafter the two communicated secretly through letters, which they passed through intermediaries. Their relationship was cloaked in romantic intrigue—which Maria probably enjoyed—while Dickens continued to wait for her declaration of love.

Dickens's letters to Maria from this time allude to an incident, a typical adolescent imbroglio in which emotions run high and every word and deed is fraught with significance. The misunderstanding involved Dickens, his sister Fanny, Maria, and her confidante, a busybody named Mary Anne Leigh. In some versions, Mary Anne flirted with Dickens to pique Maria and then told Maria about it. Letters passed furiously back and forth, with Dickens hotly accusing Mary Anne of meddling and condemning Fanny, whom "no consideration on earth shall induce me ever to forget or forgive" (because she failed to warn him about Mary Anne's mischief).

In February 1833, Dickens came of age; his mother sent out invitations for an evening of "Quadrilles." Maria probably attended, and according to an account drawn from Dickens's essay, "Birthday Celebrations," the young woman "scorched [his] brain" by calling him a boy. Their subsequent meetings were heartbreaking for him; her behavior was "little more than so many displays of heartless indifference" and "a fertile source of wretchedness and misery."

After overhearing Maria's

friends talking about him pityingly, he wrote her a letter recounting all he had done to win her love. In it he sounds more like himself: impassioned, self-righteous, proud of his unwavering devotion (in contrast to Maria's fickleness) and of his suffering: "I have been too long used to inward wretchedness, and real, real misery." (As a novelist, he would make comedic hay by parodying the melodramatic gestures of young lovers, who sound remarkably like this young Dickens.) His juvenile melodrama hides his growing conviction that the girl he loved could never reciprocate his feelings.

Maria retorted with anger and accusations; Dickens retreated with a conciliatory reply. But the damage was done. She returned his note "without the formality of even an envelope." Resigned, he wrote her his last love letter: "I never have loved and I never can love any human creature breathing but yourself." The simplicity of his language suggests, if not understanding, at least resignation.

Over twenty years later, when he tried to describe what Maria had meant to him, he found himself flooded by emotions almost too painful to write down. He had shared the secret of his unhappy childhood with his friend John Forster, but he never let him see what he had written about Maria. He put the passage in a drawer and eventually burned it. Thus the only account we have of Dickens in love is the David and Dora section in *David Copperfield*. In his autobiographical fantasy, Dickens rewrites history: Dora returns David's ardor, but it is David who realizes the error of his choice. Dora dies, and David triumphs.

Dickens's obsession and Maria's rejection would have greater implications than the young Dickens could possibly foresee. Maria's capriciousness and his subsequent humiliation influenced him to choose the placid and compliant Catherine Hogarth for a wife. No woman would ever wield that kind of erotic power over him again.

One wonders what the Beadnells must have thought when, scarcely two years later, the negligible "Mr. Dickin" became a household name. Life is rarely kind to frivolous women, and Maria was no exception. She lived with her parents on Lombard Street until February 1845, when, a thirty-four-year-old spinster, she married one Mr. Henry Winter, manager of a sawmill.*

---

* Dickens would have his revenge. Twenty-two years later, on February 22, 1855, Mrs. Henry Winter reentered his life, this time under very different circumstances. See page 272.

Sketches by Boz

☨

Sketches by Boz is an underrated book—
underrated because it is by Dickens.
—JOHN GROSS

YOU CAN CALL ME BOZ

uch of Dickens's early success can be attributed to that inimitable nom de plume, "Boz." Catchy and breezy, it grabbed the reader's imagination, suggesting the boyishness of a favorite son or an adored older brother. In fact, the name was inspired by Dickens's youngest brother, Augustus Newnham Dickens, aka Moses.

Although not generally a nickname for Augustus, the name Moses derives from a character in Oliver Goldsmith's *Vicar of Wakefield,* an adorable little boy much favored by the Victorian middle-class reader. Moses thus became a trendy nickname for any small boy. Thus in the literary Dickens' household, Augustus came to be known as Moses, which, because of the two-year-old child's adenoidal pronunciation, became Bozes, and finally Boz.

Because articles and reviews were customarily published anonymously, fledgling authors generally chose pen names that would reveal the identity of the author to family and friends. The choice of Boz was a private family joke and a tribute to his youngest brother.

Dickens's success as Boz paid for the real Boz's education and later helped him land a clerical position in an established firm. Unfortunately, Augustus inherited his father's fecklessness, along with a moral laxity that would eventually undo him. He speculated in the Crimean War—which must have infuriated Dickens, who had inveighed against wartime abuses in *Little Dorrit*—and when this failed, he left England for Illinois, thus choosing the one place guaranteed to provoke his brother's ire—Dickens had been swindled in an Illinois land deal years earlier. In America Augustus exploited his brother's fame by giving lectures on Shakespeare under the name of Boz. When this venture failed, he wrote to Dickens, begging for money.

Augustus left numerous debts in England, along with a wife who had recently gone blind. He was now traveling about the States with a woman who called herself his wife and who bore three of his children. Exasperated at last, Dickens finally gave up on the original Boz. (He did, however, help his wife.)

Augustus died in 1866, but even in death he managed to publicly humiliate his brother. When Dickens visited America in 1868, he confined his readings to the East and was roundly attacked by the press for avoiding "Mrs. Augustus Dickens" and her three children, then living in Chicago. The picture was an ugly one: Charles Dickens, champion of the poor, his pockets stuffed with American dollars, callously letting his relatives starve. Actually, he had been sending the woman—whom he had never met—50 pounds a year, but he forbade his manager to answer the newspapers' attacks.

Sketches by Boz is worth reading not simply because it is Dickens's first published book, but because it is quite remarkable in its own right. As a compilation of the vignettes and stories that Dickens, disguised as Boz, wrote for the *Evening Chronicle* and the *Monthly Magazine* from 1833 to 1834, it is the only work by a still-obscure Dickens. Shortly after its publication he began *Pickwick* and, like Byron, awoke to find himself famous.

The contradictory nature of Dickens's personality is evidenced by his two names, Boz and Charles Dickens. As Boz he was the perennial boy, untroubled, brimming with high spirits, unself-conscious. Charles Dickens was made of sterner stuff; his was the unwavering voice of England's social conscience, a man who spoke out loudly and boldly against an increasingly unjust society. But to the loyal public who adored him and had followed his career from his youth to his death, he would always be "The Inimitable Boz."

Coming to *Sketches* after reading the other novels is like seeing a picture of an old friend in youth—familiar, but so young! The Boz persona, wry, benevolent, street-smart, and perpetually inquisitive, is one of Dickens's finest inventions. His insider's knowledge of London and the brisk assurance with which he introduces us to the city and its diverse inhabitants make it seem scarcely possible that *Sketches* was written by a twenty-something reporter with little formal education. At various times, Boz sounds like a literate Artful Dodger or a precocious writer for a college humor magazine. His shrewd observations on human affairs suggest the great eighteenth-century essayists for the *Tatler* or the *Spectator.* The variety of tones and types of sketches (vignettes, reportage, essays, tales) remind us that they were written by a fledgling author searching for his voice and subject matter. In his first work, Dickens finds both.

The best parts of *Sketches* are the verbal snapshots of urban life, from the

"Boz" was drawn to London's out-of-the-way and forgotten places. The haunts and habitats of high society rarely appear in his sketches.

depraved to the ordinary: door knockers, omnibuses, pawnshops, used clothing, tea gardens, abused wives, condemned criminals. Sketches are informal pieces, but here the term also suggests a preliminary version of a major opus—only in this case the work in progress is the entire Dickens oeuvre. Now-familiar Dickensian characters and scenes make their debut: dandified clerks, pompous beadles, vinegary spinsters, bluff, military bachelors, and spoony suitors. Dickens's first piece on Christmas appears here, brimming with what would become known as "Dickensian cheer." The melodrama that would plague even his greatest novels is present in such tales as "The Black Veil" (" 'Who was he?' inquired the surgeon.' 'My son,' rejoined the woman and fell senseless at his feet.' ") The extraordinary names, a Dickens trademark, appear in full glory: Mr. Tupple, a junior clerk (what else?); Signor Billsmethi, owner of a dancing academy; Mrs. Bloss (who "has an interest in" Mr. Gobler); and Nocodemus Dumps, a gloomy misanthrope.

An irrepressible people-watcher, Boz observes quirky characters when they're least conscious of being seen. He catches those unposed, unguarded moments when people are most themselves. Thus a typical sketch might begin with the chance sighting of an intriguing face, which in turn sets off a train of thought: "We were seated in the enclosure of St. James's Park the other day, when our attention was attracted by a man. . . ." And so the disquisition begins. Visiting Astley's, a popular circus, Boz finds more diversion in the family seated in front of him—particularly the eldest son, who with the labored nonchalance of adolescence tries to pretend he's not in the party—than in the goings-on in the arena below.

Boz delights in showing us everyday people and places in an alien light so that we'll never quite view them the same way again. He strips the romantic of its mystique and makes the familiar magical. In "Minor Actors by Day-light," he divests actors of their glamour, exposing the grimy man beneath the flamboyant costume. ("See them at the neighbouring public-houses or the theatrical coffee-shop! They are the kings of the place, supposing no real performers to be present.") Without losing its drollery, the piece becomes a miniature study of the contrast between illusion and reality: caught in the light of day, the "walking gentleman" is transmogrified into a "dirty swell"; the comic singer shrinks into a public-house chairman, and the leading tragedian is exposed as a common drunk. Boz takes us to that fashionable nightspot, Vauxhall, by day, and the trip becomes an unsentimental journey, a meditation on disenchantment. But in compensation he offers us the enchantment of the used clothing displayed in an "emporium" on Monmouth Street. The author stares at the motley garments and envisions their former owners and their fates. In this sartorial reverie, frocks, bonnets, and boots, now worn by their imaginary owners, assume a life of their own and whirl about in a phantasmagoric dance.

Less fantastically, *Sketches,* published in the final year of William IV's reign, offers a picture of London at a critical juncture in the city's history. Boz's London was vanishing even as he wrote about it. He chronicles the city's transition from large village to modern metropolis. In "Scotland Yard" he mourns the loss of the familiar landmark, lamenting its smart new gentrification:

> And what is Scotland Yard now? How have its old customs changed; and how has the ancient simplicity of its inhabitants faded away! The old tottering public-house is converted into spacious and lofty "wine-vaults." . . . The tailor exhibits in his window the pattern of a foreign-looking brown surtout, with silk buttons, a fur collar and fur cuffs.

The man of a thousand voices, Boz sounds like an old-timer complaining about an infestation of yuppies and coffee bars in the neighborhood.

Like the Shadow, Boz is ubiquitous, but he is mostly drawn to raffish, out-of-the-way spots such as the "back part of Walworth," the labyrinthine courts of Seven Dials, gin shops, and that urban rite of spring, Greenwich Fair. He escorts his genteel readers into terra incognita, unveiling a morality play that's enacted daily. Among other sordid sights, we are shown prostitutes being led into a police van, an abused woman still loyal to her loutish boyfriend, and most memorably, the prison cell at Newgate where Boz contemplates the fates of three condemned men, a scene that anticipates Fagin's last night alive in *Oliver Twist.* (The trio have since been identified as a murderer and two homosexuals; only the latter two were hanged.)

Most important, *Sketches* stakes out what would become known as Dickens territory, London itself: sinister, melancholy, and homely. Urban culture, street amusements, idioms and accents, taverns and chophouses, haunts and their habitués, all are observed with an intensity that makes the city the most brilliant character Dickens ever created.

Charles and Catherine

ickens biographers tend to introduce Catherine Hogarth with surprisingly little fanfare. She slipped into his life so unobtrusively that one could hardly imagine that theirs would become one of the most famous marriages of the nineteenth century.

Their initial meeting was ordinary. As a rising reporter, Dickens was invited to the home of his editor at the *Evening Chronicle,* the Scotsman George Hogarth, a music critic and minor literary figure. (He was also Sir Walter Scott's legal adviser, which must have impressed Dickens.) Dickens soon became a regular at the Hogarth household, which included ten children. (The famed Dickensian fertility apparently came from the Hogarth side.)

Dickens's ready acceptance into this easygoing family was no doubt flattering; that he should marry his boss's eldest daughter was a coup. He basked in the attention of the four Hogarth girls: Catherine, nineteen, Mary, fifteen, Georgina, seven, and the toddler, Helen. The different roles each would play in his life were still in the distant future; for now, they were simply four pretty girls who worshiped him.

The image of Tommy Traddles in his staid lawyer's lodgings romping about with his bevy of sisters-in-law in *David Copperfield* is an idealized glimpse of Dickens's youthful relations with the Hogarth daughters. Several observers have remarked that Dickens was probably in love with them all, especially Mary, the prettiest. If so, one can't blame him. As Traddles said, "The society of girls is a very delightful thing."

The warm attentions of the family were all the more welcome after the disdain he had met at the Beadnells, who had disapproved of him as a suitor to

*D*ickens with his "two petticoats," Catherine and Mary Hogarth. After his marriage, the three lived together in his chambers at Furnival's Inn, a period he recalled as the happiest in his life. Catherine stands next to Dickens, her head bowed; her husband stands straight, eyes fixed ahead, staring into the future.

their daughter Maria. The Hogarths' admiration inspired him to feats of exuberant lunacy: once, seated in the parlor, they were startled at the sight of him standing in the window wearing a sailor suit. To their further amazement, he suddenly broke into a frenzied hornpipe. Less than two minutes later, he calmly walked into the room, expressionless, as if nothing had happened; but one glance at their astonished faces and he collapsed into uproarious laughter.

We don't know what Dickens first made of Catherine, but we do know what she thought of him. After attending his birthday party, she reported to her cousin: "Mr. Dickens improves upon acquaintance . . . he is very gentlemanly and pleasant." When Dickens first saw her, Catherine, or Kate, was small and fair-haired, with a round face, heavy-lidded blue eyes, and a retroussé nose. Her overall impression was one of sleepy softness. Although given to ocassional outbursts of peevishness, she was a docile girl who was eager to please.

Catherine and Charles's courtship was nothing like his *folie à deux* with Maria. Now that he was trying to get on in his career, he needed someone to cater to him, not the other way around. Thus in May 1835, a year after his breakup with Maria, Dickens became engaged to Catherine Hogarth—a sensible choice, precisely the sort of wife for a man who had little time for feminine whims. He hoped she would make a secure home while he continued to rise. His wedding gift to her is, tellingly, a workbox inlaid with ivory, inscribed FROM CHAS DICKENS TO KATE, APRIL 2, 1836.

On a deeper, less obvious level, Catherine seems a peculiar choice. She moved slowly, while he was in perpetual motion; she was pleasingly plump, while he was boyishly slim; she was unsure of herself and lacked definition, while Dickens knew himself thoroughly and felt there was nothing he couldn't do. There are several reasons for his attraction, although it's never easy to explain why one person chooses another. There is no doubt—whatever he said later—that he loved her at the time. Not truly, madly, deeply, perhaps, but with affectionate warmth. Mr. Hogarth's position in the literary world must have cast a certain reflected glory on his daughter, and Catherine was so unlike Maria that she never would remind Charles of what he had lost. The twenty-three-year-old Dickens desperately wanted a home, and Catherine was the first suitable woman to come along. Amiable and unassuming, she wouldn't mind taking a backseat to Dickens's enthusiasms. At first he must have thought she would make a charming complement to his own personality. In time, however, it would be precisely their differences that would drive him away.

"DEAREST PIG": BILLET-DOUX FROM DICKENS

*I*f Catherine Hogarth expected extravagant billet-doux from her literary fiancé, she was surely disappointed. Neither the feverish outpourings of an undisciplined heart nor the shared exchange of ideas between intellectual equals, the letters, written in 1835–36, the year of their betrothal, are surprisingly brief and matter-of-fact. Three weeks after they officially became engaged, Dickens wrote Catherine a stern rebuke, laying down the ground rules of their relationship. Written "more in sorrow than in anger," the letter is cold, priggish, even Pecksniffian:

My Dear Catherine,
   It is with the greatest pain that I sit down, before I go to bed to-night, to say one word which can bear the appearance of unkindness or reproach; but I owe a duty to myself as well as to you, and as I was wild enough to think that an engagement of even three weeks might pass without any such display as you have favoured me with twice already, I am the more strongly induced to discharge it.
   The sudden and uncalled for coldness with which you treated me just before I left last night, both surprised and deeply hurt me—surprised, because I could not have believed that such sullen and inflexible obstinacy could exist in the breast of any girl in whose heart love had found a place; and hurt me, because I feel for you far more than I have ever professed, and feel a slight from you more than I care to tell. My object in writing to you is this. If a *hasty* temper produces this strange behaviour, acknowledge it when I give you the opportunity—not once or twice, but again and again. If a feeling of you know not what—a capricious restlessness of you can't tell what, and a desire to teaze, you don't know why, give rise to it—overcome it; it will never make you more amiable, I more

fond, or either of us more happy. If three weeks or three months of my society has wearied you, do not trifle with me, using me like any other toy as suits your humour for the moment; but make the acknowledgment to me frankly at once—I shall not forget you lightly, but you will need no second warning.

After suffering the caprices of the fickle Maria Beadnell, Dickens clearly intends to have the upper hand in this relationship. (Two years earlier he had written to Maria, "I have borne more from you than I do believe any creature breathing ever bore from woman before.") The letter is also a thinly disguised threat: Catherine is expendable. Otherwise, the letters attest to a rather uneventful courtship. Opening with "My dearest Kate," they often end with the extended Victorian sign-off:

> Believe me
> My ever dearest girl [sometimes Love]
> yours truly and affecy
> Charles Dickens.

If he feels especially affectionate, she is his "dearest darling Pig" (or "Wig"); whatever modern readers might make of the nickname, it is clearly a fond allusion to Catherine's round form:

> Love to all
> Believe Me
> Dearest Pig
> Ever yours most truly & affecy.
> Charles Dickens.

At times affectionate, sometimes paternal, occasionally scolding, the notes are perfectly proper, even bland. Most are devoted to that inexhaustible Victorian topic: health. Their love is expressed through solicitude for each other's physical well-being. He frets over her colds and various ailments and rejoices in each recovery. He recounts his own symptoms and his various medications and dosages. Once he advises her to dose herself with "camphor Julep"; when a sore throat threatens to become serious, he announces, "I *must* see you, and *will not be prevented*." His high-flown language, straight out of melodrama, shows his enjoyment in playing the paterfamilias.

The notes are loving without being in the least romantic (or even personal); not one is an actual love letter in the strict sense of the word. Perhaps she complained of his lack of ardor, for one letter begins: "You must not be surprised at the brevity and matter-of-fact style of my letters, for we have so much to do."

The year of his engagement was both exhausting and exhilarating. He was finishing *Sketches by Boz,* reporting for several newspapers, and writing *The Pickwick Papers.* Much to her displeasure, Catherine had to take a backseat to her fiancé's numerous activities. During a typical Victorian courtship, the betrothed could expect her fiancé to visit every night. Dickens tried, but he was often fatigued, ill, or rushing to make a deadline. Thus many of his letters are excuses or explanations for cancellations, delays, or absences: "It is I fear but a tiresome repetition of an old story to say that I am too tired, and dispirited to write more than a brief note" and "A recollection of the advanced state of the month compels me with a very bad grace to stay at home until the evening, when, please God, I shall be with you about seven." In a letter of October 30, 1835, he sounds almost desperate, pleading with her to let him stay at home to nurse a cold: "If it should be a damp night, and the fog should continue, would you advise me to stay at home, take some gruel, try hot water for my feet, and go to bed early?—Let me know." Only the cruelest woman could demand a visit after such a litany.

*C*atherine Dickens at twenty-seven, from a painting by Daniel Maclise. Scholars, interpreting her body language, note that Catherine's bent head and lowered eyes suggest her docile and submissive nature.

But on many occasions Catherine was not pleased, and she resorted to complaining in a baby talk designed to mitigate the harshness of her anger. There are frequent allusions to her displeasure: "I hope . . . my dearest girl, and that you have no new complaints either *bodily* or *mental:* indeed I feel full confidence after last night that you will not have a renewal of the latter." (One wonders what happened "last night.") One letter begins, "I am sorry that you are 'coss' "; while another ends on a more loving note: "10,000 kisses—not 'coss' I hope."

Twenty-two years later, Dickens claimed that he had never loved Catherine, but what these notes suggest is not that he never loved her, but that he probably was never *in* love with her. Compared to Thomas Carlyle's epistolary rages to his fiancé, Jane, or the impassioned outbursts of Robert Browning to Elizabeth Barrett, or even Dickens's own lovesick ramblings to Maria Beadnell, these notes, neither funny nor ardent, lack the famed Dickensian charm and could have been written by almost any young man.

Novels by the Numbers

🌴

Make 'em laugh, make 'em cry, make 'em wait.
—WILKIE COLLINS

o Englishman in the middle class of life *buys* a book," noted a writer in the *Athenaeum* in 1828, almost a decade before *The Pickwick Papers* was published. In the years before *Pickwick,* novel buying was a shockingly expensive proposition. Only the very rich could afford to buy books, let alone stock a library. Hence a "good" library was a status symbol, indicating taste and affluence. When Dickens was a boy, the price of a volume was a half guinea, or 10½ shillings, where it stayed until *Pickwick.* This doesn't sound too bad until you realize that a novel was published in three, sometimes four, volumes. It is difficult to state what a pound was worth at any time in history; some have estimated that in terms of purchasing power, a half guinea was roughly equivalent to 100 modern American dollars, thus making the cost of a complete novel somewhere between $300–$400.

Avid readers belonged to circulating libraries, where for a fee they could read the latest fiction. The most popular of these was Mudie's. Mr. Mudie, a typical businessman of the age, was a tight-fisted, hymn-writing entrepreneur who could make or break a book. (In the 1870s he refused to take many of Wilkie Collins's sensational novels on the grounds that they were unsuitable for family reading.) The sheer quantity that Mudie's ordered—even before a book was published—often kept publishers afloat. (Mudie appreciated the triple-decker novel because it meant that three different subscribers could take out the same novel at one time.) Circulating libraries opened the market for fiction and helped a flourishing and literate middle class develop a taste for fiction, whether pulp or refined.

The triple-decker novel was the only format available until *Pickwick* made part publication, or serialization, respectable—and profitable. Until then only louche works or reprints ever appeared in serial form. Chapman and Hall's coup with *Pickwick* forced other publishers to change the way they published and marketed their books, the way authors wrote them, and the way readers read them. Serials appeared in monthly or weekly magazines, as many of Dickens's did, or individually in a "wrapper" decorated with scenes from the novels. Each novelist was given his own color, and when the sales of *David Copperfield* topped William Makepeace Thackeray's *Pendennis,* the latter graciously told a friend that "the green chap had beaten the yellow chap this month hollow." Part publication, while not the only means of publication in Victorian England, reigned for more than fifty years, with Dickens's death marking the beginning of its decline.

The serial's primary advantage was its low price. By paying a shilling a month, a reader eventually got an original, illustrated, 300,000-word novel for a pound. Spread over nineteen months—and sales for *Pickwick* often reached more than 40,000 for one number—that one shilling grew into a fortune, netting Chapman and Hall a hefty 10,000 pounds—far more than any of their three-deckers, or the deluxe illustrated sporting books that had previously been their staple. *Pickwick* showed publishers that if they were willing to print cheap fiction, there was a market eager to buy it. Serialization made novels, once exclusively for the rich, what the critic John Sutherland calls a "cheap luxury," the perfect commodity for a rising middle class seeking to mimic its betters.

Sales figures for a successful number are enough to make any modern novelist weep with envy. One number of *The Old Curiosity Shop* alone sold more than 100,000 copies—in one month! Publishers depended on such large sales, since each part was so inexpensive. But ironically, readers paid more for *Pickwick* than they would have for an expensive three-decker novel—it just didn't seem that much.

This new, inexpensive fiction, combined with the rise in literacy throughout the century and the development of an industry that could make books cheaper and faster, meant that book prices generally stayed low. As a result, the reading public swelled, and an industry was born to accommodate it. Dickens's monthly numbers were in a green wrapper decorated with scenes from the novel. With the exception of the final "bonus" number, each contained thirty-two pages and two illustrations, along with special offers and suitable advertising. Seasonal events were tied into the plot. The famous Christmas at Dingley Dell incident in *Pickwick* occurred in the December number; Sam Weller's Valentine's Day took place, naturally, in February. Readers could thus feel as if their experiences paralleled those of their fictional heroes.

A successful serial would always appear later as a book, either as a three-decker or a single volume, or, as in the case of *Great Expectations,* both. Around the middle of the century, publishers began producing inexpensive reissues (called bookstall editions) under such names as "Railway" and "Cheap" editions. Books of this sort were designed not only for less affluent readers but for a new type of consumer, one for whom books were a replaceable commodity—something to fill the leisure hours in a railway car—rather than an object to treasure.

MUSE AND METHOD

Some authors, notably Dickens, were temperamentally suited to the pace of serials. Others, through sheer discipline and doggedness, transcended the form's limitations and excruciating demands. Month after month, year after year, they produced thousands upon thousands of words, creating, if not masterpieces, then at least readable, profitable works—without word processors, secretaries, carbons, photocopy machines, or typewriters—often in drafty rooms by candlelight or in the half-shadows of gaslight. (Anthony Trollope, that unrivaled literary athlete, completed his morning stint by seven o'clock and then went to his "day job" at the postal service. He wrote most of his sixty novels in his spare time—when he wasn't reorganizing England's postal system!)

Today we tend to assume that a literary style emerges out of an author's genius, temperament, and perspective on the world, or we simply attribute it to the mysteries of inspiration. The Victorian novel was a collaboration between muse and method. What we call artistry was at least partly a response to the demands of the serial form. We'll never know to what extent a masterpiece like *Bleak House* was affected by workaday concerns such as printer's deadlines, pagination, readers' taste, the need for continuity, and word count. *Hard Times, Great Expectations,* and *A Tale of Two Cities* were influenced by the fact that they were written for a weekly rather than a monthly periodical. A weekly publication gave the writer less space and less need to pad; the action had to move swiftly, and every word counted. These novels are thus the most economical Dickens wrote, with none of the *longueurs* that turn off many readers. Dashed off at the last moment, *Great Expectations* is at once Dickens's most economical and most lyrical novel; all its poetry is compressed into a dramatic, tightly knit plot.

UNITY

Our experience in reading *Bleak House* is different from that of the Victorian reader, who got his plot spooned out in monthly dollops. Today we read at our own unhurried pace and can even jump forward a few chapters if so inclined. A serialist needed to provide unity in an extended work that was created piecemeal. One way he did this was through recurring imagery, such as the fog that pervades *Bleak House,* which slowly gathers meaning as an unforgettable metaphor for moral, social, and legal obfuscation.

CHARACTER TRAITS AS MNEMONICS

*M*odern novelists don't need to reintroduce a character each time he or she appears, but the serialist couldn't be certain his readers would remember a character after an absence of three or four months. As a mnemonic device, which became his signature, Dickens stamped each character with a memorable catchphrase, an identifiable verbal tic, a characteristic gesture, or an arresting feature, and then mentioned it practically every time the character appeared. These recurring signatures were leitmotives that provided unity and jogged the reader's memory. Every time Mrs. Gummidge appears in *David Copperfield,* she sighs for the "old one": "I'm a lone lorn, creetur and everythink goes contrary with me." When Mr. Turveydrop mentions the word *Deportment,* his entire character is recalled in a flash. Mrs. Sparsit, the aristocratic housekeeper to the parvenu Mr. Bounderby, possesses a pair of "dense, black eyebrows" and a "Cariolarian nose," which are mentioned whenever she comes on the scene. The nose become an emblem of all things Sparsitian: superciliousness, cruelty, snobbery, bitterness. Other examples include

Mr. Murdstone's luxuriant black whiskers, a symbol for domineering male sexuality; Mr. Carker's glistening white teeth, which evoke his predatory nature; and Mr. Vholes's black gloves, which he removes as though skinning his hand in a grotesque image of sinister gentility. All these act as mnemonics, much as the repetition of a phrase in Homeric poetry served as a frame of reference for the speaker. Each time the character appears, the same detail is produced, gradually accumulating meaning until an entire personality is condensed into a set of teeth or a pair of gloves.

WHY ARE VICTORIAN NOVELS SO LONG?

*C*ontrary to popular belief, Dickens did not get paid by the word. One simple explanation for the size of Victorian novels is that everything about the Victorians was gargantuan and prolific. They did nothing by halves, particularly Dickens, although his most popular book, *A Christmas Carol,* is also his shortest. But a more practical reason for the Victorian novel's length is that many novels originated as serials, and each installment consisted of thirty-two pages of fifty lines each. Moreover, thrifty Victorians expected a lot of book for their money. To people without television or movies, books were a major source of entertainment, and the longer they lasted the better. Also, the major novels of Dickens, Eliot, and Thackeray usually have multiple plots and thus require more space.

SERIALS AND SALES

*T*he serial reader was reading a work in progress, and thus, to a certain degree, he was able to participate in the writing process in a way we could never do today. If sales dropped, an author knew he was doing something wrong and could change it. When Dickens saw that Sam Weller's appearance boosted sales of *Pickwick,* he immediately shoved the original Pickwickians aside and gave Sam center stage. Trollope once told how he came to kill off the meddlesome Mrs. Proudie of the Barsetshire novels: as he sat writing in his club, he happened to hear two clergymen complaining about his recurring characters, particularly that High Church battle-ax, Mrs. Proudie. The author rose, introduced himself, and promised the startled men that he would kill Mrs. Proudie "before the week was over." And so he did. Later he regretted his rashness, but unlike writers of modern soap operas, he never tried to resurrect her with a lame excuse.

*A*fter weeping over the death of Paul Dombey, Victorian readers could look down and find an advertisement for ladies' undergarments or hair tonics, a typically Victorian mix of sentiment and pragmatism. Serials, like television today, reached the widest possible audience and were shrewdly used to sell everything from indigestion pills to corsets. Richard Altick, an authority on Victorian reading habits, notes that the advertising supplement to one *Pickwick* number promoted Rowland's Macassar Oil, for those who "court the GAY AND FESTIVE SCENES especially during the Dance or the heated atmosphere of crowded assemblies."

Perhaps the most important instance of reader participation was the case of Little Nell. Sensing what was coming, hundreds of readers wrote Dickens, beseeching him not to let Nell die. This time he ignored his public, and gave them what he believed they really wanted, not what they thought they did. Dickens's instincts were right: Nell's death is one of the most famous moments in literature. Once, however, he did comply with a reader's demand: the shady Miss Mowcher in *David Copperfield,* a dwarfish manicurist-chiropodist who sells cosmetics (a suspicious trade), initially appears as a shady figure who arouses David's suspicions. But the clues lead nowhere, and Miss Mowcher, rather improbably, turns out to be one of the novel's more virtuous women. What happened was that the model for Miss Mowcher, a diminutive chiropodist by the name of Mrs. Seymour Hill, recognized herself in the story and complained to Dickens, who immediately changed her role in the novel.

DICKENS, THE SERIAL KING

*D*ickens was the undisputed king of the serials. With *Pickwick* he practically invented the form. Its fast pace, rapid action, and forced intimacy with the reader all coincided perfectly with his temperament and genius. He needed the dual gratification of seeing his words in print each month (or week) and receiving an immediate response from fans and reviewers. A Dickens novel stayed in the public eye for almost two years and was often reviewed and advertised several times during its run. The excitement of the serial rarely let up. Deadlines were an urgent muse, pressing Dickens on, firing his creativity or, as he put it, his "steam." According to Julia Prewitt Brown, author of *Backgrounds to the Victorian Novel,* Dickens would begin his serials by writing two or three installments, but after that it would usually be a month-by-month rush to meet the publisher's deadlines, which were usually a few weeks before publication. Sometimes he didn't know where he was going and would work several plot strains simultaneously, all of which he would ingeniously tie together in a dramatic and satisfying conclusion.

Dickens's nervous energy was perfect for the serial form, which required two weeks of concentrated, feverish work which then freed him to do other work. On the other hand, the process, continued almost uninterrupted for almost forty years, was his undoing. As John Sutherland notes in *Victorian Novelists and Publishers,* Thackeray was completely white-haired by the age of forty. In his mid-fifties, Charles Lever declared, "I was thirty years younger ten years ago." And at forty-three, Dickens looked positively elderly. Yet despite crippling pain, illness, and despondency, he only missed two deadlines in his entire career. In May 1837 he abandoned Mr. Pickwick and Oliver while he retired to the country to mourn the death of his sister-in-law, Mary Hogarth. The other missed deadline was due to his own death in June 1870.

FED ON FICTION: WOMEN NOVEL READERS

*S*ince the biggest consumers of novels were women, "women's fiction" came into being during the Victorian age. The word *consumer* is particularly apt. The popular press delighted in portraying the female reader as ravenous, feeding on bonbons and French novels. Thus the no-nonsense

Florence Nightingale witheringly dismissed the idle woman, comparing her to a drug addict or, heaven forbid, a reader of fiction. Indolent women, she complained, "are exhausted, like those who live on opium or novels all their lives." If not an actual vice, then novel reading was at best an indulgence for those with too much time on their hands.

The feminine need for novels, writes the critic Isobel Armstrong, was seen by the Victorians as "almost an eating disorder." Women who read too much were diagnosed as having an unbridled appetite for sensation, which their own lives could not satisfy: "The woman reader gorged herself on print, on fiction in particular, which was insistently portrayed in a variety of metaphors from pastry to poison, strawberry ices, sugar plums and fiery sauces."

To continue the gustatory metaphor, women readers who fattened on fiction deprived themselves of salutary nourishment in the form of sermons, memoirs of virtuous gentlefolk, or "improving" travelogues. Sensational novels—tales of bigamy, forgery, lost wills, murder, mistaken identities, and insanity—were reviled not just as trash but as "women's fiction."

For the female fiction addict, the masculine library was a veritable garden containing the tantalizing, forbidden fruit known as "French novels."

With undisguised contempt, the fastidious art critic John Ruskin observed two females traveling from Venice to Verona. Ignoring the luscious scenery, they were, he wrote, sprawled and "writhing" amongst "French novels, lemons and lumps of sugar to beguile their state with."

Unmarried women, considered little more than children, were forbidden to read the racier novels their married sisters enjoyed. Thus for some women an important access to connubial pleasures was through the male library. A *Punch* cartoon of the period depicts a bride, still in her gown, hastily grabbing a book from a shelf as her honeymoon coach waits outside. The caption reads, "It's all right, I'm married now." (Boys, too, came under attack. Dr. Thomas Arnold, father of the poet and the most famous headmaster of Rugby, believed that both *Pickwick* and *Nicholas Nickleby* had contributed to the "decrease in manly thoughtfulness" at the school. And Samuel Taylor Coleridge, himself no stranger to indolence, wrote that "novel reading spares the reader the trouble of thinking, it saves him from the boredom of vacancy, and establishes a habit of indolence.")

The Pickwick Papers

I must own, I do hope that long after my hand is withered as the pens it held, Pickwick *will be found on many a dusty shelf with many a better work.*
—DICKENS, when the novel was only half finished

T he *Pickwick Papers* is one of those rare, unclassifiable, and irresistible novels. Actually, it isn't a novel at all in the traditional sense, as it lacks a coherent plot that moves from beginning to middle to end. It ends only because its serial run ended. According to George Gissing, a great admirer of Dickens, "*Pickwick* cannot be classed as a novel; it is merely a great book." George Orwell and G. K. Chesterton agreed. And it is simply as a book that it must be judged.

Technically, it's a disaster: a hodgepodge of escapades and buffoonery, gruesome or pathetic interpolated tales that have nothing to do with the main story, of a bald, middle-aged hero who disconcertingly changes in the middle of the novel (as Dickens recognized the limitations of his original creation).

Emotionally, however, *Pickwick* is one of the most satisfying books written. It reads with an air of unrestrained spontaneity, as if its author one day cried out, "Let's write a novel!" Its utter lack of literary pretension and its slapdash vigor make it particularly endearing, especially today, when almost every first-time novelist feels compelled to write an earnest exploration of his own psyche. Nothing in *Pickwick* is internalized or tortured. In no other work is an author's joy in his own creative powers more apparent. We know that Dickens laughed out loud while he wrote his comic episodes, and *Pickwick* fairly explodes with mirth. Behind the prose bubbles a young man's elation as he realizes his power to command an audience, and this exuberance infectiously, mysteriously, rises from the pages.

Before sitting down with *Pickwick,* you should get into a proper Pickwickian frame of mind; otherwise the book will seem merely inane instead of

A historical moment: Mr. Pickwick
meets Sam Weller in the courtyard
of the White Hart as re-created
in the 1952 movie.

inanely joyous. For the Pickwickian spirit is a joy that triumphs to
spite—and in spite of—evil. This
spirit consists of an odd double
vision: you read with the intense
pleasure of childhood, without
sacrificing the wisdom of matu-
rity. *Pickwick* does what great comedy does: it allows you to regress for a time
while remaining safely adult (a double state of being similar to that of the
novel's characters).

Surprisingly for Dickens, there's not a child in the entire novel—that role
is reserved for the adult Pickwickians, a quartet of boobies whose joys, sorrows, and appetites belong to childhood. The Pickwickian fondness for
food, drink, and comfort is legendary (mealtimes loom large in the novel);
experience with women is virtually nonexistent; and for much of the novel
the idea of evil is limited to what we would consider schoolboy pranks. The
book presents what adulthood must seem like from a child's perspective:
unlimited snacking, a series of adventures, crushes without sexual implications. The closest thing to sex in the novel is when Mr. Pickwick enters
the wrong room at an inn and, to his extreme embarrassment, discovers a
middle-aged lady in curlpapers. This is neither erotic, for the woman is decidedly homely, nor voyeuristic—Mr. Pickwick's horror as he watches her
is very real. (This is the Pickwickian version of a French farce.) But most
important, Pickwickians reside in a world without responsibility or con-

straints: they move according to their pleasure and with the aid of the ever-ready coaching schedule.

What saves *Pickwick* from silliness is the ironic, detached voice of Boz, the recipient, transcriber, and editor of the Pickwick papers, the records of club transactions and activities. It is the tension between this dry adult voice and the characters' infantile behavior that makes *Pickwick* more than just a funny book.

In ludicrously elevated diction, Boz relates Pickwickian escapades as if they were important events, presenting the zany Pickwickian perspective on its own terms. Boz's gravity is tantamount to a verbal wink that says, "Isn't all this silly?" And "this" sweepingly takes in not only the novel's world but our own as well, our society, our politics, our crushes that take on operatic proportions, our puffed-up sense of self, our follies that masquerade as wisdom, and, of course, our social pretensions.

In reflecting a fun-house mirror of reality through the Pickwickian world, Dickens mocks social conventions, institutions, and dogmas—but with a good humor not found in any of his other novels. Take Mr. Pickwick's observation of the Eatanswill elections, where the Buff and Blue parties battle with all the ferocity of "real" politicians. Their issues are Lilliputian, their platforms indistinguishable. Their sole reason for being is their opposition to each other. With his experience as a parliamentary and court reporter, Dickens brilliantly captures, and magnifies, the strategies of political rhetoric and speechifying that, a century and a half later, are re-echoed every election year. The speeches of the two candidates Samuel Slumkey and Horatio Fizkin

> though differing in every other respect, afforded beautiful tribute to the merit and high worth of the electors of Eatanswill. Both expressed their opinion that a more independent, a more enlightened, a more public-spirited, a more noble-minded, a more disinterested set of men than those who had promised to vote for him, never existed on earth; each darkly hinted his suspicions that the electors in the opposite interest had certain swinish and besotted infirmities which rendered them unfit for the exercise of important duties they were called upon to discharge. Fizkin expressed his readiness to do anything he was wanted; Slumkey, his determination to do nothing that was asked of him. Both said that the trade, manufactures, the commerce, the prosperity of Eatanswill, would ever be dearer to their hearts than any earthly object; and each had it in his power to state, with the utmost confidence, that he was the man who would eventually be returned.

This formula has remained pretty much unchanged. Refracted through the naive Pickwickian lens, which accepts everything unquestioningly, we see the insanity of the Eatanswill political system—and at the same time we can't miss the resemblance to our own party politics. In reading *Pickwick,* we discover that what seemed alien or grotesque is actually our own world.

THE PICKWICKIAN JOURNEY

*T*he novel begins on May 12, 1827, with a meeting of the Pickwick Club in full swing. Its president, Mr. Pickwick, has just concluded his paper, "Speculations on the Source of Hampstead Ponds, with some Observations on the theory of Tittlebats" (Dickens here spoofs the "learned societies," then all the rage in London). Out of the controversy of that meeting emerged an offshoot, the Corresponding Society of the Pickwick Club:

> "That while this Association is deeply sensible of the advantages which must accrue to the cause of science from the production to which they have just adverted—no less than from the unwearied researches of Samuel Pickwick, Esq., G.C.M.P.C. [General Chairman—Member Pickwick Club], in Hornsey, Highgate, Brixton and Camberwell,—they cannot but entertain a lively sense of the inestimable benefits which must inevitably result from carrying the speculations of that learned man into a wider field, from extending his travels, and consequently enlarging his sphere of observation, to the advancement of knowledge, and the diffusion of learning."

The joke is that despite the pretentious language, the Pickwickian pursuit of knowledge has only extended to Highgate and Hornsey, safe provinces of the genteel middle class. Thus it comes to pass that in the pursuit of knowledge, Mr. Pickwick, along with the club's venerable officers, Augustus Snodgrass, Nathaniel Winkle, and Tracy Tupman, venture into the world beyond suburban London.

Essential to the novel is each Pickwickian's "ruling passion," or romanticized self-image: Mr. Pickwick, dedicated to the advancement of knowledge, prides himself on his "gigantic brain"; plump Mr. Tupman is devoted to "the fair sex"; Mr. Snodgrass is a poet; and Mr. Winkle a sporting man. But Mr. Snodgrass never writes a poem or utters anything remotely poetical; Mr. Winkle aims at a rook and shoots Mr. Tupman; Mr. Tupman courts the middle-aged spinster Rachel Wardle, loses her to the adventurer Mr. Jingle, and is never seen with a woman again. And the novel's sagacious hero is continually led astray by assorted charlatans and sharks. Yet despite all the evidence to the contrary, these homely, inept men retain their belief in themselves: in the Pickwickian landscape, one need never confront the painful knowledge of one's limitations.

The knowledge Mr. Pickwick acquires on his travels consists not of observable, quantifiable facts, but of wisdom earned through direct involvement with the world. This idea is as old as storytelling itself: innocence and the temptations that beset it in a fallen world. Mr. Pickwick is a modern pilgrim, or knight-errant, and the novel follows the ancient motif of a quest. Through his hero, an innocent abroad, Dickens treats the problem of how to acquire knowledge of evil without becoming tainted by it.

As W. H. Auden has pointed out, Mr. Pickwick is a mythic character, and the novel is a comic reenactment of the Fall, but with more felicitous results. His mishaps and adventures arise from the collision between the real and the ideal. Through his encounters with the wily Mr. Jingle and his experiences in Fleet Prison, Mr. Pickwick comes to embrace a more complex view of life. Like Eve's, Mr. Pickwick's curiosity lures him out of a safe retreat, and his newfound knowledge of good and evil enables him to achieve a higher form of innocence, one based on experience, not childish credulity. In the course of the novel, he changes from an infantile stooge into a noble man capable of compassion. He becomes a rarity: someone who understands evil while remaining undiminished by it.

THE PICKWICKIANS AT LARGE

*A*fter a verbose and tedious start, *The Pickwick Papers* moves into high gear in chapter 2, when the quartet are let loose upon an unsuspecting world. Wherever they go, they wreak havoc. Their world, like that of Laurel and Hardy, is filled with comic land mines. Objects and people collide, collapse, explode, and plummet. Pickwickians get locked in, locked out, and locked up; they get lost, misled, and abandoned. And most of all they reunite, usually at mealtime. In true Dickensian fashion, the novel is filled with linguistic pratfalls, absurd lists, verbal horseplay, and inspired names: Count Smorltork, Lord Mutanhed, Mr. Smangle, Serjeant Buzfuz, Miss Henrietta Nupkins, Mr. Phunkey, and Dowager Lady Snuphanuph.

The first part of the book is packed with episodes of a somewhat arbitrary nature, most of which are tenuously linked, although one is sometimes a springboard to another. Thus a Pickwickian meets someone who invites them all for a visit. But Mr. Pickwick ends up at Bob Sawyer's bachelor digs simply because Dickens thought it would be amusing to write about Mr. Pickwick at a student booze fest. Once he's there, the reader can't imagine him anyplace else.

Pickwick, like most of Dickens's novels, is a quarry of events, tag phrases, and characters that have evolved into buzzwords, the mere mention of which sends the Dickens fan into ecstasies: Mr. Pickwick and the lady in curlpapers! Mrs. Leo Hunter's fancy-dress breakfast! Count Smorltork! The fight between Mr. Pickwick and Mr. Tupman! ("You're a fellow!" "You're another!") The Fat Boy, a prepubescent Peter Lorre, utters one of the best lines in the book. "I wants to make your flesh creep," he yells into Old Grandmother Wardle's ear trumpet.

There are more than eighty characters stuffed into this one novel—not to mention the sixteen "fictional" characters in the interpolated tales. (As one critic put it, whenever Dickens doesn't know what to do, "he throws another character on the fire.") Most of these appear in sequences that can be extremely funny—if you appreciate British humor (sort of a Victorian version of "Beyond the Fringe" cum music hall turns). In one of the best episodes Mrs. Leo Hunter, a culture vulture with "lit'ry" aspirations, recites her acclaimed poem, "Ode on an Expiring Frog."

Can I view thee panting, lying
On thy stomach, without sighing;
Can I unmoved see thee dying
*   On a log,*
*   Expiring frog!*

*   Say, have with fiends in shape of boys,*
*   With wild halloo, and brutal noise,*
*   Hunted thee from marshy joys,*
*   With a dog,*
*   Expiring frog?*

Naturally gregarious, the Pickwickians meet assorted eccentrics who lead them from one escapade to the next. Their first important encounter is with the aptly named Mr. Jingle, a bounder who sends them off on a string of quixotic adventures. Like Dickens's most memorable characters, Mr. Jingle is identified by his speech patterns. Two years earlier Dickens had taught himself shorthand, and Jinglespeech, spasmodic bursts of free-associative patter, is what shorthand would sound like if it were a spoken language. Warning the Pickwickians of danger, Mr. Jingle cries: "Heads, heads—take care of your heads! . . . Terrible place—dangerous work—other day—five children—mother—tall lady, eating sandwiches—forgot the arch—crash—knock—children look round—mother's head off—sandwich in her hand—no mouth to put it in—head of a family off. . . ." This string of breathless phrases is usually punctuated with the emphatic qualifier "very." In this instance he describes one of his amorous escapades to the susceptible Mr. Tupman:

"Many conquests, sir?" inquired Mr. Tupman.
"Conquests! Thousands. Don Bolaro Fizzgig—Grandee—only daughter—Donna Christina—splendid creature—loved me to distraction—jealous father—high-souled daughter—handsome Englishman—Donna Christina in despair—prussic acid—stomach pump in my portmanteau—operation performed—old Bolaro in ecstasies—consent to our union—join hands and floods of tears—romantic story—very."

But despite his charm, Mr. Jingle is ultimately exposed as "a serpent," the first sign that the Pickwickian garden is not as idyllic as it seems.
    The novel's most important event occurs in the fourth installment, in one of those seemingly offhand moments that make literary history. Mr. Pickwick, a portly knight-errant, has set off in feverish pursuit of Mr. Jingle, who has eloped with Rachel ("Oh! You Quiz!") Wardle. His quest takes him to the

White Hart Inn, where he bribes a "boots" (shoeshine boy) for the couple's room number. This minor figure turns out to be Sam Weller, Sancho Panza to Mr. Pickwick's Don Quixote. The archetypal duo: the pragmatic servant with street smarts teams up with an ingenuous master with dreams. (Think of the popularity of Bertie and Jeeves.) The moment, captured by the illustrator "Phiz" (Hablot Knight Browne), depicts Sam, his hat debonairly pulled over one brow, a knowing grin (or perhaps a smirk) on his face, the epitome of cockney charm and jaunty self-assurance. After Sam's appearance, the other three club members recede into the background, with the spotlight now firmly fixed on the two Samuels, Weller and Pickwick. (Incidentally, Sam's cockney surname is pronounced "veller," a pun on valor.) Their pairing leads to the turning point in the novel, and it's here in chapter 12 that Dickens begins to establish a recognizable theme and plot.

THE FALL OF MR. PICKWICK

*B*efore he can hire Sam, Mr. Pickwick must ask permission from his landlady, the marriage-mad Martha Bardell. With characteristic timidity, he leads up to the subject: "Do you think it," he cautiously asks, "a much greater expense to keep two people, than to keep one?" Through one of those comic failures of communication that so delight Dickens, she of course assumes he is proposing and promptly faints into his arms.

This brief scene is the cannon that explodes into a series of events: Mrs. Bardell's suit for breach of promise, Mr. Pickwick's encounter with the shifty lawyers Dodson and Fogg, the trial itself, Mr. Pickwick's refusal to pay damages, and his subsequent imprisonment in the Fleet. Even here, in Dickens's cheeriest novel, the author is never very far from the prison house, an obsessive image that will occur with haunting regularity in almost every one of his novels. Mr. Pickwick's experiences with the law (truly Dickensian in its perversion of truth and logic), his confrontation with suffering humanity, and the prevalence of evil, both institutional and individual, allow him (and his creator) the chance to penetrate deeper into the depths of human misery. (Incidentally, the name Fogg punningly anticipates Dickens's satire on the obscurity of the legal system that he will be set forth more fully in *Bleak House.*)

Until now, tragedy in the novel has been strictly limited to the interpolated or "introduced" tales, stories offered on the flimsiest of pretexts, i.e.: a Pickwickian bumps into a stranger, who proposes a story. Some critics condemn the tales as filler, used when Dickens was too exhausted to muster the enthusiasm for another Pickwickian adventure. Others believe that Dickens regarded them as consummate art and an integral part of the narrative. But everyone agrees that they are almost all relentlessly bleak, depicting horrors that seem out of place in this aggressively cheerful novel.

Commissioned by Chapman and Hall to write a funny book, Dickens seems able to control his tragic impulses by cordoning them off from the main narrative via these squalid little melodramas. One thinks of Mr. Dick ⟨!⟩ in *David Copperfield,* who, unable to keep his obsession with the beheading of Charles I from appearing in the legal documents he is commissioned to copy, sets aside a notebook in which he can freely indulge in his fixation. Whenever he feels the impulse to write about Charles's unfortunate end, he simply turns to his notebook, thus keeping his documents free of unwanted elements. In a sense, the interpolated tales are Mr. Dick(ens)'s "special notebooks," where he allows himself the luxury of dwelling on his own private obsessions: madness, murder, imprisonment, parricide, and vengeance.

The first, "The Bagman's Tale," is about an alcoholic clown who dies of the DTs. "The Queer Client" is a tale of monomaniacal vengeance by a man who is imprisoned for debt by his father-in-law in the Marshalsea, the prison where John Dickens spent three months when the novelist was twelve. Then there's "The Convict's Return," with the clichéd long-suffering mother who, unable to prevent her son from "going bad," dies heartbroken when he is transported for robbery. Fourteen years later he returns home, learns of his mother's death, "accidentally" meets his long-lost abusive father, and tries to kill him. Only the father's unexpected heart attack prevents the son from committing patricide. The style of the tales is very different from the unrestrained hilarity of *Pickwick* proper:

> The old man [the father] uttered a loud yell which rang through the lonely fields like the howl of an evil spirit. His face turned black: the gore rushed from his mouth and nose, and dyed the grass a deep dark red, as he staggered and fell. He had ruptured a blood-vessel: and he was a dead man before his son could raise him.

Pretty gruesome. But whatever their reason for being there, it's remarkable how many of these tales touch on ideas and images that would preoccupy Dickens until the day he died.

The effect of these unseemly tales breaking in upon the sunny narrative is similar to that of the guest who tells a tasteless anecdote in the midst of a joyous celebration. All festivity abruptly stops; the guests listen politely if disconcertedly, and then the conversation continues as if nothing happened! So too in *Pickwick:* after each teller completes his tale, the main line of action immediately resumes. It's as if such suffering and horror only belong to tales, not the real world. For instance, just as the one tale concludes with the father's blood staining the ground, Mr. Pickwick falls into a deep sleep, and the chapter ends. The next opens with a glorious morning, suggesting that the nightmare of human existence is simply a bad dream from which it is possible to awake.

This mood of unbroken tranquillity radically changes when Mr. Pickwick is imprisoned in the Fleet and discovers real, not fictionalized, sorrow. After Mr. Pickwick's imprisonment, critics note, the tales appear less frequently. Perhaps Dickens no longer needs these stories because the disasters, once so carefully segregated, have now seeped into the narrative proper. Mr. Pickwick experiences directly what the tales conveyed vicariously.

By now Mr. Pickwick should appear differently to the reader. The foolish old man who in chapter 19 is found publicly sleeping off a drunken binge in a wheelbarrow is not the hero who stands up to Dodson and Fogg. No longer a bumptious windbag, he possesses a natural wisdom and humility. Mr. Pickwick has become what Dostoyevsky, in his study of a purely good man, called an Idiot. Dickens's creation now seems less cartoonish, more mythic. W. H. Auden rather extravagantly compared him to a pagan god wandering the earth. Most often, however, the "new" Pickwick is compared to Don Quixote, and although Cervantes's creation is incomparably the greater, Dickens's hero is also an idealist in a cynical world, a man who will tilt at legal windmills, fight for the virtue of an aging spinster, and (mistakenly) defend the honor of a girls' finishing school.

Mr. Pickwick changes from childish to childlike. The first quality is anarchic, greedy, brimming with self-importance; the latter is openhearted, full of wonder, and absurdly good in the face of evil. As Dostoyevsky knew, the purely good man will always appear ridiculous to the world. And to the cynic, what could be more ludicrous than Mr. Pickwick's charity and forgiveness toward Mr. Jingle? Nevertheless, the pragmatic Dickens cannot forget that his characters inhabit a fallen world. Although he tells us what happens to all the major characters, he leaves the question of Mr. Jingle's reformation in doubt. Mr. Perker's skepticism about the possibility of change injects a sad note into what should be a jovial conclusion. There are some evils that can't be smoothed away. Mr. Pickwick gives his old enemy money, but he does so knowing that he might be taken in one last time. He would rather be benevolent and wrong than shrewd and right.

The disparity between the "two Pickwicks" suggests that if Dickens had the novel to do over, the first would have existed only in draft form. When asked about this, Dickens declared that Mr. Pickwick deepens because readers come to know him better. While this may be true, I suspect it is special pleading, the older Dickens defending the younger. Mr. Pickwick changes because Dickens did.

The question arises: would the novel be considered great if it were the only book Dickens had written? Some, including Briget Brophy, Michael Levey, and Charles Osborne, think not. Placing *Pickwick* on their list of "Fifty Works of English (and American) Authors We Could Do Without," they charge that "it appears to have been written in a series of jerkily spasmodic bouts of inane euphoria." For the many ardent Pickwickians, this exhilaration is the source of the novel's boyish charm, though it may not be to everyone's taste. The book's flaws themselves offer an unusual glimpse of a young genius at work. The furious pacing and the necessity for strict deadlines (Dickens often finished writing an installment only days before it hit the streets) meant that he could not retrospectively correct an error or rewrite a false start. This unpolished work shows us Dickens before he became "Dickensian." *Pickwick* exposes all those first attempts that might otherwise have been stashed in back drawers, erased, or thrown away.

The Pickwick Papers is Dickens's sweetest novel. It is the prototype for all good things Dickensian: frothy bowls of punch, Christmas cheer, blazing fires, welcoming inns with comely barmaids. It ends naturally with wedding bells, and—excluding the interpolated tales—there's only one death in it (a minor character, the joyless Mrs. Tony Weller). And this is the only Dickens novel in which an orphan doesn't make at least one appearance. Even Mr. Pickwick's experience with the Law, the archetypal Dickensian nightmare, is, although biting, an occasion for high comedy (viz. Mr. Winkle in the witness box). This is the novel Boz's fans wanted him to write over and over again. They longed for these happy Pickwickian days to continue in a blaze of perpetual summer.

But despite its vitality, *Pickwick* is an autumnal book, shot through with a sense of loss and an underlying awareness of time's passage. The novel ends with Mr. Pickwick's retirement to the country and the disbanding of the club. ("I am growing older, and want repose and quiet. My rambles, Sam, are over!") Its final lines are elegiac:

> Let us leave our old friend in one of those moments of unmixed happiness, of which, if we seek them, there are ever some, to cheer our transitory existence here. There are dark shadows on the earth, but its lights are stronger in the contrast. Some men, like bats or owls, have better eyes for the darkness than for the light. We, who have no such optical powers, are better pleased to take our last parting look at the visionary companions of many solitary hours, when the brief sunshine of the world is blazing full upon them. . . .

The last number, a "bumper" or double, must have been doubly poignant to those who had religiously followed the club's antics: for the first time in two years, there would be no new Pickwick adventure to anticipate.

Just as Dickens loved the contrasting images of a roaring fire set against a cold winter's night, so for him joy is always surrounded by loss. Remember: the novel's full title is *The Posthumous Papers of the Pickwick Club,* and although "posthumous" refers to the club, not its members, a sense of mortality is never very far from the book's luminous surface. The fictional adventures took place in 1824, but when Boz published his "transcription," many of the members would have been dead or aging. And the novel's final image, that of the enduring partnership between Sam and Mr. Pickwick, is a double one, containing loss within unity, permanence within transience. *Pickwick* may be elegiac, but it's not a lament. While it possesses the wistfulness of a retrospective glance, it is fueled by all the ambitious energy of a young man.

It is surprising that a young man would choose an aging one as the hero for a first novel. Green in spirit yet feeble in body, Mr. Pickwick is the reverse of Dickens, who at twenty-four must have felt already old in experience. Dickens also chose to set his novel in 1824, his *annus horribilis,* when for four months he toiled mindlessly at the blacking warehouse, an experience which, like that of Mr. Pickwick's imprisonment, marked the end of his innocence.

During the Pickwick years (1836–38), there were profound and rapid changes both in England and in Dickens's life. He began the novel a largely unknown writer; when it was finished he had become one of the most famous men in England. And although the events portrayed in the novel took place only twelve years earlier, they must have seemed like distant history to its readers. The Pickwickian world is preindustrial, the golden age of coaching and a time when London was still little more than a large village. (Dickens, however, was never one to completely sentimentalize the past; a sketch entitled "Early Coaches" opens with, "We have often wondered how many months' incessant traveling in a post-chaise it would take to kill a man.")

In one of those fortuitous coincidences that make history seem neatly compartmentalized, it was during the run of *Pickwick*—a novel that revolutionized the style, marketing, and writing of novels (see page 48)—that an old king died and a seventeen-year-old queen ascended the throne. The young novelist and the new monarch would shape the taste and temperament of an age.

❧ "I Thought of Mr. Pickwick" ❧

"I thought of Mr. Pickwick." Thus Dickens described the genesis of his first famous creation. But the story of his conception turns out to be far more complex, difficult, and interesting than Dickens's ingenuous statement implies.

The story begins not with Dickens but with Robert Seymour, one of England's leading political cartoonists, whose work had once appeared frequently in *Punch*. By the time his path crossed that of Dickens, however, he had become addicted to drugs and drink and was deeply in debt. Although he was still talented and famous, few established houses were willing to risk dealing with him. But when he approached Chapman and Hall (whose previous bestsellers included the less than memorable "Scenes and Recollections of Fly-fishing" and "A Topographical Dictionary"), they were only too eager to add him to their slim roster of mediocre writers.

Seymour proposed a picture book illustrating the high jinks of the fictitious Nimrod Club, a group of cockney sporting men who, as Dickens put it with thinly veiled contempt, "go out shooting, fishing, and so forth, and get themselves into difficulties through their want of dexterity." The book accepted, Chapman and Hall next approached several young authors to write captions for Seymour's illustrations, but one by one they refused, dismissing it as hack work.

Then in February 1836, Mr. Hall, having admired *Sketches by Boz,* visited Dickens in his tiny bachelor quarters at Furnival's Inn. When Dickens saw Hall, he screamed. Three years earlier, Hall, as part owner of a bookstore, had sold Dickens a copy of the magazine containing his first published story. The connection seemed a felicitous omen, and he accepted the offer—but only under certain conditions. He promptly informed Chapman and Hall that he was *not* a sporting man, that their idea was hackneyed, and that they would do better to let him, Dickens, have his own way. Or, as he put it, "It would be infinitely better for the plates to arise out of the text" so that he could have "a freer range of English scenes and people. I am afraid that I should ultimately do so in any case, whatever course I might prescribe to myself at starting." Thus Dickens bullied his way into literary history.

For the first number Seymour supplied the required four plates, but could only manage to finish three for the next. One, an illustration for "The Strollers' Tale," depicted a dying pantomime clown in the throes of the DTs—a far cry from the droll cockney sportsmen he had envisioned. After studying it, Dickens decided that the etching was not quite what he wanted: the clown, while suitably distressed, was *too* gruesome, apt to depress rather than intrigue readers. Fresh from his honeymoon, Dickens visited the anxious artist and after asking him to redo the picture, casually praised his ability to draw furniture. Dickens's biographer Edgar Johnson comments: "Seymour could hardly have been pleased to have been told that he could not draw people, that his true talents lay in depicting tables and chairs." Anxious to complete the illustration, Seymour worked all night. The next morning he killed himself.

No one, except Seymour's widow, blamed Dickens. The artist had been depressed before he met Dickens and only days earlier had reportedly asked his wife to try on a widow's cap. But Seymour's death is typical of the way events often turned out for Dickens. In *David Copperfield,* Dickens's fictional autobiography, seemingly immovable obstacles to happiness, such as an unsuitable wife or a rival, are conveniently removed. In art, so in life. *Pickwick* now belonged to Dickens.

✤ Seymour's replacement was Hablot Knight Browne, the man who would supply the definitive images for some of Dickens's most memorable creations. Seized by Dickens's enthusiasm, the illustrator promptly dubbed himself Phiz, a breezy sobriquet that went well with the youthful Boz. Given his genius for grotesque portraiture, the nickname is apt: Phiz, an abbreviation of "physiognomy," was Victorian slang for face—much like "kisser" or "mug."

THE PICKWICKIAN REVOLUTION

The man did not write for an audience so much as he expressed an audience's hunger—he made astonishingly vivid what an audience feared, what it dreamed of, what it wanted.
—JOHN IRVING

Boz should be compared to no one because no one has ever written like him—no one has ever combined the nicety of observation, the fineness of tact, the exquisite humour, the wit, heartiness. . . .
—ANONYMOUS REVIEWER

When Sir Walter Scott died in 1822, it seemed as if the novel had died with him. People still read fiction, but what they read was eminently forgettable. How many today have heard of, let alone read, Sir Edward Bulwer-Lytton (the man who wrote the line "It was a dark and stormy night") or the even more obscure Lady Bury, author of *The Disinherited and the Ensnared*? William Makepeace Thackeray, Anthony Trollope, the Brontës, George Eliot, Thomas Hardy—the stars of the Victorian novel—would not begin their writing careers for at least seven years after *Pickwick*. With *Pickwick,* Dickens had the field to himself.

It didn't take long for readers of *Pickwick* to realize they were in the presence of something new. Brash and boyish, Boz was a gust of fresh air into a vacuum. He was sui generis, or as he would call himself, "The Inimitable." *Pickwick* was a startling melange: social and political satire, music hall gags, melodrama, street slang, and urban legends. It also conveyed the moral of benevolence, thus establishing the Victorian taste for "elevating" fiction. And, as George Ford notes, by daring to introduce a Kafkaesque "mad-comic seriousness" into a hilarious novel, Dickens created a unique blend of light and dark, sanity and absurdity.

Pickwick did what few novels have ever done, before or since. Transcending gender, class, and age, it appealed to men, women, and children; educated and uneducated; upper, middle, and working-class. To the younger set, Boz was a cult figure; to older readers, *Pickwick* was reminiscent of the great novels of the eighteenth century. Judges read it on the bench between cases; tradesmen advertised their wares in its wrappers. Dickens's genius was to make each reader think he was writing specifically for him.

WHY *PICKWICK* WAS POPULAR

Pickwick's originality was not only an aesthetic achievement. It is a good book, a funny book, but neither good nor funny enough to account for the resulting Pickwick mania. Its newness was that of the age itself. All the latest advancements and trends in society, commerce, technology, and industry conspired to create the Pickwick phenomenon.

It is a novel of firsts: it was the first novel-as-commodity, and a popular commodity at that, with sales numbering in the tens of thousands in its first year alone. With the surge in population, the rise in literacy and leisure, there were simply more people with the time and money to read fiction. For the first time, too, a book could be read almost as soon as it was printed, in such far-flung regions as America, Canada, even India.

The story of *Pickwick* is the story of the rise of popular culture and modern marketing. As the first book read by the masses, it permeated the culture from top to bottom. Printed and bound on cheap paper, it was essentially the first paperback novel, the first work of fiction in history that almost everyone could afford.

Thus *Pickwick* was not only inspired by popular culture, it became popular culture. Sam Weller, Mr. Pickwick, and the rest of the club were as recognizable as regulars on a sitcom. Wellerisms were cited by lawyers and street urchins. Other catchphrases from the book crept into everyday banter. Seemingly overnight, an event, a person, or an experience could be pronounced Pickwickian, and everyone would understand what was meant.

Today we regard *Pickwick* as Literature with a capital L, but to its original readers it was pure fun. Dickens loved all forms of lowbrow amusements, and he thought of his early novels as entertainments not dissimilar from puppet shows, music hall revues, melodrama, even crime sheets. (At one point he actually refers to himself as Mr. Pickwick's "stage manager.") He created the demand for literary showmanship and then gave the public what it wanted. As one of the first artist/entertainers to market novels for public consumption, Dickens was the P. T. Barnum of fiction.

Pickwick profited by the advent of the new commercialism. As with blockbuster movies today, the novel's success led to the merchandising of related products, such as Pickwick coats or Sam Weller jestbooks, which in turn made the novel even more popular. More important, industry and technology made the novel, and its merchandise, widely available. New numbers were delivered by rail as soon as they came off the press. *Pickwick* was read not only in fashionable London but also in the provinces, not only in the industrial north but also in the agrarian south. Cheaper paper and new, faster methods of production meant more books to satisfy an increasingly voracious public. One need never search for the latest *Pickwick,* and back issues were quickly rereleased so that new readers could catch up.

As for matters of taste, *Pickwick* was deemed acceptable by even the most priggish readers (although there were, unbelievably, a few who complained about Mr. Pickwick's chance bedroom encounter with the lady in curl-papers!), thus conforming to the new emphasis on family values during the reign of Queen Victoria. It captured the zeitgeist almost before it arrived. For older readers, it reassuringly harkened back to the picaresque comic novels of Henry Fielding and Tobias Smollett, but it was Fielding purged of ribaldry, Smollett without the unsavory smells. In the 1838 preface to *Pickwick,* Dickens proudly asserted that there was nothing in his new novel, "no incident or expression . . . which would call a blush into the most delicate cheek." Almost thirty years later, an older, more cynical Dickens would put almost the same words into the hypocritical mouth of Podsnap, a man who blanched at anything that would "call a blush to the cheek of a young person." But in 1838 Dickens, a new family man himself, could write this without a trace of irony.

With *Pickwick* and the rise of the serials, a ritual was born: as soon as the latest number arrived, everyone would gather *en famille* to hear it read aloud. *Pickwick* would create a large part of the collective memory of a generation which would eventually view this innovative book as an emblem of a sweeter, more generous time.

Cedric Dickens and Eliot Engel maintain that it was Dickens's idea to make *Pickwick* a serial. When Chapman and Hall decided to charge a high price for the novel, Dickens told them they could make more money by stretching it out over nineteen months at a shilling per installment. Understandably, the publishers worried about how they could get readers to make a purchase each month. Dickens responded by telling them he could make them buy it by ending each number with a suspenseful moment.

Thus along with all its other marvels, *Pickwick* introduced the idea of the cliffhanger, and by extension, the soap opera. Engel's standard lecture on Dickens is fittingly entitled "From Dickens to *Dallas* and *Dynasty.*" When Michael Malone, a novelist with a Ph.D. in English literature and a soap opera scriptwriter, heard his name called out as an Emmy award–winner for best writer for his work on *One Life to Live,* he leaped to the podium and invoked Dickens as the father of the soaps. Malone insists that if Dickens were alive today, he'd be writing about nervous breakdowns, unwanted pregnancies, and messy divorces. The fertility of Dickens's imagination, his ability to crank out intricate plots, and his ear for dialogue would make him an ideal scriptwriter for daytime television.

❧ PICKWICKIANA ❧

❈ According to *The Dickensian,* volume 33, the interpolated tale "The Madman's Manuscript" became grounds for an annulment in 1937, when a husband made his wife read it on their honeymoon. Her lawyer, commenting on the cruelty of this act, remarked, "It will frizzle anybody's hair."

❈ Dickens first learned of *Pickwick*'s triumph while he was traveling outside of London. Thereafter, he superstitiously made certain to be out of town on every publication day.

❈ *Pickwick* must be the most alimentary of all Dickens's novels. According to Margaret Lane in "Pickwick on the Hearth," in *Dickens 1970: Centenary Essays,* the novel contains 35 breakfasts, 32 dinners, 10 lunches, 10 teas, 8 suppers, and not surprisingly, more than 249 references to beverages, from mulled port to milk punch. Dickens also mentions 59 inns, 33 by name.

❈ There were at least seven staged versions of *Pickwick* produced before Dickens had even finished writing the last installment.

❈ There are 865 people in *Pickwick*—roughly a new character for every page. And the plot moves through 168 places, more than any other Dickens novel.

IN THE PICKWICKIAN SENSE

*I*n *Pickwick*'s famous opening chapter, the argumentative Mr. Blotton insults Mr. Pickwick. When called to account for his hasty remark, Mr. Blotton lamely retreats with the comment, "I merely meant it in the Pickwickian sense." Dickens's original readers would have immediately caught the allusion: After disparaging a rival in a Parliamentary debate, Lord Brougham added, "I merely meant it in the Parliamentary sense." The phrase soon became a common addendum to any remark uttered in the heat of debate, giving members license to say anything they liked so long as it was "meant in the Parliamentary sense." Dickens's spoof turned out to be more than just a juvenile send-up of politicians. According to the critic Philip Collins, as soon as the members recognized themselves (in the Pickwickian sense), the practice immediately stopped. The phrase "in the Pickwickian sense" soon entered the language and is now defined (and included in most dictionaries) as any meaning other than the literal or intended one.

THE BEST-SELLER OF ALL TIME

*O*ne of the biggest champions of Pickwick *is the author's great-great-grandson Cedric Dickens, who hails the novel as the world's first paperback and soap opera.*

NE: *Can you give me some idea of* Pickwick's *success?*

CD: *The Pickwick Papers* was the best-seller of all time—of all books in the world—except probably the Bible. First, you have to invent some way of comparing a book with others at the time that it was published. So you take the number of people who could read and divide it by the number of people who bought the book. In Pickwick's day, that comes to 81 percent of the reading public. That's absolutely amazing! *Gone With the Wind* is next, with something like 40 percent. That's to give you some idea of *Pickwick* and what a wonderful book it is.

✳In addition to all the other Pickwickian novelties, there is even a Pickwickian syndrome, named no doubt by a Dickensian physician with a sense of humor. Inspired by the Fat Boy, it is characterized by obesity, hyperventilation, excessive appetite, fatigue, and sleep apnea. (And one might add, an irresistible desire to go coaching through the countryside.)

The Fat Boy has provided physicians with more diversion than any other Dickens character. Another doctor, after studying the Fat Boy's propensity to nod off at all times and places, diagnosed him as suffering from an acute case of narcolepsy. And in 1936 a Dr. Leonard Hill described the repellent child as "Greedy, sleepy, sexless and cruel," thus concluding that he suffers from a type of pituitary deficiency found only in the young. Out of all the characters in the novel, the Fat Boy "is the only one who shows no development." Dr. Hill deduces that the young servant also has a severe case of infantilism. (See also Tiny Tim disease, page 188.)

❖ In the wake of *Pickwick* mania, a parish clergyman paid a visit to console a dying man. His faith in the efficacy of prayer received a jolt, however, when on his way out, he heard the man mutter, "Well, thank God *Pickwick* comes out in ten days anyway."

❖ Dickens's books matured as he did, and one can trace his growth by reading chronologically through the canon. To complain that Pickwickian humor is sophomoric is beside the point. The joy of *Pickwick* resides in its utter abandonment. It's a world where a cold lamppost can be applied to a bruised forehead. Dickens was not a university man, and indeed he was unintellectual in his taste, habits, and humor. The Boz of *Pickwick* is more Laurel and Hardy than Noel Coward. As George Orwell so eloquently said, with Dickens, "there is always room for another custard pie."

A *Pickwick* Lexicon

With his first novel, Dickens had already begun enriching our vocabulary. Several words came out of *Pickwick* and into the lexicon. Although more popular then than now, such words as *Pickwickian* and *Wellerisms* are included in most modern dictionaries. Sam Weller, one of Dickens's most popular characters, gave his name to what is now known as a Wellerism—an assertion that opens with a solemn statement or quotation followed by an unexpected, comic sequel. For instance, " 'Everyone to his taste,' said the old woman as she kissed the cow." Or, " 'A little goes a long way,' as the nursemaid said when she dropped the baby over the Monument." *Pickwickian* signifies anything marked by simplicity and goodness.

Food, Glorious Food
(and Drink)

※

Many people ask if Mr. Dickens was a great eater, as they say he always
put such a lot of things in his books about eating—all sorts of feasts and good
dinners, they tell me. He wasn't but a light eater himself.
—WILLIAM EDRUPT, one of Dickens's office boys

ew novelists make reading about food as inviting as eating it, and
few use mealtimes as effectively. (The first and last words Dickens wrote as a novelist concern food. His first published short
story was entitled "Dinner at Poplar Walk," and the last word he
wrote in *Drood* before his fatal stroke was *appetite*.) For Dickens, often an
apple is just an apple, but sometimes his fare has moral, psychological, or social significance. For example, the edible throne of the Ghost of Christmas
Present evokes life's deepest joys, material as well as spiritual. Food is transformed into something transcendent, fare fit for a Christmas spirit:

> Heaped up on the floor, to form a kind of throne, were turkeys, geese,
> game, poultry, prawn, great joints of meat, suckling-pigs, long wreaths of
> sausages, mince-pies, plum-puddings, barrels of oysters, red-hot chest-
> nuts, cherry-cheeked apples, juicy oranges, luscious pears, immense
> twelfth-cakes, and seething bowls of punch, that made the chamber dim
> with their delicious steam.

By contrast (and not surprisingly), Scrooge sups on thin, watery gruel.

In the Dickensian universe, parties, such as the famous one in David's
rooms where Mr. Micawber whips up his celestial punch, are secular sacra-
ments with their own rites, prescriptions, and commandments. Bad table
manners, as Martin Chuzzlewit discovered in America, are not just a breach

of etiquette but a revolting form of selfishness. The act of sharing food unites disparate individuals into a festive community. The classic example of mealtime-as-communion is the most well-known feast in Dickens: the Cratchits' Christmas dinner. Organized down to the final wassail toast, each member of the family has his own part in the ceremony.

Dickens being Dickens, there is also a dark side to the act of eating, one scarcely comprehensible to the civilized mind: sometimes in Dickens's fiction *people* are regarded as food. Dickens's most compelling villains are carnivorous—casebook studies of sadistic orality: Mr. Carker in *Dombey and Son* with his gleaming white teeth relentlessly tracks Edith Dombey. Quilp in *The Old Curiosity Shop* lasciviously smacks his lips over thirteen-year-old Nell, pronouncing her a tasty morsel, and the ravenous Magwitch eyes young Pip as a potential edible: " 'You young dog,' said the man, licking his lips, 'what fat cheeks you ha' got. Darn me if I couldn't eat 'em.' " And David Copperfield avenges himself on Mr. Murdstone by biting him—hard.

FOOD AND CHARACTER

*A*s a master of quotidian detail, Dickens observed the way people eat: "Mr. Trabb had sliced his hot roll into three feather beds, and was slipping butter in between the blankets, and covering it up." Thus a minor character flares into full-bodied existence, his deft mannerisms as mincingly precise—and droll—as those of the plump film comedian Oliver Hardy.

But what and how one eats also reveals the soul. His best characters eat with gusto; his worst eat too little or too much. Gluttony (or bibulousness) almost always denotes hypocrisy, usually religious. The Reverend Chadband, the porcine prelate of *Bleak House,* gobbles until he sweats from exertion. He is always hungry because he is spiritually void. Then there's the famous Fat Boy of *Pickwick,* whose menacing drowsiness and perpetual hunger make him a darkly comic figure, like Appetite in a medieval morality play.

Sometimes food is iconically linked to a particular character: Noah Claypole's sexual mastery is evoked by oysters enticingly fed to him by the doting Charlotte. Mrs. Gamp has her "cowcumbers," Mr. Pickwick his "chops and tomata sauce," and Scrooge his gruel. (The concoction of corn and water known as gruel is pure Scroogean fare, associated with institutional deprivation—and,

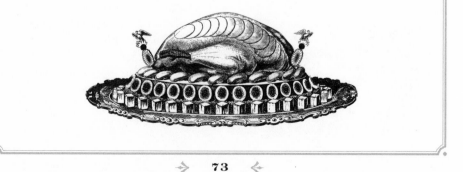

ironically, with Dickens himself. Even the word itself sounds as if Dickens invented it.) The gooey confections young Wackford Squeers gorges on make a reader feel like gagging—as do the entire Squeers family, whose collective metabolism converts the suffering of others to their own sustenance.

And food, above all else, is a key ingredient of the Victorian novel, which after all concerns itself with the substance of life as we live it. Though Virginia Woolf would deride Dickens's meat-and-potatoes materialism, the last entry in her diary concerns the reassuring presence of food in a parlous universe. Dickens would have agreed—as do Mr. Tugby and the porter in *The Chimes:*

> "Blowing and sleeting hard, and threatening snow. Dark. And very cold."
> "I am glad to think we had the muffins," said the former porter, in the tone of one who had set his conscience at rest. "It is the sort of night that's meant for muffins."

Food anchors Dickens's novels, placing them firmly in the real world of gravy, pies, puddings, kidneys, roast pig, and chops. The regular appearance of meals and teas orders his chaotic fictional landscape, making it seem more like our own. His characters eat, therefore they are.

✤Given his gustatory predilections, Dickens has naturally come in for his share of psychoanalysis. A quick glance under the heading "Dickens and Food" in the bibliography *Literature and Psychoanalysis* is enough to induce biblio-nausea. There's Dickens and Digestion and Dickens and Indigestion; Dickens and Orality, Obesity, Feasting, Cannibalism, and Excrement—the entire alimentary process in Dickens's novels from ingestion through peristalsis. One critic imagines the streets of Dickens's London as intestinal tracts, others treat Dickens's preoccupation with orality and his anticipation of Freud's theory of the anal, oral, and oral-sadistic stages of development.

✤On a pragmatic level, Dickens wrote about food because the Victorians liked to eat. During the summer of 1851, while she was awaiting the birth of her ninth child, Catherine Dickens passed the time by writing a cookery book entitled *What Shall We Have for Dinner?* Under the nom de plume Lady Maria Clutterbuck, Catherine presented herself as the widow of Sir Jonas Clutterbuck, a man of great "gastronomical experience." Her book, she explained, was intended to help the wives of finicky eaters. Her eldest son, Charley, later explained that the menus in *What Shall We Have for Dinner?* were the daily bills of fare presented at the Dickens household. No wonder Dickens suffered a stroke at a young age, and Catherine was obese and lethargic: of almost fifty recipes, only two are for vegetable dishes.

HIGH SPIRITS

I am impatient to know how the gin punch succeeded with you. It is the most wonderful beverage in the world, and I think ought to be laid on at high pressure by the board of health.
—DICKENS, letter to his manager, W. H. Wills

*M*ore than a beverage simply to quench thirst, a Dickensian drink is hospitality in a glass. These frothy potables brighten the gloomiest moments in the novels. Except on one notable occasion, Mr. Micawber is always eager to prepare a fragrant bowl of rum punch, and the Cratchits are enlivened by a steaming bowl of Christmas punch. Dickens's happiest, nicest characters are continually bringing out bottles, tankards, bowls, flagons, flasks, decanters, and mugs. In *The Convivial Dickens,* Edward Hewett and W. F. Axton suggest that the various types of nineteenth-century drinks—punches, purls, neguses, sherries, flips, cobblers, and toddies—that regularly appear in Dickens's novels reflect a more genial and relaxed era than our own, when gentlemen had the servants and the leisure for the elaborate preparations involved in concocting such drinks. Later in the century, most of these genteel potables would be replaced by that Jazz Age import, the hastily shaken American cocktail.

Preparation also involved showmanship, and concoctions with such beguiling names as Smoking Bishop, Brighton Tipper, and Dog's Nose were a major part of an evening's entertainment. With flamboyant gestures and racy patter, Dickens prepared a bowl of rum punch like a master conjurer. Abstemious himself, he relished the theatrical aspect of communal drinking: the host as Master of the Revels.

As for drink in the novels, even at its most bacchanalian, e.g., the binge at Bob Sawyer's in *The Pickwick Papers,* drinking in company has ceremonial aspects, including rousing toasts, rowdy drinking songs, and vows of undying friendship. And the communal bowl is more than a literary metaphor: whether they know it or not, the countryfolk who gather at the "snug" (one of Dickens's favorite words) Maypole in *Barnaby Rudge* participate in an ancient ritual that provides continuity from one generation to the next. Their Maypole is our *Cheers.* Dickens's public houses and taverns, with their blooming landladies, enticing aromas, and roaring fires, reflect an age-old struggle to create an enclave of light and warmth in a dark, cold world.

The Creation of
Charles Dickens

⟁

W ith the triumph of *Pickwick,* offers and proposals poured in. Intoxicated by fame, Dickens seemed either unwilling or unable to turn anything down. He was soon negotiating intricate deals with various publishers and editors, speaking out on various political subjects, and mixing with high society as if he had been born to it. It was as if he had been waiting all along to step into the role fate had provided him. The amount of work Dickens accomplished between 1834 and 1838, his first four years as a novelist, is staggering. During that time he contracted for more than twelve works, four of which would be the Victorian equivalent

of blockbuster novels. For nine months in 1837, he worked simultaneously on *Pickwick* and *Oliver Twist,* and he was also editing a literary journal, *Bentley's Miscellany.* He wrote more "sketches," the comic *Mudfog Papers,* one farce, *Is She His Wife?,* and the libretto for an opera, *The Village Coquettes.* Much to his regret, he was also editing—and mostly rewriting— *The Memoirs of Joseph Grimaldi,* a famous pantomime clown, a bit of hack work he accepted before he became famous. He also oversaw and edited the volume editions of both *Oliver Twist* and *Pickwick.* Nevertheless, except for the two months after Mary Hogarth's death in May 1837, he never missed a deadline.

CARICATURE OF DICKENS AND FORSTER
(Fac-simile of a sketch by Doyle)

*T*he relationship between Charles Dickens and John Forster, although not as celebrated as that of Johnson and Boswell, is one of literature's deepest friendships. Utterly different in temperament, outlook, and habits, the flamboyant, gregarious Dickens and the prudent, thin-skinned Forster remained best friends from 1837 to Dickens's death in 1870. Confidant, financial adviser, official biographer, and, as Forster maintained, chief literary consultant, Forster remained true to Dickens through all the latter's travails. Dickens once threw him out of his house and vowed never to speak to him again. In two days, they were again the best of friends. Although a critic and a biographer in his own right, it is rare to find Forster's name uncoupled with that of Dickens—and indeed, at times, Forster is our sole authority for what we know about Dickens today. During these early years, from 1835 to 1840, Dickens cultivated what would become known as the "Dickens Circle," a coterie of gifted artists, painters, actors, and writers who accompanied him on his many jaunts, participated in his theatricals, and saw him through each crisis. And he did the same for them in return: Dickens was a man with a genuine need for friendship.

Oliver Twist

An excellent but not faultless book. Its merit lies in the truth of its picture of the condition and sufferings of the poor; its greatest fault that Oliver Twist has no character.
—HENRY CRABB-ROBINSON

liver Twist is probably Dickens's best-known novel. The musical *Oliver!,* fine as it is, hasn't helped matters any. If you've seen only the play, the novel will seem surprisingly unjolly. If you've read only the book, it's difficult to imagine the cold-blooded Sikes as the inspiration for the lyrical ballad "As Long as He Needs Me." It's even harder to imagine Dickens's Nancy singing it. When we think about Oliver we think about a waif who asks for more. Films, comic books, and popular allusions have done their share to turn *Oliver Twist* into a clichéd picture of Victorian life. Today few adults read it, let alone appreciate it as the rich work of fiction it is.

Oliver Twist can be classified in a variety of ways. First, it's melodrama, a genre with a low rating on the cultural hierarchy. Snobbery aside, however, the theatricality of *Oliver Twist* is first-rate. The drama of the mustachioed villain and the fair-haired, helpless maiden—usually bound physically—was often performed on the Victorian stage. It was sexy and thrilling. In *Oliver Twist* the fair-haired damsel is a pale orphan bound by the tyranny of the courts, the Poor Law, and the criminal underworld. Our love of melodrama—evidenced today by the widespread addiction to daytime television—reverts to a childhood love of a story with clear distinctions between good and evil.

Melodrama thus tends to stir very powerful but uncomplicated emotions. Even today, as our appetite for violence has become slowly jaded, the ferocity of Sikes's murder of Nancy still has the power to shock. And if you cynically dismiss *Oliver Twist* as Victorian mush, remember that in another time and another medium, adults wept when an extraterrestrial squeaked, "Phone home." Shunned by polite society, Oliver for much of the story is a homesick alien.

As social commentary *Oliver Twist* is a pioneering work, one of the most incendiary books ever written, fiction's first (and still the best) exposé of child abuse, urban decay, and institutionalized cruelty. There's an "up yours" tone to the book, as if Dickens deliberately set out to offend middle-class sensibilities by flaunting an ugliness his readers would have preferred to ignore. (Lord Melbourne, upon reading the novel, voiced the sentiments of many: "It is all among workhouses and pickpockets and coffinmakers. I do not like those things: I wish to avoid them. I do not like them in reality and therefore do not like to see them represented.")

In its savage indictment of greedy, indifferent authority, *Oliver Twist* can still arouse our profound distrust of a faceless, unjust bureaucracy and its attendant demons, the self-important "Bumbles" who abuse the system as they help to run it. A subversive work, *Oliver Twist* asserts that the representatives of the queen's government, officials such as Beadle Bumble and Mrs. Corney, are just as criminal as the "real" felons, Fagin and Bill Sikes. Dickens was also among the first to condemn a centralized authority that had become increasingly complex and clogged by rules, regulations, and red tape. (As you wait in line to register your automobile, you encounter nothing that Dickens failed to foresee.) In its representation of society, *Oliver Twist* is a tale for our times. But because the novel seems so Victorian in style and tone, we tend to dismiss it as a period piece, a quaint literary knickknack.

As for *Oliver Twist*'s status as crime fiction, no one knows London's greasy, labyrinthine underworld better than Dickens. He wanted to write what *TV Guide* might call a drama of "gritty realism" (which might seem fatuous, considering the novel's cloying sentimentality), but until *Oliver Twist,* most crime stories, called "Newgate Novels" after the famous prison, were either romantic adventures of highwaymen or lurid tales of murder and revenge. (These novels, condemned as trash, were the source of vigorous debate that has a contemporary ring: Does novel reading cause violence?) In a preface to the novel, Dickens warns his readers

Here are no canterings on moonlit heaths, no merry-makings in the snuggest of all possible caverns, none of the attractions of dress, no embroidery, no lace . . . none of the dash and freedom with which "the road" has been time out of mind invested. The cold wet shelterless midnight streets of London; the foul and frowsy dens, where vice is closely packed and lacks the room to turn; the haunts of hunger and disease; the shabby rags that scarcely hold together; where are the attractions of these things?

(The singing and dancing Fagin of *Oliver!* suddenly seems inane in light of Dickens's original intention.) In its graphic descriptions of London's seedy dives and sour smells, Dickens gave his comfortable middle-class readers an urban tour they would never forget.

CHILDHOOD LOST

*B*ut *Oliver Twist* ultimately transcends the genres of crime fiction, melodrama, and social satire. It's the first novel with a child as its hero written from a child's perspective. You don't need to have been abused to empathize with Oliver. His story remains true to our own experience because it is the archetypal drama of childhood, magnified to the *n*th degree. Happy and unhappy childhoods are alike in this respect: all children are passive witnesses to their own seemingly unaccountable fates. *Oliver Twist* is about a child's vulnerability, and no one depicts the terror of a small child lost in a world of sadistic adults better than Dickens. Many have had worse childhoods than Dickens, but none have recalled their suffering with such visionary clarity.

Oliver's "progress" from institutionalized orphan to adopted son of Mr. Brownlow is a journey from helplessness to mastery, formlessness to the formulation of identity. *Oliver Twist* is the ultimate success story, a recreation of every child's fantasy of power over adults. Oliver's triumph gratifies the vestiges of our childish need for control while appealing to the primitive belief that we will be rescued by kindly adults who will banish every nightmare.

The most curious quality of Oliver is that, despite his heroic status, we have very little sense of who he is. Throughout the novel he remains a vague presence, particularly when compared to the Artful Dodger. With the exception of "Please, sir, I want some more," Oliver fails to say anything memorable. In most of his scenes he is either confused, staring, silent, weeping, asleep, or in a coma. He's the motionless hub around which the novel's action revolves. Moreover, since Dickens insists on Oliver's purity, he must make him confused and detached from the world; to do otherwise would endow him with understanding and thus implicate him in adult guilt. As a mature man, Mr. Pickwick must acquire experience, but Oliver has to remain unsullied by the world's corruption. As in *Pickwick,* the question is: can the hero preserve his virtue in a squalid world that seeks to contaminate him at every turn?

There are other reasons for Oliver's blankness. Whether as objects of charity or of sadism, children essentially "belong" to the adults who mold and mark them. With his "chalk-white" face, Oliver is a tabula rasa upon which adults inscribe—discover—their secret desires and fears. To Fagin, who would debase him, Oliver is as alluring as a blank wall to a vandal; to the sus-picious officials, he is a potential criminal, destined for the gallows; to the virtuous, he is an innocent deserving of protection. Whom will Oliver ultimately reflect? The Maylie-Brownlows? The workhouse wardens? Fagin? Oliver mirrors the adults who surround him so that we can see and judge them—not him—more clearly. He is "twisted" to fit everyone's own image. *Oliver Twist* is, to use the critic James Kincaid's witty analogy, a "story of O."

Only one person can save Oliver from utter negation. Just

after his birth, Oliver's dying mother "imprint[s] her cold, white lips passionately on his forehead," a symbolic gesture that suggests the primal bond between mother and child that never can be broken. In "marking" the infant, she gives him a fledgling sense of belonging and a memory trace which will solace him in times of duress.

OLIVER'S PROGRESS

Oliver's progress begins in the parish workhouse on the night of his birth and his mother's death. His teenage mother, as yet nameless, is unmarried, "the old story," as the doctor wearily puts it. Orphan, bastard, parish boy: Oliver registers absolute zero on the social, moral, and economic scales—the only ones that matter in utilitarian, industrialized, nineteenth-century London. Even the name "Oliver Twist" is an arbitrary designation, emblematic of the infant's nonstatus—Mr. Bumble just happened to be at the *T*s when Oliver was born. And in "badging," "ticketing," and naming Oliver Twist, Beadle Bumble has rendered the orphan powerless. Orphans, and all of Dickens's abused children, are disconnected from their names, the most basic emblem of identity. They could be called anything or anybody—indeed, at one point, Oliver is called "Tom White," a generic name suggestive of his blankness.

Oliver first distinguishes himself from the mass of workhouse orphans with his memorable plea for "more," in a scene that has been rightly called "the most famous request for seconds in history." Ironically, this act brands Oliver as a rebel, though in fact he only steps forward because the boys drew lots. It is telling that in seeking more gruel, a food that thanks to Dickens has become inextricably linked with joylessness and deprivation (Scrooge eats it), Oliver asks simply for "more." More what? Well, obviously more food. But the simplicity of his request, particularly its nonspecificity, hints at a hunger that goes deeper than physical appetite. Oliver wants more of anything that might fill the void within him. In a regimented institution, where everything is anxiously doled out, emotions such as hunger and desire are dangerous, capable of inciting rebellion and discontent. The punishment for wanting more is exile.

The nine-year-old Oliver is socialized into the adult world of work. As one of Mrs. Mann's "crops," he is hawked on the streets, a boy cheap at five pounds. No one asks him what he'd like to do; no one recognizes his skills or deficiencies. No one even sees him. Since Oliver's pale purity is an invitation to a dirty world to soil him, it's not surprising that the first offer should come from a chimney sweep.

As a sweep, the boy's striking, chalklike face will slowly turn a dingy black, the trademark of his craft. This blackening process reflects an early coarsening experience: life, as Dickens learned at an early age, can be a dirtying affair, or, as he wrote in an autobiographical fragment, a "sloppy business." The image of Oliver's dirty face must have stirred deep feelings in Dickens, whose early experience at the blacking warehouse darkened his childhood as it did his hands and face.

Oliver doesn't look like a sweep any more than the young Dickens felt like a menial, and it is his face once more that saves him. Just as an official is about to sign Oliver's indenture papers, he stares at the boy's face and, recognizing his terror, refuses to turn him over to the sweep. Thus when someone actually notices this nonentity named Oliver, he glimpses his own reflection in the boy's face. Oliver's expression elicits the man's latent kindness, and both are reprieved, Oliver from grueling work, the man from his routine indifference. (This even happens to Mr. Bumble: once—and only once—he looks at Oliver and turns away, unable to bear the humanity in a "porochial's" face.)

Oliver is next apprenticed to Mr. Sowerberry the undertaker, who also sees something in the boy's face, an "interesting melancholy" he can use to his own advantage. (The phrase is perfect: a sly dig at the Victorian middle class's gloomy pleasure in death.) Thanks to Mr. Sowerberry's marketing sense, Oliver is a miniature mourner, or "mute," specializing in children's funerals. A mute is a professional mourner, but the term suggests Oliver's voicelessness, gagged by the system that refuses to hear pleas for "more." As an epicure of death, Mr. Sowerberry is pleased with Oliver's aesthetic effect: the child's genuine sadness gives him an edge in the keen competition for the booming infant mortality trade. (Mr. Sowerberry, one of a gloriously dismal parade of Dickensian undertakers, takes a connoisseur's pleasure in his trade: " 'You'll make your fortune, Mr. Sowerberry,' said the beadle, as he thrust his thumb and forefinger into the proffered snuff-box of the undertaker: which was an ingenious little model of a patent coffin.")

This time Oliver is not blackened by dirt but draped in dark garments, the symbol of his grief. To Mr. Sowerberry Oliver is simply a mannequin, not a real person. All these various attempts to defile Oliver show children made to do the dirty work of adults. At night he sleeps in the undertaker's gloomy basement among empty coffins; by day he dumbly follows the funeral processions of fellow victims.

Dickens, however, has a plot to push forward, and so Oliver must finally act. It is significant that he strikes out not in his own defense but for his mother; by defending her character against Noah's taunts, he does for her what he cannot do for himself. No longer passive, he is now "bold," his blood is "warm," "his whole person changed." His genuine self, dormant so long, emerges. Rage liberates him from inertia, releasing all his impacted grief. Once again he is imprisoned for asserting himself, but this time he escapes. At last free to act on his own, he heads for London, a city that for Dickens was both a realm of darkness and a magic lantern to adventure.

It is in London that we meet the famous Fagin. For many readers, this is where the novel truly comes alive. Fagin is a tornado of energy in a novel that at times seems almost atrophied, and despite Dickens's moral, the crook steals the show from the orphan. His hideaway is everything the workhouse is not: anarchic, noisy with raucous laughter, inviting smells, and underworld figures such as Nancy and Bill, the Artful Dodger, and Charley Bates.

A figure of fairy tale, nightmare, and urban legend, Fagin is a wicked brew of a creature: demon, crook, gargoyle, and paranoid psychopath. His gang is a perverted version of Peter Pan's lost boys, and his den, with its food, fun, and games, is a never-never land where children lose their innocence without ever growing up.

Fagin is more than a crook with a fetish for handkerchiefs. More than a few readers have detected hints of homosexuality: his mincing mannerisms, affected daintiness, and indiscriminate bestowal of endearments—even Bill Sikes is "dear"—suggest the clichéd, lisping homosexual. Then, of course, his contempt for women is notorious. And there's a dark side to his sexuality, as seen in his jolly nest of little boys and the merry "game" in which they practice their thievery by "stealing" handkerchiefs from his back pocket. Fagin may cluck like a den mother, but he also behaves like a classic pederast.

Fagin is also a Jew, and by creating a Jewish homosexual, Dickens taps into a whole spectrum of deeply rooted prejudices. Fagin is diseased, satanic, effeminate, greedy, and has a lust for boys. Whether he actually practices sodomy is irrelevant: he is a child abuser. Initiating the innocent into adult behavior, he violates their purity and robs them of their childhood as he forces them to gratify his desires. Unable to resist Oliver's blank beauty, he sees in it something he can exploit.

Yet, dare we confess how much we enjoy him? Ironically, it's Fagin, rather than the blandly virtuous characters, who has all the fun in the novel. He's the enticing stranger who hangs around the playground, promising candy and rides in fast cars. After his rigorous stint at the workhouse, Oliver finds it difficult to resist Fagin's "courtship," and we likewise feel an odd attraction to him.

Obviously, Dickens couldn't be explicit about sex, but he could suggest its presence in his novels. Pederasty, sodomy, homosexuality, and masturbation were not unknown to him. (As Eliot Engel points out, Dickens would never have named a character Charley Bates if he couldn't call him Master Bates, a name which might have slipped past innocent Victorian readers but which never fails to draw a snigger from contemporary students.) Given the traditional Victorian belief that masturbation led to various ills and unpleasant impulses, the name Charley Bates conveys the close, unsavory airlessness of Fagin's "frowsy" den.

Until he enters Mr. Brownlow's house, Oliver lives in a shadowland of confusion. Fagin's London, like Satan's hell, is a murky kingdom that emits a fiendish light, where vice hides behind the shadows. Led through London by the Artful Dodger, Oliver catches fleeting glimpses of a city illuminated by flickering gaslights in a grimy haze. Fagin's lair, too, is sunk in perpetual night through which Oliver moves dreamily, like a somnambulist.

His first exposure to bright light is, literally and metaphorically, when he accompanies the Artful Dodger and Charley on a spree. Oliver is unjustly seized, and upon being questioned he collapses and falls into a fever. Illness is a regenerative event in Dickens's fiction, a signal that the hero's fortunes are about to change. Taken home by the benevolent Mr. Brownlow, Oliver is assured of care and attention. Here he is reborn into a new life, a realm beyond blind misery and loneliness. He awakes to a strange new world of clean linens, fresh air, and sunlight. The contrast between the serene domesticity of Mr. Brownlow's house and what has preceded it makes us almost blink in astonishment. We had forgotten such things exist, and for the first time we realize how dark Oliver's life—and the novel—has been.

His sense of his mother has been very strong throughout his long illness—as if the memory of their old connection has returned in a fever dream. He particularly feels her eyes on him; he feels her empathy, her sorrow for his pain. For the first time Oliver senses someone who feels like and with him, even if it is only in a dream. Upon his awakening, the motherly Mrs. Bedwin looks at his face and cries, "Preety creetur! What would his mother feel if she had sat by him as I have, and could see him now?" The maternal glance represents a key stage in childhood development. This mutual flash of affirmation between mother and child mirrors the child's reality, and through her eyes, he discovers his own identity. Up to this point, Oliver has been unable to identify with anyone, because no one actually looks at him or understands who he is.

Like those of a newborn, his eyes slowly start to focus on specific objects. The misty obscurity of London is replaced by a brightly lit atmosphere where details emerge with sharp clarity. In bed, he "languidly trace[s] the outline of the wallpaper." But the first thing he really notices is his mother. Agnes's face, the first object Oliver saw at his physical birth, is now the first form he notices at his rebirth. The eyes of the woman in the portrait seem "fixed" on Oliver and "make his heart beat." These eyes, although Oliver does not know it yet, will solve the mystery of his self. Oliver is the "living copy" of the portrait: "Every feature was the same. The expression was, for the instant, so precisely alike, that the minutest line seemed copied with an accuracy which was perfectly unearthly."

But what happened at Oliver's birth ten years earlier is repeated the next day. His eyes hungrily search for the loving eyes, but they are gone. When he asks to see the portrait, he is told that Mr. Brownlow has had it removed since it seemed to disturb him. If Oliver is good and recovers, he will be allowed to see the picture. Ever compliant, Oliver never asks to see it. Once again, a desire for "more" goes unsatisfied.

The next stage in Oliver's history is the famous kidnapping scene. But note a pattern emerging: Oliver had escaped the Sowerberrys and was abducted (or rescued) by the Artful Dodger and imprisoned by Fagin; then, while accompanying the two accomplices, he is allowed outdoors, where he is rescued (or kidnapped?) by Mr. Brownlow. He next becomes ill, awakens to a new life, and moves closer to understanding his identity. Now, freed on an errand for Mr. Brownlow, he is once again kidnapped and imprisoned. Whenever Oliver leaves his place of confinement, he is abducted and placed in a new home.

This time Fagin places the boy in solitary confinement, a form of imprisonment that in his writings on penal reform Dickens singles out as unusually

harsh. Fagin might well be considered a pioneer in the use of isolation techniques as a means of breaking down a prisoner's defenses. Solitary confinement,
an innovation in penal reform of the 1840s, was specifically recommended by
one prison chaplain because, as he put it,

> A few months in a solitary cell renders a prisoner strangely impression-
> able. The chaplain can then work on [the prisoner's] feelings in almost
> any way he pleases; he can, so to speak, photograph his thoughts,
> wishes, and opinions on his patient's mind, and fill his mouth with his
> own phrases and language.

In the twentieth century, Fagin's methods are used by terrorists and bullying
gurus in self-development seminars. First he subjects the boy to a prolonged
diatribe in which he tries to persuade him that his friends are his enemies and
his enemies are his friends:

> Mr. Fagin took the opportunity of reading Oliver a long lecture on the
> crying sin of ingratitude: of which he clearly demonstrated he had been
> guilty, to no ordinary extent, in wilfully absenting him from the society of
> his anxious friends; and, still more, in endeavouring to escape from them
> after so much trouble and expense had been incurred in his recovery.
> Mr. Fagin laid great stress on the fact of his having taken Oliver in, and
> cherished him, when, without his timely aid, he might have perished
> with hunger; and he related the dismal and affecting history of a young
> lad whom, in his philanthropy, he had succoured under parallel circum-
> stances, but who, proving unworthy of his confidence and evincing a de-
> sire to communicate with the police, had unfortunately come to be
> hanged at the Old Bailey one morning.

And then he isolates him:

> And so Oliver remained all that day, and for the greater part of many sub-
> sequent days, seeing nobody between early morning and midnight, and
> left during the long hours to commune with his own thoughts.
>   After the lapse of a week or so, the Jew left the room-door unlocked;
> and he was at liberty to wander about the house. . . .
>   Often, when it grew dark, and he was tired of wandering from room to
> room, he would crouch in the corner of the passage from the street-door,
> to be as near living people as he could; and would remain there, listening
> and counting the hours, until the Jew or the boys returned.

Next, Charley and the Artful Dodger call out to him:

> Oliver was but too glad to make himself useful; too happy to have some
> faces, however bad, to look upon. . . .

And finally:

> [Oliver] . . . was placed in almost constant communication with the two boys, who played the old game with the Jew every day: whether for their own improvement or Oliver's, Mr. Fagin best knew. At other times the old man would tell them stories of robberies he had committed in his younger days: mixed up with so much that was droll and curious, that Oliver could not help laughing heartily, and showing that he was amused in spite of all his better feelings.
>
> In short, the wily old Jew had the boy in his toils. Having prepared his mind, by solitude and gloom, to prefer any society to the companionship of his own sad thoughts in such a dreary place, he was now slowly instilling into his soul the poison which he hoped would *blacken it, and change its hue for ever.* [italics mine]

While Oliver was once threatened with physical dirt, now his soul is in danger of being tarnished. The pretext for Fagin's desire to hold him is the old Victorian standby of an inheritance and a lost will. Oliver will inherit his legacy "only on the stipulation that in his minority he would never have *stained his name*" [italics mine]. This is flimsy, but it gives Fagin a motive for wanting to possess and destroy Oliver. In fact, much of the novel consists of what Alfred Hitchcock called a "MacGuffin," an arbitrary contrivance which keeps the mystery chugging along. Perhaps this gratuitous motive is a stand-in for Fagin's pederasty, which Dickens could not present explicitly. (Dickens has a tendency to use plot as an excuse to write about something he wants to express.) And Fagin wants not only to debase Oliver, he also wants to destroy all evidence of the boy's past and parentage. In other words, first he will "erase" the boy and then blacken him beyond recognition.

Once again, after Oliver returns to Fagin's den, Dickens cranks up the plot machinery. Oliver is released from prison, acts as an accomplice in a robbery, falls ill, wakes up, and discovers his identity. Sound familiar? This time, however, he "robs" his aunt, not his father's best friend. And instead of seeing a picture of his mother, he sees her living likeness in Rose Maylie, her sister.

Each episode provides a piece of the puzzle of Oliver's identity. But it's his mother who fills the final empty place. Oliver's resemblance to the portrait alerts Mr. Brownlow to his true identity. Oliver learns his real name at the same time he learns his mother's identity. The two events coincide because the empty space in Oliver was that left by his mother's absence. In finding her, he finds his lost self.

In the final part of the novel, Oliver becomes a pawn between good and evil: the Maylie-Brownlow camp struggles to preserve his innocence, while Fagin and Monks seek to destroy it. The prostitute Nancy, torn between the two sides, breaks the stalemate. In Oliver's astonishing face she recalls her own lost purity, and in saving the boy, she redeems herself. Despite Fagin's efforts, Oliver has remained virtuous to the end. And, as usual in Dickens, virtue is translated into pounds and pence. The goodness inherited from his mother enables him to receive his father's monetary legacy. The story concludes with Oliver's arrival at, not the Celestial City, but the Victorian equivalent, a middle-class home and all its status. With his new name, he is restored to his rightful position, and the hateful, arbitrary "Twist" is replaced by the stolid, English-sounding "Leeford."

Some condemn Dickens for his love of bourgeois comforts: hearth, home, and prosperity. But in fact his happiest families are untraditional and makeshift. After all, Mrs. Bedwin and Mr. Brownlow are not related, and Mrs. Maylie is Rose's ward, not her mother. Oliver will be raised by his father's friend and his aunt. The households in *Oliver Twist* are thus more suited to the 1990s than to our vision of the cozy Victorian hearth. (Remember that the novel's vitality comes from people who love to break into houses.) Home, for Dickens, is not an ideal but a real place where the besieged self is protected from moral and physical contagion. Home protects individuality from a world that tends to blacken everything into a uniform drabness. Home is where Oliver's purity will remain inviolate—and here purity means not bland negation but the integrity of the self. Oliver's progress from public institution to private home reflects the growing belief that joy and pleasure are to be found in one's personal life.

But the novel's real turn of the screw is that for all his passivity, Oliver ultimately triumphs over everyone who has been bustling about to defeat him. In an aggressive world, passivity becomes an act of defiance. Like Hamlet, who bemoans his inability to act yet manages to kill practically everyone in the play, Oliver conquers everyone who opposes him. He wins just by being himself. This achievement appeals to our childish belief, often carried into adulthood, that we alone are special and will be magically saved.

Oliver Twist is a novel of wish fulfillment because it essentially reenacts the "prince and the pauper" motif, or what Freud would call the "family romance," our secret conviction that we are in fact foundlings, and one day our real parents, rich, famous, and beautiful, will claim us. Oliver discovers that he is not a workhouse orphan but a respectable member of civilized society, with a large inheritance to boot. His workhouse is young Dickens's warehouse. Although he was slogging away like any other working-class boy, he was actually a gentleman in disguise. But that isn't all. In the end, the author lovingly provides his autobiographical hero with sweet revenge: anyone who ever threatened, destroyed, or bullied Oliver is either destroyed, punished, or humiliated. "In *Oliver Twist*," Dickens wrote, "I want to show Goodness triumphing over every form of adversity." The novel bears this out, not only through its happy ending but by having been written at all. With *Oliver Twist,* the man who once worked in a warehouse celebrates his own triumph and his will to survive against all odds.

❧ TWISTIANA ❧

❖ *Oliver Twist* was Charlie Chaplin's favorite novel—which makes sense when you consider the tragicomic haplessness of the Little Tramp, and the way both Dickens and Chaplin thread pathos with humor.

❖ *Oliver Twist* was listed among contemporary police reports as an instigator of crime, and stage versions of the novel, rewritten to highlight its spicy criminal aspects, were banned by the Lord Chamberlain.

❖ When the young queen read *Oliver* in installments, she pronounced it "*too interesting,*" the Victorian adjective for anything absorbingly sordid. Despite her admiration for Dickens, she strongly disapproved of novel reading as an activity for the young.

❖ There have been at least eight movie adaptations of the novel, and throughout the nineteenth and the early half of the twentieth century, *Oliver Twist* was part of the theater's standard repertoire. The role of Oliver, like that of Peter Pan, was always played by a young woman. Indeed, the waiflike actress Winona Ryder confessed that she always wanted to play Oliver.

❖ "The Law is a ass": One of the most famous of all Dickensian phrases, it's often applied to any legal absurdity. It's Mr. Bumble's bitter response upon learning that the law holds him responsible for his wife's behavior. Usually, however, the law worked to the husband's advantage. Until 1870, a woman was regarded as little more than her husband's chattel. On her wedding day everything she owned became his, along with anything she might earn or inherit. If her husband deserted her, and she worked to support herself, her assets became his when he returned. Upon their marriage, Mr. Bumble takes possession of Mrs. Corney's assets—including the china which he had so meticulously examined during their courtship. (Most recently, the phrase was used by

It's difficult to imagine anyone working against child labor reforms, but in 1844, when the law was debated in the House of Lords, Lord Brougham argued that to legislate labor restrictions would violate the laws of nature that ensured that unworthy lower-class children would die off. As Scrooge said of such children, "[T]hey had better do it [die], and decrease the surplus population." When the Commission of Child Labor issued its report, Lord Londonderry protested what he called the report's "disgusting Pictorial woodcuts." He feared the images of women and children engaged in degrading labor would disturb genteel young ladies. It is scarcely surprising to learn that Lord Londonderry owned several of the mines featured in the report.

Senator Orrin Hatch in reference to U.S. immigration laws during the 1994
Zoe Baird hearings.)

✣ Dickens empathized with his boy-hero so much that while writing the final
pages of the novel, his childhood kidney spasms returned for the first time
in many years. With acute insight into the nature of somatic illness, he accepted his suffering as the debt he had to pay for reliving his childhood
pain through the creatures of his pen.

✣ In the final courtroom scene, Dickens has Fagin stare at a sketch artist
who is intent on capturing the criminal's likeness. The artist is none
other than George Cruik-
shank. Thus as an inside
joke between two good
friends, Dickens gives his
colleague a cameo in the
novel he illustrated. Dickens had so much respect
for Cruikshank's portray-
als of London's under-
world, it is sometimes said
that he wrote *Oliver Twist*
just so Cruikshank could
illustrate it.

The felicitous choice of the name "Bumble"
for the self-important minor official was so
apt that the term *Bumbledom* quickly entered the
language. Of Bumble, H. G. Wells wrote, "This
one supreme and devastating study of the illiterate minor official . . . was worth a hundred Royal
Commissions. . . . I would have every candidate
for the post of workhouse master pass a severe
examination upon *Oliver Twist.*"

When Cruikshank drew his masterpiece, *Fagin in the Condemned Cell,*
he used himself as a model. The artist reportedly told a friend that he
copied a mirrored reflection of himself huddling in bed, fearfully contemplating the task of drawing the final picture of Fagin, of which G. K.
Chesterton wrote, "In the doubled-up figure and frightful eyes of Fagin in
the condemned cell there is not only a baseness of subject; there is a kind
of baseness in the very technique of it. It is not drawn with the free lines of
a free man; it has the half-witted secrecies of a hunted thief. It does not look
merely like a picture of Fagin; it looks like a picture by Fagin." In a sense,
Chesterton is right: it *is* a picture by a man who thought of himself as
Fagin's double. It was not drawn with the "free lines of a free man," but by a
man driven by his need for drink and who felt imprisoned and condemned
by his self-destructive urges. In later years Cruikshank increasingly came
to identify with the old villain and would suddenly—and disconcertingly—
lapse into Fagin's speech patterns and mannerisms.

After Dickens's death, Cruikshank—whose hold on reality was tenuous
at best—claimed that he, not Dickens, was responsible for most of the
ideas in *Oliver Twist,* a claim vehemently refuted by Dickens's friends.

✣ In researching *Oliver Twist,* Dickens consulted a "statistical Magazine" that
included tables about juvenile delinquency. He also asked a friend in
charge of the press reporters for the city courts if he could be smuggled in
to watch a certain magistrate by the name of Laing. "In my next number of

Oliver Twist," he wrote, "I must have a magistrate; and casting about for a magistrate whose harshness and insolence would render him a fit subject to be 'shewn up,' I have, as a necessary consequence, stumbled upon Mr. Laing of Hatton Garden Celebrity." The result was the odious Mr. Fang, the magistrate who sentences Oliver to hard labor for the unproven charge of pickpocketing Mr. Brownlow. Of Fang, Dickens wrote, "If he [Laing] were really not in the habit of drinking rather more than was exactly good for him, he might have brought an action against his countenance for libel, and have recovered heavy damages."

❖Dostoyevsky was a great admirer of *Oliver Twist;* like Dickens, he was intrigued by the possibility of creating a character who was purely good. Oliver, like the Russian writer's Idiot, artlessly accepts life on its own terms—in contrast to the worldliness of the Artful Dodger, who can assess the price of anything in a pinch.

FAGIN: THE MONSTER WHO HAUNTS OUR DREAMS

The first thing that comes to mind when we think about *Oliver Twist* is not its waiflike hero but its villain, Fagin, his eyes blazing with cunning and greed. Like all great characters, he breaks through the confines of the work that contains him, takes on a life of his own, and enters the popular imagination. Fagin operates on various levels, from the realistic to the supernatural, and our feelings about him rise from complex sources. Indeed, he could be the hero of his own novel, albeit a very different one from *Oliver Twist.*

Like Shylock, though less obviously, Fagin rises from the dark soil of ancient prejudice, from a time when Jews were linked with Satan himself. Throughout the novel, the narrator dryly refers to Fagin as "the merry old gentleman," a traditional sobriquet for the devil. Moreover, like the devil, Fagin ensnares the innocent and unwary with blandishments. Although Dickens may have been unaware of his character's historical roots, his creature is a product of the European Middle Ages, when Jews were regarded as child killers, a point particularly relevant to Fagin, a murderer of children's souls.

To the novel's early readers, the Jew represented the archetypal outsider. As a Jewish (and probably homosexual) criminal, Fagin is the ultimate alien, beyond the reach of church, law, and community. Jewishness is less a religious affiliation than an expression of a disturbing, un-English otherness.

Fagin is a nocturnal creature of folklore and myth: the bogeyman under the bed, the gnome gloating over buried treasure, the misshapen dwarf who steals foundlings. By day Fagin looks like a carnival fun figure; by night he is transformed into something scarcely human. He rarely walks upright; he glides, crawls, skulks, and creeps: "As he glided stealthily along, creeping out of the shelter of the walks and doorways, the hideous old man seemed like some loathsome reptile, engendered in the slime and darkness through which he moved: crawling forth, by night, in search of some rich offal for a meal."

No one is ever completely safe from Fagin's clutches. As Oliver lies half-dozing amid the tranquillity of the Maylies' summer cottage, a pastoral setting far removed from urban squalor, Fagin's repellent face is suddenly framed in the window among the flowers. In this incongruous setting, he appears even more darkly grotesque, more shocking. Alfred Hitchcock once said that one of the ways he heightened Mrs. Danvers's sinister effect in the movie *Rebecca* was by never showing her walking, an act that would humanize her. Indeed, Mrs. Danvers appears with a suddenness that first disconcerts and then terrifies the innocent heroine. Dickens uses the same technique to the same effect in this scene. Fagin disappears as effortlessly as he appears, without leaving so much as a footprint.

Even more terrifying, he seems to have the power to enter children's dreams:

> Oliver knew, perfectly well, that he was in his own little room; that his books were lying on the table before him; and that the sweet air was stirring among the creeping plants outside. And yet he was asleep. Suddenly, the scene changed; the air became close and confined; and he thought with a glow of terror, that he was in the Jew's house again. There sat the hideous old man, in his accustomed corner: pointing at him.

Oliver's quandary is ours as well. Is Fagin a mythic figure or a real criminal? The boundaries that separate reverie from waking, the natural from the supernatural, are no longer quite so secure—not, that is, until the end of the novel, when in the bright light of day, Fagin seems to shrink in stature. For the first time in the novel, Dickens enters Fagin's consciousness; we almost experience the heightened perceptions of a man spending his last night alive.

It is fitting that Lon Chaney, "the man of a thousand faces," should have played Fagin, the character with a thousand masks in the 1922 silent film. With each turn in the plot he transforms himself into a new character: the maternal guardian, grasping miser, sinister spy. But in the final turn, all the masks are stripped, and he stands before us simply as himself. On the gibbet, in the full brilliance of daylight, he will stand before hundreds of eager spectators and be exposed to their curious, merciless stares.

BOB AND FAGIN

*D*ickens recalled how, on his first day at Warren's, another boy helped him learn "the trick of using the string and tying the knot" around the bottles of blacking. The boy's name was Bob Fagin, and he proved to be a good friend to Charles during his time at the warehouse, caring for him when he was sick, sticking up for him when the other boys teased him. Dickens confessed that he "took the liberty of using his name, long afterwards in *Oliver Twist.*" Why would Dickens associate his best friend with his worst villain? It could be simply that he liked the sound of the word. The critic Steven Marcus offers one explanation of how Fagin came to be named: "There is no great distance between Bob Fagin's induction of Charles on his first day of work into the secrets of wrapping and tying, and the wonderful scene in which Fagin teaches class in elementary and advanced pickpocketing." Both Fagins initiate the innocent Oliver/Charles into the mysteries of their trade, and both are linked to a dark, unhappy existence.

Warren's Blacking Warehouse was to Charles what Fagin's den was to Oliver. Dickens felt deep shame over his warehouse experience, a feeling that tainted his memories of Bob. He must have been ambivalent about their friendship; fraternizing with Bob or Mealy Potatoes meant that he was one of them, a fact that Charles desperately sought to deny. Though Dickens recalled his old friend warmly, Bob was still inextricably connected with his humiliating nightmare.

The critic must tread lightly on such delicate ground, but there may have been other, even deeper, reasons why Dickens associated Bob with Fagin. Dickens's shame over the blacking warehouse episode was so great that one wonders if it can all be attributed to snobbery. The episode was not just a part of his life he didn't talk about but something he concealed even from his wife. It was, he wrote, "the secret agony of my soul." Both as a child and an adult, Dickens felt everything more intensely than others. He was sensitive to even the slightest insult, and he would hastily reject anyone, even a friend, who wounded his pride. To the high-strung boy, working in a place as squalid as Warren's was profoundly degrading, and he was ashamed that his parents had forsaken him that way.

But perhaps, and here one can only be tentative, he felt shame about some of the activities that went on there. The fictional Fagin is a pederast who presides over a lair of boys, and his den, like prisons, English public schools, and even places like Warren's Blacking Warehouse, are all cramped atmospheres conducive to homoerotic behavior. Bob Fagin may have looked out for Charles in the same way older students in public schools dote on younger ones. Always sensitive to nuances in emotions and behavior, Charles might have sensed that Bob's feelings for him were more than that of a friend. Given his fastidiousness and his reserve with the other workers, it is unlikely that Dickens participated in any sexual activities. But he must have known about them, and as a child, he must have felt part of the sordid atmosphere, almost as if he had committed such acts himself. As Dickens revealed in *Great Expectations,* children very often feel guilt over deeds they did not commit. It just might be that Bob Fagin, the man who was such a "friend" to Charles, might not have been a friend after all.

❧ THE JEWISH QUESTION ❧

When *Oliver Twist* was written in 1837, English anti-Semitism was so ingrained that it was accepted as a natural state of affairs, as unremarkable as the filthy air Londoners breathed every day.

Thus when Jews complained about his portrait of Fagin, Dickens was shocked. Less than twenty years after *Oliver Twist* was serialized, Dickens wrote, "I know of no reason the Jews can have for regarding me as inimical to them." Dickens's attitude toward the Jews was more careless than hostile. He didn't know any, and so he casually adopted the views of his age and class.

But in 1860 he began to revise his opinion when he sold his London house to a Jewish man by the name of Davis. When he first met Davis, Dickens described him to his friends as a "Jew Money-Lender," which, while not exactly virulent, reveals the extent to which he subscribed to the popular view. But he was pleasantly surprised by Davis and his wife. After the sale, he wrote a friend: "I cannot call to mind any occasion when I have had money-dealings with any one that have been so satisfactory, considerate and trusting."

When their relations became more cordial, Mrs. Davis took Dickens to task for his portrait of Fagin. Defending himself, Dickens lamely replied that Fagin was Jewish because "it unfortunately was true of the time to which that story refers, that this class of criminal almost invariably was a Jew." But he slowly began to change his mind about the "Jewish question." In 1867–68, when the Charles Dickens Edition of the novel came out, Dickens did editorial penance for his sins: he eliminated numerous reminders of the villain's religion, substituting the simple pronoun "he" or "Fagin" for the stark epithet, "the Jew" (in chapter 39 alone, he eliminated twenty-three such references). And the famous chapter, "The Jew's Last Night Alive" subsequently became "Fagin's Last Night Alive." Later, when he gave public readings of the novel, he refrained from mentioning Fagin's Jewishness.

THE NEW POOR LAW

*T*he harshest image in *Oliver Twist* is not the fetid slums or the seedy criminal dives, but one created by the government itself: the union workhouse. They were a product of the New Poor Law of 1834, a controversial enactment that attempted a revolution in the way England treated the needy, the infirm, the elderly, and the orphaned; in short, the useless cogs in a society that worshiped work and productivity. "*Oliver Twist,*" said its author simply, "is my glance at the Poor Law." One might think—and many did at the

DIET

—ᴍ—

ickens's attacks in *Oliver Twist* were echoed in almost every newspaper and journal in England. The Poor Law commissioners were the devils of a bureaucratic age, the objects of opprobrium and ridicule. Critics of the system singled out the atrocity of the uniform national diet as created by the commissioners. *The Dietary for Able-Bodied Men and Women,* reprinted  in the Oxford edition of the novel, shows that an adult man was alloted only 170 ounces of solid food a week—less than that of a convicted prisoner. The fare itself consisted of thin gruel, potatoes, bread, suet (or rice pudding), cooked meat (15 ounces a week), soup, and cheese. One writer in the liberal *Blackwood's Magazine* wrote that workhouse inmates must be part of a large experiment designed to establish the bare minimum of food a human body requires to maintain minimum health. A "recipe" supposedly copied directly from the memorandum book of a Poor Law commissioner ran in the *Champion and Weekly Herald* of January 1837, the same month that *Oliver* was being serialized:

Take ten quarts of ditch-water, and stir it well with the body of a farthing rushlight, till it boils. Season it to your liking with old tea leaves, and it will be ready for use. The wick, which will not dissolve, is a delicious relish, and may be bottled whole, and, if you *should* want a dessert, suck your fingers.

time—that Dickens was exaggerating for dramatic effect, but the reality of this inhumane statute was far worse than can now be imagined. The historian E. J. Hobsbawn concluded that the New Poor Law "created more embittered unhappiness than any other statute of modern British history."

Under the original Poor Law, enacted in 1601, laborers with wages below subsistence level were provided with "outdoor relief," a subsidy, whether money, food, or firewood, that enabled them to stay outside the doors of the workhouse. Called the "Speenhamland System," it made up the difference between a laborer's substandard wages and the amount he and his family needed to live. It was not perfect—a laborer had to stay within his parish if he wanted relief— and it was subject to abuse— some employers purposely paid their workers less than a living wage, forcing parish ratepayers to make up the difference—yet it was still a far more humane system than what replaced it.

The Poor Law Amendment Act was a response to many factors: increased migration to the city; a growing number of unemployed children (very small children were hired as sweeps and then abandoned when they grew); accelerated urbanization; and indignation over the "free handout" that was seen as an inducement to chronic dependency.

Under the new law, the local parish was replaced by a central governing board in London that oversaw the work of local elected officials, much like Beadle Bumble in *Oliver Twist*. Parish overseers were now as obsolete as feudal lords. In keeping with the age of industry, "charity" was now regimented, subject to the jurisdiction of faceless bureaucrats who administered everything down to the last ounce of gruel. Outdoor relief was abolished: anyone who could not support himself, even those who were temporarily ill, had to enter a workhouse if he wanted relief.

Workhouses were in existence before 1834, but only the very old, the very sick, or the very young occupied them. The choice was clearly defined: live in a workhouse, find work, or starve to death outside. Many chose death.

The objective behind the New Poor Law was not to provide relief but to motivate independent working laborers and discourage "idleness"—the rationale being that any able-bodied person who did not work was lazy and lacked character. The Deserving Poor became the Undeserving Slothful. Hence the union workhouse, a place where no task was too degrading, repetitive, or meaningless. Inmates spent their days literally trudging on a treadmill, while weaker ones mindlessly twisted and untwisted rope: meaningless labor was better than none at all.

With their demoralizing, punitive atmosphere, starvation diets, enforced separation of families (including mothers from children), and harsh disciplinary regimes, these "charitable" institutions bore an unsettling resemblance to Nazi concentration camps. (The inscription over the entrance to Auschwitz, *Arbeit macht frei*—"Work makes you free"—could have been the motto for the Victorian middle classes.) The workhouse was the punishment for being poor in a society in which the sight of poverty was an affront to good taste.

Those in favor of the workhouse supported it because it efficiently sealed off the poor, decreased population growth by separating husbands and wives, and shamed the needy, all in all a system Scrooge would have admired. Indeed, when approached for a charitable donation, an affronted Scrooge replies, "Are there no workhouses?" The question is all the more ironic in light of the suffering that went on there. The Poor Law reveals the ugly Scroogean side of the Victorian devotion to labor and revenue.

The Death of
Mary Hogarth

✙

I n his fragment of an autobiography, Dickens noted that the past had made him what he was. Three events in his early life were seminal to his development: his stint at the blacking warehouse, his romantic obsession with Maria Beadnell, and the death of his sister-in-law Mary Hogarth.

On May 6, 1837, Dickens, Catherine, and Mary Hogarth returned to their lodgings after a night at the theater. They had just seen Dickens's farce *Is She His Wife?* and were still laughing at its inanities. At one o'clock they all went to bed, but as soon as Dickens and Catherine shut their door, they heard a strangled cry. Rushing into Mary's room, Dickens found her collapsed on the floor, still in her evening clothes. By the afternoon she was dead. The doctors called it "heart failure," one of those all-purpose Victorian medical terms that mean anything and nothing.

A trauma in the most precise sense of the word, it irrevocably altered the direction and meaning of Dickens's life. He abandoned himself to a grief so intense it can only be called pathological. Only her musty clothes and the hope that he might one day be entombed beside her brought him any consolation. No other death, not even that of his infant daughter, would ever affect him so profoundly. It was the only time, save his own death thirty-three years later, that he was unable to meet a deadline: Mr. Pickwick languished for two months as the Dickenses recuperated in the country. Catherine suffered a miscarriage, and the elder Hogarths grieved silently, but no one suffered more than Dickens. But then, as the actress Miriam Margolyes has pointed out, "Dickens never seemed to get over anything."

A letter Dickens wrote shortly after Mary's death on May 7, 1837. His state of mind is reflected in his script. "We are in deep and severe distress. Miss Hogarth after accompanying Mrs. Dickens and myself to the theatre last night, was suddenly taken severely ill, and despite our hot endeavours to save her, expired in my arms at two o'clock this afternoon. Faithfully yours. . . ." The rest of the letter is illegible, with the "s" in Dickens trailing downward as if the writer can barely hold on to the pen.

Dickens's description of Mary's final moments could have been lifted from any one of the popular melodramas of the day:

> She sank under the attack and died—died in such a calm and gentle sleep, that although I had held her in my arms for some time before, when she was certainly living (for she swallowed a little brandy from my hand) I continued to support her lifeless form, long after her soul had fled to heaven. . . .
> The very last words she whispered were of me.

Within seconds of her death, Dickens had slipped the ring from her finger and placed it on his own, where it remained until he died. What, one wonders, did Catherine think, seeing her sister's ring upon her husband's finger day after day? (Mary's ring is now worn by the author's great-grandson, Cedric Dickens, who displays it to ardent Dickensians.)

Even at the moment of his greatest pain, Dickens the mourner could not separate himself from Dickens the artist. His high-flown account suggests that he immediately began "using" the event, fictionalizing it, with Mary as the apotheosis of the Dickensian heroine, a child-woman of superhuman virtue. Perhaps this is the reflex of genius, a way of controlling and managing the intensity of loss. What is equally striking about Dickens's description is his own central role in the drama. Where, one wonders, was the girl's sister, Catherine? Even the dying girl exists only as she relates to Charles Dickens: "I continued to support"; "My grief"; "my name"; "my arms"; "She swallowed a little brandy *from my hand*" [italics mine]. (Ironically, Dickens seems to recognize this particular brand of egoism and would lampoon it in the widower Mr. Sapsea in *Edwin Drood,* who in praising his deceased wife speaks solely of his own virtues.)

Black-edged cards and letters were immediately sent to friends and associates, and Dickens relates the event in excruciating detail again and again. Most particularly, he describes what she meant to him:

> The dear girl had been the grace and life of our home. . . . We might have known that we were too happy together to be long without a change. Words cannot describe the pride I felt in her, and the devoted attachment I bore her. I have lost the dearest friend I ever had . . .
> The dear girl whom I loved, after my wife. . . .

The final qualifier sounds a bit like an afterthought.

His grief mingled with self-pity, and Dickens didn't just wallow in it; he nearly drowned. He solaced himself with the thought that one day he would be buried next to her; but when Catherine's brother died several years later, he gallantly offered his plot to the bereaved parents. Renouncing the burial plot was, he confessed to John Forster, like losing Mary all over again: "I feel," he wrote, "like moving her to some catacombs without telling anyone. I cannot bear the thought of being excluded from her dust."

Like many Victorian mourners, he kept her wardrobe intact. (After the Consort's death, Queen Victoria had his clothes laid out every night.) Two years after her death, he still took her clothes out to touch and look at them. "They will moulder away in their secret places," he wrote. For many years after her death, he dreamed of her almost nightly, "sometimes as a spirit, sometimes as a living creature, never with any of the bitterness of my real sorrow."

Not surprisingly, critics and scholars hover like ghouls over the event, trying to explain Mary's significance to Dickens's emotional, intellectual, and erotic life. Her death is a rare, defining moment in which Dickens's psyche is open to view, and the intensity of his response begs for inquiry. Why would the death of a sister-in-law—no matter how beautiful, good, or young—affect him so profoundly? Some argue plausibly that Mary's absence made him realize his wife's deficiencies; others insist that he was in love with Mary, that he had married the wrong sister. But their relationship was more idealistic than sexual, more loving than passionate, more companionable than erotic.

His love for Mary was intense precisely because he was *not* related to her. With her there was no residual sibling rivalry or the inevitable disenchantment one feels with a spouse. Mary had no claims on him and he was thus free simply to love her. On her side, she worshiped him and pronounced him perfection itself. And he was captivated by the delightful image of himself he saw reflected in her eyes. No one would ever look at him like that again. More than a friend, but neither wife nor sister, he believed she was the companion of his heart.

But who can ever say exactly what one person means to another? Death transformed Mary into an emblematic figure. For Dickens she became the end point of all desire, even the desire for death.

SWEET SEVENTEEN

In . . . Dicken's [sic] fiction there is evidence of some peculiar affection on his part for a strange sort of little girl; a little girl with a premature sense of responsibility and duty; a sort of saintly precocity. Did he know some little girl of this kind? Did she die, perhaps, and remain in his memory in colours too ethereal and pale? In any case there are a great number of them in his works.
—G. K. CHESTERTON

Some believe that Mary Hogarth was not the only casualty that night. For years readers of Dickens have attributed his so-called inability to create credible women to his enshrinement of Mary. "Mary," he recalled, "had not a single fault." This may help preserve pleasant memories, but it does not make for a strong and complex female character. Every Dickensian ingenue, it is said, is fashioned in the mold of Mary: Pet Meagles (who has an "air of timidity and dependence that was the best"), Madeline Bray, Rose Maylie, Kate Nickleby: all slender, shy, sweet—and seventeen. And in real life there was Nelly Ternan, Dickens's mistress, who was just seventeen when he met her. Each fictional girl is indis-tinguishable from another (odd in an artist known for his uniquely eccentric portraits). With admirable succinctness the actress Miriam Margolyes refers to these paragons as "icky."

Nicholas Nickleby

icholas Nickleby is Dickens's most theatrical novel, both literally and figuratively. Just before he wrote it, Dickens had been editing the memoirs of Grimaldi, a famous pantomime clown. No doubt a theatrical aura lingered about him, providing fresh inspiration for his new novel. Dedicated to his friend the actor William Macready, it is steeped in dramatic imagery, rhetoric, and characters and allusions, from sideshows and melodrama to tragedy and romance. Literary pirates were quick to note the tale's dramatic possibilities: in *Dickens and Popular Entertainment,* Peter Schlicke notes that before its serial run was over, six adaptations of *Nickleby* had already appeared on the popular stage. In our own century, there's a mediocre film and the historic, nine-hour dramatization, a coup de théâtre that for many turned Dickens's unread book into a "novelization" of a great play.

Nicholas Nickleby is Dickens's most joyful and effortless work, confirming its author's assertion that he was never happier than when involved with the stage. Its plot, set pieces, and characters amount to a checklist of every cliché of nineteenth-century melodrama. There's a poignant deathbed scene, a duel, a lost legacy, a father-and-son reunion. Its leads are stock character types: Nicholas, an earnest and chivalrous hero, and Kate, his maidenly sister. When Mr. Crummles, with his usual rhetorical flair, hails Nicholas, "Farewell, my noble, my lion-hearted boy!" (in blank verse), we know that Dickens is gently mocking the stage manager's exaggerated mannerisms. But what the showman says is true: Nicholas is precisely the kind of hero who could be seen every night on Mr. Crummles's provincial stage. In Nicholas, Dickens, a much

The "*Nicholas Nickleby* Portrait" (1839), so called because it graced the frontispiece of that novel. The twenty-seven-year-old author had written two best-selling novels and been acclaimed as the greatest writer in England. Painted by his good friend Daniel Maclise, the portrait was exhibited at the Royal Academy and pronounced an extraordinary likeness. (One suspects, however, that it was somewhat flattering.) It now hangs in the National Portrait Gallery.

greater stage manager, has created a noble, lion-hearted young hero—and in teasing Mr. Crummles, he draws attention to his own melodramatic posturing.

In *Nickleby,* as in all melodrama, the line between good and evil is unwavering. Pure character types, those embodying a single moral trait, evoke a gut response. Dickens doesn't want to tug at our emotions, he wants to wrench them out of us: tears, outrage, laughter, and delight. One need only recall how a seemingly sophisticated twentieth-century audience burst into cheers when Nicholas finally thrashed the odious Wackford Squeers.

AT DOTHEBOYS HALL

Squeers, the sadistic schoolmaster of Dotheboys Hall (a place name now synonymous with any brutal school), takes pride of place among the villains in Dickens's rogues' gallery. His roots go back to the medieval stage tradition of the Vice, the often humorous personification of evil. In fact, the Squeerses are the seven deadly sins rolled into one family; their household fairly vibrates with joyful viciousness. Thus the porcine Wackford junior, urged to eat until his skin glistens, is used to advertise the bounties awaiting each child at Dotheboys; Mrs. Squeers thrusts brimstone and treacle down the throats of her charges with all the tenderness of a prison matron. Fanny alone, plain, jealous, and petty, merits some sympathy—and amused contempt. (Only a modern reader could experience such a mixed response to Fanny; to Dickens and his contemporaries, a shrill and bitter woman was merely an object of comic derision.)

Dickens intended the Dotheboys section to be a scorching exposé of the so-called Yorkshire schools, those "educational" institutions situated in the remote north where parents sent unwanted children. That Squeers's evil belongs to the real world, and that it involves suffering children, momentarily lifts the novel out of the artificial realm of romance and melodrama, placing it squarely in a particular time and place. Our response to this villain is thus more complicated than just a hiss and a boo. Squeers isn't an unsmiling knave, like Ralph Nickleby, but a figure of exuberant comedy. Few writers besides Dickens, Shakespeare, or Dostoyevsky can lace cruelty with such antic humor. Even as the schoolmaster evokes our outrage, we can't help smiling at his pedagogical methods and his remarkable spelling:

> "We go upon the practical mode of teaching, Nickleby; the regular education system. C-l-e-a-n, clean, verb active, to make bright, to scour. W-i-n, win, d-e-r, der, winder, a casement. When the boy knows this out of book, he goes and does it. . . . Where's the second boy?"
>
> "Please, sir, he's weeding the garden," replied a small voice.
>
> "To be sure," said Squeers, by no means disconcerted. "So he is. B-o-t, bot, t-i-n; bottin, n-e-y, ney, bottinney, noun substantive, a knowledge of plants. When he has learned that bottinney means a knowledge of plants, he goes and knows 'em."

SCENE-STEALERS

*A*lthough Nicholas remains firmly in the center of the action, it's the minor figures who steal the show. Who can forget Mr. Mantalini, whose blandishments are a form of extortion: "What about the cash, my existence's jewel?" Or Mrs. Wititterly's "soul," or Mr. Curdle, the literary man who has written "a pamphlet of sixty-four pages, post octavo, on the character of the Nurse's deceased husband in *Romeo and Juliet*." Before he became a writer, Dickens wanted to be a comic who specialized in depicting characters, and any one of these characters and their scenes could be a skit in the "Nicholas Nickleby Revue."

Indeed, in his brilliant introduction to the Penguin edition, Michael Slater notes that "role playing is the living heart of the novel." Few see themselves or their world as it exists, and practically all create roles for themselves that they enact on their own private stage. Thus Dickens writes, Fanny Squeers "look[ed] into her own little glass, where, like most of us, she saw—not herself, but the reflection of some pleasant image in her own brain." Paradoxically, human beings are most real when they pretend to be something they're not. *Homo sapiens* is a role-playing creature.

Especially the estimable Mr. Lillyvick, a minor civil servant (a collector of the water rates) who sees himself as an important official. The scenes involving the Kenwigses, Mr. Lillyvick's poor relations, their fawning attempts to stay in his good graces—and his will—and the collector's magisterial condescension are broad comedy at its best. When the collector takes offense and threatens to break up a family party, the Kenwigses, as if on cue, fall into lamentations to great effect. One can't help but suspect that this scene has been enacted before, as indeed it has:

> But still Mr. Lillyvick . . . cried obdurately, "Morleena, my hat!" upon the fourth repetition of which demand Mrs. Kenwigs sunk back in her chair, with a cry that might have softened a water-butt, not to say a water-collector; while the four little girls (privately instructed to that effect) clasped their uncle's corduroy shorts in their arms, and prayed him in imperfect English to remain.
>
> "Why should I stop here, my dears?" said Mr. Lillyvick; "I'm not wanted here."
>
> "Oh, do not speak so cruelly, uncle," sobbed Mrs. Kenwigs, "unless you wish to kill me."

Mrs. Kenwigs's histrionics and Mr. Lillyvick's grandiosity suggest that in *Nicholas Nickleby* everyone is an actor ready to go "on." What makes the Kenwigses beguiling rather than repellent is that they honestly don't see themselves as motivated by greed. By now, they believe their own act. One can't even call them hypocrites; their scale of deception is modest and very human—they are actors in the way we all are.

THE CRUMMLES COMPANY

*B*ut the living embodiment of theater in the novel is Vincent Crummles, the manager of the acting company Nicholas joins after leaving Dotheboys Hall. Dickens loved writing about bad actors and is never better than when depicting their grand illusions, heightened mannerisms, and affectations. The Crummleses are not only actors but actors playing actors; that is, they perform onstage and off. The entire family represents the repertoire of the popular theater of Dickens's youth. In her palmy days Mrs. Crummles was known for her spine-chilling rendition of "The Blood-Drinker's Burial"; their daughter, Ninetta, "the Infant Phenomenon," who has been the same age for five years, is practicing a raucous pas de deux with the troupe's leading man entitled "The Indian Maiden and the Savage." Even the pony, boasts Mr. Crummles, "is quite one of us." An equine Barrymore, his mother "ate apple-pie at a circus for upwards of fourteen years . . . fired pistols, and went to bed in a nightcap; and, in short, took the low comedy entirely." His father, Mr. Crummles adds, "was a dancer."

Mr. Crummles and his actors find it difficult to discern where the stage ends and real life begins. Their embraces are stylized stage hugs, "which, as everybody knows, are performed by the embracer's laying his or her chin on the shoulder of the object of affection, and looking over it." Ordinary objects are potential props, and any occasion an opportunity for a staged "event." When Mr. Crummles sadly accepts Nicholas's decision to leave the troupe, his spirits rally as he begins to plan a series of farewell performances: "We can have positively your last appearance, on Thursday—re-engagement for one night more, on Friday—and, yielding to the wishes of numerous influential patrons, who were disappointed in obtaining seats, on Saturday."

Paradoxically, Mr. Crummles is sincere in his affections, which through the years have formed his identity; the actors, even with their professional rivalries and vanities, are the most genuinely kind people in the book. Next to their generosity, the ultravirtuous Cheeryble brothers seem false and insipid.

In the Crummles section, Dickens lovingly parodies popular genres, especially pantomime, romance, and melodrama. When Mr. Lenville, the leading tragedian, discreetly inquires about his part in the upcoming production, Nicholas hastily improvises a scene:

"You are troubled with remorse till the last act, and then you make up your mind to destroy yourself. But just as you are raising the pistol to your head, a clock strikes—ten."

"I see," cried Mr. Lenville. "Very good."

"You pause," said Nicholas; "you recollect to have heard a clock strike ten in your infancy. The pistol falls from your hand—you are overcome—you burst into tears, and become a virtuous and exemplary character for ever afterwards."

We laugh, as no doubt Dickens did as he wrote it. But a sneaking, even blasphemous thought persists: is this farcical concoction any more outrageous than certain scenes in any Dickens novel? What else is Nicholas's ad hoc scenario but a crude version of *A Christmas Carol* as written by a hack instead of a genius? And the just-in-the-nick-of-time appearance of *Nickleby*'s deus ex machina, the brothers Cheeryble, strains credulity to the breaking point.

We know *Nickleby* will have a happily-ever-after ending because throughout the novel we sense Dickens's presence, busily directing everything toward that inevitable conclusion. Near the end he becomes clumsy, however, like a stagehand who allows the audience a glimpse of himself as the curtain goes up. Readers tend to be troubled by the facile manner in which Nicholas and Kate's problems are resolved; they arrive at happiness rather than achieve it, and almost everything in the last part of the novel depends on fortuity. Nicholas bumps into two benefactors who like his manner, and after they give him a job in their firm, he becomes a success and marries his dream girl. Kate, her virtue intact, marries wealthy Frank Cheeryble, the brothers' nephew. Poor Smike doesn't survive, but we knew that all along.

Without treating a comic novel like a serious work of meta-fiction, it's fair to

TREMENDOUS SACRIFICE!

say that in *Nickleby,* Dickens writes on two levels. The first and most obvious one, the adventures of a virtuous hero named Nicholas Nickleby, draws us in simply by the forward drive of its plot and its dazzling ingenuity. On another level, Dickens pokes fun at the conventions he so felicitously uses—and we are constantly aware of the "stage machinery" behind the illusion of reality. Thus *Nickleby* is a morality play about goodness and a flamboyant, almost camp work that self-consciously flaunts its comic artistry.

Nickleby may be comprised of clichés and conventions, but it also transcends them. Dickens's ability to bring this sort of thing off is one reason he's an extraordinary artist and a popular success. Only Dickens can take the ingredients of soap opera—bathos, predictability, coincidence—and miraculously create a work that defies traditional highbrow/lowbrow distinctions. Of all the great novelists, only Dickens so unabashedly turns clichés to such good account.

*W*ith Bosch-like grotesquerie, George Cruikshank illustrates the diabolical conditions of the millinery establishments, which were little more than sweatshops for women. The working conditions of such places— poor ventilation, long hours, scant pay—forced women into the streets. Milliners were often fronts for brothels, and the two establishments were almost the same thing in the public mind. A millinery meant a very different thing to Dickens's public than it does to us today—and Dickens's use of it shows how he telegraphed sexual or unmentionable subjects to a family audience.

Adapting *Nickleby*

⫯

INTERVIEW WITH DAVID EDGAR

n 1978 David Edgar was approached to write a play based on a Dickens novel. The play turned out to be the Royal Shakespeare Company's 1981 dazzling, unprecedented The Life and Adventures of Nicholas Nickleby, *a production that made theatrical history. At nine and a half hours, it was among the longest plays ever written, and unlike any other Dickens adaptation, Edgar's version keeps all the minor characters and subplots intact.*

People who could never sit still for a nine-hour bout with a Dickens novel were enthralled as his story sprang to life on the stage. It sounds blasphemous, but Edgar's production went even deeper than Dickens's novel, introducing a chorus that interjected social commentary applicable to the ages of both Queen Victoria and Prime Minister Margaret Thatcher. While Edgar reduced the novel's sentimentality, he retained its great emotional power. When Smike died, most members of the audience were left weeping, and almost everyone reports leaving the theater dazed and disoriented. Edgar also fleshed out the female characters, making them more spirited and "real." Nevertheless, his dramatization was at once innovative, nostalgic—and faithful to the Dickensian spirit.

NE: *Why did you choose* Nicholas Nickleby?

DE: I didn't choose it. The choice was made by the directors [Trevor Nunn and John Caird] and they had whittled it down to *Our Mutual Friend* and

Nicholas Nickleby. They didn't want to do a well-known novel, and there had just been a successful small theatrical version of *Bleak House. Great Expectations, David Copperfield, A Tale of Two Cities* were knocked off for the same reason. *Oliver Twist,* again, too well known. They also wanted something with a large number of very good parts.

The other thing, of course, was that *Nicholas Nickleby* had the Crummles's theater company. Whatever one got wrong, at least one had the Crummles. There's nothing more entertaining than watching good actors playing bad actors. Another reason—which sounds silly but was quite real—is that almost everybody in *Our Mutual Friend* drowns or nearly drowns. We thought that all our time would be spent trying to find ways of making people drown on dry stages.

NE: *How did you make these sentimental relationships seem real to a modern audience?*

DE: I think we did a great deal to take the curse of sentimentality off the novel. One does have the problem of children's deaths in Victorian novels. We did this partly by a little judicious evasion—there were various sentimental things we avoided. We tried to make Smike as real as possible. David Threlfall [the actor who played Smike] portrayed someone who had all the symptoms of rickets as well as severe nutritional and environmental deprivation. It was a very naturalistic portrait of someone who had been emotionally and physically abused since early childhood. I had already decided that one way to make Smike work was to develop those aspects of his dialogue that were at least equivalent to the medically observable behavior of retarded or schizophrenic people.

So we didn't have the golden-haired, blue-eyed child dying in someone's arms. There's one other thing we did—and we didn't realize we had done it till afterward (I would recommend this to anyone who wants to move an audience): first you make an audience laugh at something, then you do the same thing again, but in a sad context. In so doing, you make people cry. In *Nickleby,* Nicholas is trying to teach Smike the apothecary scene from *Romeo and Juliet.* Smike is struggling to learn the lines, and it's very funny. Throughout the play the lines become a sort of running code between Nicholas and Smike. But these lines become Smike's dying words: "Who calls so loud?" ceases to be a line from a play. It becomes real, since it relates to Smike looking up and seeing the angels call him to heaven.

NE: *How is that different from Dickens's scene?*

DE: The two main differences between my version of Smike's death and Dickens's is in my use of Shakespeare. The lines become a poignant replay of a crucial moment in their friendship. Also, the *Romeo and Juliet* story relates to Smike's love for Kate. The second difference is that Kate is there. In the novel Nicholas and Smike go alone to Devon, but I thought Kate's presence was important because in a sense Smike dies for love of her.

NE: *Did you find Dickens's characters flat?*

DE: Dickens wrote *Nickleby* when he was twenty-six, and the first half of the novel contains as many great characters as any normal novelist would expect to produce in a lifetime. So to sit around and complain is ridiculous. But there's no doubt that he does some things better than others. And he does grotesques very well indeed. As for women, he does shrews and older women a great deal better than ingenues. His heroines are weak, and we had to do a lot of work on Kate. And we practically had to invent a character for Madeline Bray. For instance, in Dickens's novel, during Madeline's greatest crisis, you hear a thump from upstairs: it's Madeline fainting. At the end of the scene Nicholas carries her out. During her biggest moment, her supposed marriage to Gride, she's comatose. So we had to wake her up—literally.

NE: *What else did you do to make the characters more vivid?*

DE: Dickens often tells readers what characters think but don't say. We transformed their thoughts into speech. For instance, I made Kate's thoughts into spoken lines. Kate suffers terribly. She nearly gets raped, and she is employed in a fiendish millinery establishment, which in Dickens's day destroyed women. If you were to describe a woman who endures all this with accuracy, you end up with a much braver figure than the woman who comes off Dickens's page.

NE: *Is it true that no one else had ever staged a complete Dickens novel before?*

DE: Well, that certainly was the rhetoric. *Nickleby* let us do a theatrical event on a scale that allowed people to feel as if they were participating in an entire vision of society. That was its great virtue. There have been multiple plots in stage adaptations, and certainly it's been done on British television. People thought that to do *Nickleby* you had to lose the Mantalini and the Kenwigs plot. But they perform the function of Shakespearean subplots. They are comic reflections on the serious main plot, and their inclusion makes the novel—and the play—more considerable.

NE: *Why isn't* Nicholas Nickleby *generally considered great Dickens?*

DE: Well, one reason is that people don't really know it. They know bits from the films, and *Nickleby* has been rather badly served in this way. The thirties film isn't good. And you know, there was an awful musical called *Smike*.

NE: *What did you mean when you wrote in an essay in* The Dickensian *that* Nicholas Nickleby *is about Charles Dickens?*

DE: We didn't want Dickens to be a character in the play, but by using his narrative voice, we suggest that his England is an imaginary place. It is not quite as obviously imaginary as Tolkien's Middle Earth or a fantasy like that, but it's not a documentary, or indeed even a particularly realistic view of Victorian England. It is a place of fantasy, and paradoxically, it tells us a lot about Victorian England. For instance, London was not as socially nervous, nor was the countryside as idyllic, as Dickens portrayed them. But clearly, people had an acute perception that there *was* a movement from a rural paradise into a disruptive, teeming city where no social relationship was secure.

NE: *What are some of the parallels between 1830 and the late 1970s and early '80s?*

DE: I don't want to overdo this, but the play originally opened during Margaret Thatcher's triumphal first year. Businesses were closing, and there was a depression going on. People wanted to see another view of the world. They wanted the old things we regard as sentimental and silly to be validated. And I also think there was another element: *Nickleby* portrays the very beginning of the industrial era, and we are now at the end of the process that was just starting to become apparent in the novel.

The 1830s were in many ways a mirror of our own times. It was the decade when the great technological revolution that had been brewing for fifty years suddenly flapped its wings and flew. Two years before *Nickleby* was begun, Samuel Morse built the first telegraph; four years before that, Michael Faraday discovered electromagnetism; in that year Charles Darwin set off on his voyage of the *Beagle*. And *Nickleby* was finished only ten years after the first steam locomotive line opened in the United States.

NE: *Does* Nickleby *portray the world as it could be, as a community of potential goodness?*

DE: That again is where *Nickleby* is a work of the imagination. The Cheeryble brothers are simply not possible. The great thing about Dickens is that he manages to use fairies and monsters, yet he puts them in a place that at least looks something like the real world. But it isn't the real world, only an imitation of it.

NE: *What did you learn about Dickens's methods by using his material?*

DE: I got to know him quite well. Because he wrote for serialization, he writes himself into the most appalling corners. We got rid of a lot of meandering stuff, particularly in the second half, when Dickens is clearly padding the length of each episode. He clearly had no idea till quite late that Smike was going to turn out to be Ralph's son. His energy is that of somebody going through the jungle with a machete. What I found terribly exciting was the way he got himself out of different situations. I like the muscularity of it. The sentimentality I could do without.

Playing Nicholas

ᴛ

INTERVIEW WITH ROGER REES

oger Rees is a brilliant actor and a shrewd observer of drama, acting, and literature. He began his career with the Royal Shakespeare Company, cast usually as the virtuous friend or sidekick. He
finally became a hero of heroic proportions when, in 1981, he
played Nicholas—and won a Tony for his performance in The Life and Adventures of Nicholas Nickleby, *the stunning nine-and-a-half-hour dramatic version
of Dickens's little-read novel. Rees is onstage for most of the time, and his performance is shockingly good. Unlike any other actor, he has made one of Dickens's
male "ingenues" seem like a flesh-and-blood man, not a mannequin of virtue.
Rees's Nicholas matures from an overly proud and at times insensitive adolescent into a man.*

NE: *You once wrote that in the first millisecond after a part is offered to you, as
soon as you hear the character's name, you mentally shuffle through a card index
of actors who have already played the role and then quickly start shaping the
character. With* Nickleby *you had no tradition to follow. How did you see
Nicholas in that first second?*

RR: Other people, of course, have played it. Henry Irving did it, and Derek
Bond was in the movie. Henry Irving did excerpts. It was very, very popular
in the Victorian theater. Dickens loved the theater so much that he often went
and saw pirated versions of his novels long before they were even completed

A heartrending scene from the Royal Shakespeare Company's production of *The Life and Adventures of Nicholas Nickleby:* Smike (David Threlfall) and Nicholas (Roger Rees) have just escaped Dotheboys Hall. Smike begs to accompany Nicholas "anywhere. The world's end. To the churchyard grave . . . You'll let me. Come away with you. . . . You are my home."

in their monthly form. So there have been many people who played the part before. Dozens probably, although we don't know who they are or where they did it. After I got the part I really didn't do anything but complain that I didn't think I looked like him. I was thirty-six when I played him, and he's nineteen. There were lots of young men in the company who looked more as I imagined Nicholas would look.

NE: *Did you read the novel before you undertook the part?*

RR: I read the novel as we did the project, sure. But don't you understand we rehearsed the play for seven months before we knew what part we played? Everyone played everything. Girls played Smike, boys played Mrs. Crummles. So there was no question about who was going to do what. We tried to remove one whole aspect of an actor's life, the part that says, "Ooh, I want to play that part." You've seen Bottom in *A Midsummer Night's Dream,* so you understand what actors want: they want to play everyone's part. So when I got the part, I thought, All right, so that's it.

NE: *[The playwright] David Edgar said that each one of you researched bits of Victorian life.*

RR: That's right, but it wasn't as petty as that. It was really, really much more vigorous. We were doing a complete season at Stratford with seven major plays and thirteen other smaller plays of modern writers and nineteenth-century Russian playwrights. At the same time we were researching and reading as much about Dickens and the period, 1840, as one could possibly do. It was a vigorous and exciting time. It wasn't in little bits and pieces. People were very committed, sometimes wrongly, but it was interesting. We found out about the sewage system and lighting and social mores and opera. Someone made an opera of that time and put it on. Everyone performed different characters, and through that we discovered a form, a way of dealing with a narrative, how to make the novel into a three-dimensional stage play.

NE: *Why did the production require so much background?*

RR: Because it was a novel, not a play. The play grew out of our improvisa-tions. David *politicized* our group work. The scenes were created by a group of actors. It was made into a play by the group.

NE: *Yet it's Edgar's dramatization.*

RR: It was essentially David's. We would work on one scene for many days, and then he would go away for a day and come back with a scene or a version of it, and then it would be changed. But I think he recognized that he couldn't have done it without the spadework of the group. That's why it turned out to be so good, really.

NE: *Why do you think a late-twentieth-century audience responded so wildly to the play?*

RR: Except for the language change, there's no difference in people then and now. An interesting point: people were paying $100 to come see this on Broad-way while they were stepping over tramps and dead bodies in Times Square to get to the theater on time. Isn't that what Dickens was talking about? The haves and the have-nots, the poor and the rich. Also, there's the problem of vi-olence in the streets. People went to a restaurant and then stabbed a night watchman as a matter of course. They wouldn't think twice about it. It's very similar to the gangs in Los Angeles. And I think high society is still as obscene and unapproachable and stupid as it ever was, you know, and life and death are all around us. What was nice about doing *Nicholas* is that it embraced all those things within itself. Actors died while we were doing it, people got married, people left, people arrived. It had laughter and tears in its making.

NE: *Is Dickens in danger of becoming extinct?*

RR: There's no one writing today who is as interesting, who has the vision and the imagination. It's okay, but it's just that we move further away from him. Cars go faster, planes go swifter. I think we can be influenced by Dickens's anger, the strength you can find in his fury. It's a good solace to find. I think that's what people need now. That's why people read him now. If he isn't read now, it's because people don't read.

NE: *What about the charge that Dickens creates flat caricatures, as opposed to Shakespeare, who creates fully rounded, psychological characters?*

RR: People are not able to see the reality of Dickens. Sometimes you gasp when you read Shakespeare, thinking, "Oh, I feel like that!" That's true of Dickens too. I don't think he'd be here now if that wasn't the case.

NE: *What is* Nickleby *about? It's so episodic, it's hard to say.*

RR: Nicholas meets interesting people and learns from them. The play will confound people like you for years to come. You are not able to compartmen-talize it. That probably means there is a splendid sanity about it. Nicholas is always renewing himself. There are little lessons all along the way. He ends up marrying a plump bride; they get money. Sort of horrible really. But they all seem to end like that.

NE: *What about the sentimentality? Does that turn modern audiences off? Most of us don't weep over the death of Little Nell.*

RR: You won't own up to it. People won't own up to their true affections without cynicism.

NE: *It takes a lot for people to weep.*

RR: Why? Because you are out of touch with your body? Or your feelings? I don't find it difficult. Dickens makes you cry; I don't think he was ashamed of that. If you are, that would seem to disqualify you from this area. Popular sentimentality will always be around. "Is Little Nell dead?" they yelled from the docks in New York, when the latest serial came out. It doesn't matter if you are forced to cry or are exploited. You should glory in the ability to cry. It motivates you.

NE: *Did you feel frustrated because there wasn't enough complexity or ambivalence in Nicholas?*

RR: No, far from it. I think Dickens is very eloquent in his treatment of a boy who has yet to get the keys to the car from his father. Boys that age *know* they can drive, but their father won't let them have the keys. It's a very interesting point in a man's life, and I think that is exactly what Dickens was describing . . . somebody who is ill at ease with authority, with himself, and much happier being pleasant and sentimental with his mother and his sister. He's scared of responsibility, scared of it and attracted by it. He's scared of sex, and attracted by it, you know. One of the actors says to Nicholas about Miss Snevellicci, "She has a very coming-on disposition." I know from my life, it's exactly what we say to a boy at that time. I think there's lots there for Nicholas to do, there's lots of nervousness and a kind of strength all at once.

NE: *The women seem more vivid in the play than in the book, more real, somehow. I noticed this particularly with Fanny Squeers, whom I think Dickens treated rather badly.*

RR: Women get a rough deal in Dickens because they got a rough deal at that time. You have to see beyond that. It's easier when you have actresses who can personify the characters. The women in the films or onstage are so much greater simply because they are *there.*

Fanny Squeers has a bad life. She's in a terrible place. She is going to grab anything in trousers. Her predicament is very moving. She, of course, cannot do the thing you suggest about Nicholas. She can't be heroic in protestation. Of course you care about her, that's why you laugh! You only laugh at someone you care about. I don't think Dickens is ever cruel without also being kind. Look at Gride: Gride wants a young woman. He needs what he's lost: beauty and youth. It's tragic and sad. It's what comes to us all. Squeers is a thrilling character. He's very contented but blind to his own flaws. He is terrible, but fabulous.

The Prodigal Father

⚯

How long he is, growing up to be a man.
—DICKENS, on his father

———◆·◆◆·◆———

he story of Charles Dickens and John Dickens is a tale of a prodigal father. By the time he was eleven, Charles Dickens had already developed a precocious sense of duty toward his father, and through most of their lives their roles would be reversed: the angry son would repeatedly give his father loans, handouts, and allowances, while the wayward father, alternately sheepish, playful, and abusive, always came back.

By 1839, Dickens was famous enough for his ever-impecunious father to try to cash in on the family name. In his own inimitable manner, John Dickens believed he could get away with anything as long as it was done with flair. He began clipping his son's signature from private letters to sell to autograph dealers; in 1843 he sold a piece of Dickens's juvenilia, a trifle called "O'Thello," to a manuscript collector. Worse, he would write imploring letters to Dickens's wealthy friends, such as Angela Burdett-Coutts and the publishers Chapman and Hall, melodramatically informing them that he was but one step from "perdition" and "disaster." Even the most pinched circumstances could not curb his rhetorical flourishes, which his son would later immortalize in Mr. Micawber:

> Contemporaneous events of this nature place me in a difficulty from which, without some anticipatory pecuniary effort, I cannot extricate myself. . . .

But the flowery language could not disguise that these were shameless appeals for cash. One wonders if John Dickens viewed "anticipatory pecuniary effort[s]" as anything so crude as "loans." In one letter there is even a suggestion of blackmail: writing to Chapman and Hall, he reminds them of "how much your interests are bound up with my son," and hints at "fatal consequences" if they refuse him.

Apparently, neither Miss Burdett-Coutts, nor her bank, nor Chapman and Hall could save John Dickens from financial ruin. In November 1839, just as his father was about to be arrested for debt—not for the first time—Dickens rescued his parents, providing them with a cottage in the Devonshire countryside and paying off their creditors. But they hated the country, resented their exile, and blamed their son, writing him letters filled with self-pity and threats. Dickens diligently continued to pay his father's creditors: "And so it always is," he wrote to John Forster, "directly I build up a hundred pounds, one of my dear relations comes and knocks it down again."

John Dickens, however, refused to play the country squire and would periodically break out and arrive in London with more beggarly appeals. Dickens, who controlled everyone—publishers, wife, friends, and children—could not restrain his father: "The thought of him besets me, night and day," he wrote in February 1843 (after the "O'Thello" incident), "and I really do not know what is to be done with him. It is quite clear that the more we do, the more outrageous and audacious he becomes." Finally, Dickens found one thing he could do. In November of that year, an advertisement appeared in all the major newspapers: "Henceforth Charles Dickens will not discharge . . . debts . . . save those of his own or his wife's contracting."

Yet Dickens was an attentive son until the day his father died. When he became editor at the *Daily News* in 1854, he hired his father to supervise the reporters and, despite his incompetence, kept him on the payroll. One reporter remembered Dickens senior as "obese, fond of a glass of grog, full of fun, never given to much locomotion. . . ." Later, when his father was sixty, Dickens found him a minor position at his journal *Household Words,* probably to keep him under a watchful eye.

John Dickens has usually been portrayed as lovable old rogue, a "character" much like Mr. Micawber. Certainly he displayed Micawberesque tendencies: his linguistic contortions, his fecklessness with money, his uncanny knack of evading creditors, and his geniality and warmth of spirit. But characters in fiction are often softened versions of their living counterparts, and unlike Mr. Micawber, who always remains endearing, Dickens senior could be calculating, greedy, and insensitive to his son's position. Dickens's feelings toward his father were complicated: he complained about him even as he rescued him. In later years he recalled the old man's foibles with tenderness, remarking, "My father was a much better man than I thought him."

CANNIBALISM

Dickens, as his biographer Fred Kaplan points out, felt "cannibalized" by his tribe of dependents, which, beginning with his parents, eventually expanded to include several adult offspring, his wife's separate household (after 1858), a brother who had inherited their father's spending habits, assorted nieces and nephews and in-laws, and even his brother's mistress. And then he supported his own mistress and *her* family. At an early age he had acquired the habit of assuming responsibility for others, whether he (or they) liked it or not.

Of his parents and siblings he wrote, "They and all of them, look upon me as a something to be plucked and torn to pieces for their advantage. They have no idea of, and no care for, my existence in any other light. My soul sickens at the thought of them." This image of either being plucked, shorn, ravaged, savaged, eaten, or swallowed recurs throughout his letters and novels. His family and all his dependents were a swarming horde that threatened his very existence.

He also spoke for and gave to numerous guilds, charities, causes, and funds: "For a good many years," he complained in 1865, "I have suffered a great deal from charities, but never anything like what I suffer now." Why did he do it? Dickens was an extremely generous man who found it difficult to refuse anyone in need. He also liked having others in his debt—it made him feel powerful and influential; for the Victorians, largesse meant success.

But it was also a burden; his expenses were phenomenal, and he never stopped struggling for more money. The shadow of his father's fate haunted him. No matter how much he had, it was never enough. Less than two years before he died, against the wishes of his friends, he made a reading tour of America, solely on the promise that it would net him 15,000 pounds. Some say it was the strain of the trip and the dramatic readings that killed him. If so, then he had been right all along: the importunate relatives and numerous parasites had gotten him at last.

The Dickensian
Freak Show

꘠

hen Dickens was in New York in 1868, he visited P. T. Barnum's
"museum," where, among other attractions, he saw such
"human curiosities" as an albino family, the Last Aztecs, the
Swiss Bearded Lady, the Highland Fat Boys (an attraction reminiscent of the Fat Boy of *Pickwick* fame) and Barnum's star feature, "What Is
It?," a mentally retarded black man who was billed as a "lower order of man, a
higher order of monkey!"

The nineteenth century was the golden age of the peep show, a shameless
exploitation of "human oddities," "curiosities," and "nature's mistakes." Any
of these "human oddities" would not have seemed out of place in a Dickens
novel. *The Old Curiosity Shop,* for instance, is a carnival sideshow of disturbing "attractions": Sally Brass is the bearded lady; Quilp is the amazing dwarf
who eats hard-boiled eggs, shell and all! There are also dancing dogs, a
Punch and Judy show, a waxwork museum of notorious criminals, and the female counterpart of Tom Thumb, a tiny woman dubbed the "Marchioness."

Any display of human curiosities today would be high art (such as a Fellini
film or a Diane Arbus photograph), bad taste, or simple cruelty, but to the Victorians it was pure entertainment. Dickens exploits the human desire to
gawk, taking us beyond the limits of what is "normal." Thus in a telling scene
in *The Old Curiosity Shop,* Short and Mr. Vuffin, a sideshow owner, discuss
the fate of elderly giants:

"What becomes of old giants?" said Short, turning to him again after a little reflection.

"WHAT IS IT"?

Is it a lower order of MAN! Or is it a higher order of MONKEY! None can tell! Perhaps it is a combination of both. It is beyond dispute THE MOST MARVELLOUS CREATURE LIVING. It was captured in a savage state in Central Africa, is probably about 20 years old, 4 Feet high, intelligent, docile, active, sportive, and PLAYFUL AS A KITTEN. It has the skull, limbs and general anatomy of an ORANG OUTANG and the COUNTENANCE of a HUMAN BEING.
TO BE SEEN AT ALL HOURS AT BARNUM'S MUSEUM

"*H*uman oddities" such as Barnum's "What Is It?" were popular exhibits at carnivals and peep shows. In *Martin Chuzzlewit* Sairey Gamp reflects upon a pickled baby in a bottle along with "a pink-eyed lady, Prooshan dwarf, and livin skelinton" displayed at Greenwich fair; Short in *The Old Curiosity Shop* ponders the fate of elderly giants. And in several novels, Dickens refers to Sarah Biffin, a woman without arms or legs and who wrote with her teeth. Outside the context of their novels, many of Dickens's most successful creations would be considered freaks.

"They're usually kept in carawans [sic] to wait upon the dwarfs," said Mr. Vuffin.

"The maintaining of them must be expensive, when they can't be shown, eh?" remarked Short, eyeing him doubtfully.

"It's better then letting 'em go upon the parish or about the streets," said Mr. Vuffin. "Once make a giant common and giants will never draw again. Look at wooden legs. If there was only one man with a wooden leg what a property *he*'d be!"

"This shows, you see," said Mr. Vuffin, waving his pipe with an argumentative air, "this shows the policy of keeping the used-up giants still in the carawans, where they get food and lodging for nothing, all their lives. . . ."

By having Short pose such a question, Dickens satisfies even the most baroque imagination. For a small price, the author provides a behind-the-scenes peek at a peep show, thus revealing the unthinkable to those unable to think it.

This scene also says something important about Dickens's own art: quite simply, Dickens markets the marvelous, and his stories are freak shows that display human oddities for our delectation. By reading a Dickens novel, we hear all the details of a child's deathbed, see the greasy remains of a victim of spontaneous combustion, overhear the business dealings of a mortician, discover what dancing dogs do when they're off duty, eavesdrop on a conversation between two carnival hands, and meet a dwarfish manicurist who saves the nail parings of royalty.

Dickens saw nothing amiss with enjoying lowbrow amusements. *Hard Times,* a cautionary tale about the dangers of abstinence, opens with Tom and Louisa Gradgrind, the products of a stringent utilitarian upbringing, staring at the forbidden spectacle of a circus through a peephole in a fence. When caught by their father, the soul-crushing Thomas Gradgrind, they are punished for their curiosity. By depriving his children of clowns, fairy tales, and sideshows, Mr. Gradgrind turns *them* into freaks, children who lack the capacity to wonder. The Dickensian moral is clear. As Mr. Sleary, the circus owner, lisps: "People mutht be amuthed."

DICKENS'S DIVERSIONS

*D*ickens's inquisitiveness drove him to seek other "diversions" not officially sanctioned for public consumption. As journalist, philanthropist, or tourist, he visited morgues, jails, crime scenes, graveyards, hospitals, gallows sites, insane asylums, and institutions for the handicapped. When in Paris, he didn't go to the Louvre but to the celebrated morgue, where he mused upon the bloated bodies of the drowned and unclaimed suicides laid out for viewing. Dickens needed to be shocked, to be pushed to the edge. After a jaunt to Paris, Dickens admitted that he felt "dragged by invisible force into the Morgue . . . with its ghastly beds, and the swollen saturated clothes hanging up, and the water dripping, dripping all day long, upon that other swollen saturated something in the corner, like a heap of crushed over-ripe figs." And what made Dickens, of all men, visit a morgue on Christmas Day? He never visited it again.

*I*n *Martin Chuzzlewit,* Dickens has Mrs. Gamp describe a traveling exhibit that boasted a "sweet infant" preserved in a bottle of spirits, a pink-eyed lady, a Prussian dwarf, and a living skeleton. Placed in another Dickensian context, that "sweet infant" might have been the subject of one of the author's famous sentimental set pieces. The flip side of Dickens's tendency to sanctify dead children is his inclination to view them as exhibits in a freak show. In that sense, Little Nell and Paul Dombey are freaks. Dickens could write an affecting juvenile deathbed scene and then turn around and portray a similar tableau with macabre mockery. The ability to view the world from various, opposing perspectives, often at the same time, is typically Dickensian. A tendency to weep does not preclude the desire to laugh.

The Old Curiosity Shop

 f the Italian director Federico Fellini had been an English novelist writing in the age of Victoria, *The Old Curiosity Shop* could have been his *La Strada*. Dickens's novel is a curious work, by turns a circus and a funeral. Like a reverie, a nightmare, and a vision—and the shop itself—the novel brings together startling, contradictory themes, images, and objects. While writing the novel, Dickens was haunted by images from what he called his "mental museum," i.e., his unconscious. The tale itself emerged from an idea that he couldn't get out of his mind:

> In writing the book, I had it always in my fancy to surround the lonely figure of the child with *grotesque* and *wild,* but not impossible companions, and to gather about her innocent face and pure intentions, associates as *strange* and *uncongenial* as the *grim* objects that are about her bed when her history is first foreshadowed. [italics mine]

This hardly sounds like the sticky-sweet novel derided by those who have never read it. Like Little Red Riding Hood in the forest or Alice in Wonderland, Nell is Purity threatened by Evil. Her peril, like theirs, is far greater and far more disturbing than a mere physical threat.

The novel resists easy explication. Why is the idea of a solitary girl living amid dust and decay so potent? And why does she collect a coterie of worshipful, elderly men? The Nell cult includes characters called the single gentleman (or the younger brother), the grandfather, the schoolmaster, the gravedigger, and the sexton—all aging, neutered bachelors or widowers. (Kit

Nubbles and Dick Swiveller are the only specimens of normal male sexuality in the novel—and they seem positively rude with health.) More curious still, why do these elderly men lack real names? It's an odd omission for an author with a genius for naming.

Nell's grandfather, the novel's second most important character, is called simply "Nell's grandfather" or "the old man," and few readers remember his or Nell's surname (Trent). Their lack of names distances us from these men, making them less individualized than characters in a realistic novel and more like those in a fairy tale. (Does Red Riding Hood have a real name? Does her grandmother?)

The virtuous heroine, Nell, is a dream child, mirroring the unconscious needs of those who are drawn to her. To every man who sees her, she becomes an object of desire, whether sacred or profane. Quilp, the malevolent dwarf with the big cigar, can view Nell only with lecherous eyes. A Dickensian Humbert Humbert, Quilp sees Nell as a nymphet, "a chubby little bud," and a "tasty morsel" over whom he smacks his lips. (Actually, the character in *Lolita* that Quilp most resembles is the unregenerate Quilty.) And when Quilp moves into

"Quilp's Wharf." Dickens's London is a decaying, ramshackle, melancholy place.

the curiosity shop, he chooses to sleep in Nell's bed. There is something tempting about young innocence that makes a man like Quilp yearn to defile it. But set

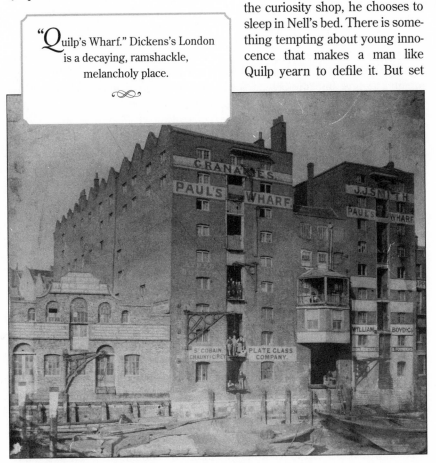

against Quilp's bristling sexuality are all the neutered men who desexualize Nell, elevating her to the status of angel or saint. (Quilp's plot to replace Mrs. Quilp with the young Nell is eerily prophetic; eighteen years later Dickens would replace his wife with the young Nelly.)

We are thus given two contrasting views of Nell: Dickens's favorite—and most beloved—heroine is poised precariously in that idealized state in which she is both sweet little girl and nubile young woman. Only death can preserve such perfection. Nell Trent, age thirteen, lives alone with her grandfather amid musty curios.

The contrast between Nell and her musty setting intensifies her youth, her beauty—and her isolation. The shop's other inhabitant, Nell's grandfather, is as ancient as the treasures that surround him: "The haggard aspect of the little old man was wonderfully suited to the place; he might have groped among old churches and tombs and deserted houses and gathered all the spoils with his own hands. There was nothing in the collection that looked older or more worn than he." But unlike the twinkly old gents of the Pickwickian mold, Nell's grandfather is a secret compulsive gambler who, he later insists, gambles in the hope of making his granddaughter a lady. For her grandfather, Nell is a convenient excuse to continue his vice.

Throughout most of the narrative, Nell exists in a state of terrible isolation. And just as she is the only blooming young thing in the shop, so there is no one else like her in the novel. David Copperfield finds solace among like-minded friends, but no one can speak or help Nell because no one ever understands her. Characters seem to speak *at* rather than *to* Nell; they look past her, seeing only what they want to see.

When Quilp learns that the grandfather can't repay the debt he owes him, the dwarf seizes control of the shop, holding Nell and the old man prisoner, terrorizing them with his threats. No one comes to their rescue, and Nell (whose reputation as a fluttering, frail heroine is unwarranted) takes control of the situation and escapes with her grandfather. Thus they leave behind the claustral confines of the shop and the dirt of the city for the freedom and the excitement of the open road.

In the course of her travels, Nell, like Alice in Wonderland or Dorothy in Oz, meets a veritable fantasia of remarkable creatures who, like the Cheshire Cat, the Mad Hatter, and the March Hare, follow their own peculiar logic. Like Alice, Nell is the reader's guide, a normative frame of reference in a bizarre world. Two of the most popular characters in the Dickensian gallery are the Punch and Judy men, Codlin and Short, who vie for Nell's favor. (Short's repeated injunction to Nell, "Short's the friend, not Codlin," became a favorite catchphrase for the novel's early readers.) They also encounter a homeless visionary who hears voices and music in the fire he has tended all his life; and the jolly Mrs. Jarley, the proud owner of Jarley's Waxworks, which contains such sinister delights as an image of Jasper Packlemerton "of atrocious memory, who courted and married fourteen wives, and destroyed them all by tickling the soles of their feet when they was sleeping in the consciousness of innocence and virtue."

No one in this novel is what he should be, and practically everyone defies our expectations. Women seem like men, and men like women (e.g., Sally Brass, the hirsute legal assistant, and her effeminate brother, Sampson). Puppets simulate people, and people—like the addicted grandfather or the eerily compliant Mrs. Quilp—behave mechanically, as if propelled by unseen forces.

Veering wildly between melancholia and mania, the novel leaves the reader emotionally dizzy. As in all Dickens's novels, tragedy and terror accompany humor and joy. It's packed with memento mori, with much of the action taking place in an attenuated realm inhabited by a grandfather, a sexton, a gravedigger, a middle-aged bachelor, a celibate schoolmaster, and dying children.

But it also teems with vitality. A vertiginous landscape of physical delights, it consists of waxworks, dancing dogs, puppets, gamblers, and a virile villain whose ingenuity is matched only by his sadism. These extremes finally meld with the demise of the two opposing forces in the novel: Quilp dies because he is evil, Nell because she is good.

Reduced to its simplest form, *The Old Curiosity Shop* is a journey. But in contrast to Oliver Twist's progress from parish boy to child of fortune, Nell begins her odyssey as a healthy young girl and slowly moves westward, toward the symbolic realm of the dead. Nell's final destination is the village of Tong, a place of peace, stasis, and, finally, death. After suffering so long, Nell has reached a nirvana that is beyond struggle—Tong, the endpoint of all desire, is a land beyond time itself. Dickens plays variations on the theme of antiquity and mortality. The village seems to consist solely of an ancient priory, churchyard, ruins, church, and graveyard. Although there is a school, we never see it. The focal point of the town is the burial yard where Nell plants flowers on overgrown, neglected graves. The Tong section is a drawn-out elegy concluding with the death of Nell.

Behind all the dust, graves, and epitaphs, one senses Dickens, the great materialist, struggling to express something holy and ineffable. Nell dies in the dead of winter— just before the single gentleman, Kit, and Mr. Garland, after a long pilgrimage, reach her. In awe, the three men approach her tower, drawn by a solitary light in the church window. They are Nell's Three Wise Men, the light her Star of Bethlehem. They find Nell in her bed: "Sorrow was dead indeed in her, but peace and perfect happiness were born."

The Old Curiosity Shop, like a good fairy tale, presents unhappy truths in a manner exaggerated, fantastic, and sentimentalized. For instance, the plight of the Marchioness, told in naturalistic terms, is one of child abuse and parental abandonment. The nameless, illegitimate offspring of two freaks, Sally Brass and Quilp, the Marchioness (so named by Dick Swiveller) is held captive in her mother's cellar until her release by Dick. Dickens defuses the horror by treating the Marchioness's ordeal as if it were a fairy tale with a happily-ever-after ending. Miss Sally, or as Dick calls her, the "Dragon," guards the cellar door where the tiny maid is kept. " 'This is a most remarkable and supernatural sort of house!' said Mr. Swiveller, as he walked into the office. . . . 'She-dragons in the business, conducting themselves like professional gentlemen; plain cooks of three feet high appearing mysteriously from underground. . . .' " The tiny girl's lack of a name distances us from her situation—she is not an enslaved child like Oliver Twist, but an imp who, enchanted and imprisoned by unnatural fiends, is freed from her spell by a prince who introduces her to the delights of beer, cards, and cribbage.

The trick to enjoying this remarkable work is to view it not as a syrupy period piece or a realistic novel but as a fairy tale for adults, filled with unsettling elements, startling, inexplicable symbols, and dark meanings just below the surface. Like all tales of enchantment, it transforms unspeakable and primal anxieties and taboos—such as incest, freaks, sadism, separation anxiety, and death—into something manageable and strangely compelling.

Dickens obviously resembles his autobiographical alter ego, the virtuous David Copperfield, but he also has much in common with Daniel Quilp, the lip-smacking monstrosity who tries to hold Nell and her grandfather in thrall. Uncannily, Quilp's attraction to Nell, whom he hopes to marry as a replacement for Mrs. Quilp, anticipates Dickens's separation from Mrs. Dickens, whom he replaced with the eighteen-year-old Nelly Ternan.

No wonder that for many readers, Quilp is the best thing in the book. In contrast to the limpid sadness of the Nell crowd, he is a bundle of sadistic energy. Freudians cite Quilp as an embodiment of sadistic orality: he swallows hard-boiled eggs, shell and all, smokes enormous pipes and cigars, and devours "gigantic prawns with the heads and tails on." He also eyes Nell as a delectable morsel. But he has other pleasures as well: for amusement, he drives a red-hot poker through a wooden figurehead of an admiral, kept especially for the purpose. He can't pass a chained dog without teasing it by dancing around it while making hideous faces. And he tortures his wife for the sheer fun of it.

Quilp is an antidote to the pathos of the novel; he is the source of humor, vigor, and color. "Quilp," the critic John Carey writes, "is Dickens's way of

---

DICKENSIAN ELIOT ENGEL ON THE SECRET OF QUILP'S SUCCESS

—✠—

NE: *What is it about Quilp? He's a dwarf, he's ugly, yet women seem to find him irresistible. Was Dickens making a subtle point about female sexuality?*

EE: He's good in bed! He's powerful; he dominates women. You know, there are some women who are looking for a monster like that. As one critic once said, not everything about Quilp was necessarily tiny.

---

avenging himself upon the sentimental set-up of *The Old Curiosity Shop,* upon all that part of his nature that reveled in angelic, plaster heroines, the deaths of little children, and touching animals." The average reader, weary of Nell's sappy virtue, might find himself applauding Quilp, especially when he threatens to wring the neck of Nell's pathetic little bird. For Carey, Quilp is a self-portrait of the author, another man who thrilled to violence and who loved writing about murders, wife abuse, fires, and riots. Quilp and Dickens both possess, in Carey's words, "a fine demonic rapture."

✵WHO WOULD NOT WEEP FOR LITTLE NELL?✵

With the death of Nell, the ardent Dickensian is forced to either defend or apologize for Dickens's undeniably morbid sentimentality. Her death is offered up as the classic case of Victorian necrophilia, the diseased fixation on premature death and mourning. Nell's deathbed scene evokes another era, when it was still possible for men to weep "manly" tears, and ladies resorted to bottles of sal volatile. The manner in which Nell's death is presented—the *longueurs,* the florid prose, and the association between premature death and spotless virtue—is pure Victoriana. For us, reading the "Death of Nell" is like opening a time capsule filled with Victorian curios: a sickly-sweet odor fills the air.

Everyone has heard of Little Nell, though few today have read *The Old Curiosity Shop,* once one of Dickens's most beloved novels. She's the girl with the most celebrated deathbed scene in literary history. Even Camille, with her last anguished gasp, can't top Nell's slow wasting away. One of literature's great set pieces, it's like Hamlet in the graveyard, lampooned, sneered at, and cherished.

Today, few if any care or even think about the death of Nell, and it's hard to imagine a time when her fate mattered. But the overwhelming response to her death is more than a comment on Victorian taste (or, as some would have it, the lack of

> ## TWO MAJOR MISCONCEPTIONS
> ### ABOUT *THE OLD CURIOSITY SHOP*
> —⁓—
>
> ✤Contrary to popular belief, the novel does *not* end with Nell's death. Dickens unfortunately still has one more chapter to go: he thus drags Master Humphrey back into the action. Accustomed to providing a surprise revelation at the end of his novels, Dickens clumsily reveals that Master Humphrey is in fact Nell's great-uncle. By this time, however, no one cares. Nell is still dead, and everyone has forgotten Master Humphrey.
>
> ✤As surprising as it may seem, Nell never has a real deathbed scene. She dies offstage, and her final moments are recounted by her grandfather.

it). It is also proof of the extent to which readers loved and identified with the fictional creations who entered their homes at regular intervals. The death of a fa-

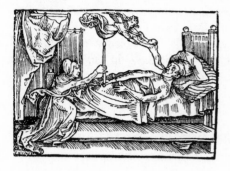

vorite character was the loss of a friend. Those who journeyed, suffered, and wept with Nell for fifty-three weeks hoped she would find the happiness she deserved at the novel's end. That her destiny was death and not marriage was a violent denial of readers' expectations.

In December 1841 readers began to sense the melancholic turn the novel was taking, and as Dickens reports, they "inundated [him] with imploring letters recommending poor little Nell to mercy." It is said that when the number containing her death was delivered in New York, people hovered anxiously on the docks, crying out, "Is Little Nell dead?" For the novel's original readers, the heroine's end was not a question of taste but a matter of life and death. For modern readers, Nell's fate may be more open-ended. In a recent *New Yorker* cartoon, one man says to another, "When we have interactive books, the first thing I'm going to do is rush Little Nell to the hospital."

Nell's death makes psychological as well as aesthetic sense. Put simply, she is too pure to live. As the novel progresses, she becomes increasingly rarefied, until it is impossible to imagine her growing up, marrying, or bearing children. One reason why adult men were so touched by Nell was that she represented an image enshrined in the male collective unconscious: a prepubescent virgin, "a young bud," poised on the brink of sexual flowering. Nell is the Victorian Lolita. This ideal, both sexy and sacred, recurs throughout Victorian fiction, in cheap novels as well as literary "texts." Her death only adds an extra erotic fillip to the novel. Deathbed scenes were euphemistically called "interesting," and in Victorian fiction it is but a small leap from the interesting to the prurient.

DICKENS AND NELLY

The death of "Nelly" meant a great deal to Dickens and his friends. To him, she symbolized all that was good in a corrupt world. After one of his feuds with John Forster, Dickens reminded himself of Little Nell and wrote his friend at once:

> I felt this death of Little Nell as a kind of discipline of feeling and emotion which would do me lasting good . . . you and I have sometimes had nasty

differences . . . but certain am I, that if, at any time hereafter, a word or tone that might possibly give you pain should threaten to rise to my throat, I'd gulp it down in the memory of Little Nell.

Ironic: we think of the Victorians as repressed, as if sexuality is the only taboo. We are more emotionally reticent than Dickens's contemporaries, who reveled in every lugubrious detail. A story wasn't considered good unless it had the power to move its readers to laughter or tears, preferably both. Dickens's friend Lord Jeffrey begged him to write more in the "Nelly vein"; the famous mesmerist, Dr. John Elliotson, confessed that he "cried a deluge . . . we all agreed that you must be a good man to be able to write thus." (Victorian axiom: good novels are written by good men.)

Nell's death was not simply a literary matter but an intense emotional experience for Dickens. He felt every word he wrote. He loved the girl he called his child, but in killing her he almost killed himself. Before he sat down to write, he would work himself into a fever pitch of grief.

SENTIMENT AS CRIME

—⁓—

According to Freud, sentimentality is displaced rage. It forces readers to *feel* something, whether they want to or not; literature as emotional blackmail. The death of the unconvincingly virtuous little Dick in *Oliver Twist* is tantamount to extortion. In fact, Dickens seems at times to court our pity, saying in effect, "I'll kill him, and *then* you'll be sorry," the last words of a suicide. And perhaps the grief he wants us to feel over the death of neglected little Dick is the compassion and pity that we *should* have extended thirteen years earlier for the abandoned little Dickens.

To paraphrase the poet Gerard Manley Hopkins, it is Dickens whom he weeps for.

"I am," he confessed, "for the time, nearly dead with work and grief for the loss of my child." And as he progressed, his sorrow deepened:

> You can't imagine (gravely I write and speak) how exhausted I am to-day with yesterday's labours. I went to bed last night utterly dispirited and done up. All night I have been pursued by the child; and this morning I am unrefreshed and miserable. I do not know what to do with myself.

When he finished the novel, he cried, "Nobody shall miss her like I shall."

While Dickens was "breaking [his] heart" over a fictional girl, the daughter of his friend the tragedian William Macready died. This, however, wasn't as real or as wrenching to him as the plight of Nell. When John Forster, the child's godfather, gave in to his sorrow, Dickens professed himself bewildered by such an "amazing display of grief." Unthinkingly, he wrote the child's father: "I am slowly murdering that poor child [Nell] and grow wretched over it. It wrings my heart. Yet it must be." Thinking about his own daughter, Macready begged Dickens to spare Nell, but Dickens was inexorable—and continued to lament his own loss. Nell was as real to Dickens as the daughter of his friend, perhaps more so.

✲Whether intentional or not, Nell's name is a pun on one of the most poetic parts of the Anglican service for the dead, the death knell. And, for generations, Nell *was* a knell that summoned thoughts of mortality. Poems, paeans, songs, and lyrics were written in honor of the child. They all sound alike: saccharine, maudlin, and uniformly bad, they insist that death is not really the end, but the beginning of eternal life.

Sleep on, Sweet Nell
Sleep on, Sweet Nell, sleep on:
Life's but a dream,
While death's the door
Through which we pass
To bliss immortal.

Sleep on, Sweet Nell:
Death's but a sleep
From which we wake
To our real life,
In realms eternal.

—FRANK SPEAIGHT, 1905

The Erotic Child

✥

INTERVIEW WITH JAMES R. KINCAID

rofessor Kincaid is Aerol Arnold Professor of English at the University of Southern California. Rare among academics, his books are fun—and disturbing. His tone is irreverent, his scholarship impeccable, and he'll use anything to make his point, from* The Brady Bunch *to Dickens. Professor Kincaid is the author of the brilliant and unsettling* Child-Loving: The Erotic Child in Victorian Culture *a study of how the Victorians—and we—eroticize children.*

NE: *I want to talk about Dickens and sex. To be blunt, what was sex like for the Victorians?*

JK: I'll begin by saying that the past might provide us with a way of unloosening our smug attitudes about our own lives. That is, when we read about the nineteenth century, we assure ourselves that our own way of seeing things seems perfectly natural, normal, and clear. We interpret classic commentary on Victorian sexuality as a way of handling our own personal anxiety, and we make the past very reassuring to us. For instance, thinking of the Victorians as repressed is a convenient way of seeing ourselves as liberated.

It is very profitable to think of the Victorians, their sexual attitudes and practices, as being as diverse and as different as our own are, so that instead of providing us with security, they might help us to look closely at our own practices and assumptions. Take masturbation. There were probably many

*P*ortrait of a nude child as an aesthetic object. Smut is in the eye of the beholder. For all their so-called prudery, the Victorians would not have considered this photograph pornographic.
Oscar Gustav Rejlander, *Artist's Study, Nude Child, Rear View (c. 1860)*.

Victorians who were hysterical about this subject. But some surely weren't. Others are silent about it. They don't think it's important. Or there are some who promote it as healthy. These various views suggest that there is an enormous range of opinion, including indifference, on any of these subjects. The Victorians were excited about the issue of sex in ways we no longer are. They thought there was a lot to find out. Naturally that also made some people very anxious. It's useful and interesting for us to think of the Victorians as being more open, liberal, curious about the possibilities of this general field than we are.

NE: *Do you mean middle-class Victorians or the intellectuals who were exploring sexuality?*

JK: I don't see any reason to limit this to intellectuals or the middle class. Some people think that the middle class were very anxious to think of the working class as dangerously sexually loose in their activities, but there is evidence to suggest that the working class was much more careful, more puritanical in their activities than the upper class.

NE: *Sometimes in reading Victorian diaries and letters, you come across sexually charged language applied to children. We are much more guarded in the way we think about children. Was Lewis Carroll, for instance, aware of his attraction when he photographed nude little girls?*

JK: How aware are we today about Shirley Temple or the Coppertone Kid? I don't know how knowing *we* are. I think Victorians were being rhapsodic when they wrote like that. We also display willful naïveté toward the way children are exposed in our culture. One possibility is that the Victorians had less need to police themselves than we do. Maybe they were more comfortable with a wider range of categories. The feelings of parents toward children could be partly erotic.

NE: *What about Dickens's fictional children? Oliver Twist, Paul Dombey, Little Nell—are they also eroticized?*

JK: The way we read Dickens is the way we read our culture. He isn't separate from it, so even people who haven't read *The Old Curiosity Shop* know a considerable amount about Little Nell. With Dickens, the cultural vision we have of these children is that they are middle class, androgynous, enormously passive. Dickens's boys are almost always passive and generally abused.

NE: *And die.*

JK: And die—exactly. To a certain extent, this parade of boys is repeated in the children on *The Brady Bunch* or *Little House on the Prairie,* or actors like Freddie Bartholomew. They are children of perfect beauty, almost featureless, like David Copperfield or Oliver Twist, at least as they are usually portrayed. There are some exceptions, like the David Lean film of *Oliver Twist.* Look at the child actor in the musical *Oliver!* It's hard to find a blanker face. But that face is startingly like the faces of idealized children in American culture as well. Cindy Brady, for instance, looks a lot like that child! The Dickens child, the Shirley Temple child, there's a certain congruence between all of them. I don't mean to say they all derive from Dickens, but they seem to be similar.

NE: *What about the girls?*

JK: Nell has been constructed in our culture and presumably in the culture of her time as an innocent victim. But she's an innocent victim in the sense of . . . oh, you know, "those whom the gods love die young." It's easy to see Little Nell as a victim of a capitalistic, patriarchial culture that just hounds her to death. Because in fact, she is *not,* unlike Oliver or David, passive. She takes her grandfather and gets him the hell out of there, she makes money, she knows where to go and is very courageous in evading people who have designs on her body or on her money. So she is a survivor; she just wears out. The later heroines, Florence Dombey or Amy Dorrit, become more and more assertive. They are not just objects to be looked at.

NE: *What about the criticism that Dickens can't create convincing women?*

JK: I think it's a political statement. I don't think it's Dickens so much as the way *we* have constructed these characters. From another point of view many of these women are competent, strong, and working well against enormous forces. The ideal of passive angels in the house is a patriarchal one. The test case might be a character like Agnes Wickfield—I mean, it's *David's* voice that describes her, that wants to see her as a passive angel. Aunt Betsey is a tough character with an abusive alcoholic husband who manages to exist on her own. She sees what's going on, and she knows that Agnes is not simply waiting for David but trying to send out signals.

NE: *But is it David's image of Agnes or is it Dickens's that we are given?*

JK: If we make it Dickens's, that's our choice. I think there are ways of making Dickens's women more interesting. The question is, why do we *want* to see his heroines as passive, or rather why have they been seen as dull, flat, and uninteresting? It becomes a question about our culture rather than one about the Victorians or about Dickens. There are scholars now who are talking about Dickens's women in new and different ways.

NE: *But didn't Dickens have a "problem" with women, as they say? Was it in fact the death of Mary Hogarth that made him create such idealized creatures?*

JK: Dickens was an omnivorous person who would take any personal event, literary tradition, or philosophical current and push it—*hard.*

NE: *Can you name a sexy moment in a Dickens novel?*

JK: Sure, when Mr. Murdstone beats David.

NE: *Then there's the intensity of David's feelings for Steerforth.*

JK: Yes. And I almost forget that Estella is in *Great Expectations,* because for me, the novel is all about men. Pip and Herbert, Pip and Joe, Pip and Magwitch. There are powerful moments of homoerotic bonding. These are moments that might be embarrassing to some people, like when Magwitch is dying, and he and Pip are holding hands. Those are exquisite moments of death, eroticism, and self-fulfillment.

NE: *But you would never say Pip is gay!*

JK: Oh no! They were not confined by labels like "gay."

NE: *So would you say that the Victorians are erotic about everything but heterosexual love?*

JK: Right! Well, they idealized marriage, husband, wife, and the family so much that they washed it free of all erotic feeling. Meanwhile, those feelings went everywhere else.

How Many Children Did Dickens Kill?

꘏

*[In Dickens's novels] an interesting child runs as much risk . . .
as any of the troops who stormed the Redan.*
—FITZJAMES STEPHENS

—•◆•—

*No man can offer to his public so large a stock of death-beds adapted
for either sex and for any age from five-and-twenty downwards.*
—*Saturday Review,* May 8, 1858

—•◆•—

Between ourselves, Paul is dead.
—DICKENS, in a letter to Miss Burdett-Coutts, confiding the fate of Paul Dombey

—•◆•—

THE CASUALTIES (AGE 25 AND UNDER)

1. Little Dick, *Oliver Twist.*

2. Smike, *Nicholas Nickleby.*

3. Nell Trent, *The Old Curiosity Shop.*

4. Schoolmaster's pupil, *The Old Curiosity Shop.*

5. Tiny Tim, but only in the vision of Christmas Yet to Come in *A Christmas Carol.*

6. Paul Dombey, *Dombey and Son.*

7. Clara Copperfield Murdstone's infant son, *David Copperfield.*

8. Dora Spenlow Copperfield (David's "child-wife," scarcely more than twenty when she died), *David Copperfield.*

9. Jo, the street sweeper, *Bleak House.*

10. Jenny's baby, *Bleak House.*

11. Richard Carstone, *Bleak House.*

12. Laborer's child, *A Tale of Two Cities.*

13. Lucie Darnay's oldest son, *A Tale of Two Cities* (a Dickensian deathbed, complete in one paragraph).

14. Johnny, *Our Mutual Friend.*

FADING AWAY

*W*e share with the Victorians an excessive interest in the bedroom, but while for us the bed evokes sex, for them it meant death. The Victorian novel is filled with death because death added a racy interest and a pleasing melancholy—a tableau for the reader to linger over with prurient fascination. One might call it funereal porn.

Victorian deathbed scenes, usually those involving children or women, are written with the charged emotionality that we reserve for erotic interludes. Victorian death is often transfigured into a blissful experience, a swooning away into another, higher state. A child's death scene packed a wallop, loaded with submerged implications.

Death and sex have always been inextricably linked in the unconscious mind. Both are perceived as a loss: an orgasm is a little death, *un petit mort;* Elizabethan slang for intercourse is "to die," for the Victorians it was "to spend." For Shakespeare "Th' expense of spirit [semen] in a waste of shame / is Lust in action": with each ejaculation a man shortened his life by a few minutes. Likewise, the Victorians thought that orgasm depleted them of the thing they valued most: energy.

Considering that in the middle of the nineteenth century, almost half of all the deaths recorded in London were those of children under ten years of age, Dickens's concern with juvenile death doesn't seem so ghoulish. To his readers, Paul's or Nell's death was an exalted version of what most of them had already experienced.

In the Victorian novel, an "interesting" death is when the deceased is overcome by exhaustion or a loss of will. It's a gentle swoon rarely disturbed by the ugliness of either blood or pain. Death was eroticized as a form of surrender; the dying waste away, pine, wither, and ultimately submerge and unite with larger forces. Water imagery or death by drowning was often used to express a death that was like a peaceful release, a violent submersion, or a slackening of willpower. Saintly Paul Dombey dies still wondering what the wild waves are saying. The taciturn and lowly Barkis in *David Copperfield* ebbs with the tide; in the same novel, the Byronic, sexually tempestuous Steerforth drowns in stormy seas.

David Copperfield's first wife, the fetching Dora, the "Little Blossom," withers and dies after suffering complications after a miscarriage, which Dickens only alludes to through coy periphrasis, yet readers would understand the underlying connection between sex and death.

Dora's pet name, "Little Blossom," carries all manner of erotic implications (Dickens's other sexy girl/child is named Rosa Bud), and the youthful Dora wilts—rather conveniently—just as her husband realizes that marriage based on sexual desire alone, or as he put it, his "undisciplined heart," can only be temporary. Blossoms fade when the bloom is off.

David's mother, Clara, yields to the titanic will of her domineering husband and so dies. The sickly Smike pines away for love of Kate Nickleby, and Little Nell simply fades, exhausted by her earthly travails.

To the Victorians, who worshiped work, common sense, and probity, sex was a temporary—and death an infinite—surrender to a realm without struggle or care. Victorian death scenes are thus subtly sexualized, with the lingering disease acting as foreplay to the grand, climactic moment of ultimate release.

Fading Away, a popular photograph depicting a girl on the verge of womanhood, "fading away" from consumption. Death was often portrayed as a vaporization or a languorous drifting. This 1858 photograph, by Henry Peach Robinson, was displayed at the Royal Exhibition.

Barnaby Rudge

arnaby Rudge must be the least-read—and least-attractive—novel in the Dickens canon. Except for three silent films, it's never been dramatized, and there will probably never be a musical called *Barnaby!*—at least one hopes not. The titular figure—one can't call him a hero—is a rarity among Dickens's protagonists: he doesn't make a fortune, fall in love, or marry. He is what used to be called an "idiot," but he's neither a Forrest Gump nor a Prince Myshkin. Uncharacteristically unsentimental, Dickens avoids the cliché of equating simplicity with virtue. The reader thus finds it difficult to identify with an agitated man who suffers from an "absence of soul," and the lack of a sympathetic hero or a strong moral center makes *Barnaby Rudge* an unlikely choice for a cozy read.

Like Forrest Gump, Barnaby is swept along by the historical current, in this case the "No Popery!" riots over Catholic emancipation instigated by Lord Gordon in the 1780s. Oblivious to the idea of religious persecution, Barnaby is an idiot without a cause. Perhaps this is Dickens's point: revolutions are full of sound and fury, political and religious rhetoric are meaningless, leaders are wrongheaded, followers are dupes.

As in *A Tale of Two Cities,* Dickens is concerned with historical change, how the old inevitably, and often violently, gives way to the new—for better or worse. This theme resonates in the generational tension between father and son, John and Joe Willet. Whereas John initially refuses to acknowledge his son's manhood, he eventually yields and allows the next generation a chance to assume its rightful role in the ongoing historical drama. Willet's Maypole Inn, a symbol of "merrie old England," is pillaged by rioters, rebuilt, and taken over by Joe, thus suggesting that a balance between change and continuity can be achieved—but not without violence.

But any reassurance *Barnaby Rudge* may offer is lost amid scenes of mayhem and butchery. After all their difficulties, Joe and Dolly Varden finally declare their love, but the moment is tempered by the fact that Joe has lost an arm in the riots. Gabriel Varden's apprentice, Sim Tappertit, "entertains great admiration" for his shapely legs, but by the end of the novel they are crushed and amputated. If that isn't grisly enough, his wife, the widow of a rag-and-bone merchant, tosses his wooden legs out the window. And when a rioter's head literally broils, Dickens can barely control his glee. Then there's Dennis the hangman, who adorns himself in his victims' clothes, and Hugh, the bestial ostler at the Maypole, who tries to molest the delectable Dolly. "Something will come of this. I hope it won't be human gore," mutters one character. Gore and fomentation, however, inspire some of Dickens's most electrifying prose. He felt his rioters' bloodlust while describing it. "I have just burnt into Newgate," he wrote to John Forster, "and am going in the next number to tear the prisoners out by the hair of their heads." A week later he wrote, "I have let all the prisoners out of Newgate. . . . I feel quite smoky when I am at work." More than any other novel, *Barnaby* allowed Dickens to indulge his penchant for violence. At his best moments, Dickens seems to write from the viscera rather than from the brain. As the critic John Carey points out, Dennis the executioner "provides Dickens with ample opportunity for anecdotes about the dreadful apparatus and its operation." The "dreadful apparatus" itself invokes hideous imagery: nooses dangle, Dickens writes, "like loathsome garlands." And although Dickens intends to rail against capital punishment, it's obvious that he enjoyed writing about its victims. This is not the friendly author of hearth and home but an aggressive man drawn to scenes of savagery and terror.

Barnaby Rudge is part historical novel, part gothic tale of terror. In addition to the riots, it includes two startling father-and-son reunions, a feud between two families, two love stories, an abduction, and a murder mystery. But the novel's quirky features and freakish characters linger in the reader's memory long after its ponderous plot is forgotten: Gabriel Varden's skirmishes with his snappish wife, a religious fanatic who's never without her *Protestant Manual;* Grip, Barnaby's familiar, modeled on Dickens's pet raven, prone to oracular utterances and probably the source of Poe's more famous bird; Dolly Varden, a charming heroine, the sweetheart of 1841, who inspired fashions, dances, a painting by W. P. Frith, and a cake.

Barnaby Rudge is to the Dickens canon what the disturbing "problem plays" are to Shakespeare's. Dickens's position is similarly indefinite: at times he sympathizes with the Catholic underdogs, whose church he nevertheless hated; he despairs of wanton savagery while relishing its anarchic energy; he hates organized "causes" while using the novel to champion his own. Except for the mob riots, the novel never truly comes alive, and like its titular character, it seems empty, devoid of soul and lacking the robust comedy we expect from Dickens. There is little laughter in this book, which, despite its many devotees, remains a blip in the Dickens oeuvre.

"GRIP THE CLEVER, GRIP THE WICKED"

*B*efore writing *Barnaby Rudge,* a novel in which the titular hero has a pet raven, Dickens bought a raven so he could observe the bird's habits. He named it Grip: "Grip the clever, Grip the wicked, Grip the knowing." Dickens was so taken with the bird's antics that his friend Edwin Landseer, the famous painter of animals, pronounced him "raven mad." (Dickens never did anything by halves.)

When the novel appeared in America, it was favorably reviewed by Edgar Allan Poe, who, as a raven maven, couldn't resist making a few suggestions: Dickens's raven was playful and droll where it should have been sepulchral. Although Dickens's bird never utters the memorable pronouncement "Nevermore," it is likely that Grip inspired Poe's famous poem, which was published in 1845, four years after *Barnaby Rudge.* Perhaps Poe was trying to counteract Dickens's chatty bird with his own saturnine prophet.

Grip died on March 12, 1841. That he had immortalized Grip in *Barnaby Rudge* was not enough for Dickens, who promptly had him stuffed and mounted under glass. In his usual mock-serious way, Dickens wrote his friend

*D*ickens's pet raven, which he had stuffed after its death. Grip was the real-life model for the fictional bird in *Barnaby Rudge,* and, some say, the inspiration for Poe's famous poem. Grip is on permanent display at the Philadelphia Free Library.

the artist Daniel Maclise a description of the bird's final days that wickedly parodies the Victorian penchant for minute-by-minute deathbed accounts:

> You will be greatly shocked and grieved to hear that the Raven is no more. He expired to-day at a few minutes after Twelve o'Clock noon. He had been ailing for a few days, but we anticipated no serious result, conjecturing that a portion of the white paint he swallowed last summer might be lingering about his vitals. Yesterday afternoon he was taken so much worse that I sent an express for the medical gentleman, who promptly attended and administered a dose of castor oil. Under the influence of this medicine he recovered so far as to be able, at 8 o'Clock, p.m., to bite Topping [the coachman]. His night was peaceful. This morning, at daybreak, he appeared better, and partook plentifully of some warm gruel, the flavor of which he appeared to relish. Towards eleven o'Clock he was so much worse that it was found necessary to muffle the stable knocker. At half-past, or thereabouts, he was heard talking to himself about the horse and Topping's family, and to add some incoherent expressions which are supposed to have been either a foreboding of his approaching dissolution or some wishes relative to the disposal of his little property, consisting chiefly of half-pence which he had buried in different parts of the garden. On the clock striking twelve he appeared slightly agitated, but he soon recovered, walked twice or thrice along the coach-house, stopped to

EDGAR ALLAN POE & *BARNABY RUDGE*

—⁊⁊⁊—

Edgar Allan Poe, an admirer of Dickens and *Barnaby Rudge,* wrote two reviews of the novel. The first, published on May 1, 1841, in the *Philadelphia Saturday Evening Post,* was written after Dickens had completed about a quarter of the novel. Nonetheless, the master of mystery deduced the identity of the murderer from just the clues given in the first chapter—and Poe had no compunction about giving away the mystery. Eight months later, in the next review, he bragged about his prediction, which was proving to be true. The critic Barry Westburg notes that Poe's predicted ending, which was more "elegant" than Dickens's, might have prompted the novelist to change his mind about the outcome of his novel.

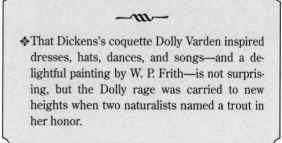

—⁊⁊⁊—

❖ That Dickens's coquette Dolly Varden inspired dresses, hats, dances, and songs—and a delightful painting by W. P. Frith—is not surprising, but the Dolly rage was carried to new heights when two naturalists named a trout in her honor.

bark, staggered, and exclaimed "Halloa, old girl!" (his favorite expression) and died.

A month after Dickens's death the stuffed bird went up for auction with the rest of his possessions. *Photo News* of August 1870 excitedly reported that Grip was the "subject of hot rivalry" in the Christie and Manson's salesroom, and was "eventually knocked down to Mr. Nottage of the London Stereoscopic Society for one hundred and twenty guineas! The result called forth cheers from the assembled company." Mr. Nottage of Cheapside was engaged in a "spirited competition" with a Mr. Andrew Halliday, who lost the bird by a mere 30 shillings. The Stereoscopic Society immediately photographed it in an "admirable manner," and assured its readers, "There is no doubt that the portrait of the memorable bird . . . will be eagerly sought after." But the unknown writer's prediction of Grip's enduring fame proved wrong. Few today read *Barnaby Rudge;* even fewer have heard of Grip. Our knowledge of great ravens in literature is limited to Poe's poem.

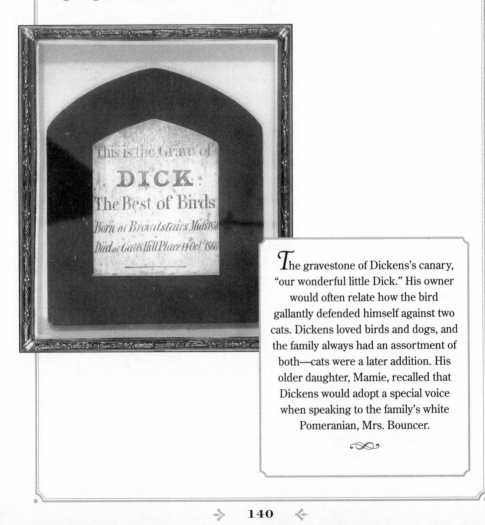

The gravestone of Dickens's canary, "our wonderful little Dick." His owner would often relate how the bird gallantly defended himself against two cats. Dickens loved birds and dogs, and the family always had an assortment of both—cats were a later addition. His older daughter, Mamie, recalled that Dickens would adopt a special voice when speaking to the family's white Pomeranian, Mrs. Bouncer.

Public Executions

good hanging, preferably of a famous criminal, made for high drama in Victorian England. Constance Kent, a governess who murdered her employer, drew thousands to her execution. Although the audience knew the "star" would be killed, there was always some doubt as to how he or, even more excitingly, she would acquit herself at the end. Betting on whether the condemned would die "chicken" or "game" was common and added a macabre relish to the sport. Social critics decried the barbarity of the spectacle, but the public was reluctant to give up one of its few free pastimes. It took more than sixty years of incremental reform before public hangings became an extinct custom, fondly recalled by those who had lived during their heyday.

Dickens opposed public hangings on the ground that they exploited the inbred and inhumane craving to see a fellow creature trapped and condemned. He argued that such displays encouraged rather than discouraged vice: public executions lured pimps, pickpockets, and prostitutes, all of whom did a booming trade. (The Artful Dodger does some of his best work at the hangings of fellow thieves.)

But it's typical of Dickens that while he inveighed against public executions, he was also drawn to them. The secret threshold between death and life tantalized him, and he was obsessed by the idea that a man could know with certainty the exact hour of his death. Instruments of fatal justice—the guillotine, the gibbet, the noose, and the rope—recur throughout his fiction.

Dickens willingly attended at least four public executions. In July 1840 he had witnessed the execution of a Swiss murderer named Courvoisier, a nauseating

A broadside containing the details of T. H. Hooker's crime, trial, and hanging, including verses composed for the latter occasion. It would have been hawked at Newgate, where the execution took place.

spectacle that inspired his graphic account of the gallows in his next novel, *Barnaby Rudge*. Nine years later he turned out along with 30,000 other spectators to watch the joint hanging of Mr. and Mrs. George Manning, convicted of conspiring to kill Mrs. Manning's lover. Billed as the "Hanging of the Century," it was the first time a married couple had been executed together in more than 150 years. Afraid of missing anything, Dickens rented an apartment high over Horsemonger Gaol where he could watch the scene in comfort with friends, and arranged for a supper party at a nearby coffeehouse. He even arrived the night before so he could watch the workmen as they prepared the scaffold for the Mannings' last bow and observe the crowd, which at first light began bellowing the new tune "O Susannah!," substituting Mrs. Manning's name in the lyric.

The day after the spectacle, he penned an angry letter to the *Times* complaining about "the wickedness and levity of the crowd" who came to gawk at the two miserable creatures. Two days later he was still sufficiently aroused to write another letter. Dickens must have convinced himself that his presence at the execution was of a higher order than that of the hordes below. Dickens was not a hypocrite: he was just often of two minds regarding most matters. He deplored the unsympathetic, frenzied vulgarity of the crowd, but he was rarely able to resist an intense emotional experience. He was, as he once put it, "attracted to repulsion."

For some reason, whether a constitutional quirk, a genetic tendency, or the result of some psychological trauma, Dickens identified with both mobs and murderers. He may have watched the Manning hanging in genteel comfort, but part of him was down below, screeching with the mob. Thus his portrayals of the riots and mobs in *Barnaby Rudge* and *A Tale of Two Cities* have an immediacy that captures not only the passion of the scene but also the author's intense involvement with it.

His descriptions of executions seem almost demonically inspired. His portrayals of the shouting hordes, the condemned man as he awaits his doom, and the step-by-step mechanics from noose to trapdoor reveal a concentration of vision, an ability to zoom in on minute details, all the while remaining undistracted by noise or squeamishness.

At the Manning hanging he observed the two corpses as they "turned quivering in the air," and he even discerned a difference in the way the two forms swayed and dangled in the wind: "the man's, a limp, loose suit of clothes as if the man had gone out of them; the woman's, a fine shape, so elaborately corseted and artfully dressed, that it was quite unchanged in its trim appearance as it slowly swung from side to side." Horror is submerged into fascination as the two emotions combine into a finely realized picture.

❋ When traveling, Dickens wasn't interested in the usual tourist haunts, preferring instead murder sites, prisons, and execution yards. In Boston, he asked to see Harvard College, not because of its reputation as a seat of learning, but because he wanted to see the laboratory where Professor Parkman killed, dismembered, and buried a rival colleague. Dickens needed to stand on the spot where heinous deeds took place so he could visualize them, perhaps because proximity in space produced for him the illusion of proximity in time.

❋ Murder wasn't the only crime punishable by death. In "A Visit to Newgate" in *Sketches by Boz,* Dickens relates how he stood in front of three cells, observing three prisoners who were condemned to death. The three have since been identified as Robert Swan, convicted of armed robbery, John Smith and John Roberts, convicted of homosexual offenses, probably sodomy. Swan was reprieved by the king. The other two were hanged in November 1836.

American Notes

I never knew what it was to feel disgust and contempt 'till I travelled in America.
—DICKENS, 1842

I t would be a good thing, wouldn't it, if I ran over to America about the end of February, and came back after four or five months with a one volume book?" wrote Dickens to his editor in September 1841. With that casual statement, he would embark on a voyage that was as much a journey inward as it was outward, changing him in ways he could never imagine. He left England an exuberant idealist and returned a weary cynic.

In January 1842 Dickens left England in search of "the republic of [his] imagination" and found a nation of bores and boors. His trip to America, a land, or so he believed, of liberty and liberalism, and the book it spawned, *American Notes,* was a public relations nightmare. It would take decades to repair the damage.

Boz's jubilant arrival in America was the Victorian equivalent to the Beatles' inaugural tour in 1964. Having read pirated editions of his novels, Americans were suffering from an acute case of Bozmania, and Dickens's tour was surrounded by hype unprecedented in American history. Even before landing he was already inundated with dozens of requests and invitations. In one of his first letters home, he wrote, "How can I give you the faintest notion of my reception here, of the crowds that pour in and out the whole day; of the people that line the streets when I go out; of the cheering when I went to the theatre; of the copies of verse, letters of congratulations, welcomes of all kinds, balls, dinners, assemblies without end?"

Although gregarious, Dickens was essentially a private man, and the violation of his privacy, by the press and well-wishers, unnerved and finally an-

Georgina Hogarth, Dickens's sister-in-law. Shortly after the Dickenses returned from America, Catherine's fifteen-year-old sister, "Georgy," moved in with the family. She stayed for more than twenty-five years, remaining with Dickens—and braving scandal—when he and Catherine separated. She was by his side at his death.

gered him. American effusiveness offended his British reserve: in Cleveland, Dickens could only glare as a party of curiosity-seekers peered through the window of his steamboat cabin while Catherine was still in bed and he was washing. It was even whispered that Dickens's barbers sold locks of his shorn hair.

Tension exacerbated and finally peaked when he introduced the subject of international copyright into his conversation and after-dinner remarks in one city after another. Expecting Bozian hilarity, the formally attired guests were told that they were conspirators in theft. They ascribed Dickens's ingratitude to his lack of breeding and his concern with copyrights to greed.

Dickens's dislike for America seems to have increased with each mile. In response, Americans found Boz disappointingly "vulgar," or what they called "rowdy." Dickens in turn had nothing but contempt for the behavior of the country's natives, finding them malodorous and mercenary. He also found them boring: "I am quite serious," he wrote, "when I say that I do not believe there are, on the whole Earth, besides, so many intensified bores as in these United States. No man can form an adequate idea of the word without coming here."

Eager to find the much-vaunted American democracy, he saw instead rapacity and "Pecksniffery on a national scale," a worship of the dollar and a pretense of equality in a land of snobbism and slavery. Americans, he complained, were hungry for praise and unable to laugh at themselves. They did, however, enjoy laughing at their famous guest: caricatures of Dickens appeared in newspapers and magazines throughout the country, and Dickens, seeing himself portrayed unflatteringly, was not amused. Perhaps, as his biographer Peter Ackroyd maintains, the monolithic identity Dickens ascribed to America, the republic as a young land, was actually a self-portrait of the artist as a young man. In its landscape and people he saw what he disliked most about himself.

He saved his most acidulous prose for slavery, politicians, the press, and the American habit of spitting. Many celebrities today would agree with his opinion of the American press; few, however could express their disgust so pungently:

What are the fifty newspapers which these precocious urchins are bawling down the street? What are they but amusements? Not vapid, waterish amusements, but good strong stuff; dealing in sound abuse and blackguard names; pulling off the roots of private houses. . . . pimping and pandering for all degrees of vicious taste, and gorging with coined lies the most voracious maw; imputing to every man in public life the coarsest and vilest of motives; scaring away from the stabbed and prostrate body-politic every Samaritan of good conscience and good deeds; and setting on, with yell and whistle and the clapping of foul hands, the vilest vermin and worst birds of prey.

Dickens rarely gets much angrier than this. The truth is, he made good copy, and the press, following him everywhere, noted everything about him, from his clothing (foppish) and features (handsome but coarse) to his long, waving hair (effeminate). Everything he did made the papers. After the Great Boz Ball in New York, the *New York Herald* put out an extra edition devoted to the event. "If I were to drop a letter in the street, it would be in the newspaper the next day," Dickens complained.

For the fastidious Dickens, the American habit of spitting was as aesthetically offensive as it was unhygienic. While riding on a train, he bitingly observed that "the flashes of saliva flew so perpetually and incessantly out of the windows all the way, that it looked as though they were ripping open featherbeds inside, and letting wind dispose of the feathers." Dickens regarded spitting and other uncouth habits as examples of the national tendency to confuse a disregard for the sensibilities of others with individuality of expression. Thus in *Martin Chuzzlewit,* Americans slurp, spit, and guzzle with abandon. When Martin protests after another diner licks the communal butter knife, he is chided for lacking a democratic spirit. Only Europeans, he is told, are bound by such elitist, artificial conventions as table manners. Watching Bostonians eat, he noted that "the gentlemen thrust the broad-bladed knives and two-pronged forks further down their throats than ever I saw the same weapons go before, except in the hands of a skilful juggler."

"American leaders," wrote Dickens, are the "lice of God's creation." Party politics in the United States was contaminating everything, even the way its citizens educated their young and cared for their infirm. And, he asserts, its leaders "bow down" before any idea, no matter how barbaric or idiotic, so long as it represents "Public Opinion." Thus Dickens reviled not only the barbarism of slavery but also its attendant hypocrisy: jingoistic natives bragging about liberty and democracy while condoning the practice of slavery. The Declaration of Independence, he concluded, is a sham, and America is based upon a lie. Many critics now agree that Dickens's American experience was almost as crucial in shaping the author's identity as his traumatic childhood. The journey, during which he turned thirty, was the watershed separating his youth from his middle years, and it reinforced his sense of himself as an Englishman and an English writer. But the trip had other ramifications as well: the hostile response to *American Notes,* which devastated him, forced him to change his perception of himself and his relationship to the public. He was no longer England's chosen son and wunderkind, immune from criticism, but a mature writer who had to assume responsibility for his words. For the first time, he couldn't hide behind his fictional alter ego: *American Notes* was written by Charles Dickens, not the lovable Boz.

Dickens's journey to America, a fall from innocence, profoundly affected the temper of his work. In his earlier novels, evil is personified and his villains resemble grotesque fun-house figures, but after 1842 he exhibits a keener sense of the reality of evil, which does not always wear a human face and which often exists on a vaster scale than he had previously imagined. As the later novels reveal, moral corruption permeates an entire society. After the hilarious *Martin Chuzzlewit,* Dickens's writing deepens, and his view of life darkens. In the end, he does not find in America the land of his imagination, but he does discover a new imaginative terrain within himself.

✤ While in America, Dickens engaged in an epistolary marathon, sometimes writing up to 8,000 words per day. Unlike many novelists, he preferred writing letters to keeping a diary. His detailed letters, which he collected from friends upon his return, form the basis of *American Notes.* This is typical of the convivial Dickens: a diary was not enough; he needed a reader to inspire him.

I AM A TAPE RECORDER

With his unerring ear for dialect and speech rhythms, Dickens in both *American Notes* and *Martin Chuzzlewit* captures American speech in its infinite variety. To his British ears, American English (with the exception of that spoken in New York and Boston) sounded drawling and lazy, lacking sonority and precision. In *American Notes* he relates his encounter with a shoemaker, gleefully preserving the man's oafish localisms. Suspiciously scanning the author's British-made boot, the man says, "You an't partikler, about this scoop in the heel then? We don't foller that, here." And his parody of the American dialect in *Martin Chuzzlewit* is merciless: " 'The name of Pogrom will be proud Toe jine you. And may it, My friends, be written on My Tomb.' He was a member of Congress of our common country, and was acTive in his trust."

DICKENS'S DUNKIRK

*A*merican Notes *caused all Yankee-doodledom to blaze up like one universal soda water bottle.*
—THOMAS CARLYLE

*A*s soon as he returned to England, Dickens began writing *American Notes,* the repository of all his grievances against his host country. He asked Forster his opinion about the dedication: "I dedicate this Book to those friends of mine in America, who, loving their country, can bear the truth, when it is written good humouredly and in a kind spirit." Dickens was indeed optimistic about American forbearance.

"The most trashy . . . the most contemptible . . . the essence of balderdash reduced to the last drop of silliness and inanity," wrote one reviewer in the *New York Herald,* squelching Dickens's hopes for an impartial reading. Few could bear the truth, and the "kindliness" of Dickens's spirit is suspect. Even his friends found the book unsporting, not to mention un-Bozlike. As the scholar Ada Nisbet put it in 1952, *American Notes* was Dickens's Dunkirk.

Critics on both sides of the Atlantic attacked the book as libelous, spiteful, and ignorant. They wondered at the author's audacity in offering up "informed" opinions about American institutions after briefly touring only a few schools, prisons, and asylums. Even more wounding, some questioned his motives, claiming that Dickens railed against slavery only to get back at Americans. Why, they wondered, did he remain silent on the subject while in the United States, when he had no qualms about speaking out there about international copyright? Despite the bad reviews and the disputes with friends, Dickens—and it's pure Dickens—wrote to an American friend: "The American book . . . has been a most complete and thorough-going success."

Was Dickens so naive as to think that Americans would appreciate having their national flaws pointed out by a young foreigner who had spent a mere six months in their country? Dickens found himself in the ridiculous position of resembling his own Count Smorltork, the superficial travel writer in *Pickwick Papers.*

Reading *American Notes* today, more than 150 years after Dickens's journey, one is struck by how simultaneously funny and painful it is. His accounts of slavery have the stark horror of cinema verité, yet at times the book rings comically true in its portrait of the American eccentricities (which he would later put to good use in *Martin Chuzzlewit*). In any case, *American Notes* reveals how the United States appeared to Charles Dickens—and that, of course, should be enough.

International Copyright

❧

Is it not a horrible thing that scoundrel-booksellers should grow rich [in America] from publishing books, the authors of which do not reap one farthing from their issue, by scores of thousands? And that every vile, blackguard, and detestable newspaper—so filthy and so bestial that no honest man would admit one into his house, for a water-closet doormat—should be able to publish those same writings side by side, cheek by jowl, with the coarsest and most obscene companions? I vow before high heaven that my blood so boils at these enormities, that when I speak about them, I seem to grow twenty feet high. . . . "Robbers that ye are"— I think to myself, when I get upon my legs—"here goes!"
—DICKENS

 s the first important writer to champion copyright, Dickens did more to protect authors' rights than any lawyer or politician. At the time, there was little conception of intellectual property. A writer had no recourse against literary pirates, nor could he prevent a foreign publisher from printing an unauthorized version of his work without paying royalties.

Words, Dickens insisted, were property—not portable property, as Mr. Wemmick might say, but no less real for that—and as property they could be protected and sold only by the owner himself. The romantic view that art transcends monetary considerations, along with the greed of unscrupulous publishers, had kept copyright laws from being taken seriously. The law in Dickens's day, unchanged for more than two centuries, was inadequate to serve the demands of modern authorship.

After *Pickwick,* Dickens realized that he was helpless to stem the flow of imitations and pirated editions of his work. At first he was philosophical: "Well, if the *Pickwick,*" he wrote, "has been the means of putting a few shillings in the vermin-eaten pockets of so miserable a creature, and had saved him from a workhouse or jail, let him empty out his little pot of filth and welcome." But he quickly soured as he realized that he was unable to collect royalties from these imitations. If he sued the offenders—as he once tried to do—any money he might collect would go for legal fees.

Dickens encouraged his friend, the parliamentary member Thomas Noon Talfourd, to introduce a bill that would extend copyright for sixty years after an author's death and provide for an international copyright as well, but the bill did not pass, and throughout Dickens's lifetime his novels were reprinted and plagiarized even before their serial runs were over. In 1842, however, a new copyright law shifted ownership from the publisher or printer of a work to the author. Thereafter, an unscrupulous publisher could not sell an author's copyrights.

International copyright laws were even more difficult to pass and enforce, since they involved foreign publishers reluctant to give up easy sources of revenue and less susceptible to control from afar. International copyright, as Dickens soon learned, was an incendiary subject. His visit to America in 1843 was marred by his outspoken appeals for this protection. At his first speech in Boston, he alienated hosts and fans who wanted to hear the comical, carefree Boz, not a serious man who insisted on receiving his due. The next day the press denounced his remarks as ungrateful and "unmanly." Americans argued that copyright protection would raise the price of books, making them prohibitively expensive for poor people; and, more important, America was undergoing a serious economic recession and could not afford to send capital overseas, particularly for books. Of course, the American publishers who had been fattening off Dickens for the last decade vehemently opposed the bill.

Dickens heatedly replied that recessions were nothing new—Americans were always complaining of economic depression—that American authors would also benefit from such a law, and that a great injustice was being done to all authors (reason enough in itself).

In the same year as his first trip to America, Dickens formed the Society for the Protection of Authors, a guild solely for writers. Its purpose, like that of PEN today, was to secure and maintain authors' rights and provide legal services to writers. Dickens was not sanguine about achieving the first goal. To his American colleague Henry Wadsworth Longfellow he wrote, "I quite agree with you, that we shall never live to see the passing of an international Law." Dickens was right. Copyright was not legally enforced, and international copyright did not come into existence until 1891. It wasn't until 1954 that all countries joined the system.

Almost single-handedly, Dickens turned fiction writing into a profession worthy of a gentleman. Men of high birth, like Horace Walpole, Sir Walter Scott, Sir Edward Bulwer-Lytton, Percy Bysshe Shelley, and Lord Byron, could write poems and novels, but they were independently wealthy and did not *have* to write. They were therefore artistes, men who wrote out of inspiration and not for cash. By contrast, those who scribbled for a living were seen as Grub Street hacks. They were men who wrote to order: the louche, the loungers, the bohemians—never the gentlemen. That is, not until Dickens. By promoting authors' rights, organizing guilds, creating pensions for elderly authors and their families, and, as editor, by paying his own authors an amount commensurate with their abilities, Dickens legitimized writing as a serious and worthy profession. Practitioners of the craft began to receive the same rights and considerations as those in law or trade.

Dickens's stature as man of letters, public figure, and philanthropist was influential in raising the status of the literary profession. But even more important in the public mind, he was extraordinarily rich—and he had become so by writing.

Martin Chuzzlewit

༺༻

*There can be few pieces of literature where the good
and the bad jostle so closely.*
—R. C. CHURCHILL

n 1844 Dickens wrote optimistically, "In a hundred years, I hope to be remembered as the man who wrote *Martin Chuzzlewit*." Does anyone read *Martin Chuzzlewit* anymore? At one time—not so long ago—the names "Sairey" Gamp and Mr. Pecksniff were as familiar as Bugs Bunny or Mickey Mouse. Mention of the Gampian catchphrase, "Leave the bottle on the chimleypiece, and . . . let me put my lips to it when I am so dispoged," was enough to provoke at least a smile of recognition. *Martin Chuzzlewit* is Dickens's most hilarious, free-spirited, and inventive novel; it also has the most erratic, incoherent, and witless of plots.

Dickens's readers are more divided about *Chuzzlewit* than any other of his novels. The novelist William Boyd hailed chapters 8 and 9 as "the most sustained passage of comic writing in English literature," while the critic Albert Guerard cited the novel's first chapter as the "worst opening of any important English novel."

What's best about the novel is the extravaganza of Chuzzlewittian grotesques, tricksters, knaves, and fools who exist to amuse us, not to serve the demands of an inane plot. Mrs. Gamp, Mr. Pecksniff, Tigg Montague (née Montague Tigg), Chevy Slyme, the Spottletoes, Putnam Smif, Augustus Moddle, Jefferson Brick, and the undertaker Mr. Mould are so over-the-top that they overshadow any story Dickens could devise. As the writer Mick Imlah observed, "The best of it is magnificent irrelevance." Don't be alarmed if you can't remember what happens next: in *Chuzzlewit,* character is king. You read it for its broad comedy, its extended set pieces, and Dickens's satirical portrait of America and Americans. You do not read it to find out what happens next.

In *Pickwick,* Dickens takes us on a wild ride; in *Chuzzlewit,* he practically hijacks us. The action shifts abruptly from one setting and set of characters to another, from Salisbury to America to London, and then round again for another turn. Martin's American trek points up the haphazard nature of the novel. When a decline in sales suggested that Dickens's anemic plot needed a transfusion of adventure, he suddenly packed Young Martin and his good-natured valet, Mark Tapley, off to the "US of A" (as his Americans say), where some of the novel's most wicked satire takes place.

The novel's tone blends Pickwickian hilarity with the grimly sardonic voice of the novels yet to come. The mature voice of Charles Dickens, the conscience of England, begins to be heard. The critic Alexander Welch, who sees *Martin Chuzzlewit* as a turning point in Dickens's career, attributes the change to the author's disillusionment after his trip to America in 1843. He arrived as an idealistic radical in search of "the Republic of my imagination," and left enraged and disgusted by a country he termed a "vast counting-house" populated by "humbugs and bores."

One reason for *Chuzzlewit*'s mania is that, even in this, his sixth novel, Dickens is still struggling to master the multiple-plot structure—a technique he didn't perfect until *Bleak House. Nicholas Nickleby* has its share of varying strands, as does *Barnaby Rudge,* but neither novel is as intricate or as involved as *Chuzzlewit.* What holds the novel together is its circus troupe of recurring characters. Its parts are bigger than its whole, and the critic can do it justice only by describing those parts without attempting to weave them into a coherent whole.

The novel presumably centers around the question of Old Martin Chuzzlewit's estate and the attempts of various predatory relatives, most notably the monstrous hypocrite Mr. Pecksniff, to insinuate themselves into his good graces—and his pocket.

The novel begins as the Chuzzlewits, drawn by the smell of money and death, swoop down on the village where Old Martin lies—they hope—dying. A greasier, more ill-favored clan you'll never find. The name of one branch of the family, the Spottletoes, suggests a species of rodent. Traveling with Old Martin is his companion and nurse, Mary Graham. The family senses she is a potential rival and holds a council to figure out how to oust her. In the meantime Mr. Pecksniff, hoping to worm his way into Old Martin's affections, has taken on his grandson as an architectural apprentice. Young Martin, the old man's heir, has fallen in love with Mary and is disinherited, thus igniting the plot by leaving the way clear for Mr. Pecksniff's machinations and his own adventures.

In the tradition of the great eighteenth-century novels Dickens loved, Martin sets off to make his fortune, first as an architectural apprentice to Mr. Pecksniff (who never teaches anything and passes off his student's work as his own) and then, after his dismissal (at Old Martin's instigation), in America. In a sense the novel is a bildungsroman, tracing Martin's growth and self-discovery. But it also branches off into various subplots: there's the unselfish Tom Pinch's blind loyalty to his employer, Mr. Pecksniff, and his eventual awakening; Young Martin's arrogance and his eventual fall in America; Mercy Pecksniff's marriage to the sadistic Jonas Chuzzlewit, and her eventual come-uppance; Anthony Chuzzlewit's realization that in teaching his son the credo of selfishness, "Do other men, for they would do you," he has created a monster who lives for his death ("having been long taught by his father to over-reach everybody, he had imperceptibly acquired a love of over-reaching that venerable monitor himself"); Montague Tigg's insurance scam; and, most famously, Mr. Pecksniff's schemes to seize control of Old Martin's estate. Add to this a murder, an attempted parricide, a gin-swilling midwife, a false death, a real one, and various love plots.

One way readers try to disentangle what Welsh calls "Chuzzlewit Madness" is to cite Dickens's explanation that the novel is about "self" or selfishness. But this explanation is as helpful as saying that *Hamlet* is about revenge. The novel is about money and the power it exerts over people. To be precise, what draws all the characters and incidents together are the themes of delusion, illusion, and deception, both willful and innocent. In *Chuzzlewit* Dickens removes public masks, revealing our lively capacity to deceive and be deceived. Deception exists on many levels in the novel: Mr. Pecksniff is an individual fraud; the Anglo-Bengalee Disinterested Loan and Life Assurance Company is a corporate racket; and America is a scam on a national scale. Individual swindles, business chicanery, and a political system called democracy all amount to the same thing.

An air of mystery surrounds the novel, as if the story itself is a mask hiding some deeper, mythic meaning. In a sense the novel itself is duplicitous, existing on several levels of reality at the same time. For instance, Old Martin *seems* like any old man full of crotchets and jealousies, but there is also a touch of wizardry about him; Todgers's boardinghouse *seems* like a mundane establishment for traveling businessmen, but it is located in a London that can't be found on any map (see page 164). The enigma of Todgers's is never explained, lending an intriguing aura to a novel that is half fantasy, half reality.

Chuzzlewit's London is filled with realistic details, but it's also a place where each character confronts his secret self with its attendant desires and terrors. To Ruth Pinch and John Westlock, it is a lovers' pastoral, with purling fountains and wild beasts; but to Jonas Chuzzlewit, London is a place of spies and whispers, where his own shadow pursues him through winding streets. London is a place of unexpected nooks and crannies, such as the hideaway where Tom finds a private pleasure dome of books to be sorted, cataloged, and shelved—his favorite pursuit.

The characters, like the city that draws them, appear in many moods and guises. Almost everyone in the novel possesses a secret self. Some seem split into two different people; others, through strange offstage metamorphoses, become entirely different characters. In *Chuzzlewit* human beings are not only alienated from one another, putting up false fronts to disguise their true intentions, but also in many cases disconnected from themselves. No one truly knows another because no one is ever truly himself. Identity is not fixed but fluid, capable of being modified at will or by necessity.

Montague Tigg exhibits the most protean dexterity in the novel. First seen as a shabby ne'er-do-well, he magically transforms himself into Tigg Montague, the sartorially splendid head of the Anglo-Bengalee Disinterested Loan and Life Assurance Company. (In a novel where there's no assurance about anything and everyone pursues self-interest, the name of Tigg's phony company is pointedly ironic.) Chevy Slyme, crook and freeloader, disappears early in the book and, in a surprise cameo, reappears at the end as the constable who arrests Jonas Chuzzlewit. Jonas, after murdering Tigg, splits into two beings: murderer and victim. "He was so horribly afraid of that infernal room at home. This made him, in a gloomy, murderous, mad way, not only fearful *for* himself, but *of* himself."

The most comic instance of split identity is that of Mrs. Gamp and her alter ego, Mrs. Harris, to whom she attributes her most cherished opinions and anecdotes. Then there's the duplicity of Dickens's Tartuffe, the oily Mr. Pecksniff, who spouts precepts while plotting to seduce Mary Graham and seize Old Martin's estate. (Mr. Pecksniff speaks in an idiom one can only call "Bible-ese," a precursor of televangelistic oratory: "Oh, Calf, Calf . . . Oh, Baal, Baal! Oh my friend Mrs. Todgers! To barter away that precious jewel, self-esteem, and cringe to any mortal creature—for eighteen shillings a week!" At one point, to emphasize Mr. Pecksniff's duplicity, Dickens even describes him as warming his hands "benevolently before the fire as if they belonged to somebody else." In a telling moment, Old Anthony Chuzzlewit, congratulating Pecksniff on his perfection of the hypocrite's art, says, "I swear, you believe yourself sometimes."

Names, Dickens's specialty, illustrate the way in which one character may play many parts. The Christian names and nicknames of the Pecksniff girls reflect their private and public selves: Charity/Cherry and Mercy/Merry suggest the pious facade that hides the giddy girl. Despite the virtuous implications of her name, Charity is really a sour Cherry, a bitter spinster who lives only to spite her prettier, more marriageable sister. She does, however, remain true to the letter, if not the spirit, of her given name: at the novel's end she's unwillingly attending her despised father, in his "drunken, squalid, begging, letter-writing" old age. Merry, true to her nickname, marries the sadist Jonas as a lark and is almost destroyed by her silliness. Dickens, however, offers her redemption: through suffering she undergoes a moral conversion and becomes worthy of her Christian name, a woman capable of compassion and true mercy.

Given that almost every character possesses at least two names, it's significant that two different characters are named Martin Chuzzlewit. Why would Dickens, usually so fertile with names, do this? By giving grandfather and grandson the same name, Dickens suggests a lineage of virtue that won't die out with Chuzzlewit senior but, like his name, will be carried into the succeeding generation.

The doubleness motif is even carried out in the way characters look: eyes, which, as Dickens points out, usually come in matched sets, are in *Martin Chuzzlewit* not always evenly paired. Zephania Scadder, for instance, the agent of the fraudulent Eden Land Corporation, has one eye in perpetual motion, the other perfectly still. Each of Mrs. Todgers's eyes seems to belong to two different people: her benevolent one warmly beams, the calculating one coldly stares. Each reflects a contradictory side of her character. Ultimately the benevolent eye triumphs, and as she becomes true to herself, she emerges as one of the novel's few kindhearted women.

In *Martin Chuzzlewit* nothing is as it seems: the apparently solid Assurance Company is only a bubble, and America, which advertises itself as a land of opportunity, turns out to be a land of opportunists. With the last of his savings, Young Martin purchases a land package in the town of Eden and discovers that it's actually a pestilential swamp. In this false paradise, Martin sheds his vanity and sees himself for the first time.

He lands in Eden because of his grandiose ideas and his selfish gullibility, and he can leave only when he sheds his vanity and admits he needs help. It is, in short, like Dante's Purgatory, where shades are doomed to do penance for their folly and greed before they can be released. This Eden is a perverted pastoral where, instead of being protectively enclosed, Martin is enmired in a pestilential swamp, a "place of fever, ague and death."

Martin's foil, the unselfish Tom Pinch—who, despite the novel's title (another deception!), is the book's true hero—discovers that he too has been living in a false paradise, Pecksniff's menage. Martin's opinion of himself and his belief in America are as unfounded as Tom's faith in his employer. This balding, middle-aged clerk has spent his adult life living as a dependent child whose innocence has made him susceptible to Pecksniffian guile. In a fallen world, innocence is unprotected against evil. This theme continually recurs in Dickens's early fiction: How can the good man (or boy) preserve his innocence while protecting himself against wickedness?

Tom has taken Mr. Pecksniff at face value, and has valued base coin. Living for a kind word from his idol, he thinks it an honor to be Mr. Pecksniff's flunky. In a climactic scene in the church,

Chuzzlewit is so crammed with characters that each reader seems compelled to choose a favorite. During Dickens's lifetime, *Chuzzlewit* was not rated as highly as his other novels, but everyone loved Mrs. Gamp. The "decadent" poet Algernon Swinburne, connoisseur of sadomasochistic practices and Dickens enthusiast, singled out Jonas as a special favorite. Swinburne, one assumes, must have known what he was talking about: "Jonas Chuzzlewit has his place of eminence for ever among the most memorable types of living and breathing wickedness that ever were stamped and branded with immortality by the indignant genius of a great and unrelenting master."

he sees Mr. Pecksniff, snakelike, crouching among the pews, dart up and try to seduce Mary Graham. He has to see the true Mr. Pecksniff and confront the evil before he can believe what others have known all along. At last the scales fall from his eyes. Disillusioned, Tom undergoes his own personal Fall.

Like Adam, he is exiled from his shelter, and like the typical Dickensian hero, he heads for the urban wilderness of London.

Alone in London, Tom experiences Dickens's version of existential angst. Life without Mr. Pecksniff seems pointless. His disillusionment reaches a peak when, upon finding himself at the Monument to the Fire of London, he pays a shilling to see the legendary "Man in the Monument," only to find that the tower is as empty as Mr. Pecksniff. Tom must discover that the world is a far more ambiguous and complex place than he originally thought: truth must be discerned on a case-by-case basis. Nothing is simple, nothing is quite as it appears.

Both Tom at Mr. Pecksniff's and Martin in his noxious Eden confront their own stagnation: they only find themselves when they leave their false paradises and head for the place—London!—where each man finds what he is looking for. Martin learns to love others, while Tom learns to love more wisely.

But the biggest revelation is saved for last. Midway through the novel Old Martin, who originally appeared unforgiving and selfish, suddenly turns into a doddering fool, entrapped in Pecksniffian snares. But his assumed personalities have allowed his true self to go into hiding while he secretly tests loyalties, discerning the virtuous from the vicious, the true from the false. Old Martin "awakens" from his false dementia, seizes control of the plot, and dispenses fortunes, judgments, and marriages. Perhaps this seems too pat, but Dickens manipulates us so that we don't mind. Readers who suffered—or relished—Pecksniffian cant and humbuggery for almost 600 pages are now dying to see his comeuppance. In one crowning moment, with all the characters assembled in one place, all masks are dropped: Mr. Pecksniff is seen as the sanctimonious phony he is—though to give him his due, he retains his mask even as he lies sprawled on the floor. Jonas's crimes come to light, Tom Pinch's hidden virtue is revealed—even Mrs. Gamp is called to account—and everyone, for the first time, sees each other plainly, face to face.

❧ CHUZZLEWIT LORE ❧

One of the most undeservedly neglected Dickens novels, *Martin Chuzzlewit* is also one of the most important. If *Pickwick* is a novel of "firsts," then *Chuzzlewit* is one of "lasts." It was the last novel Dickens published under the pseudonym Boz; the last, for a while anyway, to be published by his *Pickwick* publishers, Chapman and Hall; and the last slapdash novel he would ever write. Henceforth, starting with *Dombey and Son,* he rigorously planned each installment, carefully referring to copious working notes, which he called "mems" (see page 199).

✳ The screenwriters Lowell Ganz and Babaloo Mandel loved *Martin Chuzzlewit* so much they decided to update it and adapt it for film. The result was the 1993 movie *Greedy,* starring Michael J. Fox and Kirk Douglas. The *Los Angeles Daily News* warned its readers that the movie's plot might seem familiar because it was based on a novel by Charles Dickens. It's hard to imagine the average American turning to his neighbor and remarking, "Isn't this like *Martin Chuzzlewit?*" In an interview with the *Daily News,* Ganz said, "Fortunately, Dickens isn't alive to ask any questions, so we were free to take the story and make it completely our own."

❋In 1843, the year *Chuzzlewit* came out in serial form, the book industry was in a serious recession, and Dickens's serial never sold more than 23,000 copies a month, a marked contrast to the 40,000–100,000 monthly sales of his earlier novels. Then as now, a novel's success or failure often depends on the work that immediately precedes it. *Chuzzlewit*'s failure may be partly due to the fact that it followed *Barnaby Rudge,* Dickens's least-popular novel. Thus by December 1843 Dickens decided to augment his income and raise funds by writing a Christmas book. If *Martin Chuzzlewit* had been a best-seller, *A Christmas Carol* might never have been written.

❦CHUZZLEWIT'S YANKEE-DOODLEDOM❦

*M*artin Chuzzlewit's America is a mad-house:
but it is a mad-house we are all on the road to.
—G. K. CHESTERTON

Martin lands in America just as Alice tumbles down the rabbit hole into Wonderland. Mr. Jefferson Brick, Major Pawkins, and Mr. La Fayette Kettle are just as absurd in their way as the Mad Hatter and the March Hare are in theirs. At one point, surrounded by Americans, Martin turns to his valet and wonderingly asks, "Touch me, will you. Am I awake?" Dickens's America and Wonderland are absurd places where ordinary reason does not apply and sane visitors are caught in a circuitous logic from which they can never hope to escape. Martin encounters an American gentleman who confidently asserts that Queen Victoria resides in the Tower of London; when Martin corrects his misunderstanding, the American informs the Englishman that he has fallen "into an error not uncommon among his countrymen," and that he, Martin, is the dupe of a widespread conspiracy. In one paragraph Dickens captures the uniquely American tendency to uncritically accept conspiracy and coverup, no matter how preposterous.

With Swiftian savagery, Dickens exposes our native flaws and indigenous characters. Nowhere is he more brilliant, or prophetic, than in his picture of Putnam Smif, whose rhapsodic literary style anticipates the lyrics of Walt Whitman, twelve years before the poet wrote *Leaves of Grass:*

I was raised in those interminable solitudes where our mighty Mississippi (or Father of Waters) rolls his turbid flood.

I am young, and ardent. For there is a poetry in wildness, and every alligator basking in the slime is in himself an Epic, self-contained. I aspirate for fame. It is my yearning and my thirst.

❧ THE WORLD ACCORDING TO GAMP ❧

The very quintessence of Dickens's genius.
—GEORGE GISSING

Sarah "Sairey" Gamp was to Dickens's time what any of the recurring characters on *Saturday Night Live* are to our own. She has her tag lines, her signature expressions and gestures; each time she appears, she goes through a routine with a predictability audiences can depend on. (For Henri Bergson, such mechanical predictability was the essence of comedy itself.) To explicate humor is to kill it: if you don't find Mrs. Gamp funny, there is nothing anyone can do to make her so. But for generations, Sairey Gamp was regarded as the pinnacle of drollery.

Mrs. Gamp is purely English: you can still find her in shops, tearooms, and pubs, gossiping with neighbors or anyone who will listen.

Mrs. Gamp Propoges a Toast, one of the finest—and drollest—drawings of Phiz (Hablot Knight Browne). He was at the peak of his powers when he illustrated *Martin Chuzzlewit.*

("Then he said, then I said," and so on.) One of England's most recognizable comic types, Mrs. Gamp can be heard on *The Benny Hill Show,* in Peter Cook and Dudley Moore's skits in *Beyond the Fringe,* even in T. S. Eliot's *The Waste Land.*

A nurse before Florence Nightingale made the profession respectable, Mrs. Gamp, whose hygienic practices are suspect, attends "a lying-in or a laying-out with equal relish and zest."

With an eye ever on business, Mrs. Gamp, with a wink and a leer, presses business cards into the hands of blushing brides (or any nubile young woman—"just in case") and flatters the local undertaker Mr. Mould, with whom she has a professional relationship. Spying the three marriageable Mould girls, she waxes sentimental, recalling earlier days: "Ah! the sweet creeturs!—playing a berryins down in the shop and follerin' the orderbook to its long home in the iron safe!" (In *Martin Chuzzlewit,* death is inextricably linked to cash.)

Pleased with herself, her treats, and her gin, Mrs. Gamp is ready with an aphorism for every occasion: "[Death] is what we all come to; as certain as being born, except we can't make our calculations so exact." Despite her relish for living, she repeatedly refers to life as a "wale of tears" and has a morbid curiosity about other people's affairs. But there's another side to Mrs. Gamp: her false sentimentality disguises a tough practicality. Nursing a man at the point of death, she regards him with professional detachment:

> By degrees, a horrible remembrance of one branch of her calling took possession of the woman; and stooping down, she pinned his wandering arms against his sides, to see how he would look if laid out as a dead man. Hideous as it may appear, her fingers itched to compose his limbs in that last marble attitude.
>
> "Ah," said Mrs. Gamp, walking from the bed, "he'd make a lovely corpse."

While recuperating from an illness, young Mamie Dickens was permitted to occupy the sofa in her father's study while he worked. One day while she lay there quietly, Dickens apparently forgot she was in the room:

> Suddenly [he] jumped up, went to the looking-glass, rushed back to his writing-table and jotted down a few words; back to the glass again, this time talking to his own reflection, or rather to the simulated expression he saw there . . . then back again to his writing. After a little while he got up again, and stood with his back to the glass, talking softly and rapidly for a long time, then *looking* at his daughter, but certainly never *seeing* her, then once more back to his table. . . . It was a curious experience, and a wonderful thing to see him throwing himself so entirely *out* of himself and into the character he was writing about.

"Hideous as it may appear," indeed. But funny, too. Dickens takes what is potentially threatening, the unnameable mysteries of birth and death, and through this snuff-stained, gin-swilling nurse makes them the stuff of comedy. The man who created mawkish deathbed scenes could also fill the sickroom of the terminally ill with gallows humor.

Whereas her indifference to suffering should provoke the outrage aroused by the workhouse authorities in, say, *Oliver Twist,* we instead find ourselves smiling at Mrs. Gamp's outrageous abuses of her profession. She does not reside in that inferno of evil occupied by Bill Sikes or Jonas Chuzzlewit—which is one reason why we can laugh at her. For Dickens, absolute evil belongs to calculating "adults" like Jonas Chuzzlewit, those who are incapable of giving and receiving pleasure, those who lack zest for life, and those who abuse children. We enjoy Mrs. Gamp because, unlike the workhouse officials and Jonas, she enjoys herself. In her infantile fondness for comfort, sleep, food and drink, she disarms as well as charms. In Mrs. Gamp, Dickens achieves something rather daring: he creates a likable character who skirts the edge of cruelty—and at times the edge is particularly fine. She provokes ambivalence: we laugh because she is funny, but our laughter is laced with a slight edge of disgust, at her—and ourselves.

❖Mrs. Gamp is more than a Dickensian grotesque. Her work habits are an accurate portrayal of nursing in the early part of the century, when nurses were basically "watchers," poor women hired to watch a patient, administer medicine, and call a doctor when necessary. They were untrained, often drunk, and usually dirty. They could do little for patients but watch them die. Although Dickens intended Sairey as a comic character, he also used her to point to some of the abuses of the nursing profession. Some of her characteristics are derived from a queer old nurse that Dickens had heard about from his friend Miss Burdett-Coutts. This unknown caretaker also wore a yellow nightcap and was partial to gin and snuff.

MRS. HARRIS

*W*hat readers tend to remember about Mrs. Gamp is her remarkable friendship with Mrs. Harris. Actually, Mrs. Gamp has two close friends: first there's Betsey Prig, the working "pardner" who shares her cases and, as a day nurse, provides advance warning of the cuisine served at each job. Then there's Mrs. Harris. Part of Mrs. Gamp's appeal comes from her continual references to this friend, who never actually makes an appearance in the novel, for the reason that she simply does not exist. Nevertheless, Mrs. Gamp has a powerful ally in Mrs. Harris: as a projection of Mrs. Gamp herself, she is ready whenever Mrs. Gamp needs her, to bolster her opinions and stories, to urge her to take one more drink, to tell her that she works too hard, and to praise her generosity of spirit:

"Mrs. Harris," I says, at the very last case as ever I acted in, which it was but a young person, "Mrs. Harris," I says, "leave the bottle on the chimley-piece, and don't ask me to take none, but let me put my lips to it when I am so dispoged, and then I will do what I am engaged to do, according to the best of my ability." "Mrs. Gamp," she says, in answer, "if ever there was a sober creetur to be got at eighteen pence a day for working people, and three and six for gentlefolks—night watching," said Mrs. Gamp, with emphasis, "being an extra charge—you are that inwallable person."

When modesty forbids self-praise, Mrs. Harris rushes to the rescue with a few well-chosen remarks; when Mrs. Gamp politely refrains from advertising hours and rates, Mrs. Harris has no such scruples. And she is always available to give credibility to Mrs. Gamp's anecdotes, or what we might call "urban legends." She's that imaginary being, "the friend of a friend" to whom preposterous things always happen (e.g., the friend of a friend who accidentally incinerates the poodle in the microwave). In one instance, Mrs. Harris is a relation of a pickled baby:

"Mrs. Harris as has one sweet infant (though she did not wish it be known) in her family by the mother's side kep in spirits in a bottle; and that sweet babe she see at Greenwich Fair, a travellin' in company with the pink-eyed lady, Prooshan dwarf, and livin skelinton."

Who but Dickens could imagine a woman with an imaginary friend with a relation on "the mother's side" whose baby is preserved in a bottle of spirits and displayed in a sideshow? Unstoppable now, Mrs. Gamp expounds on Mrs. Harris's supposed feelings upon discovering the bottled infant:

"which judge from her feelins wen the barrel organ played, and she was showed her own dear sister's child, the same not bein expected from the outside picter, where it was painted quite contrairy in a livin state, a many sizes larger, and performing beautiful upon the Arp, which never did that dear child know or do: since breath it never did, to speak on, in this wale [vale]."

In one of the funniest scenes in all of Dickens, Betsey Prig, emboldened by drink, challenges the existence of Mrs. Harris (the accompanying drawing of the two drunken women, entitled *Mrs. Gamp Propoges a Toast,* is among Phiz's best):

"Bother Mrs. Harris!" said Betsey Prig.
Mrs. Gamp looked at her with amazement, incredulity, and indignation; when Mrs. Prig, shutting her eye still closer, and folding her arms still tighter, uttered these memorable and tremendous words:
"I don't believe there's no sich a person!"

Mrs. Gamp all but collapses at such perfidy:

> "Wot I have took from Betsey Prig this blessed night, no mortial creetur
> knows! . . . The words she spoke of Mrs. Harris, lambs could not forgive.
> No, Betsey!" said Mrs. Gamp, in a violent burst of feeling, "nor worms
> forget!"

Within minutes, however, she manages to pull herself together sufficiently to
recount the incident, and the assault upon Mrs. Harris, about whom she is
now holding forth at great length.

Mrs. Harris is nothing less than Mrs. Gamp's self-serving double, the
specter-self who provides convenient rationalizations for all occasions, that
still, small voice urging us to have the extra slice of cake. In short, she is the
mouthpiece of appetite.

SETH PECKSNIFF, HYPOCRITE EXTRAORDINAIRE

Seth Pecksniff is, to borrow a phrase once applied to U.S. Speaker of the
House Newt Gingrich, a "libertine in prig's clothing." Hailed as the English
Tartuffe—Molière's religious hypocrite and the prototype of the canting char-
latan—Mr. Pecksniff, with his phony smile, is one of Dickens's most famous
characters. In Tartuffian fashion, he tries to worm his way into Old Martin's
household, seizing control of his estate, his money, and his companion, the
lovely and virtuous Mary Graham.

He has many faces, all ready to be assumed at a moment's notice: the
Beaming Paterfamilias, Outraged Virtue, Ingenuous Honesty, and the Widower Devoted to the Memory of "She." This is one of Dickens's favorite types,
the humbug with monstrous pretensions to virtue.

Few have a keener ear for moral cant than Dickens, and in Mr. Pecksniff, as
in the preacher Mr. Chadband (*Bleak House*), he captures the rolling rhythms
of the false prophet. These duplicitous figures speak a disguised language:
statements are never direct and simple but oblique, polysyllabic, and allusive.
Just telling Martin that he's going to London involves circumlocution: " 'We
shall go forth tonight by the heavy coach—like the dove of old, my dear Martin—and it will be a week before we again deposit our olive-branches in the
passage. When I say 'olive-branches,' observed Mr. Pecksniff, in explanation,
'I mean our unpretended luggage.' "

Unpretended indeed! For the Pecksniffs of the world, words are like fancy
costumes: the more words they use, the more they can avoid exposing their
naked souls. Visiting London with the sole aim of insinuating his way into
Martin's heart, he says, "It is not often . . . that my daughters and I desert our
quiet home to pursue the giddy pleasures that revolve abroad." Mr. Pecksniff

is incapable of uttering a direct statement. Words are crucial to the hypocrite, for they are often substitutes for benevolent deeds. "Mr. Pecksniff," Dickens writes, "was a grave man, a man of noble sentiments and speech." Notice that Dickens doesn't say anything about his deeds; words for Pecksniff are divorced from actions.

Echoes from Pecksniffian Wounded Virtue oratory appear in Nixon's famous Checkers speech. Confronted by those whom he has cheated, lied to, and deceived, Mr. Pecksniff artfully makes himself out to be the injured party, more sinned against than sinning:

> "I know the human mind, although I trust it. That is my weakness. . . . And if you ever contemplate the silent tomb, sir, think of me. . . . If you should wish to have anything inscribed upon the silent tomb, sir, let it be, that I—ah, my remorseful sir! that I—the humble individual who has now the honour of reproaching you, forgave you. That I forgave you when my injuries were fresh, and when my bosom was newly wrung."

His speech patterns are also heard in the sonorous rhythms of televangelists and in the excuses of politicians caught with their pockets full and their pants down.

❧ TODGERS'S ☙

George Gissing said that when he passed the Monument, it was never of the fire of London that he thought, always of Todgers's.
—GEORGE ORWELL

"Surely there never was, in any other borough, city or hamlet in the world, such a singular sort of place as Todgers's." And, one might add, surely there never was, in any other novel, myth, or tale, a more inviting prelude. Located in the heart of London, within the shadow of the Monument, Todgers's boardinghouse *should* be readily located on any city map. But although Dickens provides us with a precise locale and an immutable landmark, Todgers's is impossible to find because only part of it exists in the London we know; the other part resides in pure fantasy.

Todgers's is somewhere in London, but where is anyone's guess. Removed from the city that surrounds it, the Todgerian world exudes a desolate stillness, where time is measured not by clocks or calendars but by the succession of life and death: "Here, [in the churchyard] paralysed old watchmen guarded the bodies of the dead at night, year after year, until at last they joined that solemn brotherhood."

In the search for Todgers's, both readers and characters are thrown into a hallucinatory landscape where nothing is where it's supposed to be:

> You couldn't walk about in Todgers's neighbourhood, as you could in any other neighbourhood. You groped your way for an hour through lanes and bye-ways, and court-yards, and passages; and you never once emerged upon anything that might be reasonably called a street. A kind of resigned distraction came over the stranger as he trod these devious mazes, and, giving himself up for lost, went in and out and round about and quietly turned back again when he came to a dead wall or was stopped by an iron railing, and felt that the means of escape might possibly present themselves in their own good time, but that to anticipate them was hopeless. Instances were known of people who, being asked to dine at Todgers's, had travelled round and round for a weary time, with its very chimney-pots in view; and finding it, at last, impossible of attainment, had gone home again and with a gentle melancholy on their spirits, tranquil and uncomplaining.

Dickens takes the most mundane of settings and transforms it into the archetypal anxiety-provoking dream: you are lost in a familiar neighborhood with recognizable signposts that fail to lead you anywhere except another maze. Every street is impossible to follow, leading only to cul-de-sacs and walls. This passage is remarkable for a subtlety of tone (the search induces a "gentle melancholy of the spirit") and its fantastic premise. The conflation of the supernal and the ordinary is pure Dickens.

Besides, is this passage only about people looking for a boardinghouse? Dickens suggests that he saying something deeper, perhaps something about the meaning of life. Or is he? The digression is irrelevant to the novel, and Dickens never reveals why the boardinghouse is so hard to find; the passage leads nowhere, leaving us in a state like that of the Todgerian seekers. Perhaps something has been omitted or left unexpressed. There is poetry in the passage that hints at the desolation of a city filled with seekers and missed opportunities. Something sought has not been found—yet perhaps it was of no great matter.

And it isn't. When we finally penetrate the mystery of Todgers's, we find that there is no mystery at all. It's simply a boardinghouse for commercial travelers—young sparks with pretensions to high society, just the sort of "gentlemen" that Dickens likes to lampoon. Presided over by the redoubtable Mrs. Todgers (whose husband "had cut his matrimonial career rather short, by unlawfully running away from his happiness, and establishing himself in foreign countries as a bachelor"), Todgers's is a veritable heaven for the boy-crazy Pecksniff girls, who rarely get to shine in their own little hamlet.

Among the "gentlemen" (Dickens uses the term with gentle irony) lodgers are the self-appointed wit of the house, Mr. Gander, and a "gentleman of a theatrical turn," who had once entertained serious thoughts of coming out, but had been kept in by the wickedness of human nature." There are also men of various turns, each embodying a different humor or type, from the youngest, the spoony Augustus Moddle, to the oldest, Mr. Jinkins, "a man of superior talents" who "always takes the lead in the house."

The Todgers's section contains the famous set piece, the "Great Dinner Party at Todgers's," a fete in honor of the new arrivals, where the commercial gentlemen vie for the attention of Charity and Mercy, in their element among so many bachelors. The Todgerian feast provides the usual Dickensian list of comestibles: "Quarts of almonds; dozens of oranges; pounds of raisins; stacks of biffins; soup plates full of nuts. . . . Oh! Todgers's could do it when it chose! Mind that." The evening concludes with "a large china bowl of punch, brewed by the gentleman of a convivial turn." More punch flows, enthusiasm reaches a height, and speeches are called for. The company, now thoroughly drunk, toasts one another, and all raise a glass to Mr. Pecksniff. "What saith Mr. Pecksniff? Or rather let the question, What leaves he unsaid? Nothing. More punch is called for."

Masterpiece Theatre

꙰

INTERVIEW WITH DAVID LODGE

ew literary critics make good novelists, and vice versa. Even fewer *are hilarious. As Honorary Professor of Modern English Literature at the University of Birmingham, David Lodge can write about Dickens—and write like Dickens. He is the author of nine novels and many works of criticism.*

Lodge is also one of the few writers who could bring Dickens's obscure novel about greed and hypocrisy, Martin Chuzzlewit, *to life on television: American viewers saw his adaptation of the novel on* Masterpiece Theatre *in April 1995.*

NE: *What is your favorite Dickens novel?*

DL: Hard question, really. But if I had to pick one, I'd pick *Bleak House.* Technically, it's very impressive, particularly for a popular Victorian novelist. And it has all the Dickensian ingredients at their best: wonderful authorial rhetoric (I don't think he ever wrote better than in those parts of the novel) and terrific comic characters. *And* a very powerful theme. I think that *Little Dorrit, Our Mutual Friend,* and *Great Expectations* are all in the same league, and at a different times one might have a different preference.

NE: *You chose all late ones.*

DL: I suppose those appeal to the modern reader. And as an academic critic, one goes for the later books because they're teachable. I just finished adapting

Martin Chuzzlewit for BBC Television; I would have hesitated if I had been asked to do one of the later novels. But the early novels are so theatrical, and you don't feel you're taking liberties with a masterpiece.

NE: *What is* Martin Chuzzlewit *about exactly? It seems like a hodgepodge of a book.*

DL: Thematically? It's the first of Dickens's novels to have an abstract theme, and it's hammered in very heavily. It's greed, the awful effects of greed as displayed in a family and its fortunes. It's also about hypocrisy and appearance and pretense. Many of the characters put on masks and pretend to be other than what they are. There is a great unmasking process going on in the novel. The most unequivocally good character is someone who doesn't pretend to be anything other than what he is. That's Tom Pinch.

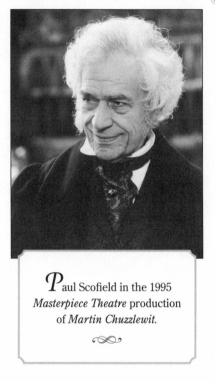

*P*aul Scofield in the 1995 *Masterpiece Theatre* production of *Martin Chuzzlewit.*

NE: *How can you make Tom seem real? He seems too perfect to be believable.*

DL: He's not altogether easy for a modern reader to accept because his goodness seems improbably extreme. He avoids seeing the evil around him. As a dramatist, the only way to handle this is to make it a sort of comedy—Tom as a holy fool. I think—and this is a commonplace—that Dickens's presentation of good characters is less acceptable to us than his presentation of evil characters.

My director and I had a struggle about this. He wanted more Dickensian moralizing. He managed to get more time out of the BBC, so I was able to meet him on it, and I think the script benefited as a result. If you cut out the good characters too much, then there's no tension. There is none of the identification that I think an audience—as distinct from a reader—needs. Audiences want characters to identify with. That's the problem for any modern adapter or teacher of Dickens: to overcome a certain resistance we have to his slightly excessive presentation of goodness.

NE: *Have tastes changed that much? When Dickens read aloud from his novels, grown men wept.*

DL: People *did* cry more easily then. They were more easily moved by dramatic or narrative entertainment. Dickens was drawing on a dramatic tradition of melodrama, which to us seems artificial and often ludicrous. It's hard to take melodrama straight. This is simply something that is as remote to us as the Alexandrine couplet of Racine. It's a convention. Those long speeches like arias in which characters . . . well, for instance, when Mary denounces Pecksniff in the church, it goes on for pages, long, long speeches. The modern reader will think this unnecessarily explicit. The rhetoric is also rather unrealistically well formed for a girl who is supposed to be in distress. The Victorians were prepared to sacrifice realism for the sake of the moral catharsis they got from these scenes. Well, part of a literary education is getting people to make these allowances. They should go with the flow as much as possible. They shouldn't act as if Dickens was writing yesterday.

NE: *What about sentimentality?*

DL: Yes, that's part of it, isn't it? The sentimentality seems to go with the melodrama. What it comes down to is this: sophisticated readers today resist sentimentality in movies as well as in literature. Unsophisticated audiences are still easily open to sentimentality in movies and television, but they don't read classic fiction because they find the vocabulary and the allusions too difficult and off-putting. If they could get past that, they would probably enjoy it in the same way they enjoy soaps. *A Christmas Carol* continues to work in all kinds of ways for audiences. There is a huge popular responsiveness to sentiment if it's focused on a genuine story.

NE: *Why do we still read Dickens today?*

DL: He's a wonderful comic writer. Why comedy is therapeutic is rather mysterious business. Dickens's observation of folly, affectation, hypocrisy, self-deception, deception of others, and the way in which people manipulate language to these ends just tickles one. Dickens does what comedy has always done: it both exposes imperfections in the world and reconciles us to it by making something entertaining out of it.

He extends your knowledge of the world. He has a journalistic curiosity for turning up odd corners of reality. He is a great novelist of the city. He has this extraordinary metaphorical imagination that makes the physical appearance of the city poetic. He transforms it into a kind of apocalyptic vision of civilization at the end of its tether. A teacher might demonstrate that from the opening of *Bleak House*—the way in which a drab London street passes through all kinds of mythical and historical allusions and is transformed into the world after the flood, the world at the end of creation: "The death of the sun . . ." It's just incredible. The richness of it all: the novels do so many things at once. They entertain, they provoke thought, they give you a good story, they give you memorable characters, wonderful dialogue, they're very funny. You have to take all these novels as an oeuvre, as an extraordinary accumulating world.

NE: *Has Dickens influenced your own writing?*

DL: I humbly place myself in a tradition of English fiction that runs from Fielding, Smollett, Sterne, Austen, Dickens. It's a largely comic tradition. It uses comedy to explore serious issues. Dickens is very important to that great tradition of the English novel and therefore to me personally. *Nice Work* is modeled on the English industrial novel, such as *Hard Times*. Anthony Burgess wrote a very nice review of it which he finished by saying, "Some people may say it's too English, but then so is Dickens." I took that as a compliment. Some critics think I am rather inclined to sentimentality, that my happy endings are slightly contrived. Maybe that's an inheritance from Dickens.

NE: *Which scenes and characters in Dickens strike you as funny?*

DL: I think I told you my introduction to Dickens was *Pickwick*. Well, I suppose the Fat Boy is stuck in my mind—he's one of my favorite characters. I like Dickens's grotesque old people, so I would pick the Smallweeds from *Bleak House*. Flora Finching [*Little Dorrit*] I like. As for scenes: Wopsle's *Hamlet* in *Great Expectations;* in *Martin Chuzzlewit,* which is obviously chief in my mind at present, I pick the Great Dinner at Todgers's—one of my favorite pieces— and the showdown scene between Mrs. Gamp and Betsey Prig.

NE: *What would the world look like through Dickensian eyes?*

DL: Distorted. When I think of Dickensian, I think of those illustrations as much as I think of the text. The illustrations are interesting because Dickens usually chose his artists with some care and collaborated with them—and presumably approved of them. The drawings were useful in our television production. It's interesting that the good characters look slightly anemic, and the comic and evil ones look slightly grotesque.

NE: *Do people read Dickens as they once did?*

DL: Dickens's length discourages most people, and the books that tend to get read are usually the short ones, like *Oliver Twist*. By the way, do you know the apocryphal story of the popular paperback edition of *Oliver Twist*? There's a girl in a torn shift on the cover with the caption, "He wanted more, more, more . . ."

NE: *What interests you most about Dickens?*

DL: He had a kind of demon in him that had to be satisfied. *Why* did he go on doing these readings when they were killing him? How much did he *really* need the money? He needed the adrenaline. He was drunk on his power over audiences. That fascinates me, that side of Dickens—his interest in dramatics and theatricals and so on. And his extraordinary tireless energy. The long walks . . . these novels were huge efforts. They weren't easy for him. He had to build up a lot of steam, and they went on for so long! *And* he was doing all sorts of business things at the same time. I don't think anybody like that is going to be happy in the normal sense of contented. He had moments of great satisfaction, but he was never satisfied. Such a person never could be.

The Illustrated Dickens

Modern readers are apt to regard Victorian book illustrations as quaintly juvenile, charming in their way but outmoded. When we encounter such drawings we tend to pass them over, eager to get back to the plot, perhaps because in the pages of a narrative, we value words over pictures and find the two incompatible.

That book illustration has gone the way of the pianoforte is attributable to two factors. First, modern reproduction techniques make illustrated books prohibitively expensive. The other reason has to do with the nature of modern fiction.

*D*ickens's illustrators, particularly Phiz, have imprinted their images of a character on the public's imagination. Actors still tend to model their appearances on those early visual conceptions. Lennox Pawle, Mr. Dick in George Cukor's 1935 *David Copperfield,* poses side by side with Fred Barnard's version of the same character.

Although a picture may express a thousand words, it would take a thousand pictures to illustrate just one scene from a modern novel. Citing Thomas Pynchon's *Gravity's Rainbow* as an example, Julia Prewitt Brown points out that a drawing could never do justice to its complex psychology, symbolic patterns, and abstract ideas. And few illustrators could even begin to capture the sense of the numinous that hovers over an Iris Murdoch novel. In the modernist tradition, the material world is not the only one that matters; in the Victorian it is all. The nineteenth-century novel deals in the corporeal, objective world, a realm that *can* be visually represented.

To the Victorian reader, illustrations were an integral part of the reading experience, enhancing and complementing the text. They not only depicted Dickens's words, they also illuminated them.

Readers expected four drawings in each installment of a Dickens novel. To them, Phiz's *Mrs. Gamp Propoges a Toast* in *Martin Chuzzlewit* or his illustration of Nell's deathbed added an important dimension to the text, enhancing

*C*ruikshank's remarkable engraving *Fagin in the Condemned Cell* prompted G. K. Chesterton to remark that the picture looked as it had been drawn by Fagin himself. Dickens's accompanying text reads, "His eyes shone with a terrible light; his unwashed flesh crackled with the fever that burnt him up."

its comedy or its pathos. Though Dickens provided artists with a general description of how he wanted a scene portrayed, the artist was an imaginative interpreter of the text, sometimes seeing things Dickens hadn't imagined or been able to express. Michael Steig notes that the diabolic Quilp in *The Old Curiosity Shop* embodies the unbridled energies "unleashed by Dickens's imagination."

Some illustrations—often poorly reproduced—are regarded as masterpieces of the genre, like the satiric drawings of William Hogarth or Honoré Daumier. To the unaccustomed eye, they appear scratchy, cartoonish, grotesque. But ugliness serves a purpose. George Cruikshank's famous engraving *Fagin in the Condemned Cell* is terror incarnate, as arresting as Edvard Munch's *The Scream*. As G. K. Chesterton remarked, the drawing not only depicts Fagin, it also looks as if it were *drawn* by him.

In his famous essay on Dickens, George Orwell writes, "Many children begin to know his characters by sight before they can read, for on the whole Dickens was lucky in his illustrators." Those original faces are forgotten today, yet they are still recognized through movies and stage productions. We don't know *how* we know what Mr. Pickwick looks like—we just do. David Lean's Oliver looks like Cruikshank's, and the actor James Hayter seems to leap from Phiz's original drawing. And although we see W. C. Fields when we think of Mr. Micawber, it is really Phiz's creation that we see.

A Christmas Carol

Christmas Carol is a phenomenon, an industry, and a ritual. It is also one of the most compelling tales ever written, far more profound than its cheerfully bland annual productions suggest. The story, an archetypal journey from death to rebirth, recounts the cleansing transformation of a man who, deadened by experience, is surprised by joy. Neither just a tale for Christmas nor a ghost story for children, *Carol* touches our deep desire for a second chance at life.

In his preface Dickens is forthright about his intentions: "I have endeavoured in *this Ghostly little book, to raise the Ghost of an Idea,* which shall not put my readers out of humour with themselves, with each other, with the season or with me. May it haunt their houses pleasantly, and no one wish to lay it by" [italics mine].

As a "Ghostly little book," the tale should haunt us, just as the ghosts haunt Scrooge, and to precisely the same effect. The spirits give Scrooge—just as

Dickens gives us—a story with a linear plot that moves through past, present, and future; the experience of reliving his story changes Scrooge, as the experience of reading it should change us, for the better. *A Christmas Carol* is designed not to make us think or see or know, but to make us feel. For Dickens, the power of the imagination expressed through fiction is, like the ghosts, an agent of regeneration.

Stave One: The Beginning of the Story

The first "stave" (Dickens divides his "carol" into musical staves rather than chapters) begins with one of the most famous first sentences in English literature: "Marley was dead, to begin with." It's an opening designed to make a listener draw his chair closer, or a reader nestle down. The narrator next digresses a bit, giving us time to digest this fact, and then, with an apology, returns to his original point: "Old Marley was as dead as a doornail." Addressing us directly ("Now mind!"), Dickens draws us in and makes us feel that we are participants in the story. He quickly gets down to business and introduces Scrooge:

> Oh! but he was a tight-fisted hand at the grindstone, Scrooge! a squeezing, wrenching, grasping, scraping, clutching, covetous old sinner! Hard and sharp as flint, from which no steel had ever struck out generous fire; secret, and self-contained, and solitary as an oyster.

"Squeezing, wrenching, grasping, scraping, clutching," Scrooge is a man who never gives up, relents, submits, or lets go; the gerund form further emphasizes that his behavior is ongoing. Scrooge is as tightly wound as a machine, a perfect product of the industrial age. As he is unwilling to risk involvement in human affairs, his emotional life is similarly cramped. Scrooge is defined in terms of negation.

Although Scrooge dismisses all human interaction as "interference," he is, however, involved with others in one way: through money. As a moneylender, he controls others by keeping them in his debt. (As another Dickensian usurer, Ralph Nickleby, observed, to have a man owe you is to have him in your power.) His relations with his fellow human beings are based solely on what the Victorian philosopher Thomas Carlyle called the "cash nexus."

Dickens offers three reasons for Scrooge's miserliness. First, as a representative of his age, he embodies the Victorian policies and beliefs that Dickens hated most. Second, Scrooge is the Dickensian Adult-as-Villain, a man who, without fancy or emotions, has forgotten the lessons of childhood as embodied in the Christmas spirit. The third reason is more psychological and subtle. Misers accumulate and hoard out of a need for control and a fear of loss. Fear and mistrust of the world have created a man who, barricaded in his counting room, embraces only those things he feels he *can* count on: pounds, pence, guineas, and shillings. The only joy and pain he understands is the kind measured in terms of profit and loss.

As his uncle's foil, Fred is everything Scrooge is not. "Open, free and frank," he falls in love with and marries a penniless girl, a fate that the young Scrooge rejected, and the old one comes to regret. For Dickens, openness implies various qualities: a childlike openness to experience, the heartiness of

*A*n American Scrooge: Reginald Owen in the MGM's 1938 *A Christmas Carol* with Leo G. Carroll as Marley's Ghost. Lionel Barrymore was originally cast as Scrooge, but ill health forced him to drop out.

the open hand of charity, and the generosity of spirit evoked by the open door of hospitality. Fred honors the spirit of Christmas, "a time in which each man and woman opens their shut-up hearts freely."

In response to Fred's wishes of good cheer, Scrooge snarls his famous "Bah, humbug!" The expression, indelibly associated with the character, is Scroogean shorthand for denial. Everything beyond bottom-line materialism is denounced as humbug: false, foolish, unnecessary. Scrooge can't comprehend any reality outside the material world; but his grasp of reality, which now seems fixed and secure, will soon be shattered.

Scrooge's encounter with Fred reveals his disdain for familial bonds, just as his treatment of his clerk, Bob Cratchit, expresses his indifference to the ties that bind employer to employee. But his encounter with two benevolent gentlemen seeking charitable donations is crucial to the story, because, more than anything else, it illustrates Scrooge's feelings about humanity at large. Scrooge's dispute with them reveals that Dickens did not intend his protagonist to be the comical, eccentric, or even curmudgeonly figure he is generally made out to be, but rather a cold-blooded shark feeding off the defenseless poor. His is the human face of institutionalized cruelty. When asked for a charitable contribution, Scrooge asks in mock surprise, "And the Union workhouses? Are they still in operation?"—queries now synonymous with heartlessness. Few today can appreciate the depths of meaning behind those questions, but Victorian readers, familiar with the inhuman conditions of union workhouses, would have immediately understood the nature of Scrooge's callousness. The workhouses were the ugly products of the New Poor Law (see page 93), an act that Dickens detested and had attacked earlier in *Oliver Twist*. When Scrooge is told that many of the poor would rather die than go to these institutions, his reply is Dickens's bullet aimed at Malthusianism: "If they would rather die ... they had better do it, and decrease the surplus population." Welfare disturbs natural law, which necessitates that the "overflow" must die so others can live. Scrooge adds, "It's not my business. . . . It's enough for a man to understand his own business, and not to interfere with other people's." His belief that assistance is a form of interference is a by-product of laissez-faire Victorian government, a "do-nothingism" at its height when Dickens was writing. As Scrooge slams the door on the two gentlemen, the darkness and the fog thicken even more.

"The city clocks had only just gone three, but it was quite dark already. Foggier yet, and colder!" The atmosphere is tenebrous and foreboding; an air of apocalyptic expectancy hangs over London. Dickens repeatedly reminds us of the unnatural darkness, and his tone suggests that something momentous is about to happen. Through the fog come the muffled sounds of the city clocks, a reminder that time is slowly running out for all of us. Christmas Eve will be a night of reckoning for Scrooge.

As regular as the clocks, Scrooge makes his way home at closing time, and for the first time in his adult life he is jolted out of his closed, routinized existence. Suddenly, his door knocker turns into an apparition of Marley's head. The door knocker—an object of almost talismanic significance for Dickens—hangs over the threshold that Scrooge must cross before he can undergo his transformation.

Called liminal spaces by anthropologists, thresholds, passages, and doorways play an important role in rites of passage (hence mistletoe hanging over doorways and grooms carrying brides over thresholds). For a second Scrooge cannot trust his formerly reliable senses, yet he refuses to be shaken. With a "Bah, humbug!"—a refrain with an almost incantatory effect—the world reverts to Scroogean dimensions.

But there are other portents: Marley's head appears again, this time on the chimney, and unaccountably, all the city bells begin to toll. Then the ghost of

*A*lec Guinness as Marley's ghost in the 1984 television film.

 Marley himself makes its dramatic appearance, entwined in chains, dragging cash boxes, and with a kerchief tied below his jaw to prevent it from flapping open. Despite the apparitions, the bells, and the appearance of his dead partner, Scrooge staunchly maintains his bravado: Marley can't exist, because Scrooge refuses to believe he does.

First he rationalizes Marley's appearance: the ghost originates from some gastrointestinal upset, a figment arising from "an undigested bit of beef, a blot of mustard, a crumb of cheese, a fragment of an underdone potato." Although he sees the ghost standing in front of him, he is still incredulous and battles his own senses. He puts up a good fight, but in the end he succumbs, falling on his knees and pleading for mercy. The night is beginning to work its bizarre magic.

But Scrooge still doesn't get it. In response to Marley's portentous talk of regret and missed opportunities, Scrooge can only lamely assert, "You were always a good man of business, Jacob." Marley's retort becomes the crucial lesson Scrooge will learn this night: "Mankind was my business."

Why, one wonders, does Marley return to reclaim his partner? Why is Scrooge worth saving? Like Samuel Taylor Coleridge's Ancient Mariner, he chooses the guest most likely to profit by his instructional tale. Marley selects Scrooge because for all his partner's sins, a germ buried within him is still capable of heeding the Ghosts' wisdom.

Scrooge's hold on reality is shaken by the appearance of Marley; next his sense of time itself is undermined. Falling asleep at two, he awakes just as the clock strikes twelve. Disoriented, unable to determine whether it is day or night, he at first thinks that something has happened to the sun. He lies awake, waiting for the stroke of one, the time Marley told him to expect the first spirit's haunting.

STAVE THE SECOND

The Ghost of Christmas Past is a hybrid creature, part child, part old man. As the incarnation of memory itself, he is both fresh and ancient—a reflection of a past event that returns to the present reinvigorated.

The first sign that Scrooge is beginning to relinquish control occurs early in the story. First, he trusts that Marley is a ghost and not a bit of undigested matter; second, by believing in ghosts, he is forced to admit that there is more to life than he once thought. Finally, he is ready to risk everything and put his new beliefs to the test. Holding on to the robes of the ghost, Scrooge jumps out the window—and flies.

Hours earlier, Scrooge trusted no one, much less a ghost. The grasping man would have held the windowsill tightly, refusing to let go. But as he steps through the window and into the night sky, he makes a leap of faith that goes beyond a physical jump. He lets go of the material world's constraints, preoccupations, and cares and enters an alternate, invisible world where time, gravity, and matter itself are subject to different laws. He lets go of his need for control and allows the strange being to take him where it will.

Just before he jumps, Scrooge makes what for him is a startling admission: "I am a mortal and liable to fall." These words take on double meaning. Scrooge confesses that he is like everyone else, mortal, a member of the human race and therefore subject to death and decay—a foretaste of the vision the Ghost of Christmas Yet to Come will show him. And also, as a mere mortal, Scrooge is liable to fall, or sin.

The journey back in time speaks to the seemingly universal idea—as seen in such theories, methodologies, and beliefs as the "inner child," psychoanalysis, and reincarnation—that true change can only come about through a return to the past. The Ghost of Christmas Past not only shows Scrooge his past, but also restores his emotional memory so that he can feel exactly as he did as a child. The ghost does for Scrooge what a madeleine did for Marcel Proust (who admired Dickens's use of what he called the "music of memory"): his past is not simply remembered but recaptured. All the feelings of childhood return like sensation to a paralyzed limb: "He was conscious of a thousand thoughts, hopes, and joys, and cares, long, long forgotten!"

Gently, like a teacher, a Zen master, or a psychoanalyst, the spirit prompts his disciple, "You recollect the way." The religious implication of *way* would not be lost on the reader; Scrooge has indeed strayed from the path of virtue. The fanciful, dreamy boy has lost his way, growing up to become the calcified materialist.

Scrooge runs to the schoolhouse and finds a desolate child, whom he immediately recognizes. In drama, the heart-stopping moment when a parent recognizes his long-lost child is called a recognition scene. The recognition scene in *Carol* is thus all the more potent: the adult Scrooge recognizes his forgotten child-self. Seeing the boy he once was, he breaks down and sobs. But in a moment he leaps up, ecstatic at the once-familiar sight of Ali Baba, Robinson Crusoe, and the parrot, his fictional companions. The characters are presented as real because for the boy Ebenezer they were just as real as Ebenezer Scrooge should be to us, the readers. By vicariously becoming a child again, Scrooge is given the chance to reclaim his lost innocence, which for Dickens is associated with imagination and wonder. Adult cares, avarice, and selfishness have deadened Scrooge's imaginative power. The adult Scrooge, we are told, "had less fancy about him than any man in London."

The Ghost of Christmas Past brings together several uniquely Dickensian motifs: the importance of memory, the need for adults to retain childlike qualities, and the connection between memory, imagination, and compassion. Scrooge first remembers his past and recovers his ability to feel; next, his imagination is quickened by the presence of his make-believe friends. Memory plus imagination prompts compassion—itself a form of imagination, since it allows us to transcend ourselves and feel what

others feel. It is precisely at this moment that Scrooge recalls a young caroler he had sent away earlier:

"I wish, . . . but it's too late now."
"What is the matter?" asked the Spirit.
"Nothing," said Scrooge. "Nothing. There was a boy singing a Christmas carol at my door last night. I should like to have given him something: that's all."

If Dickens, the ghostly author, works his magic properly, what happens to Scrooge should now be happening to us—in other words, the author is to us what the ghosts are to Scrooge. Scrooge sympathizes with his child-self just as he once identified with the fictional Ali Baba, and in so doing he is able to extend his compassion to the young caroler. We identify with Scrooge, also a fictional character, and by vicariously feeling his loneliness, we feel compassion for real human beings.

In revisiting his past, Scrooge watches a tragicomedy that evokes in him both tears and laughter. He sees his dead sister young and strong (and it's at this point that we realize that Fred is Fan's son); the joyous young laughter of the Fezziwig Ball, his breakup with Belle, his increasing indifference to humanity, and his growing love of gold. Scrooge not only witnesses past mistakes but relives them—and with that horrible, sinking feeling of "if only."

At the Fezziwig Ball Scrooge sees the employer he might have been, a man who loves and is beloved by his employees. At Belle's house he sees a happy family, the children he might have had. These scenes, particularly those with Belle, are harrowing; Scrooge must passively watch himself creating his desolate future. Watching the shadows of the past is so unbearable that Scrooge is practically blinded by raw pain, as if he were staring directly at the sun. It's at this moment of intense agony that he physically quenches the ghost's flame, crying out, "Haunt me no longer!" Although this is a tale of the supernatural, Scrooge's pain is familiar; who has not also been similarly haunted? *All* memories are ghosts, shadows of the past that haunt the present, reminding us of what might have been.

It is strange that the *Carol* is regarded as a child's tale. It portrays the ache of regret, nostalgia, and longing that can only be experienced by adults.

STAVE THE THIRD

*T*he scenes with the Ghost of Christmas Past are so essential and moving that readers tend to dismiss the next two spirits as inconsequential. But Scrooge must live through his past, his present, and his future before he can be reborn on Christmas morning.

Scrooge must pass through the stages of his life because *A Christmas Carol* is a parable of the generations, exhorting us to care not just for our own children but for all needy children before it is too late. Otherwise, we create a world where Ignorance and Want thrive, and men like Scrooge flourish.

The first ghost quickens Scrooge's dormant tenderness and prompts his compassion for those who remind him of himself. But the second ghost goes even further, showing him his immediate circle, the Cratchits and Fred, his wife and friends, and then widening the circle by taking him to remote places of desolation and suffering, of joy, abundance, and fellowship. First, they walk the city streets, where all, rich and poor alike, are united in their celebration of Christmas.

We see the city through Scrooge's newly opened eyes. Everything, from the "piles of filberts, mossy and brown" to the "Norfolk Biffins, squab and swarthy," is portrayed with loving attention to detail. The surface of ordinary life gleams with the Christmas spirit.

They go to the Cratchits', and then to Fred's party. The homely Cratchits, with their shabby clothes and meager food, have a radiance that emanates from their own domestic warmth. At Fred's the joy is so contagious that even Scrooge forgets himself and joins their parlor games as if he were actually present. Bob Cratchit and Fred are no longer simply Scrooge's clerk and poor relation, but men with real lives of their own. Scrooge enters into their worlds, seeing them from a new perspective, and he begins to care about them: "Spirit," said Scrooge with an interest he had never felt before, "tell me if Tiny Tim will live." "I see a vacant seat," replied the ghost, "in the poor chimney-corner, and a crutch without an owner, carefully preserved." "No, no," says Scrooge. "Oh, no, kind Spirit! Say he will be spared." To which the ghost answers, echoing the old Scrooge's words, "If he be like to die, he had better do it, and decrease the surplus population." Scrooge's precious theories, utilitarianism and Malthusianism, which stress the masses over the individual, dwindle to nothing when that individual has a name and is known and loved. The poor are no longer an anonymous mass. As Scrooge learns, it is very hard to be indifferent when one mingles with one's kind. Since he hadn't visited his nephew or the Cratchits before, Scrooge never imagined that they had real lives. This is why he could dismiss them as "surplus population," or relegate them to prisons and workhouses.

But the ghost widens Scrooge's circle ever further: he is now taken below the earth, where miners celebrate the season; to wild seas, where lonely mariners have their bit of cheer; and to the rude, uncivilized places on the globe where the seasonal spirit lights the darkness.

The climactic moment in stave 3 occurs precisely at the end, leaving us, and Scrooge, much to think about. Suddenly, the ghost opens his robe and reveals the shocking sight of two bestial children called Ignorance and Want. They are not cute Dickensian waifs like Oliver:

They were a boy and girl. Yellow, meagre, ragged, scowling, wolfish, but prostrate, too, in their humility. Where graceful youth should have filled their features out . . . a stale and shrivelled hand, like that of age, had pinched, and twisted them, and pulled them into shreds.

The horror of this description may be one reason why this scene is usually cut from dramatizations and film versions. We like our *Carol* sweet and un-cluttered, untainted by bitterness. But such portrayals are gross distortions of the *Carol* Dickens wrote. Just as the ghost hides the children beneath his luxuriant robes, the Victorian age, Dickens believed, hid social ills with a show of prosperity.

The first spirit revealed personal sorrow; this spirit discloses a public shame. With all the righteousness of an Old Testament prophet, he expresses the author's anger toward those who would forget and ignore their obligation to such children. "Have they no refuge or resource?" cries Scrooge. To which the ghost, wise teacher, replies, "Are there no prisons? Are there no work-houses?" So stave 3 ends, with the echo of Scrooge's own words ringing in his ears.

STAVE THE FOURTH

*I*n no time the third phantom appears, looking like Death in an Ingmar Bergman film. Draped in sepulchral black robes, he is a hooded shape who mutely communicates with Scrooge by throwing out one long arm. By this time Scrooge has been stripped of all his defenses. He is now in a realm beyond language.

It is Christmas Day, sometime in the future. We realize, as Scrooge does not, that he is dead. In *It's a Wonderful Life,* George Bailey is shown what life would have been had he never been born; Scrooge is now shown what life will be after he dies. Whereas Bailey once saved someone from dying, Scrooge sees a death he might have prevented. After the Ghost of Christmas Present's exhortation, Scrooge realizes that he alone is responsible for Tiny Tim's death.

In stave 1, Scrooge recognizes his child-self and weeps; in the fourth and final stave, he cannot find himself at all. All he knows is that someone has died, unloved and unmourned, and although he doesn't know the dead man, he begs to be shown one person who "feels some emotion caused by this man's death." But "the only emotion that the ghost could show him was one of pleasure." The dead Scrooge aids the poor in a way he never did in life: his bed curtains and linens are stolen by his charwoman; his shirt is stripped from his corpse and sold. As carrion to be picked over and exchanged for cash, Scrooge is now used in death as he once used others in life.

The final moment is a recognition scene with a vengeance: Scrooge at last understands that the strange dead man is himself. The deeds of the past have led inexorably to this vision of the future. Scrooge begs the ghost, "Oh, tell me I may sponge away the writing on this stone!" If *Carol* were a tragedy, the answer would be no, the writing on the stone indelible. But since it is a tragi-comedy, the date and words are not yet fully chiseled. Scrooge has more story left in him yet.

THE FINAL STAVE: THE MORNING AFTER

Scrooge's awakening reads like a sigh of relief from the tension that has been building through the last four staves. With a rush, he realizes that he is not dead, that it's still Christmas, and that above all, he has been given a future full of Christmases in which to atone for the past. The rhythm of the prose captures Scrooge's rising excitement as he touches everything, testing its tactile reality. "Yes! And the bedpost was his own. The bed was his own, the room was his own. Best and happiest of all, the Time before him was his own, to make amends in." If *Carol* were set to music, the tempo of each movement would accelerate to this head-spinning finale. The sense of relief is a sense of release. The formerly hardened, tight-lipped Scrooge is unhinged and babbling: "I am as light as a feather, I am as happy as an angel, I am as merry as a schoolboy. I am as giddy as a drunken man. A merry Christmas to everybody." Given a second chance, Scrooge is reborn: "I am quite a baby," he cries.

Scrooge doesn't waste a minute bewailing lost years or brooding over the past (like the embittered Miss Havisham of *Great Expectations*) but lives from this moment solely in the present. The miser who saves for an illusory future now lives—and spends—today. The dimensions of time unite in the eternal Now: "I will live in the Past, Present and Future," he vows.

Most important for Dickens, the story ends with Scrooge's assimilation into the community. No longer estranged from society, his first gesture after he wakes up is to go into the streets and greet his fellow citizens. Unlike a modern hero for whom self-discovery is an end in itself, Scrooge's new wisdom affects the entire community.

❖ ❖ ❖

Why has this slight tale endured and inspired such fanatical devotion, remaining as fresh and timely as the day it was written? One reason may be that the story provides the catharsis of great tragedy without its horror and pessimism. In so doing, *A Christmas Carol* speaks to all of us in a way that *King Lear* and *Hamlet,* for all their magisterial greatness, do not. We watch Scrooge undergo his grueling ordeal, identify with him, and leave the theater or the book cleansed and renewed. *Carol,* in short, is a tragicomedy, not tragedy (which portrays a world in which one choice irrevocably leads to a future that can never be altered). Lear's howl, "Never, never, never, never," is the essence of tragedy. Scrooge's cry is not "never," but rather an optimistic "maybe."

Scrooge will never recover his wasted years, but he can change his present, and thus his future. He has been given a reprieve. *A Christmas Carol* leaves us, or should leave us, with an apocalyptic sense of urgency to love our neighbors before it is too late. It moves us because it reassures us that no matter how old or hidebound we've become, change, even wondrous change, is possible.

HISTORY OF A STORY

One of literature's little ironies: Dickens's parable of a reformed miser was written for the money. *Martin Chuzzlewit,* his current serial, was falling in sales, and in an effort to boost his flagging income, Dickens dashed off a tale for the Christmas of 1843 in about six weeks. The manuscript for his "Ghostly little book" is a scant sixty-six pages, as compared to the usual eight hundred for the typical Dickens blockbuster, yet it is the biggest seller he ever wrote.

Which doesn't mean he didn't believe passionately in what he was writing about. The previous summer he had visited a "ragged school," part of an evangelical movement to provide basic instruction to poor children. Although he disapproved of religious indoctrination, believing that the poor need a bath more than a psalm, he firmly held that ignorance is inseparable from want. The school was Fagin territory: the children, poorly clothed and underfed, were already pimps, prostitutes, and thieves—hardly the cherubic waifs associated with Dickens. The sight of such wretchedness horrified and unnerved him: "I have very seldom seen in all the strange and dreadful things I have seen in London and elsewhere, anything so shocking as the dire neglect of soul and body exhibited in these children."

In a piece for the *Examiner,* he wrote, "Side by side with Crime, Disease, and Misery in England, Ignorance is always brooding." Thus the germinating image of *A Christmas Carol* was not that of the ghosts, Scrooge, or even Tiny Tim, but the two "monsters," the allegorical children Ignorance and Want. Dickens had intended a tract on education for the poor, but he now decided to write a story that, he announced with justifiable hyperbole, would hit his readers over the head like a "sledge-hammer."

This sledgehammer of a Christmas story is a reminder that Dickens is one of the few, if not the only, examples in literature of someone who did well by doing good. Like the old Scrooge, Dickens was a man of business, and like the reformed one, he never forgot that mankind was his business.

Dickens worked like a demon to have the tale in the stores before Christmas. *A Christmas Carol* was published by December 19, 1843, and by Christmas Eve more than 6,000 copies had been sold. By January of the new year an extraordinary 9,000 copies were in print. But in February Dickens learned that he had only earned 230 pounds for the first 6,000 copies. He had, he confessed, "set [his] heart and soul upon a Thousand clear." The book was beautifully and expensively packaged, and most of his royalties were absorbed by printing costs, which he paid himself. To add to his disappointment, the literary parasites were quick to swarm around the story, spewing out imitations, parodies, spin-offs, and sequels, from which he never received a cent.

Though critically well received, *Carol* did not do as well in the United States as Dickens had hoped. Americans, still smarting over his attack on their country in *American Notes,* were not yet ready to buy another Dickens book.

Haunted by the specter of his impecunious father, Dickens believed he was ruined. The financial failure of both *Carol* and *Chuzzlewit* embittered him, and deciding that it would be cheaper to live on the Continent, he packed up his entire family and moved to Italy, where the bells of Genoa made him long for home. Thus in yet another great irony, the story that epitomizes English warmth helped drive its author abroad.

But ultimately *A Christmas Carol* did not fail him: years later his dramatic readings of that one tale earned him more money than any of his books.

A WINTER'S MORALITY TALE

Spine-chilling tales should not be a solitary vice; they are meant to be told or read aloud. And what better time to do so than at Christmas, which has a long association with ghostly visitors in folklore? Dickens, however, was the first to link a ghost story with Christmas, and other writers have since followed his lead. In Henry James's *The Turn of the Screw,* one of the most terrifying tales ever written, the ghost story is recounted to guests in an ancient manor on Christmas Eve. M. R. James and Robertson Davies devised many of their spectral tales as Christmas entertainments. Perhaps the ancient association between the holiday and ghost stories arose from the superstition that on Christmas Eve "no spirit dares walk abroad" (*Hamlet*); thus the time itself was propitious, allowing one to talk freely of unearthly matters without fear that an infernal eavesdropper might take revenge.

A Christmas Carol is different from other specimens of the genre and has almost none of the chilling features that constitute the classic ghost story. It is a cautionary tale with ghosts as agents of reformation rather than of revenge. The haunting of Scrooge is intended not merely to frighten its audience but to scare them into virtue.

DICKENS'S OWN CHRISTMAS

Like the converted Scrooge, Dickens religiously kept Christmas each year, particularly Twelfth Night, the feast of the Epiphany, the last night of

Christmas. As his son Charley commented, "My father was always at his best at Christmas." The season brought out all of Dickens's most endearing qualities—his hospitality, graciousness, generosity, sense of fun, and genius for entertaining. No one knows why this particular holiday meant so much to Dickens. But it's worth noting that the worst day of his childhood was December 25, 1822, the day he traveled from Chatham to London, leaving behind the happiest days of his life. Perhaps the fevered celebrations of his adulthood were a way of undoing and forgetting his own miserable childhood holidays.

In 1843, the year he wrote *A Christmas Carol,* Dickens hosted a yuletide saturnalia that no one who was there would ever forget. After plugging away at *Chuzzlewit* and *Carol* without a break, his pent-up spirits broke out like Niagara after a thaw. Conjuring, dancing quadrilles, mixing milk punch, his face beaming with mirth and mischief, Dickens celebrated with a vengeance that year. He can barely contain his excitement as he recounts the events to Miss Burdett-Coutts:

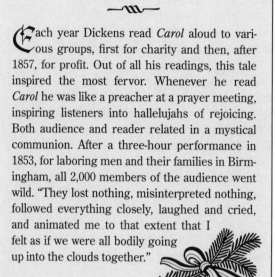

Each year Dickens read *Carol* aloud to various groups, first for charity and then, after 1857, for profit. Out of all his readings, this tale inspired the most fervor. Whenever he read *Carol* he was like a preacher at a prayer meeting, inspiring listeners into hallelujahs of rejoicing. Both audience and reader related in a mystical communion. After a three-hour performance in 1853, for laboring men and their families in Birmingham, all 2,000 members of the audience went wild. "They lost nothing, misinterpreted nothing, followed everything closely, laughed and cried, and animated me to that extent that I felt as if we were all bodily going up into the clouds together."

> Forster is out again; and if he don't go in again after the manner in which we have been keeping Christmas, he must be very strong indeed. Such dinings, such theatre goings, such kissings out of old years and kissings in of new ones never took place in these parts before.

Never one for niggling qualifiers, his self-descriptions are peppered with such expressions as "No one has ever seen" and "You have never seen." Whatever he does, it's never like what anyone else has done. With Dickens such hyperbole often proves justified.

Even the acerbic Jane Carlyle, wife of the philosopher and a dour party guest, confirmed Dickens's account. Watching the proceedings in awe, she declared that Dickens and Forster "seemed *drunk* with their efforts . . . the *very* most agreeable party that I was ever at in London."

A "CHRISTMASSY GUY"

*I*n 1905, G. K. Chesterton (who tended to get misty when it came to Dickens) wrote, "The mystery of Christmas is in a manner identical with the mystery of Dickens." What he meant by this is itself a mystery, but he was accurate about one thing: Dickens is inseparable from Christmas. Even in his own lifetime, he was regarded as the presiding genius of the season of comfort and joy. It's been said that when Dickens died, children all over England asked if the holiday would die as well. The association between Dickens and Christmas is so strong that Chesterton approvingly called the author's ebullient side (as opposed to his dark, political or sardonic one) the "Christmassy Dickens."

But Dickens and Christmas are not all sweetness and light. As he aged, his outlook became less syrupy, more sour. Pip's Christmas in *Great Expectations* is one of the more miserable in literature, and the worst holiday ever was probably the one spent, or rather not spent, by murder victim Edwin Drood in Dickens's unfinished mystery.

> *The next time someone tells you he longs for a typically Dickensian Christmas, ask him if he has in mind the kind of Christmas Eve Dickens gave to Edwin Drood.*
> —BILL VAN DE WATER, CBS News archivist

🍃 CAROLIANA 🍃

❋ *Carol* has had a profound effect on audiences ever since Dickens started reading it aloud in 1843. For some listeners, the impact was not merely dramatic but a conversion experience. When Dickens read *Carol* in Boston in 1867, a Mr. Fairbanks, a manufacturer of scales, was so moved that he vowed to "break the custom we have hitherto observed of opening the works on Christmas day." True to his word, he closed his factory that Christmas and, in keeping with his new Scrooge spirit, dispensed holiday turkeys to all his workers.

✣In 1993 SCROOGE—the Society to Curtail Ridiculous, Outrageous and Ostentatious Gift Exchanges—was founded. Members of SCROOGE, according to E. S. Turner in *Unwrapping Christmas,* encourage sensible gifts such as smoke detectors, first-aid kits, and gift certificates for self-improvement courses.

✣The famous phrase, "and Tiny Tim who did NOT die," was actually an afterthought on Dickens's part. At the time, critics thought Dickens should have left the boy's fate open: "The fate of Tiny Tim," sniffed one critic in the *Dickensian,* "should be a matter of dignified reticence. . . . Dickens was carried away by exuberance, and momentarily forgot good taste." Dickens felt compelled to tie up every loose strand of a story, no matter how minor. To leave an audience in doubt violated a crucial Dickensian tenet.

✣The cynical Robert Benchley, who made reading *Carol* an annual ritual, wrote that he cried "not at the sad parts, but at the parts that are so glad that they shut off your wind."

✣The cheery tone Dickens affected in his annual Christmas books was often a strain. He found it difficult to interrupt the novel he was working on with a sprightly story in accord with the happy season. When he had difficulties writing the aptly titled "Battle of Life," and had fallen behind in his labors, Dickens, with forgivable cheerlessess, groused: "I am in the preliminary seclusion and ill-temper of the Christmas book."

*T*he classic Scrooge: Alastair Sim, who seems more tormented than malicious—perhaps a result of the 1950s craze for psychoanalysis (1951).

✣W. C. Fields, a natural for the part, agreed to play Scrooge, but only if he could stop before he was redeemed.

✣The poignant illnesses that appear so frequently in Victorian novels are usually given vague diagnoses such as "brain fever" or "wasting disease." Tiny Tim is called "crippled" or "lame," without any further explanation. Despite the crutch, it may not have been Tim's legs that were diseased, but rather his kidneys. According to at least one modern physician, Tiny Tim suffered from an advanced state of distal renal tubular acidosis (type 1). Dr. Donald Lewis of the Medical

College of Hampton Roads in Norfolk, Virginia, "examined" Tiny Tim to show his medical students how to diagnose children. Here are the symptoms that led to Dr. Lewis's diagnosis:

1. Tiny Tim was small, like his father, who was also described as short. Tim was, however, perfectly proportioned.

2. He used only one crutch, so presumably only one side of his body was affected.

3. His weakness and withered hand suggest a disturbance of the nervous system.

4. Tim's prognosis was bad, but when Scrooge offered medical assistance, he survived. The disease is lethal if left untreated.

❋ There is another Tiny Tim disease: excessive sentimentality. The queen of Norway was already in an advanced stage of the illness in 1906 when she proclaimed, "No one can be really bad who can cry over Tiny Tim. Whenever I feel a wee bit selfish I read *A Christmas Carol* through and then I feel as though I must do something to brighten the lives of the many brave-hearted little cripples there are in the world." Every Christmas she would send gifts to poor children bearing a card, "With Tiny Tim's Love."

IS THERE NO PROZAC?

In a piece for the *Boston Globe* called "Scrooge on the Couch," Madeline Drexler asked two psychologists for their "clinical impressions" of Scrooge's anti-social behavior. She first describes her subject: "The Patient: Ebenezer Scrooge, Presenting Symptoms: 'Edges his way along crowded paths of life, warning all human sympathy to keep its distance; secret and self-contained' . . . persistent use of epithet 'Bah Humbug!' "

John G. Norcross, a specialist on behavioral changes, offered the following diagnosis: "I would say Ebenezer Scrooge is a classic anal-retentive with antisocial and narcissistic features—self-importance, lack of empathic capacity, egocentric perception. . . . [Scrooge's] facade developed as a defense against hurt. He takes out his emotional pain on the rest of the world."

Philip Levendusky, director of ambulatory care at McLean [Psychiatric] Hospital in Belmont, Massachusetts, comments: "The world was not a loving place, a place he could trust. He was probably a fragile sort of child. He developed a rough, crusty style. I would think of the likelihood of Scrooge having an abuse history. . . . We're probably also talking a low-grade obsessive-compulsive disorder."

❋ Not even Tiny Tim's creator was immune: when reading *Carol* aloud, Dickens never failed to weep when he came to the part about Tiny Tim. Late in life he would resort to opium to calm his nerves after reading that part of *Carol*.

✤In 1992 a mock trial was held in the San Francisco Court of Historical Review and Appeals to determine whether it was fair to use the name "Scrooge" as a synonym for greed. Although the ghost of Jack Benny was invoked for the defense, Municipal Judge George T. Choppelas refused to clear Scrooge's name.

✤*Kristnakska Sonoraddo: Rakonto de la Glora Angla Autoro, Charles Dickens. Esperantigita de Martyn Westcott.* For those who don't recognize it, this is the title of *A Christmas Carol* in Esperanto. A 1908 review in the *Dickensian* hailed this latest effort as "invaluable" for those who know *Carol* by heart but who would like to become more conversant in Esperanto. The famous opening, rendered in the universal language, reads: "Marley estis seuviva. Neuia dubo pri tio. La protokolo pri lia enterigo estis subskribita de le pastro, la ekleziulo, la cerkforisto kaj la cef-ploreguls. Scrooge gin subskribis. Kaj la nomo Scrooge multe estis lakaota pri ia aju afero en la Borso." An Esperanto expert assured Dickensians that the translation was not only true to the spirit, "but also, to an extent infinitely greater than [the original]."

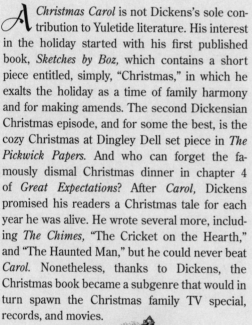

A Christmas Carol is not Dickens's sole contribution to Yuletide literature. His interest in the holiday started with his first published book, *Sketches by Boz,* which contains a short piece entitled, simply, "Christmas," in which he exalts the holiday as a time of family harmony and for making amends. The second Dickensian Christmas episode, and for some the best, is the cozy Christmas at Dingley Dell set piece in *The Pickwick Papers.* And who can forget the famously dismal Christmas dinner in chapter 4 of *Great Expectations?* After *Carol,* Dickens promised his readers a Christmas tale for each year he was alive. He wrote several more, including *The Chimes,* "The Cricket on the Hearth," and "The Haunted Man," but he could never beat *Carol.* Nonetheless, thanks to Dickens, the Christmas book became a subgenre that would in turn spawn the Christmas family TV special, records, and movies.

✤In December 1994 the Ethics Panel of the Graduate School of the College of Business at the University of Denver published an essay in the *Rocky Mountain News* in which Scrooge was hailed as "a successful business person." As proof, they cite his "considerable wealth" and his ability to "run a tight ship.... His offices were kept cool to save on fuel (an early conservationist, no doubt) and his employees were paid the 'going wage.'" In giving Bob the day off, Scrooge showed his willingness to engage in "participative management."

✤Albert Finney's 1970 musical *Scrooge* is a *Carol* for the swinging youth culture. Finney, even in makeup, is the youngest, best-looking Scrooge ever, more middle-aged than elderly.

*A*lbert Finney, one of the youngest Scrooges ever, in the 1970 "psychedelic" musical, *Scrooge.*

❧ "Are there no workhouses?" replies Scrooge when asked for a charitable donation. A century and a half later the question once again becomes timely. In 1994, the Speaker of the House of Representatives, Newt Gingrich (a name worthy of Dickens!), recommended the return to orphanages as a solution to the rising numbers of unwanted children. As proof of their worthiness, he cited the movie *Boy's Town.* The Democrats told him to read *Oliver Twist.* Gingrich was portrayed as Scrooge on the cover of *Newsweek,* and journalists everywhere compared him to the famous skinflint.

*M*y premise is that the first Ghost is the one who does the converting, not the other two. The one who brings Scrooge back to his childhood is the one who has the deepest effect. The others are booster rockets.
—ROGER ROSENBLATT

*R*ob Roger's *A GOP Christmas Carol,* with Ebenewter Scrooge. Dickens's tale has been adapted for political purposes almost from the day he wrote it. *The New York Times,* November 27, 1994.

His *fifteen longer novels languish on the bookshelves in comparison*
to the perennial popularity of A Christmas Carol. *Today we don't read*
the best of Dickens or the worst of Dickens: we read the least of Dickens.
—ELIOT ENGEL

You *try to lead a good life. But it's that knowledge of our weaknesses that*
gives us compassion. My favorite line is that last line. The thing about,
"And they say no man could keep Christmas as well as Ebenezer
Scrooge." I think that would be a nice way to live.
—JAY LENO (who confessed he reads the story annually), *Parade,* December 1993

I *could never see why people were so happy about Dickens's* A Christmas
Carol *because I never had any confidence that Scrooge was going to*
be any different the next day.
—KARL MENNINGER, *A Psychiatrist's World*

Shall *we ask what Scrooge would actually be like, if we were able to follow*
him beyond the frame of the story? Unquestionably, he would relapse into
moroseness, vindictiveness, suspicion. He would, that is to say, reveal
himself as a victim of a manic-depressive cycle, and a
very uncomfortable person.
—EDMUND WILSON, "The Two Scrooges"

Reading *Carol*

INTERVIEW WITH PATRICK STEWART

P atrick Stewart is one of the founders of the Royal Shakespeare Company and has played roles as diverse as Prospero in Joseph Papp's The Tempest *(1996) and Captain Jean-Luc Picard on* Star Trek: The Next Generation. *For the last nine years he has, like Dickens, induced tears and laughter with his dramatic reading of* A Christmas Carol, *which he has performed in London, on Broadway, and at numerous theaters and campuses across the United States.*

When Stewart tells the story of Scrooge's downfall and reformation, no one is ashamed to weep over the death of Tiny Tim, and the gravity of his rebuke as the Ghost of Christmas Present could shake the conscience of a sociopath. His choking, wheezing, sputtering rendition of Scrooge's first laugh as a new man sends shivers down an audience's spine.

His Carol *has won the New York Drama Critics Award, and broken box office records for a one-man show on Broadway.*

NE: *Why do you feel you must do* A Christmas Carol *every year?*

PS: This is going to be a long answer. I was on location in Derbyshire, and I was on standby, sitting in this little hotel waiting to be called. All they had in the lounge were some dog-eared paperbacks, and I was absolutely desperate for something to read. I pulled out this [holds up *Carol*] because it

*L*ike Dickens, Patrick Stewart "reads" *A Christmas Carol,* playing more than 200 different parts, from Mrs. Fezziwig to Tiny Tim.

was the thinnest volume in the house. Thank God I was never called that day. I read all through the morning, all through coffee and all through lunch with the book propped up at my table, and then on into the afternoon hours. What surprised me was that the story was something very different from all the adaptations I had ever seen. All along I had carried around a sense of what *A Christmas Carol* was—a marionette version, a rather jolly, eccentric bit of mid-Victorian writing about some slightly bizarre and amusing characters—a harmless, soft piece of work. It's interesting about *A Christmas Carol:* It's like *Hamlet*—half the world knows "To be, or not to be," but very little else. Everybody knows "Bah, humbug!" but not the real *Carol.*

NE: *When did you decide to make it a one-man show?*

PS: After I started doing *Star Trek,* I wanted to do something so I wouldn't lose my theater skills. I was asked by my brother, who sings in the choir at a small northern town in England, if I would perform something for their organ restoration fund, and I didn't know what the hell to do. It quickly occurred to me that here was an excellent subject, an opportunity to get to know the

piece. What impressed me was that on a bitterly cold December night, people were visibly moved. I was moved, too. Even now after eight years there are two or three sections of the story that overwhelm me emotionally, simply take me apart whenever I come to them. There are two moments—there are a lot of them—but there are two in particular that affected me that night in that church.

NE: *You make it sound like the mystery of conversion. What are those two scenes?*

PS: The most potent occurs just toward the end of the Cratchits' Christmas Day; just after Tiny Tim sings a song [which Stewart sings in the reading in a high-pitched, sweet treble]. Dickens writes, "They were not a handsome family, they were not well-dressed, their shoes were well-worn, their clothes were scanty, but they were happy, pleased with one another and contented with the time." It overwhelms me, that moment. There is something about the affirmation of domestic happiness that I find very, very moving. The other is when Bob Cratchit breaks down when he talks about visiting the cemetery where Tiny Tim is buried. But there are other places too: the moment of Scrooge's most intense terror in the graveyard, when he tries to avoid looking at the grave and then he finally reads his name.

NE: *How did you prepare the text?*

PS: During the late summer, early autumn of 1987, I would work on the text every weekend. Looking back, those were some of my happiest days. And the more I worked on it, I felt I could almost feel the characters demanding that I get on my feet and perform. I found myself wanting to become the characters—they started to inhabit me. I put Dickens's reading version and mine side by side, and it was a *fascinating* study! To have done mine blind, and *then* to see what Dickens did! Because in so many places our cuts were *identical!*

NE: *Is there anything Dickens cut that you left in?*

PS: He changed as the years went by. What is most interesting is that he sentimentalized it; he started taking out everything that was hard, dark, grim, or uncomfortable. One reason for this was that he used *Carol* during the first half of his reading as an introduction to the murder of Nancy. So he was essentially trying to keep everything in the first part frothy, fun, and fantastical so he could heighten the dramatic effects in the second half. To my unimaginable horror, I discovered that during the last years of his readings, he never mentioned the two children, Ignorance and Want.

NE: *Isn't that an important moment?*

PS: Ahh, it is for me, certainly; it is one of the two or three critical moments of the whole evening, that moment when he produces the two children. Because if the audience doesn't get that, they won't get anything I have to say.

NE: *So the problem with our understanding of* Carol *is that we focus on Tiny Tim and "God bless us, every one" and not on the social horrors that Dickens is trying to expose?*

PS: Well, they aren't seen for very long. One moment Scrooge is traveling around seeing all these wonderful Christmases with the Ghost of Christmas Present, and then out of nowhere he is confronted by these two—as he calls them—Monsters. And he asks the question, "Have they no refuge?" This is a question that he never would have asked hours earlier.

NE: *Why is* Carol *so potent? Is it because Dickens writes about the kind of change we all secretly desire?*

PS: I don't think it is so much reformation as redemption.

NE: *Then is it because Dickens essentially affirms that redemption is possible? Is that why we return to this story, for solace?*

PS: Well, Dickens wasn't the first to do this. In many respects the story is like a lot of late Shakespeare. In the same way that Shakespeare needed elements such as magic, ghosts and spirits, and wild coincidence to complete his fables, so Dickens made the same choice with the meaning of his story. In *The Tempest,* and, most potently, *The Winter's Tale,* the heroes are given [whispers] *a second chance!* I think we all possess a very fundamental, ancient hunger to believe that we can be saved.

NE: *So it's really about getting a second chance?*

PS: *Yes!* That's what's so powerful about it! What happens to Scrooge is not that he's told, "You're going to die, mate." It has already *happened!* He's dead! The grave is *already* overgrown! *That's* what's so powerful about the scene at the graveyard! That's why his waking up at the end is all the more powerful.

NE: *What is this point that Scrooge finally "gets"?*

PS: [Long pause.] He has a feeling, he has a gentle feeling about someone else.

NE: *He feels tenderness? So the key is that he empathizes with himself, too, and through that feels for others.*

PS: That's *exactly* what he does. He says, "I wish, I wish," . . . and the ghost says, "What?" And Scrooge remembers the boy he sent away earlier.

NE: *Does your audience go out afterward and do good deeds?*

PS: I'm told they do. Joan Rivers came into the dressing room and said, "I am now going to do the typical Broadway audience leaving the theater: 'Get out of my way. It's my taxi!' " Mean, snarling, angry, irritable. Then she said, "I've just come out of the theater, and I've seen people say, 'No, no, after you. You go first, would you like to share my taxi?' I heard people say these things, they looked at one another and smiled as they walked out of your show."

NE: *Is that your goal?*

PS: Oh, absolutely. Well, no, I do the story for myself. I am compelled to tell the story over and over again. And twice on Thursdays and Saturdays. It kills me to do it. It terrifies me. Every performance terrifies me. The aftereffect is one of absolute exhaustion, but it's a story I have to tell for myself.

MIDDLE
Years

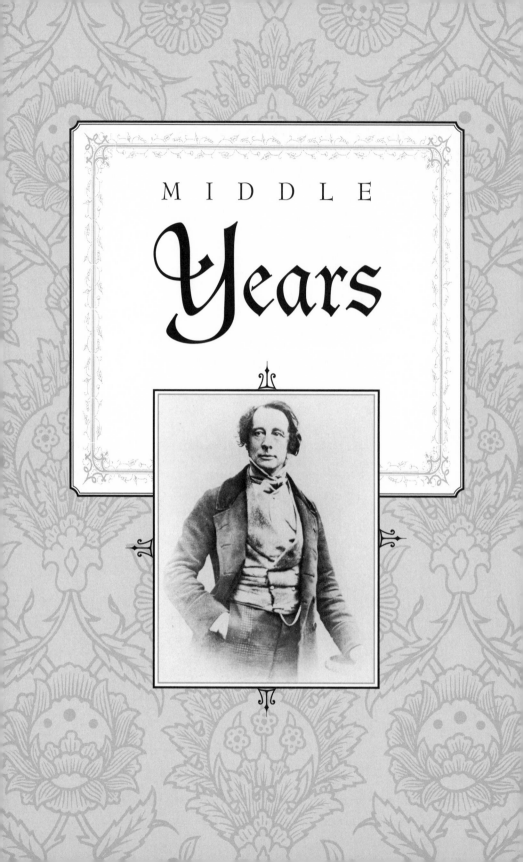

"Those Carefree, Memless Days"

♌ *Martin Chuzzlewit* was the last full-length novel "edited" by Boz. *Dombey and Son,* Dickens's seventh serialized novel and his first attempt to write serious fiction, proudly announces "By Charles Dickens" on its frontispiece. To move from *Pickwick* to *Dombey* (1845) is to witness a rite of passage from Boz, youthful humorist and entertainer, to Charles Dickens, mature author and conscience of England. He would never return to the high-spirited Pickwickian vein again.

The spontaneity and carnival atmosphere of *Pickwick, Nicholas Nickleby, The Old Curiosity Shop,* and *Martin Chuzzlewit* give way to the self-conscious artistry of *Dombey and Son* and *David Copperfield.* These in turn lead to the even more mature *Bleak House* and *Little Dorrit,* novels that reveal a willingness to probe deeper into human experience and demonstrate an acute awareness of society as a man-made disease. After *Chuzzlewit* a new tone slowly emerges, not only more mature and confident but also at times subversive and vituperative. Dickens's jaundiced view of society coexists with his belief in humanity's inherent goodness, and he creates novels in which darkness and horror reside uneasily with virtue and laughter.

What caused the change? The critic Alexander Welsh attributes Dickens's new cynicism to his disillusioning trip to America. Others maintain that Dickens was sufficiently perturbed by the commercial failure of *Chuzzlewit* to want to try more ambitious works. Moreover, his philanthropic efforts in the London slums may have forced him to confront realities that would have been impossible to ignore in his writing. Or perhaps Boz simply grew up.

Some readers welcomed the social critic and reformer, but most of his fans yearned for the Boz of *Pickwick*. It is an indication of contemporary taste that Dickens's current reputation rests almost entirely on the last six novels. Had he written nothing after *Dombey,* we would probably have regarded him as a humorist of genius, but certainly not a great novelist on the order of Tolstoy or Dostoyevsky.

With the publication of *Bleak House* in 1853, Victorian critics pounced on Dickens, declaring that he had abandoned his true gifts. In "Remonstrance with Dickens," J. C. Jeafferson mourned: "We sit down and weep when we remember thee, O *Pickwick*!" He was not alone. A critic at the *Saturday Review* wrote, "We admit Mr. Dickens has a mission, but it is to make the world grin, not to recreate and rehabilitate society."

IMAGING FORTH

*I*n the early years, from *Pickwick* to *Chuzzlewit,* Dickens occasionally wrote brief outlines, setting down ideas and plans for future installments, but mostly he relied on what he called "imaging forth," a form of intense concentration. (Thus Dickens hit upon a writing method that was later developed into a technique known as "using the right side of the brain" or "creative visualization.")

In January 1841, just as he was about to begin *Barnaby Rudge,* he glumly wrote, "Sat and thought all day; not writing a line; imaged forth a good deal of *Barnaby* by keeping my mind steadily upon him." (Dickens dreaded writing *Barnaby Rudge,* and had put off the novel for three years.) The imaging probably helped him get started. It required an unwavering focus on one idea or subject until it conformed to his will. By intently concentrating on an as-yet-unformed fictional subject, he could force it into a living presence.

Usually he devoted one day to determined mental effort, with the next given over to actual writing. He allowed his ideas to flow until he "ran out of steam," at which point he stopped and waited until the flow started again.

MEMS

*W*ith *Dombey and Son,* Dickens began his long habit of writing out copious working notes, or as he called them, "mems," an abbreviation of "memoranda." Mems contained outlines for future chapters, lists of potential fates for certain characters, questions concerning timing and pacing, and lists of possible names and titles. Sometimes a mem would take the form of a question, left to be answered at a later date: "Dora to die in this No? Yes. At the end." A mem might also be an imperative to himself:

Back to the opening chapter of the book, *strongly.*

or:

Smash Uriah Heep, by means of Mr. Micawber.

A mem is a record of a Dickensian brainstorm in which he sets down various plot possibilities that have been boiling in his imagination. It's as if he's talking to himself on paper, firing questions, answering them, raising new ones, arguing with himself, and finally reaching an answer.

As a mature artist, he would recall his early years as his "carefree, memless  days," when inspiration flowed. Harry Stone, editor of *Dickens's Working Notes,* makes the point that *Dombey* is the first novel "to exhibit that profound and sustained integration of theme, fable, image, and mood that would characterize all his later works. Whether the number plans enabled Dickens to achieve this new complexity or whether the new complexity made number plans mandatory is now impossible to tell." One suspects that there was a synchronicity between the two: Dickens's desire to write more ambitious fiction converged with and demanded that he write voluminous working notes. As he became famous and more aware of himself as an artist, he no longer allowed himself to write whatever came into his head. The inspiration that once happily flowed, unchecked, was now policed, reexamined, and weighed. He had, after all, a reputation to uphold.

In the mems for *David Copperfield,* some of his most detailed, he worries about the fate of the Murdstones. In the mem for the twelfth number, he writes: "Miss Murdstone Mr. Murdstone Not *yet.*" Then, in the fifteenth installment, he jots: "No, Consider for next No." While planning the next number, he raises the Murdstonian question once more: "No," he vehemently writes, adding a characteristic slash for weight. In the seventeenth number, he returns to the problem, reminding himself that it as yet remains unresolved. More decisively, he answers himself: "Not Yet." By the eighteenth number, the fate of the Murdstones is sealed: "No, Last No."

Dombey and Son

༜

ombey and Son is the closest Dickens ever came to writing a feminist novel. Despite its title, *Dombey* is about not a son but a daughter, and through her the novel celebrates the triumph of the feminine. In it Dickens strikes out against such male prerogatives as primogeniture and supremacy in marriage (though he does not go so far as to advocate female suffrage). In the Dickensian universe, good men and women remain in their separate spheres. The female draws inward, representing abstract virtues like fidelity, truth, and love; the male reaches out, creating railways, businesses, bureaucracies, and empires.

The novel opens with the events that bracket human experience: the birth of Paul Dombey and the death of his nameless mother. She is simply "Mrs. Dombey," and Paul is "and Son." Mr. Dombey, a Victorian Donald Trump, can only see the world in relation to the House of Dombey. He doesn't want a loving family but a commercial dynasty; to him women are born to breed, and marriage is a "matrimonial alliance" and a "social contract." As far as he's concerned, having done her wifely duty and delivered an heir, Mrs. Dombey can now die.

Dickens is no D. H. Lawrence, rhapsodizing over earth goddesses. But for him, as for Lawrence, women represented man's connection to the primitive: birth, nurturing, death. The bond between mother and child is like the gravitational pull between moon and sea, and the rupture of that tie at birth is the direct cause of Paul's decline and premature death. In the most profound sense of the word, he is weaned too soon. Paul doesn't die so much as ebb back into a watery womb. As he nears death, he cries out, "[H]ow the river runs, between its green banks and the rushes, Floy! But it's very near the sea. I hear the waves!"

Mr. Dombey's denial of the feminine and his lack of connection to basic elements of life leads to his downfall. By contrast his daughter, Florence, is intimate with the mysteries of love, birth, and death. But as a girl she is "nothing to speak of," a "bad boy," a "base coin" that "couldn't be invested." A girl is unable to turn herself into anything valuable, whereas a male heir is true currency. Florence is modest, affectionate, and faithful, but in Mr. Dombey's male-dominated world such values are dross.

As Mr. Dombey gloats over his new son, the six-year-old Florence embraces her dying mother. He watches uneasily, for Florence represents everything he is not, reminding him of a deficiency in his own nature. She personifies yearnings that Mr. Dombey has long since buried and forgotten.

These two female figures reside in a self-contained world in which Mr. Dombey's presence is superfluous. Throughout the novel Florence receives affections that rightly belong to him, and his two wives and son turn to her and recoil from him. Down the years his disquiet turns to hatred and disgust.

Paul Dombey is both his mother's son and his sister's child. Dreamy, preternaturally thoughtful, even effeminate, he deflates his father's dream of a vigorous successor to the House of Dombey. When he suddenly asks, "Papa! What's money?" the usually unflappable Mr. Dombey struggles to explain: "Gold, and silver, and copper. Guineas, shillings, halfpence. You know what they are?" But Paul replies, "Oh yes, I know what they are. . . . I don't mean that, Papa. I mean what's money after all?" With that question the child undermines everything his father stands for—the monetary yoke that ties society together.

Paul is often regarded as the epitome of mid-Victorian sappiness, a male Little Nell, languishing forever on a deathbed. But he is also the forerunner of such modern characters as Thomas Hardy's suicidal little Father Time and Thomas Mann's Hanno Buddenbrook, the wise child, weary of existence itself. These children of the twilight are too exhausted to carry their parental legacy into the next generation; they are emblems of a dying race and the need for a new order. Through the death of "the Son," Dickens suggests that Mr. Dombey's way of life is also destined for extinction.

After Paul's death, the novel focuses on Florence and her yearning for her absent father as Mr. Dombey's adventures take a different turn. In need of a

Dombey and Son marks Dickens's break with his Boz persona and his first attempt to write serious fiction. It's a transitional work, lacking the exuberance of the youthful fiction, while hinting at darker themes to come. For the first time, Dickens braids several stories into a coherent plot, tying them up neatly—perhaps too neatly—at the end. Dombey repays a second and even a third reading—but, as Mr. Dombey's sister would say, an effort is required.

new family, he "buys" a wife on the marriage market. His bride, Edith Skewton Granger Dombey, intelligent, sensual, and self-destructive, is one of Dickens's most complex portraits of a lady. In Edith, Mr. Dombey meets his match. Through her, Dickens presents marriage from the perspective of a proud, independent woman who must marry to survive. With rare insight for a Dickens heroine, Edith sees through the illusions of romance. For her, courtship is another word for negotiation and marriage is simply a business contract. The night before her wedding, she informs her mother:

> "You know he has bought me. . . . Or that he will tomorrow. He has considered of his bargain; he has shown it to his friend; he is even rather proud of it; he thinks that it will suit him, and may be had sufficiently cheap; and that he will buy to-morrow. God, that I have lived for this, and that I feel it!"

With her mother as her bawd, she has been hawked at spas until, as she puts it, "The last grain of self-respect is dead within me, and I loathe myself." This sort of marriage is just another act of self-degradation. And, to emphasize further the correspondence between matrimony and prostitution, Dickens creates a double for Edith in her fallen cousin, Alice Marwood. Legal marriage and prostitution differ only in degree.

Edith ultimately takes her revenge: she publicly humiliates her husband by eloping with his manager, Mr. Carker, and then, just when Carker is poised for seduction and gloating over his prize, she in turn derisively abandons him. Both Florence and Edith, the novel's central women, strip arrogant men of their power, leaving them defenseless and essentially castrated. Thus in one of those classically Freudian scenes that validate psychoanalytic symbolism, Carker is dismembered just after Edith humiliates him.

Throughout the novel other male voices are heard, each sounding a different version of masculinity. Major Joe Bagstock's bluster is a byword of masculine egoism and sexual bravado:

> He was mightily proud of awakening an interest in Miss Tox, and tickled his vanity with the fiction that she was a splendid woman who had her eye on him. This he had several times hinted at the club: in connexion with little jocularities, of which old Joe Bagstock, old Joey Bagstock, old J. Bagstock, old Josh Bagstock, or so forth, was the perpetual theme. . . .
>
> "Joey B, Sir," the Major would say, with a flourish of his walking-stick, "is worth a dozen of you. If you had a few more of the Bagstock breed among you, Sir, you'd be none the worse for it. Old Joe, Sir, needn't look far for a wife even now, if he was on the look-out; but he's hard-hearted, Sir, is Joe—he's tough, Sir, tough, and de-vilish sly!"

And Mr. Carker, with his monstrous "regiment" of glistening white teeth, represents the carnivorous male at his ugliest.

But of course there are other men in the novel besides Messrs. Carker and

Dombey and Major Bagstock. Florence escapes her father's gloomy house to Sol Gills's instrument shop, where she finds different types of men: the self-effacing Mr. Toots with his repeated disclaimer, "It's of no consequence," and the sexless yet nurturing bachelors Sol Gills and Captain Cuttle. These men share a love for Florence that approaches veneration. Outside the Dombey circle, women are all-powerful—sometimes to the point of comedy: Captain Cuttle lives in perpetual terror of his virago landlady, Mrs. MacStinger; Mr. Toots defers to the intellectual superiority of his wife, Susan Nipper; and, finally, Walter Gay, a modern Dick Whittington, the poor boy who grew up to be Lord Mayor of London, marries Florence Dombey, daughter of the richest man in town.

The battle of wills between Edith and Mr. Dombey ultimately leads to Florence's flight, Mr. Carker's grisly mutilation, and the destruction of the House of Dombey. Mr. Dombey is "ruined" and "fallen"—adjectives typically applied to women. Stripped of his property, he is feminized, symbolically castrated.

Edith may be his nemesis, but in the end Florence is his savior. Up to now, she has been portrayed as a sympathetic girl, hungry for a father's love. Now a woman with children of her own, she assumes more mythic and powerful proportions than any one character can—or should—in a work. She becomes the embodiment of Woman, the life-giver to whom Mr. Dombey, chastened and childlike, now turns. She becomes her father's mother, nursing the broken man back to emotional and physical health. Like King Lear, Mr. Dombey is restored to his daughter—but he must lose everything first.

Finally, Mr. Dombey's singular affection for Florence's daughter, Little Florence, suggests that he has learned to treasure the feminine, and in the end the true inheritors of the House of Dombey are daughters. The triumph of the feminine is joyously summed up by Miss Tox's resounding cry: "Dombey and Son is a daughter after all!"

🐚 FATHERS AND DAUGHTERS 🐚

In *Dombey,* Dickens goes beyond childhood desolation and focuses on one of the most poignant themes in literature: the unique relationship between father and daughter.

When stripped of sentiment and melodrama, *Dombey* is an accurate and moving portrayal of a sensitive girl's yearning for an absent father, or what psychologists call "father hunger." According to the psychoanalyst Sydney Greenspan, the father's task is to help his daughter emerge from her symbiotic immersion with the mother and guide her into the world beyond. But when Florence rises from her mother's deathbed, there is no outstretched hand, and she remains fixed in the past, locked in the realm of the dead. After her brother's death she waits passively in her house, eager for her father's return. Like a sleeping fairy-tale princess, or Tennyson's Mariana of "the moated grange," she is suspended in time, unable to grow up and take her place in the world.

Like many neglected children, Florence blames herself for her father's inability to love her, and she struggles to find a way to unlock his frozen heart. In her innocence, she believes that there is something she can do, one special act that will win his love.

> Florence hoped that the more she knew, and the more accomplished she became, the more glad he would be when he came to know and like her. Sometimes she wondered, with a swelling heart and a rising tear, whether she was proficient enough in anything to surprise him when they should become companions. Sometimes she tried to think if there were any kind of knowledge that would bespeak his interest more readily than another.

The decisive break comes when her father, in his hatred and rage, knocks her down and makes accusations so ugly that there can be no turning back.

> She looked at him, and a cry of desolation issued from her heart. For as she looked, she saw him murdering the fond idea to which she had held in spite of him. She saw his cruelty, neglect, and hatred dominant above it, and stamping it down. She saw she had no father upon earth, and ran out, orphaned from the house.

When she finally realizes that the father she yearned for never existed, she can renounce her neurotic attachment. Liberated from her father-obsession, she flees his house with its echoes of the dead and transfers her affection to a more felicitous substitute.

Shortly after her epiphany, Walter Gay is conveniently "resurrected"—he was thought to have drowned—and the two are soon married. The tolling death-knell sound of "Dom-bey" is replaced by the lilting "Gay," and with her new name, Florence is reborn. The father, discarded and alone, has become what the daughter once was, and the generational roles are reversed, with the daughter the mother to the man.

✤Dickens was no Mr. Dombey; unlike many men of his generation, he favored daughters over sons. Upon being presented with his seventh son in March 1852, he glumly wrote, "I am partial to girls, and had set my sights on one—but never mind me." Of all his children, he was closest in temperament and appearance to Katey, his second daughter.

The Great Reformer

Dickens has done more to ameliorate the conditions of the English poor than all the statesmen Great Britain has sent into Parliament.
—DANIEL WEBSTER

He was an independent Dickensian, a sort of unphilosophical radical.
—GEORGE BERNARD SHAW

 ith the creation of Sam Weller, Mr. Pickwick's valet, Dickens became the first novelist to give importance to that lowly being, the servant. At the time Dickens was writing, servants were invisible presences, both in the home and in the novel, and few valets would have presumed to take the kind of liberties Sam does with such cheeky grace. Mr. Pickwick may be the master, but Sam is the boss. In an essay entitled "Why We Need a New Dickens," Matthew Cooper points out that the scene in which Mr. Pickwick hires Sam reads like a "Who's on First?" shtick, which suggests that Sam employs Mr. Pickwick instead of the other way around. And Mr. Pickwick (whose affinity with his valet is mirrored by their mutual first name) accedes to each of Sam's demands.

As one of his contemporaries put it, Dickens had the ability to make a "washerwoman as interesting as a duchess," a comment that reveals as much about Victorian life as it does about Dickens's genius. In the world of the pre-Dickensian novel, all laundresses are alike, and each duchess is unique. But the forceful presence of the lower classes in Dickens's novels reflects and foreshadows their increasing power in society itself. Dickens saw the need for social rank, but he never regarded people as abstract members of a class. Each character he created was unique, with his own perspectives, quirks, and values. Cooper writes, "Dickens stuck to the simple proposition that no class had a monopoly on smarts or morality or decency or humor." The Dickens novel is a miniature democracy, in which all characters are created equal. He

THE BURNING OF EFFIGIES AT THE MODEL PRISON, PENTONVILLE—FROM P. 171.

*D*ickens's interest in penal reform probably dates from the moment his father entered the gates of the Marshalsea Prison in 1824. He denounced Pentonville's acclaimed "solitary system" with its single cells and enforced silence. Reformers found the method dehumanizing and predicted it would ultimately lead to despair, not reformation. With a macabre quality evocative of Edward Gorey, the unknown artist portrays a suicide in mid-flight. By 1851, however, Dickens's views had hardened: In *David Copperfield* he mocks the easy life of prisoners who clamor for better food.

⌒≫⌒

spends as much time creating *Bleak House*'s Lady Dedlock as he does the humble Jo—and both are equally crucial to the novel's plot.

Dickens's grandmother was in service, and he himself worked in a blacking factory while his father was in debtor's prison. But John Dickens worked in the Navy Pay Office, owned books, and went to the theater. The Dickenses were more genteel than the "real" poor, yet they experienced real poverty. Thus at an early age Dickens could observe the underclass from the perspective of a sort of sympathetic outsider. As a result, David Copperfield's nurse, Peggotty, Mr. Plornish in *Little Dorrit,* and Jo, the crossing sweep, possess a raw dignity that raises them above their so-called betters.

In Dickens the poor found a champion who portrayed them as they wished to be seen. When Dickens died, there was no one to take his place (there still isn't). On the day of his funeral a cabbie turned to one of the novelist's sons and cried, "Ah! Mr. Dickens, your father's death was a great loss to all of us— and we cabbies were in hopes that he would be doing something to help us."

❖ ❖ ❖

As George Orwell noted, Dickens's sympathies are always with the underdog—even when, as in *A Tale of Two Cities,* the underdogs are the rich aristocrats he had condemned only a few pages earlier. In almost every novel, Dickens attacked a new social ill. In *Oliver Twist* it was the Poor Law and the union workhouses; in *Nicholas Nickleby* it was the notorious Yorkshire schools that were little more than concentration camps for unwanted children. (After the novel came out, one such academy, the model for Dotheboys Hall, was investigated and shut down.) In *Hard Times* it's factory bosses and unionism; in *Bleak House,* it's the coiling nightmare of a Chancery suit. Dickens was not merely a concerned bystander but an active participant in almost every major issue of the day: education for the poor, penal reform, sanitation reform, child labor, prostitution, copyright laws, capital punishment, bureaucratic red tape, union workhouses. Dickens was always on the side of the downtrodden.

Radicals like George Bernard Shaw have nourished themselves on Dickens's subversive tendencies, turning a blind eye to his less progressive views. But conservatives can also cite Dickens chapter and verse. As he grew older, he gradually modified his opposition to capital punishment, conceding that it might be useful in some cases. Despite his elevation of the poor, he believed in the class system and wanted his sons to be gentlemen. Although he advocated workers' rights, he distrusted unionism. And a few of his opinions are an embarrassment today. He was ambivalent about Jews, he saw blacks as intellectually inferior, and he jokingly dismissed the idea of women's rights. But what Dickens said is not always what he did: he hired the best women writers of his age, paying them what they were worth; he atoned for his anti-Semitic portrait of Fagin with one of a good Jew in *Our Mutual Friend;* and after his first trip to America, he denounced the abomination of slavery with the zeal of an abolitionist. Yet as he aged and became more crotchety and conservative, Dickens became more of a racist. His biographer Peter Ackroyd writes, "In modern terminology Dickens was a 'racist' of the most egregious kind, a fact that ought to give pause to those who persist in believing that he was necessarily the epitome of all that was decent and benevolent in the previous century." But it is absurd, not to mention ahistorical, to hold Dickens to standards of a very different time. Dickens may not have been the epitome of probity and justice, but through his writings and what he has meant to readers, he has probably influenced more people to do good than any other writer.

It is said that when the seventeen-year-old Victoria was told that her uncle, William IV, was dead and that she was now queen, her first words were "I will be good." Few statements describe the sensibility of an age so succinctly. Victoria was not always "good," but she never forgot what goodness was. For the Victorians, unlike most modern Americans, virtue was an absolute, and the moral self was a very real entity. The Victorian ethos was essentially a belief in the importance of virtue—and that means good by nineteenth-, not twentieth-century standards.

One can't doubt Dickens's sincerity when he writes about kindness and charity. When David Copperfield, Dickens's fictional self, finally finds a loving home, he vows that he will never be homeless again—and that he will never forget the homeless. The two vows are inseparable. Dickens never forgot that wealth, fame, and genius were responsibilities as well as gifts. No matter what his underlying motives may have been, Dickens, like many of the "greats" of his generation, heeded the call to service.

Fallen Women
Raised Up

There is much more good in women than in men, however ragged they are. . . . People are apt to think otherwise, because the outward degradation of a woman strikes them more forcibly than any amount of hideousness in a man.
—DICKENS

E very evening from her window in Piccadilly, the wealthy spinster Angela Burdett-Coutts would watch as flocks of women and girls appeared as if by instinct on the streets. Perturbed by the sight, in May 1846 she suggested a project to Dickens that, she hoped, would alleviate what was then known as the "Great Social Evil." By November 1847 Dickens and Miss Burdett-Coutts officially opened Urania Cottage, "a home for homeless women" in Shepherd's Bush, just outside of London.

Dickens's involvement with Urania Cottage would last more than ten years. Despite deadlines, editorial duties, personal difficulties, and depression, he closely supervised its day-to-day maintenance, approaching it as if nothing less than the collective fate of fallen womanhood hung in the balance. His goal, as he wrote to Miss Burdett-Coutts, was to reform its inmates and send them "to distant parts of the World . . . for marriage."

Marriage was indeed the Victorian crown of success, proof that a prostitute had changed her way of life. Unlike many of his contemporaries, Dickens believed that a prostitute was not an incubus of desire but a woman with a disease rather like madness, who, if treated with "particular gentleness and anxiety," could in fact be "cured."

Thus the idea of home played a crucial role in an inmate's redemption. Like many of his own generation, Dickens invested homemaking with almost sacramental value. At Urania Cottage, then, women would learn cookery,

thrift, discipline, punctuality, cleanliness, and order-
liness—habits that, in time, would "by God's blessing" lead to a home of their own.

Household management was the essence of female virtue. Dickens believed that a "monotonous
round of occupation or self-denial" would eventually
culminate in the sinner's reformation. (It's easy to
see why there was such a high dropout rate.)

As his plans for Urania Cottage took shape, Dickens took on a prodigious amount of work. During
his tenure there he oversaw every detail, no matter
how minute—clothing (which he personally se-
lected), reading material, music, and diet. Every
Tuesday he met with the governing board to discuss special problems such
as one inmate's tendency to relapse, another's drunkenness, the problem of
secret assignations, and the question of whether or not to expel an inmate for
bad behavior. There were eighteen girls at the home at one time; he knew
their names, histories, and personalities. He talked with them, counseled and
disciplined them. He was a tireless letter-writer on their behalf—his correspondence for the Cottage would have been enough to occupy a full-time secretary.

Saving prostitutes from disease and degradation may have appealed to Dickens's reformist's imagination, but he was no Don Quixote who saw a queen in
an Aldonza. Idealism, romanticism, and sentimentality never blinded him to
the grimy truth of a fallen woman's existence and her slender chances of reha-
bilitation. On one occasion, his response to a rebellious woman shows how un-
yielding he could be when his authority was challenged. One Miss Isabella
Gordon, after violating various house rules, saucily "danced upstairs . . . holding her skirts like a lady at a ball." Upon learning of her behavior, Dickens
closely examined Miss Gordon's case and concluded that the rules of the
house were paramount and that the defiant girl, who had already been expelled and readmitted once before, had to be dismissed. Though adamant, he
couldn't help recording her departure in all its heart-sinking detail:

> Her going away was a most pitiable sight. They [inmates and matrons]
> cried bitterly. . . . The girl herself, now that it had really come to this,
> cried, and hung down her head, and when she got out at the door,
> stopped and leaned against the house for a minute or two before she
> went to the gate—in a most miserable and wretched state. As it was im-
> possible to relent, with any hope of doing good, we could not do so. We
> passed her in the lane, afterwards, going slowly away, and wiping her
> face with her shawl. A more forlorn and hopeless thing altogether, I
> never saw.

When an inmate demonstrated a willingness to renounce her former habits,
two problems remained: first, moral reformation could never be considered

permanent. No matter how virtuous and determined a woman seemed upon leaving Urania Cottage, there was always the possibility that she would return to her former life. More important was the question of where she would go after her departure, and on this point social reformers disagreed. Some, like Angela Burdett-Coutts, believed that such women should never marry; Dickens, however, advocated emigration to either Canada or Australia, where they could bury their past and begin a new life with a new identity. But emigration was itself fraught with moral pitfalls. The long voyage was an arduous test, and the women, their resolve still shaky, were assigned chaperones. Even so, many fell again before arriving safely on shore: temptation, in the form of sailors, often proved irresistible.

In our post-Freudian age, it is easy to search for dark motives behind Dickens's efforts, and one can't discount the unconscious thrill he may have derived from the proximity to "dangerous women." But in his concern for prostitutes and other social outcasts, he was very much in tune with the tenor of the time. One also senses that as a novelist—and an uncommonly curious man—Dickens was intrigued by these specimens of womankind with their "peculiar and strangely made character." "A most extraordinary and mysterious study it is," he wrote, "but interesting and touching in the extreme." His interviews with fallen women permitted him almost unlimited access to the minds of remote and unfamiliar beings. On one occasion he secretly followed a woman who had been expelled just to observe her reaction as she walked away.

Yet this access did not change the way he portrayed female sensuality in his fiction. Philip Collins writes, "No one would have guessed, from reading *David Copperfield* or any of the other novels which contain 'fallen' or delinquent girls, that their author really knew what he was talking about."

✤ Dickens's attitude toward fallen women seems patronizing, but he is less judgmental than most of his contemporaries, both men and women. Consider his friend John Forster: after a party, Forster wished to donate leftover food to poor women on the street—but only after inquiring into their background and manner of living. When Dickens heard this he roared with laughter.

The Proper
and the Improper

n our "broad-minded" times, the term *Victorian* evokes the odor of smelling salts or faded violets. The Victorian reputation for prudery is so ingrained that we forget that prudery is relative, depending on what offends you. For some Victorians, it was Shakespeare: many middle-class Victorian homes contained the Reverend Thomas and Harriet Bowdler's *Family Shakespeare,* an expurgated edition in which anything violent, scurrilous, or sexual was carefully excised. (Hence the word *bowdlerize.*) *Hamlet* was too bawdy, *Macbeth* too violent, and *King Lear* too upsetting. Published in 1818, *The Family Shakespeare* went through thirty printings and was a staple in every genteel library. *Robinson Crusoe,* now esteemed as a children's classic, was also expurgated, and even sections of the Bible such as the paeans to physical love in the Song of Solomon were not exempt from a few well-chosen cuts.

Middle-class Victorians, however, didn't lack for erotic thrills. If their pleasures were more temperate, they were no less exciting. Reticence is not synonymous with repression; silence does not mean ignorance or prudery. As the critic Julia Prewitt Brown points out, Victorian sexual discourse was more varied and imaginative than our own, which seems confined to either medical terms or obscenities. What seem like neutral words to us had erotic implications to Victorians. A mere word could melt the frozen reserve between a woman and a man, transforming them from friendly acquaintances into lovers. For example, since a gentleman did not call a lady by her first name until he had "intentions," the sudden change from "Miss" to a first name was like a verbal caress, signaling warmer intimacies to come. An experience did not have to be explicitly sexual to convey an erotic aura: mere proximity could have the sensuality of a long kiss. Leading a woman across the street, helping her into a carriage, or the slight touch of a finger could signify a world of meaning.

No discussion of Victorian sexual mores would be complete without mentioning Mrs. Grundy, the imaginary busybody who personified public opinion. Mrs. Grundy was the specter everybody feared, yet paradoxically she *was* everybody. Dreaded like a wrathful deity, she could ruin careers and shatter marital opportunities. Mrs. Grundy, portrayed as a gossip, is a telling symbol in an age when it didn't matter so much what one did as what was known about it. People had skeletons, but they tried to keep them in the cupboard.

The Victorians may not have talked about sex, but they certainly engaged in and enjoyed it. The stale joke "Lie back and think of the queen," often cited as evidence of Victorian prudery, is ironic in light of the queen's connubial joys. After the birth of her ninth child, she delicately asked her doctor how she could avoid another pregnancy. When he—equally delicately—advised abstinence, she reportedly said, "Oh, doctor, can I have no more fun in bed?"

There was such a wide variety of attitudes on sex that one can't ascribe to the Victorians any monolithic perspective. Some virgins, led terrified to their wedding beds, found the physical side of marriage an unexpected delight. Some physicians theorized that "good" women were sexually unresponsive, but others firmly held that women could not conceive unless they experienced orgasm. Considering the large size of the average Victorian family, one could well believe that most women were motivated by more than a sense of duty.

If the Victorians had one view of sex, it was that sexual energy is volcanic and should therefore be contained in discreet and appropriate ways. What we deem prudery, they would have called common sense. And perhaps this is the source of the celebrated Victorian energy. Libido, theorized Freud (himself a Victorian), has to be channeled in *some* direction. Perhaps for the Victorians it went into building railways, reforming the government, and conquering new territories.

PORNOGRAPHY

While the Society for the Prevention of Vice, founded in 1802, scoured the streets for obscene material and brought it to the attention of the police, underground pornography dens were doing a booming trade. It's no coincidence that the golden age of euphemism was also the *grande siècle* of smut. Naughtiness, denied the front door, entered through the back.

The greatest pornophile of all time was a Victorian, Henry Spencer Ashbee. In a lifetime devoted to compiling, collecting, and cataloging erotic literature, he wrote the definitive annotated bibliography of pornography, a massive three-volume work weighing in at four pounds, which was privately printed in 1877. Upon his death in 1900 he left his 15,000-volume library to the British Museum, with one caveat: the Museum had to accept his collection of erotic literature, or else the entire library would be dispersed. Ashbee was  a true Victorian aristocrat, a connoisseur of exquisite taste and refined sensibilities, who treated his subject as serious literature. He had read every source cited in his trilogy, his comments on each are models of diligence, and his bibliography is as scholarly—and titillating—as can be.

The pornography of a given period reveals much about the age's anxieties and desires. Running through all these stories and novellas is a streak of orientalism. To men living in an industrialized city where the sun rarely shone, the East evoked erotica: incense, pashas, perfumes, harem girls. The plots were formulaic: a modest English virgin (much like Dickens's own virtuous maidens) is abducted into a seraglio and forced to perform acts she grows to love and crave.

In ordinary life the nude form was permitted in art, when draped in gauze and depicted in a suitably remote, preferably classical, setting. Fleshy cherubim and Grecian maidens were permissible; nude adult women were not. Portraits of naked children, one of our biggest taboos, were not only acceptable but also pronounced charming and adorable. The photographic studies of prepubescent girls taken by the mathematician, clergyman, and author of the *Alice* books, the Reverend Charles Dodgson (Lewis Carroll), would be confiscated if exhibited in galleries today.

THE MYTH OF "VICTORIAN GOODY-GOODY PRIGGERY"

Neatly summing up an entire era with the phrase "goody-goody priggery," Bertrand Russell said farewell to the Victorian age writing from the vantage point of the enlightened Edwardian. Until recently, most would have agreed with Russell's assessment. For decades people assumed that Victorians were all prudes whose risible inhibitions allowed us to congratulate ourselves on our own splendid enlightenment.

But recent studies suggest that Victorian sexual stuffiness was largely a myth created by intellectuals of the pre–World War I generation, rebelling against their parents and their stuffy childhoods. In every age there is a sharp division between what people say and what they do, and the Victorians were no better or worse than others. In fact, they simply may have been more private about sexual matters.

In the past few decades, studies of nineteenth-century sexuality have focused on the dualities of the age: the cramped parlors, the frilled pants on the piano legs, the antimacassars, the Sunday afternoon prayers for servants, all were set against a steamy underworld of scarlet bordellos, a famous madam  named Skittle, pornographic dens, and flagellation chambers. The divided world, popularized in Steven Marcus's *Other Victorians* (1966), has until recently been the popular image of Victorian life.

The image of Victorian naughtiness—the bustier beneath the buttoned-up frock—pervades our culture. The presence of Victoria's Secret in almost every mall in America attests to the enduring power of this seductive myth. One could even argue that the Victorians had more sexual options than we do today. Harriet Taylor and John Stuart Mill enjoyed a blissful if nonsexual union, and a man could be a bachelor without anyone assuming he was gay.

SEX AND THE ENGLISH NOVEL

*W*hen John Forster praised Dickens's novels as suitable reading matter for children, Wilkie Collins took him to task:

> If it is true, which it is not, it would imply the condemnation of Dickens's books as works of art, it would declare him to be guilty of deliberately presenting to his readers a false reflection of human life. If this wretched English claptrap means anything it means that the novelist is forbidden to touch on the sexual relations which literally swarm about him, and influence the lives of millions of his fellow-creatures, [except when] those relations are licensed by the ceremony called marriage. One expects this essentially immoral view of the functions of the novelist from a professor of claptrap like the late Bishop of Manchester. But that Forster should quote it with approval is a sad discovery indeed.

Dickens's awareness of sexuality is not expressed in his portraits of "fallen women," but more subtly, through, as a Victorian critic put it, "innuendoes, winks, and nods." Rosa Dartle's blighted sexuality in *David Copperfield,* the sexual predatoriness of Messrs Steerforth and Carker, Miss Murdstone's frigidity, Miss Wade's lesbianism in *Little Dorrit,* Fagin's pedophilia in *Oliver Twist,* the masturbatory impulses of Uriah Heep in *David Copperfield* and the boys of Dotheboys Hall in *Nicholas Nickleby,* and Quilp's sexual prowess in *The Old Curiosity Shop* are all expressed through gestures (such as Heep's wriggling, clammy hands), symbolism (Rosa's scar), or iconic objects (Quilp's long cigar with its brightly glowing tip).

David Copperfield

*A man's character is discernible in the mental or moral attitude
in which, when it came upon him, he felt himself most deeply and
intensely active and alive. At such moments there is a voice
inside which speaks and says: "This is the real me!"*
—WILLIAM JAMES

I f you really want to hear about it, the first thing you'll probably want to know is where I was born, and what my lousy childhood was like, and how my parents were occupied before they had me, and that David Copperfield kind of crap." Thus Holden Caulfield begins his confession to a psychiatrist in *The Catcher in the Rye,* J. D. Salinger's famous novel about growing up. Created almost a century apart, Holden and David are both troubled youths, each typical of his generation. And although David writes his memoirs as an adult, he might as well be speaking to a shrink.

David Copperfield was Freud's favorite novel, which says as much about the book as it does about Freud. Dickens believed (like Freud) that memory is the key to self-knowledge, that by exploring the past one can achieve emotional maturity. Through the ministrations of *his* psychiatrist, the Ghost of Christmas Past, Scrooge sees the man he is—but only after he returns to the boy he was. And Dickens's lesser-known Christmas tale for 1843, "The Haunted Man," is about someone who begs to be rid of his memories. Granted his wish, he finds that, more than a cluster of events and experiences, the past is the essence of identity itself.

Like Holden Caulfield, David Copperfield is uncertain about his role in life, or as William James put it, "the real me." In one of the most famous openings in literature, he makes a startling declaration: "Whether I shall turn out to be the hero of my own life, or whether that station will be held by anybody else, these pages must show." It's an incredible statement that takes the reader completely by surprise. The novel's complete title, *The Personal History of David Copperfield,* naturally leads us to assume that David is the novel's hero.

But perhaps that depends on how you define the term. The "personal history," David's adventures and experiences, form the novel's plot, but its underlying theme, the spine that holds it all together, is that of self-discovery and the triumph of the self over confusion and loss. David's history traces his growth from naïf and dupe into a forceful man who masters his own fate by writing about it. David's task is to assume control of his own narrative.

From the outset, he admits that as a child he could only "observe in little pieces, as it were; but as to making a net of a number of these pieces and catching anybody in it, that was, as yet, beyond me." Like Saint Paul, whom he paraphrases, David can only partially see himself, the people he loves, and his experiences; but as a man, when he puts away childish "pieces," he sees truth face-to-face, variegated, multidimensional, whole.

HE IS BORN

*T*he chapter heading "I Am Born" is deceptively artless. Packed with details, the chapter introduces many of the themes and motifs that will recur throughout the novel. The story of his birth, both a personal creation myth and a once-upon-a-time fairy tale, shapes David's sense of himself and his place in the world.

A funereal air of expectancy hangs about the house, as if a death rather than a birth is imminent. The expectant mother, clad in deep mourning, sits frightened and weeping on a rainy November night. Her husband, David Copperfield senior, died six months earlier, and like a book published after its author's demise, David enters the world a "posthumous child." The tempestuous night, the anxious expectancy, an uncanny visitor, and the midnight birth all suggest a supernatural event. The infant cries as the clock strikes the hour, a conjunction of sounds that suggests that time itself, at least from David's perspective, begins at the moment of birth.

David's nativity is attended by numerous predictions and portents: old wives declare that Friday's child is ill-fated, but counterbalancing this dire prediction is the fortuitous caul, a membrane that sometimes covers the head of an infant at birth. According to superstition, a caul grants its possessor a charmed life and assurance against drowning, and cauls were actually sold as good-luck charms at seaports. Thus immediately after his birth, a "piece" of David is detached and sent into the world, where ten years later it is purchased by an "old lady with a hand-basket" for five shillings. David recollects being at the auction and feeling "uncomfortable and confused, at a part of myself being disposed of that way." The *disjecta membra* foreshadows how easily parts of David will be cut up, scattered, and disposed of.

The caul's protection against drowning, of course, prefigures the most dramatic moment in the novel, the death of Steerforth. But death by drowning symbolically suggests a submersion into a larger force, a threat David continually faces in the novel. The major obstacle to his heroic status is his tendency to subjugate his own idea of himself to the ideas others have of him. The caul suggests that although David's identity may be scattered and diffuse, he will never drown. There will always be a net to gather him up and save him.

One part of David is sent to an auction. Another, his father, is buried in the churchyard near the house. And then there is another self, one that never even came into being. When Aunt Betsey learns that her hoped-for niece, Betsey Trotwood Copperfield, is in fact a nephew named David, she leaves in a fury, and the phantom girl, the child David was supposed to be, dies with her. In Aunt Betsey's eyes, David is a mistake; the wrong child is born that Friday night. Growing up with this family legend, David feels that he should have been someone else.

At first it might seem strange that a chapter about birth should end with such a sense of emptiness and loss. The narrator mourns for the father he will never see, and for the ghostly sister, his other half, who never was:

> I lay in my basket, and my mother lay in her bed; but Betsey Trotwood Copperfield was for ever in the land of dreams and shadows, the tremendous region whence I had so lately travelled; and the light upon the window of our room shone out upon the earthly bourne of all such travellers, and the mound above the ashes and the dust that once was he, without whom I had never been.

The emptiness he experienced at birth is a void David will strive to fill for much of his life.

THE TWO CLARAS

Four chapters into the novel, Dickens reveals that both Peggotty and David's mother, the two maternal figures, are named Clara. Clearly Dickens, a man with a genius for names, wouldn't perform this doubling act without good reason. The "coincidence" is Dickens's way of showing how David perceives women. Both are named Clara because, on an unconscious level, they are two halves of one woman, each fulfilling a mutually exclusive need. His mother is beautiful, vain, and flighty. Peggotty, although homely and a servant, is faithful, and most important, believes in David and provides him with a comforting sense of constancy through all his roles and adventures. (In a memorable scene, she secretly visits him during his imprisonment, and they kiss through the keyhole.) David's earliest life is one of utter contentment: one Clara satisfies his desire for romance, the other, his equally strong need for stability.

But it's the birth mother who has the greatest effect on him. Called "a wax doll," "a baby," and "a poor little fool," Clara Copperfield—whom David physically resembles—is a silly creature who manipulates her son, alternately treating him like a man, a dupe, or an ally, rather than a child who needs her protection. In one of her many skirmishes with Peggotty, for instance, she uses David as a weapon, inciting him to tears and anger on her behalf. David exists to admire and to love her—in other words, he doesn't exist at all in his own right. Later, after her marriage to the odious Mr. Murdstone, she never stands up for her son but silently witnesses his suffering. No wonder David feels as if he doesn't exist.

BROOKS OF SHEFFIELD

The close-knit triumvirate is shattered by the arrival of the aptly named Mr. Murdstone, who casts a long shadow over David's young life. To David's imaginative eyes, Mr. Murdstone is a terrifying, Svengali-like figure: "I see him turn round in the garden, and give us a last look with his ill-omened black eyes." *David Copperfield* has been called Dickens's most Freudian novel, and certainly David's situation closely parallels the triangular Oedipus complex, with the son vying with an older man for his mother's attention:

As my mother stooped down on the threshold to take me in her arms and kiss me, the gentleman said I was a more highly privileged little fellow than a monarch—or something like that; for my later understanding comes, I am sensible, to my aid here.

"What does that mean?" I asked him, over her shoulder.

He patted me on the head; but somehow, I didn't like him or his deep voice, and I was jealous that his hand should touch my mother's in touching me. . . .

Mr. Murdstone is defined by qualities and features suggestive of brutish masculinity: with his thick black whiskers—a Victorian symbol of virility—his persistent emphasis on firmness, and his deep voice, he's an all-powerful male archetype who obliterates the small child in nightmares, myths, and fantasies. He is, moreover, one of the few characters to call David by his Christian name. Unlike his mother's softened "Davy," Mr. Murdstone's use of "David" sounds like a rebuke addressed to a serving boy. His refusal to preface the boy's name with the customary "master" is also telling: he strips David of his courtesy title because he can't (or won't) apply the word *master* to anyone but himself.

The courtship between Clara and Mr. Murdstone is admirably compressed, but one scene stands out, the day David accompanies Murdstone on a business trip to Lowestoft. Among the men there (one of whom, Mr. Quinion, will become David's employer), the child is jokingly dubbed "Brooks of Sheffield," a disguised allusion to David as an obstacle to Mr. Murdstone's pursuit of the pretty young widow. Mr. Murdstone does what many adults do in using a code to speak over the heads of children, but the scene painfully reveals David's isolation and turmoil: as the men raise their glasses, they force the boy to say, "Confusion to Brooks of Sheffield!" Unknowingly, David laughs at himself as though he were someone else.

Of course, Mr. Murdstone triumphs over "Brooks of Sheffield" and marries Clara Copperfield. As soon as the honeymoon is over, he begins to train the household over which he now presides. With his mannish sister Jane, a "metallic lady" with a purse that snaps shut like a mantrap, he bullies David's mother until she loses control of her home, her child, and finally her own will. In his desolation, David retreats to fiction (as the young Dickens did), escaping from the terrible real world into one of the imagination. As a defense against anxiety and loss, he impersonates his favorite characters, transferring his pain onto another person, a hero more glamorous and brave. Life is glossed over, its jagged edges smoothed by denial. David's ability to immerse himself, whether in fiction, in love, or in terror of Mr. Murdstone, is the source of his greatest gifts and his keenest sorrows.

SALEM HOUSE DAYS

One of the saddest episodes in the novel is David's long, uncomfortable carriage ride to school. There is some confusion about his name at the coaching inn where the passengers stop for dinner. Apparently there is no David Copperfield on the reservation list. A meal, however, has been ordered for a "Master Murdstone," an unfamiliar being whom David has never heard of, but who nevertheless turns out to be himself. The small episode illustrates David's pliant sense of identity and his disconnection from himself. His feeling of powerlessness is complete when the waiter, with one pretense after another, tricks David into giving him each course, from wine to pudding. Though David never gets anything to eat, the other passengers turn his apparently gargantuan appetite into a running joke for the rest of the ride. Unable to stand up for himself, he goes hungry from embarrassment. He would rather conform to their false image than assert himself by declaring the truth. The boy lives under a reign of silence in which he is never allowed to explain himself or offer his side of the story.

STEERFORTH I

It may well be Steerforth, not Dora, who is the love of David's young life. After arriving at school demoralized, convinced he's a criminal, and craving affection, David is introduced to the others as a violent boy to be shunned. The imperious Steerforth, however, sneers at authority and honors the boy with his patronage, making David his pet.

One of Dickens's most fascinating characters, J. Steerforth embodies insouciant perfection—he's everything the earnest, innocent David is not and yearns to be. The boy exists to love and admire his friend—and, of course, to bask in the reflected glory cast by such an illustrious personage. Steerforth is one of David's fictional heroes come to life. The boy "carried a spell with him to which it was a natural weakness to yield." And the softhearted David is always ready to yield to another. But the spell he casts over David ultimately enslaves him. David, no less than little Emily, is seduced by a modern cavalier with perfect manners.

Much has been made of the homoerotic implications of the friendship, and as the critic Norman Talbot notes, Steerforth exploits and feminizes David. Steerforth calls David "Young Copperfield," a condescending epithet that evokes David's youthful vulnerability. Throughout their friendship, Steerforth will always be the experienced one, David the trusting naïf. Their relationship resembles intense male friendships at English public schools in which older boys favor and protect younger ones, who are thus obligated to do their bidding. Nightly, David stays up to play Scheherazade to Steerforth's sultan, beguiling his lord to sleep with tales. David's blind love for Steerforth is the first indication of the way in which his "undisciplined heart" will lead him astray. One instance stands out: unable to keep a secret from Steerforth, David confides that the mother of Mr. Mell—the school's most kindly master—lives in a workhouse, a fact Steerforth later uses to humiliate the teacher and instigate his dismissal. Standing between the homely teacher whom he respects and the handsome friend whom he adores, David undergoes a psychic struggle that will be repeated over and over again until he gets it right. As yet he is blind to Steerforth's entire character, preferring to focus on one piece of him.

DEATH, MURDSTONE, AND GRINSBY

*D*avid's romance with Steerforth abruptly ends with the death of his mother and half brother. He is now completely on his own—he is no one: no one's son, no one's brother, no one's friend. He exists in a limbo of idleness while the Murdstones figure out what to do with him. He dreams of "being a hero in the story" and running away, but he is instead sent to work as a common drudge at the warehouse of Murdstone and Grinsby. Once again, David's real self is lost as he begins to lead a life that is seemingly meant for another; again, he is not called by his given name but is referred to by the other workers as "the little gent" or "the young Suffolker." At the age of ten he is as lightly disposed of as the caul.

A narrative pattern begins to emerge. After each major section, David must undergo a change in status and identity that he must assimilate into his larger sense of self. Each section ends with a loss and a movement forward. He moves from adored child to abused stepson to schoolboy, and now, the most radical change of all, to orphan and child laborer. The latter is so foreign to his idea of himself that he almost forgets who he is.

His landlords, the feckless Micawbers, engaging as they are, see past the boy, regarding him more as a fellow sufferer of "pecuniary difficulties" than a child who needs care. Mr. Micawber calls David "Copperfield," as though the boy were a man. Only when they are about to part does Mrs. Micawber see David as he is: a friendless child.

Aunt Betsey: He Is Born, Again

*T*he point in David's story when he *does* emulate "the hero" of the story is when he sets out for Dover to find Aunt Betsey. His journey, which includes the theft of his luggage by the Donkey Man (an episode adapted by Kafka in *Amerika*) and the Munchian screams of the Goroo Man, is a surreal rite of passage in which David strips himself of his old self just as he rids himself of his clothes: "I . . . was on the Dover Road: taking very little more out of the world, towards the retreat of my aunt, Miss Betsey, than I had brought into it, on the night when my arrival gave her so much umbrage." By the time he arrives, he is unrecognizable.

Aunt Betsey adopts and shelters the child she had rejected ten years earlier, remaking him, at least partially, in a new image. An older David will recall: "That little fellow seems to be no part of me; I remember him as something left behind upon the road of life—as something I have passed, rather than actually been—and almost think of him as someone else." And so the old David seemingly disappears, discarded like so many other of his other selves.

So closely does Aunt Betsey embrace the boy that she renames him "Trotwood Copperfield," a name suggesting a combination of Copperfieldian pliancy and Trotwoodian sturdiness. Aunt Betsey's goal, to turn David into a "firm fellow with a will of [his] own," means a complete repudiation of his former self, a boy who would do anything for love.

The episode concludes with the adult David's summation: "Thus I began my new life, in a new name, and with everything new about me." And thus the novel begins again with David, now Trotwood, and a whole new cast of characters.

Agnes

*P*oor Agnes. She's the most despised of all Dickens heroines, the one most often cited as an example of Dickens's inability to create convincing female characters. George Orwell called her "disagreeable," the "legless angel of Victorian romance." George Bernard Shaw saw her as "decidedly the most seventh-rate heroine ever produced by a first-rate artist." But Agnes found a champion in the writer Peter Gay, who confessed in the *New York Times Book Review* that he had been in love with her since he read *David Copperfield* as a child. Surely Gay can't be the only one. Agnes's failure to win over readers may not be Dickens's fault as an artist so much as David's as a man. We are, after all, seeing her through his eyes—and he does have a tendency to idealize whomever he loves.

Agnes presents a contrast to the other women in David's life. When we first see her as a young girl, she is carrying a complete set of household keys. Such keys are talismanic objects for Dickens, signifying a woman's authority in her own home. When Miss Murdstone imperiously strips Clara Copperfield of her keys, we know that she has lost all power; and although the dimwitted Dora has a set, they are more like toys, as useless as the coins Mr. Dick jingles in his pocket. Unlike these flighty child/wives, Agnes is strong and stable—the only mature woman in the book.

Agnes's self-possession, her serenity, and her mildness indicate to David that she transcends the storms of human passion. Callously, the adolescent David confesses all his little crushes to her, never thinking that Agnes could possibly be an object of desire herself, or realizing the pain he causes her. His failure to see that she loves him is almost cruel. If he weren't so innocent, he'd be a cad, with Agnes playing Rosa Dartle to his Steerforth.

"Blind, blind, blind" is how David's shrewd aunt assesses her nephew's taste in women. Drawn like his father to pretty dolls, David is incapable of seeing Agnes as she is, preferring instead to enshrine her as a saint. His early association of her with a stained-glass church window precludes any erotic feelings for her. His view of her is one-dimensional; once again, he can only see in "little pieces." No doubt Agnes would appreciate less adoration and more passion. Whenever David praises her virtue, she only smiles sadly, recognizing that he has turned her into a "legless angel." (David writes: "I love little Em'ly, and I don't love Agnes—no, not at all in that way—but I feel that there are goodness, peace, and truth, wherever Agnes is . . .") When he tells his aunt that he's engaged to Dora, David feels a slight ache, "a vague unhappy loss or want of something." This yearning, although he is still too callow to recognize it, is for Agnes, his best self and other half.

LONDON, ONCE MORE

Like so many of Dickens's heroes, David finds—and loses—himself in the city of confusion, London. Prophetically, on his first night there he attends a play called "The Stranger" and becomes so entranced by the drama that he doesn't recognize himself in the mirror when he gets home. Self-conscious about his youth, he is sensitive to the slightest threat to his identity and, more particularly, his manhood. His control over his environment is so shaky that even his landlady intimidates and cheats him. Her persistent refusal to get his name right shows just how negligible a figure this clean-shaven boy, "Mr. Copperfull," presents. Uriah Heep subtly belittles David by continuing to call him "Master Copperfield," a term reserved for young boys. (For Dickens, mistaking someone's name is the ultimate putdown: twenty-five years earlier, when he was about David's age, Mrs. Beadnell, the mother of his beloved Maria, humiliated him with her brisk dismissal, "And now Mr. Dickin, we'll wish you good morning.")

When David unexpectedly meets Steerforth in London, the older man plays white knight to David's damsel in distress, rescuing him from loneliness, boredom, and snooty waiters. The night he discovers his old schoolfriend, David dreams of "ancient Rome, Steerforth and friendship," a trinity that hints at David's desire for forbidden pleasures, along with a touch of homoeroticism. Steerforth is the pleasure principle in human form. (At one point he hails David as "my little Bacchanal.")

"Daisy," the girlish and gently mocking nickname Steerforth confers upon David, suggests that their friendship imperils David's integrity and manhood. As Daisy, David is a feminized innocent abroad, ripe for seduction and betrayal. In the chapter entitled "My First Dissipation," Steerforth initiates David into bachelor life in the city. Disoriented by his overindulgence in cigars, wine, and food, David views himself with the detachment of a stranger. His slurred homage to his friend, the "guidingstarofmyexistence," suggests exactly the opposite: Steerforth is steering David astray.

The evening (which might also have included a trip to a brothel) is brought to a sobering close with the surprise appearance of Agnes. At the sight of his true guiding star, David returns to his senses. Agnes reminds him of his true self and puts him back on track when he's lost his way. It may not be a very glamorous role, but, like Mr. Mell, she sees through Steerforth's charm.

DORA

"*I* Fall Into Captivity": thus David describes his encounter with literature's most memorable bimbo, the maddeningly adorable Dora Spenlow. For David, love means bondage, loss of control, and complete abandonment of the self to the beloved. He is both captivated and captured. (Actually, David is so susceptible to female charms that he has been falling in and out of love regularly since his early teens.) Seduced by the idea of love, he imagines a fairy-tale romance and then tries to live it. Their courtship, with its parental objections, clandestine meetings, oaths of unswerving passion, and even a go-between, is conducted according to all the clichés of bad fiction—and is a wonderful study of how seriously the young take themselves. But Dora and David's relationship comes down to earth when Agnes advises him to forgo the trysts and secret letters for honesty and openness. While the young David gives himself over to his ardor, the older records it with an irony that makes this section one of the funniest—and the sweetest—in the book.

If Agnes is associated with repose, Dora is all motion, with fluttering ringlets, flounces, and petulant pouting. Wherever she goes, she creates a delightful chaos—particularly within David. Her pet name for him, "Doadie," implies that his attachment to Dora is a regression to infantilism and a flight from responsibility. She represents the "lack of firmness" in him that Aunt Betsey hopes to correct. Any eroticism is defused by their childishness. The besotted Doadie cuts a ridiculous figure, one minute tearing his hair and threatening suicide, the next rhapsodizing upon Dora's curls. The two communicate in a fatuous prattle that leaves them both at cross-purposes—fine for young love, but not for the serious business of marriage. When David tries to talk about his work, his goals, or even domestic practicalities, she looks at him in horrified incomprehension. Torn between the practical and the romantic, he gives himself over to the idiocies and raptures of "a Fairy's bower," as he calls the improbable world of first love.

Thus Steerforth's "Daisy" marries Aunt Betsey's "Little Blossom," and like two flowers, their time together is brief. They dreamed, as Aunt Betsey put it, "of a party-supper-table kind of life, like two pretty pieces of confectionary." But a sobering dose of reality soon sets in: in their domestic life, they are clumsy children trapped in a grown-up world. Although married and working, David is still unable to seize control of his own affairs. Servants, shopkeepers, accounts, and possessions prove unruly, and David confesses that he and Dora ultimately "corrupt" others through their "want of system and management."

After all his reveries about domestic life, David is stunned by the ordinariness of marriage—Dora even wears curl papers! Life, as it turns out, is not the story with the happy ending he had imagined. Fairy bowers of "tra la la and guitars" are unsuitable for a man of substance, and upon awakening from his dream of fairies, he finds he is alone with a pretty girl with whom he has little in common. For the first time, he sees Dora as separate from himself, and the realization makes him sad and lonely. Treating the "Little Blossom" like a hothouse plant, he tries to force her maturation, shaping her into someone he can talk to, a companion or soulmate—someone, in fact, very much like Agnes. Drilling her unmercifully, he sounds like an anemic Mr. Murdstone. But people—and David should know this better than anyone—cannot be cut to measure. David grows up when he accepts his "child-bride" as she is, not as a figure of romance but as a real woman. But in doing so, he must confront what he fears most: separation and loss.

David never admits that he no longer loves Dora, but he alludes to a vague, hollow feeling, a want of something that he can't name: "The old unhappy feeling pervaded my life. It was deepened, if it were changed at all; but it was as undefined as ever, and addressed me like a strain of sorrowful music faintly heard in the night." Love based solely on youthful allure is doomed, whereas love based on mutuality of interests endures.

Thus Dora, the blossom of spring, conveniently dies—ostensibly from a miscarriage, but actually because both Dickens and David need her to. It's a cheap shot on Dickens's part, sentimental and bathetic—yet Dora's death says something meaningful about the limitations of love. Knowing that David would soon cease to love her if she survived, Dora, with unexpected wisdom, tells him, "It's better this way."

STEERFORTH II

*W*ith Dora's incompetence and Steerforth's betrayal of the Peggottys, the delusions of romantic love and hero worship collapse. Both Dora and Steerforth have duped the gullible "Daisy/Doadie," and the deaths of Steerforth and Dora signal the end of his innocence. (In this case innocence is not virtue but blindness.) In death he is able to see the objects of his desire as they were, with all their flaws and their virtues, not as creations of his own desires.

Steerforth's drowning is as dramatic as Dora's death is melodramatic. The tiny boat founders; the furious storm and the unnatural darkness parallel David's despair. Shell-shocked, he goes abroad, wandering from place to place, a Byronic figure bearing a nameless guilt. Agnes's sturdiness and Aunt Betsey's self-reliance are lessons that David must now learn for himself. His epiphany, his realization that he loves Agnes, is not only a tidy conclusion but also a reflection of his maturity and a true homecoming. He takes control of his life and becomes its hero—but only when he realizes that life is not a romance. He grows up when he can love a woman, not a child.

Despite her reputation as a pallid prig, Agnes is capable of an intensity of feeling unmatched by any other woman in the novel; her final outburst to David, "I have loved you all my life!" is the most passionate utterance in the novel. After all his searching, David has discovered his other half, his best self, and the old unhappy ache is soothed. As the critic Sylvere Monod points out, the similarity between the names Wickfield and Copperfield suggests the mutuality that Dickens insists is essential for a happy marriage. David's life, when we leave him, is ordered and secure.

Most important, through Agnes, David realizes his true vocation. At her urging he transforms grief into art, writing an autobiographical novel that helps others while it consoles and cures himself. His book establishes him as a writer (one very much like Dickens), while it makes him the hero of his own life story. The old Steerforthian ideal, the self-destructive, Romantic poet manqué, gives way to the earnest mid-Victorian gentleman personified in David Copperfield. Through work and love David finds happiness and his "real self." This point is happily brought home when Mr. Micawber, now in Australia, writes with his usual flourish to "David Copperfield, AUTHOR." For the first time he is addressed by his given name in its entirety. As a celebrated author, David has literally made a name for himself.

The novel's ending, while happy, is nevertheless shot through with pain. David brings us up to date: beloved characters are older; deaths (at least ten) are remembered. But the reappearance of the "Crocodile book" that the child David once read to Peggotty reassures us that the past can be reincorporated into the present. Finally, in writing his memoirs, David reminds us and himself that loss can be sustained and the self discovered through memory and art.

DAVID COPPERFIELD

COPPERFIELDIANA

❊In the *Life,* John Forster notes that shortly after Dickens began *David Copperfield,* he decided to change the name of his infant son from Oliver Goldsmith to Henry Fielding in a "kind of homage to the style of his new novel." And in its own Dickensian way, *David Copperfield* is *Tom Jones* without the sex.

❊Less than a century later, novelist Robert Graves remedied the lack. In a case of reverse bowdlerizing, Graves "updated" the novel, spicing it with bedroom scenes and deleting its sappier parts.

❊Agnes Wickfield has been the object of more derision than any other Dickens heroine—and at one point or another each has had her share of abuse. Few critics have failed to note that lamentable moment when she points her finger upward. Given the amount of controversy her gesture has caused, one might well wonder which finger Agnes is pointing. Even in 1869, R. H. Hutton pro-

---

*A*ristotle divided life into two forms: that which is unstable and in a dynamic state of becoming, and that which is complete and in a state of repose or arrival. *Pickwick, Nicholas Nickleby, The Old Curiosity Shop,* and *Martin Chuzzlewit,* although finished, seem impromptu efforts, more like works in progress. Boz rushes through them helter-skelter, eager to ingratiate himself with the reader. They have a driven, maniacal quality, as though the plot were leading the author rather than the reverse. Although funny and joyous, they lack the profundity and grace that only comes with from experience.

David Copperfield, on the other hand, is a work of arrival. We don't sense Dickens in the background feverishly struggling to amuse or touch us. There is a steadier hand guiding the work, one that is in full command of his material. It is, in many respects, Dickens's *Hamlet.*

nounced Agnes a "detestable" woman who "insists on pointing upward." Despite his admiration for Dickens's heroine, the historian Peter Gay concedes that Agnes's gesture must be the "most awkward moment in *David Copperfield.*" But the Dickensian critic Alexander Welch sees Agnes's gesture as a defining moment in the novel. Finally, Michael Slater in *Dickens and Women* writes, "The disastrously voulu nature of the presentation of Agnes remains a rock ahead, even for the most ardent Dickensian."

✻ "I did for myself what psychoanalysts do for their patients. I expressed some very long felt and deeply felt emotion. And in expressing it I explained it and then laid it to rest." So wrote Virginia Woolf after completing *To the Lighthouse,* the autobiographical novel in which she confronts and buries the ghosts of her parents. Dickens's early novels did much the same thing for him. Like psychoanalysis, novels provided an arena in which he could reenact old fantasies, memories, and traumas; at times they were a form of wish fulfillment that enabled him to exact revenge on those who had hurt him. In *Oliver Twist* he relived his early childhood abandonment; in *The Old Curiosity Shop* he reexperienced his grief at Mary Hogarth's death; in *Barnaby Rudge* he reenacted a young man's struggle to supersede his father. *Nicholas Nickleby* is the young Dickens searching for a vocation, and *Martin Chuzzlewit* reproduces the mature Dickens's disillusioning experiences in America. All these "autobiographical" memoirs culminate in *David Copperfield,* Dickens's midlife novel, in which he confronts and releases his past by projecting it on his fictional double, David Copperfield—who, as John Forster pointed out, has Dickens's initials in reverse.

In *Copperfield,* Dickens writes about his early years and at the same time confesses his secret anxieties. Self-knowledge in *David Copperfield* is closely linked to married love. The novel's concern with misalliances, thwarted desire, and the sorrows and errors of love will dominate the next half of Dickens's life much as his childhood anguish did the first.

For the first time Dickens adopts the first-person voice; his narrator is a mature man, a novelist, who reflects on how the past has contributed to his present identity. David's sufferings are portrayed with a genuineness and a lack of sentimentality that's rare for Dickens. Wilkins and Emma Micawber, based on the novelist's parents, are portrayed without rancor, and even with good humor. He notes their flaws, but values their strengths. The generosity with which Dickens depicts the ever-optimistic failure Mr. Micawber suggests that he had at last understood and made peace with his father. By writing about his parents and reliving his childhood, Dickens triumphed over his past. He would never again need to make a neglected child the central focus of a novel.

✻ From her fluttering hair ribbons to her ubiquitous lap dog (whose name was changed to Jip from Daphne), Dora Spenlow is a portrait of Dickens's first love, Maria Beadnell. Although the juvenile romance between David and Dora is the stuff of comedy, Dickens never underestimated the depth of his feelings for Maria. When Forster reproved him for exaggerating the torments of young love, Dickens testily replied:

> I don't quite apprehend what you mean by my overrating the strength of the feeling of five-and-twenty years ago. If you . . . will only think what the desperate intensity of my nature is, and that this . . . excluded every other idea from my mind for four years, at a time when four years are equal to four times four; . . . then you are wrong, because nothing can exaggerate that. . . . No one can imagine in the most distant degree what pain the recollection gave me in *Copperfield*.

Dora's marriage to David and her death was the author's way of enacting fantasy and exacting revenge.

✤ Everyone knows that David Copperfield is Dickens's alter ego, but few suspect his affinity with the obsessive writer and wise fool, Mr. Dick. As Alexander Welsh points out, "the name is a giveaway." In the novel's early stages the character was Mr. Robert, but by changing the name, Dickens deliberately creates a droll double for himself. Both men are writers, and both are working on autobiographies, Mr. Dick has his Memorial, a petition to the Lord Chancellor recounting the abuses he endured from his family, and Mr. Dickens his novel, in which he relates *his* childhood wrongs.

Mr. Dick's Memorial never progresses; whenever he begins to contemplate distressing matters, he obsessively begins writing about the beheading of King Charles I. Instinctively, Dickens anticipated a crucial precept of psychoanalysis: the neurotic, beset with anxiety over the past, will often allay his psychic pain by symbolically projecting it onto an obsession that will distract him from the true source of his neurosis. Most psychoanalysts would view the recurring

*D*ickens's novels spawned songs, dances, fashions, and fads. Numerous odes were penned to Nell, Paul Dombey, Dora, and Dolly Varden, the heroine of *Barnaby Rudge.*

*A*n impressive photograph from J.E. Mayall's 1852 daguerreotype of the forty-year-old Dickens at the height of his fame. He has just completed the first work of his maturity. His face still unlined, he looks confident yet relaxed. Later photographs reveal a bewhiskered, careworn man.

image of King Charles *da capo* as an unexpressed wish to kill (and castrate) the father. That the king is named Charles further complicates the matter.

❖What would a psychoanalyst make of the Dickensian gallery of characters? In *David Copperfield* alone, there's Dora's infantilism, Annie Strong's father complex, and Mr. Micawber's delusional optimism. Aunt Betsey must be a repressed lesbian, and Mr. Dick . . . well, one can't say enough. In a note entitled *The Kite as the Symbol of Erection,* Sandor Ferenczi, a disciple of Freud, writes:

> A patient relates of his uncle who suffers from delusions of persecution and that although the latter was already more than thirty years of age he always played with boys, and would sometimes show them his member, and was particularly fond of, and skilled at, constructing gigantic paper kites with long tails.

Ferenczi compares the paranoid uncle to the frolicsome Mr. Dick, who also likes little boys and kites.

❖Dickens arrived at the artless title *David Copperfield* only after a long and circuitous search; its various mutations reveal how the idea of the book evolved in the author's mind. How, one wonders, would the novel be different if Dickens had chosen

"Mag's Diversions."
Being the personal history, adventures, and observation, of
Mr. David Copperfield the Younger
And his Great-Aunt Margaret.

Writing *Copperfield* was Dickens's most intense endeavor to date, submerging him in a shadow world of the past, evoking memories and sensations he thought he had forgotten. "Coming out of Copperfield," as he put it, was a wrenching experience. Two days before he finished the novel, he wrote to John Forster, "Oh my dear Forster, if I were to say half of what Copperfield makes me feel to-night, how strangely, even to you, I should be turned inside-out! I seem to be sending some part of myself into the Shadowy World." Like David's caul, the book was being detached from him and sent out into the marketplace. Dickens loved all his books, but *Copperfield* was his "favorite son."

❖Dickens claimed that of all his public readings, "The Drowning of Steerforth" affected him the most. He could scarcely read the tempestuous scene without weeping. One wonders what Steerforth, beautiful yet flawed, meant to Dickens—and to David. The treatment of David's affection for Steerforth is almost Jamesian in its nuanced complexity. To describe it as homoerotic is too simplistic and obvious. Steerforth is a precursor of the modern character who behaves in ways even he cannot understand, and he is one of the few characters for whom Dickens provides a past that would explain his psychology. This resplendent yet careless young man is stained *and* beloved. He is a sinner, not a villain. And unlike Dickens's other sinners, Steerforth never succumbs to remorse. We hope he died unrepentant. Guilt belongs to David, not the effortlessly beautiful Steerforth. Twenty years after he created this flawed young man, Dickens still wept for him.

ON BEING 'UMBLE

*U*riah Heep may be the creepiest figure in English literature. With his writhing, eel-like figure and clammy, restless hands, he exudes an aura of something unclean. The exact nature of his nastiness, which is partly sexual (see page 216), is felt but not known. It is not, as some critics maintain, snobbery alone that evokes our—and Dickens's—distaste for this defective product of charity schools. Nor is his cringing, groveling posture enough to account for our feelings of disgust. There's something more, a disquieting air of menace behind the lashless gaze and the softly ingratiating voice. Uriah's sly pride in his masochistic posture, his secret pleasure in deprivation, and his lack of vitality deny all that's joyous and abundant—in short, everything Dickens's novels celebrate. Uriah's presence dampens the human spirit, turning the world dank and ordinary.

Someone once complained that Dickens couldn't understand sin unless it was a crime. But Uriah is not simply a felon, he's perversion incarnate. The telltale red hair, regarded by the Victorians as a suspicious oddity and traditionally associated with the devil, Shylock, and Judas, confirms Uriah's status as an outcast from wholesome society. Wizened, cadaverous, he is old and fallen before fifteen.

Uriah Heep ultimately transcends his own clichés—not simply an "'umble" law clerk who rubs his hands, but an insidious, nameless evil, diabolic and unsavory. One scene in particular captures the peculiar Heepian essence: Heep, David, and Aunt Betsey have just arrived at the Wickfields', and leaving Uriah in charge of the pony, they enter the house. From the window, David watches a bizarre dumbshow: "I caught a glimpse of Uriah Heep breathing into the pony's nostrils, and immediately covering them with his hand, as if he were putting some strange spell upon him." Behind that eerie pantomime lies a world of meaning.

Heep has entered the dictionary not merely as a character but as a character type. His name has become shorthand for any obsequious act or person, evoking all the craftiness of people who would lick the boot that kicks them. Those who have been likened to Uriah Heep are legion, the most prominent being Richard Nixon. Nixon's famous Checkers speech, with its sentimental toadyism, is perhaps the acme of Heepism in our century. Nixon has thus been referred to as "Uriah Heep giving a press conference" and "a statesman masquerading as Uriah Heep" (Mark Feeny, *Boston Globe*). Tom Wolfe once called Lyndon Johnson "Uriah Heep with a tab collar," and Joe Klein described the abject former Clinton aide Dick Morris as "Uriah Heep on the couch."

—m—

*O*n what not to do at a job interview:

A Uriah Heep handshake portrays a lack of self-confidence. It's a poor way to initiate a cordial relationship even on a temporary basis and can be a chilling experience that is carried over throughout the interview.
—J. I. BIEGELEISEN,
San Jose Mercury News, May 25, 1986

A Question
of Character

Even during his lifetime, readers argued whether Dickens's characters were "good," i.e., true to life. Good characters are emotionally complex, but Dickens's are one-dimensional. Does this mean Dickens lacked artistry?

The novelist E. M. Forster divided characters into two types: flat and round. Whereas round characters possess an inner life, flat ones are static representations of a single humor or type—like Faith or Despair in a medieval mystery play. Flat characters are mechanical dolls who spring into the same action each time they appear. Thus Uriah Heep will always rub his clammy hands, and Agnes will always be pointing upward. But for Forster, Dickens is unique. Even though all his characters are flat ("Nearly everyone can be summed up in a sentence") and therefore *should* be bad, they still manage to evoke

> this wonderful feeling of human depth. Probably the immense vitality of Dickens causes his characters to vibrate a little, so that they borrow his life and appear to lead one of their own. It is a conjuring trick. . . . [Dickens] ought to be bad. He is actually one of our big writers, and his immense success with types suggests that there may be more in flatness than the severer critics admit.

> For G. K. Chesterton, such "flatness" is a source of Dickensian charm. Figures like Mr. Pickwick, he argues, reside "in a perpetual summer of being themselves. It was not the aim of Dickens to show the effect of time and circumstances upon a character." George Orwell—who loved Dickens—agreed:

Dickens's characters, unlike those of Tolstoy, don't tell us about ourselves. Tolstoy "is writing about people who are growing"; Dickens's characters are "already finished and perfect":

> They never learn, never speculate. In my own mind, Dickens's people are present far more often and far more vividly than Tolstoy's, but always in a single unchangeable attitude, like pictures or pieces of furniture. You cannot hold an imaginary conversation with a Dickens character.

Admittedly, one cannot hold an imaginary conversation with Tiny Tim, but then again, who would want to? Nor have we burning issues to discuss with Mr. Pickwick—he's already said everything we want to hear. Dickens's characters, as Orwell suggests, are inanimate objects like pictures or furniture—but are no less companionable for it. Like the favorite toys of childhood, they are reassuringly constant in our minds, providing fixed points of reference throughout our lives.

*D*ickens's people are alive, not merely clothed ideas or symbols.
—VLADIMIR NABOKOV

Showing the intricate workings of a mind is not the only way to display character, and even though a Dickens character may lack psychological depth, he or she often exhibits a precise insight into human nature. Dickens's creations do not reveal an individual psyche but the human condition. We might not identify with David Copperfield, the man, but we can identify with his childhood loneliness and his wayward heart. Pip may not seem "real," but for many he is the epitome of young manhood, at once callow and kind, and his agonizing obsession with Estella may be all too real for some of us.

Dickens's characters may not prompt self-knowledge the way Shakespeare's do, but they are a magnifying mirror in which we can see—and smile at—our own flaws and virtues. He catches human beings off guard at the moment when they are most themselves: no grandeur, just small people trying to seem important or big people revealed as all too small. Mrs. Plornish of *Little Dorrit* talks loudly in childish syntax and is convinced she is speaking Italian. (" 'Why,' enquired Mrs. Plornish, reverting to the Italian language, 'why 'ope bad man no see?' ") The irresponsible Harold Skimpole of *Bleak House* airily dismisses pounds and guineas as too complex for his childish nature, while he calculatingly sponges off friends. Mrs. Gamp might not possess much of a psyche, but she is a recognizable character type, the self-serving gossip who rings true down to her linguistic contortions and snuff-stained gown. The lawyer Mr. Vholes is "only a type," yet this soft-spoken predator with an "elderly father in the Vale of Taunton" is also a perfect specimen of his kind.

More than any other novelist, Dickens relies on external details to convey a character's inner life. Thus the sadistic Miss Murdstone's mantrap of a pocketbook ("she kept the purse in a very jail of a bag which hung upon her arm by a heavy chain, and shut up like a bite"); the spinster Rosa Dartle's wasted frame; and the twinkly Pickwick's pleasing rotundity—such details make a character spring into life. In fact, Dickens's physical depictions were so exacting that several of his real-life models, much to their distress, recognized themselves when they read his books.

Admittedly, Little Nell is not a mimetic portrait of an adolescent girl, yet when the final numbers of *The Old Curiosity Shop* arrived in New York, people allegedly gathered at the dock, crying out, "Is Nelly dead?" Tolstoy's characters live and breathe, but it's hard to imagine a crowd crying out, "Is Anna Karenina dead?" Dickens's characters aren't "real," but generations of readers have cared about them as if they were.

EVERYONE (LITERALLY!) IN DICKENS

Since Dickens's death, "Dickens Dictionaries," listings of all his characters, have become a veritable subgenre. In 1995, with a Macintosh SE and an ink-jet printer, George Newlin published the list of all lists, making previous ones obsolete. His masterwork is the three-volume *Everyone in Dickens*—a definitive listing of every character, imaginary or real, ever mentioned in the Dickens canon, including magazine pieces, travel writing, speeches, plays, poetry, and collaborations. The total comes to a staggering (but not surprising) 13,143 characters. Those who think Dickens wrote only the fourteen novels and some short stories are in for a surprise: according to Newlin, there are over five hundred titles in Dickens's oeuvre.

Everyone in Dickens lives up to its name: in its 2,568 pages, the concordance lists not only named creations but also the legions (4,000, to be exact) of uncelebrated cheesemongers, parlormaids, waiters, mob members, and assorted extras. Newlin distinguishes each with a one-line sketch: "Child, very astonished" or "Professional gentlemen," or "A threesome attempting a glee." His descriptions are quirky—few readers would recognize Bill Sikes, the vicious housebreaker in *Oliver Twist,* as a man "admired by his dog."

Dickensian Names

Generally, Mr. Dickens, as if in revenge for his own queer name, does bestow still queerer ones upon his fictitious creations.
—ANONYMOUS REVIEWER, *Macphail's Ecclesiastical Journal,* January 1849

No writer can match Dickens when it comes to the names of characters. His names are so apt that it's impossible to imagine his characters with other names. In fact, the name *is* the character, as with Wackford Squeers, Seth Pecksniff, Uriah Heep, Ebenezer Scrooge, Mrs. Gamp, or Mr. Podsnap.

For Dickens, the art of naming was a mysterious process inseparable from the act of creation itself. To name is to know, and he couldn't begin to imagine a character until he had found the *nom juste,* his search for which often led to long lists that sound like the nonsense poems of his contemporaries Edward Lear and Lewis Carroll. Thus "Chubblewig," "Chuttlewig," "Chuzzlewig," and "Chuttlewig" finally led to "Chuzzlewit." He sometimes arrived at a name by free-associating on a character's qualities. One doesn't need to read the novels to know that Flintwinch, Gride, Scrooge, and Squeers are all knaves and misers.

Some Dickensian names are portmanteau words, packing several meanings into one. Mr. Vholes's (*Bleak House*) name is a chilling blend of *vulture, ghoul,* and *vampire,* as well as a homonym for *vole,* a small rodent. Murdstone, David's sadistic stepfather, unites murderer, *merde,* and stony. Of the nurse in *Martin Chuzzlewit,* Stephen Leacock wrote, "What is Gamp—is it *gruesome* and *damp?*" Perhaps, but the name conjures up a range of meanings greater than the sum of its suggested parts. "Gamp's my name and Gamp's my natur," she announces.

Dickens also seems to have had a private code in which certain letters or sounds connoted meanings known only to himself. As a boy he attributed various traits to each letter of the alphabet. Rarely used letters, like *Q,* were disagreeable, and therefore not surprisingly, the only "Q names" in the Dickens canon belong to Mr. Quinion, Mr. Murdstone's friend and David Copperfield's employer, and Quilp, the sadistic dwarf in *The Old Curiosity Shop. B* usually signifies bragging, bombast, and bumbling: hence Beadle Bumble, Major Bagstock, and Josiah Bounderby, bunglers all.

> In his column of January 25, 1995, "Dickens with a C," Russell Baker notes that after having read a lot of Dickens, he is struck by the abundance of Dickensian names in the real world. "What's worse," he confesses, "I waste hours, puzzling over what kinds of characters Dickens would have built for these names, Cito Gaston for one." The real Mr. Gaston manages the Toronto Blue Jays, but in Baker's dream of a Dickensian universe, Gaston is a "Lancashire businessman posing as a French count to con a snobby London banker into refinancing his chair factory." Baker proposes a parlor game for Dickens fans, asking them to list ten famous people whose names have the true Dickensian ring, and then imagine the personality that Dickens would have created to go with them.

The true Dickensian name is a form of linguistic phrenology. Like protuberances on a cranium, sound and allusory meanings are an index to character. The meaningless word *Quilp,* a perfect example of Dickens's use of onomatopoeia, sounds as ugly as its owner, but it also produces a sound like a gulp or a swallow, expressive of the character's vicious orality. And what could evoke balmy, quivering formlessness better than the extraordinary name Jellyby? This quixotic do-gooder changes social causes as though they were bonnets. Her loyalties are gelatinous, as opposed to those of Mr. Boythorn, whose solid-sounding name implies his inflexibility of purpose.

Other delicious Dickensian names include Mrs. General, who commands Amy Dorrit into gentility, and Volumnia Sparsit, the spiteful spinster of *Hard Times,* whose first name denotes her patrician background, while her last suggests her pinched existence and her martyred satisfaction in her spartan life. For Mr. Murdstone, the tyrant who marries Clara Copperfield, Dickens wanted a name connoting hardness and homicide. Lady Dedlock in *Bleak House* is locked in a loveless marriage, her passions deadened. Drood, a compound of dread and brood, is the very sound of doom.

Whenever there's a hypocrite in a Dickens novel, one can be sure he has a biblical name: Uriah Heep, Seth Pecksniff, Josiah Bounderby. Mr. Gradgrind in *Hard Times* sounds like a utensil for grinding. One must grit one's teeth just to say it. As a proponent of utilitarianism, he ignores the individual spirit for the common good and is thus a human mill that crushes everything into uniform drabness. His associate in educating the young is Mr. McChoakumchild.

In *Dombey and Son,* Mr. Carker's name derives from the rarely used verb *cark,* to trouble or worry. But it also evokes *canker,* an oral sore, a source of corruption and decay, and a disease that destroys young plants. Mr. Carker is indeed a destroyer of innocence. In keeping with his voracious sexuality, his name also suggests *carnivore* and *carnal*.

Magwitch and his alias Provis in *Great Expectations* are fittingly cryptic names. A combination of *magus* and *witch,* he is a necromantic figure who transforms a blacksmith's apprentice into a gentleman. But, the alias suggests that his legacy carries a proviso, a requirement or qualification that Pip must be prepared to meet.

Bleak House

Nothing prepares us for *Bleak House,* a novel both horrific and sublime, the jewel in the crown of nineteenth-century English literature. Shakespearean in its grandeur, Kafkaesque in its sense of the absurd, it is both realistic and fantastic, one of the finest examples of urban gothic ever written. The London of *Bleak House* closely resembles the "real" city, yet it has all the lurid secrets and supernatural terrors of Renaissance Italy in a gothic romance. With its elaborate plotting and accelerating action, *Bleak House* is the biggest page-turner in the Dickens canon.

But it's also much, much more. Reading *Bleak House,* one has the disorienting feeling that the novel's overt story hides deeper meanings that one can grope toward but never fully grasp. Terse, cryptic chapter titles, "A Progress," "Closing In," "Moving On, "Signs and Tokens," "The Appointed Time," and "Beginning the World," intensify this impression. *Bleak House* may be the first detective novel, but its mystery is more than a simple whodunit. It abounds with blind alleys, dead ends, and plot lines that lead nowhere. And the novel's main plots, the mystery of Lady Dedlock and the lawsuit *Jarndyce and Jarndyce,* are two lines of action, which, defying the reader's expectations, never intersect.

TWO VIEWS: AN EXPERIMENT

*F*or the first and only time in his career, Dickens breaks with his usual style and uses two alternating narrators to tell his tale. Thirty-four chapters are given to an omniscient narrator, and thirty-three are "written" by the aptly named Esther Summerson, who recalls events of seven years earlier. Esther's fidelity to cherished Victorian virtues is balanced against the first narrator's harsh view, which threatens to undermine such values. It is typical of this slippery novel that we never know whom to believe. Much maligned as one of Dickens's goody-goody girls, Esther is an indispensable part of the narrative: without her comforting presence, the omniscient narrator's vision of society would be too terrifying to contemplate.

FOG AND MUD

*T*he London fog that opens the novel is both a meteorological phenomenon and a manifestation of metaphysical foreboding. The afternoon gaslights, winking in unnatural darkness, evoke not only an aura of doom but Doom itself. True to the novel's realistic tradition, the narrator first orients his reader, supplying a precise time and setting for the action: "London. Michaelmas term lately over, and the Lord Chancellor sitting in Lincoln's Inn Hall. Implacable November weather." That done, he proceeds to describe a landscape dense with disorienting meanings and portents:

> As much mud in the streets, as if the waters had but newly retired from the face of the earth, and it would not be wonderful to meet a Megalosaurus, forty feet long or so, waddling like an elephantine lizard up Holborn Hill. Smoke lowering down from chimney-pots, making a soft black drizzle with flakes of soot in it as big as full-grown snow-flakes—gone into mourning, one might imagine, for the death of the sun. Dogs, indistinguishable in mire. Horses, scarcely better; splashed to their very blinkers. Foot passengers, jostling one another's umbrellas, in a general infection of ill-temper, and losing their foot-hold at street-corners, where tens of thousands of other foot passengers have been slipping and sliding since the day broke (if this day ever broke), adding new deposits to the crust upon crust of mud, sticking at those points tenaciously to the pavement, and accumulating at compound interest.

Literally, Dickens describes a raw afternoon in November; figuratively, he hints at the social ills that afflict humanity; metaphysically, he prepares us for the Last Judgment that will occur in London sometime after Michaelmas term. All three levels unite in the pervasive images of fog and mud.

All that's wrong with industrial London—the grime, the anonymity, the disintegration of social relationships—coalesces in one fog-bound afternoon. Fractious pedestrians grope through mist, barely seeing, let alone acknowledging or helping one another. The foul smoke, a metaphor for the muddle of bureaucracy, obscures individuality, turning human beings into angry shapes. We are heading into T. S. Eliot country, a Dickensian Waste Land, where hordes of benumbed people are in perpetual motion with nowhere to go. (The imperative, "Move along," continually addressed to Jo, the crossing sweep, applies to everyone.)

As for the metaphysical dimension, the cumulative effect of mist, dirt, and debris suggests that London and its inhabitants are returning to entropy, the state of randomness and uniformity. The first twelve chapters overflow with descriptions of haphazardness, putrefaction, and ruin: Krook's rag-and-bottle shop, the original Bleak House, Tom-All-Alone's, Miss Flite's mind, Mrs. Jellyby's closet, Chancery itself.

Thus an ordinary cityscape, with pedestrians, horses, and dogs, resonates with apocalyptic meanings: it is almost winter, the season of death; the waters are retreating from the earth; prehistoric monsters waddle up Holborn Hill; the sun, a mere squib, is dying; and darkness descends at noon. People flounder through the mist, a reminder that nothing solid holds; all guideposts are blotted out, leaving everyone, directionless and alone, to fend for himself.

According to Mr. Guppy, the fog is called "a London particular." Despite Mr. Guppy's taxonomy, this fog is *not* particular to London: it is, in fact, descending all over England, blinding the country in a murky haze.

JARNDYCE AND JARNDYCE

*A*t last Dickens narrows in on his subject as the literal fog melts into the metaphorical: "Never can there come fog too thick, never can there come mud and mire too deep, to assort with the groping and floundering condition which this High Court of Chancery, most pestilent of hoary sinners, holds, this day, in the sight of heaven and earth." The interminable Chancery lawsuit involves an ancient dispute over an inheritance bequeathed by an unnamed member of the Jarndyce family. It's curious that Dickens, master of the irrelevant detail, fails to provide concrete particulars about the central case of his novel, leaving us in doubt about its origin, the property in question, the original legatees, and on and on. Such a grave omission reinforces the notion that the suit rests on nothing but ambiguity and confusion.

In the middle of this muddle, in all his "foggy glory," sits the Law, personified by the Lord High Chancellor—the highest legal official in the land—called "M'lud" by his minions, a slurring of words that confirms his Lordship's affinity with the muck that surrounds him. (This association has a long history with Dickens: in his first novel, Mr. Pickwick's shyster lawyer is named Fogg.) Law, the infrastructure of society, is reduced to vaporous be-fuddlement (or, as Mr. Jarndyce calls it, "Wiglomeration"), a state of affairs confirmed by an administrator named Mr. Tangle and officials such as the in-terchangeable Mizzle, Chizzle, and Drizzle.

The case at hand—the one always at hand—is the notorious *Jarndyce and Jarndyce,* which, depending on one's perspective, is tragic, comic, or cosmi-cally absurd. *Bleak House* is usually interpreted as Dickens's exposé of Chancery, with the fog "standing for" legal and moral obscurity. This is one way to interpret the novel, and it's certainly part of Dickens's intention. But the meaning of the lawsuit, like concentric rings in water, grows wider and wider each time you read the novel. As a case of internecine fighting, the law-suit is a metaphor for the atomized state of human relationships in the Bleak Housian world. The British vision of chaos, as its history shows, is that of a family divided. In modern times families don't wage war, they litigate. And in such a world, judges and lawyers are kings.

But here they are tyrants presiding over a diseased society. In an upper-class British accent, "Jarndyce" sounds remarkably like "Jaundice," a pun that mediates between the novel's legal theme and its disease motif; moreover, as a verb, *to jaundice* means "to prejudice, invoke envy, or arouse anger." Pre-cisely Dickens's point: "How many people," the narrator asks, "out of the suit, Jarndyce and Jarndyce has stretched forth its unwholesome hand to spoil and corrupt, would be a very wide question." Even those not actively engaged in evil are tempted into something just as bad: a flabby acceptance of the status quo. Those who have contemplated the case "from the outermost of such evil have been insensibly tempted into a loose way of letting bad things alone to take their own bad course, and a loose belief that if the world go wrong, it was, in some off-hand manner, never meant to go right." The reader is left wondering: is England's collapse inevitable? Can anything or anyone set it right, and if not, what if anything can be salvaged from the wreckage?

THE LAST JUDGMENT

Calendar and clock time, years, months, days, and minutes dwindle into in-significance in the face of Jarndycian time, in which a lifetime passes in the wink of an eye:

> Innumerable children have been born into the cause; innumerable young people have married into it; innumerable old people have died out of it. Scores of persons have deliriously found themselves made parties in Jarndyce and Jarndyce, without knowing how or why; whole families have inherited legendary hatreds with the suit. The little plaintiff or de-fendant, who was promised a new rocking-horse when Jarndyce and Jarndyce should be settled, has grown up, possessed himself of a real horse, and trotted away into the other world.

The suit into which people are born and die is a metaphor for life itself, and ultimately one is judged by how he responds to *Jarndyce and Jarndyce*'s evil allure. Those who are immune, like Esther and Mr. Jarndyce, are blessed; those like Richard Carstone, Miss Flite, and Mr. Gridley, helplessly drawn beneath the wheels of the juggernaut, are in Purgatory; but those like the lawyer Mr. Vholes, a suburban vampire who quietly drains his clients' blood, belong to the lowest circle of hell.

The legal and the cosmic realms merge when mad Miss Flite—Dickens's sibyl—speaks of the unsettled case as the "Sixth or Great Seal," an allusion to the Book of Revelation and Judgment Day. In this novel, dispensation, death, judgment, and verdicts (both secular and profane) resonate sympathetically and suggest meanings beyond their ordinary context. Years earlier, Tom Jarndyce, one of the case's principal suitors, had remarked, "I am much depressed; my cause is on again, and I think I am nearer Judgment than I ever was." He then walks into a Chancery coffee shop and blows his brains out. When the case's verdict is finally read, Richard Carstone, the young ward in Chancery, dies, released from his bondage to the suit. And Miss Flite sets her captive birds free.

SECRETS AND PREDATORS: THE MYSTERY BEGINS

It seems a giant leap from the squalid nooks of the Court of Chancery to Chesney Wold, the landed estate of Sir Leicester and Lady Dedlock, but both realms are "things of precedent and usage." (The novel quickly jumps from one setting and group of characters to another, requiring the reader to connect them all, as in the childhood game of "dot to dot.") Sir Leicester, the custodian of moldy tradition, approves of *Jarndyce and Jarndyce* as "a British constitutional kind of thing." And, Dickens implies, the Dedlocks with their ancient lineage are also a "British kind of thing"—leading a moribund existence that drags on simply out of tradition.

It is raining at Chesney Wold, a relentless downpour, a symbol of the deluge that will wash away the arid Dedlockian way of life. Lady Dedlock—an inspired name—has buried and locked her past, forcibly deadening herself to genuine feeling. Dickens's sketch of what Lady Dedlock sees as she gazes out the window tells us, and reminds her, what such self-possession has cost her:

My Lady Dedlock (who is childless), looking out in the early twilight from her boudoir at a keeper's lodge, and seeing the light of a fire upon the latticed panes, and smoke rising from the chimney, and a child, chased by a woman, running out into the rain to meet the shining figure of a wrapped-up man coming through the gate, has been put quite out of temper.

The keeper, his wife, and his child shimmer in the wet countryside, emblems of fertility and vitality in a desiccated and artificial world. Dickens slips in the parenthetical "who is childless," a phrase that, placed where it is, begs to be noticed. The Dedlock line might be dead, but as we will learn, My Lady is *not* childless.

Through the years she has acquired an icy composure that is not shaken until the night in question. Bored and disdainful, Lady Dedlock sits by her husband and Mr. Tulkinghorn, the city's most powerful lawyer, as they study inconsequential legal documents. Suddenly she does something unusual—she acts on instinct:

> My Lady, changing her position, sees the papers on the table—looks at them nearer—looks at them nearer still—asks impulsively:
> Who copied that?
> Mr. Tulkinghorn stops short, surprised by My Lady's animation and her unusual tone.

In the stagnant Dedlockian realm, any show of animation is certain to arouse suspicion. Without her inscrutable mask, Lady Dedlock is like a hunted animal without protective coloration. The voracious lawyer, noting her unusual interest in the handwriting, is right on her scent—that is, he smells a secret. Mr. Tulkinghorn's calling is "the acquisition of secrets, and the holding possession of such power as they give him." To know someone's secret is to own them.

Mr. Tulkinghorn, whose name suggests a furtive, skulking beast, tops the legal food chain, followed by the lesser predators, Mr. Guppy, Mr. Vholes, the Smallweeds, and Mr. Weevle, names evocative of predators and parasites. Everyone in his own way is after something: letters, wills, documents, secrets.

From now until the end of the novel, he relentlessly pursues Lady Dedlock, threatening her with disclosure and ruin. It is ironic that this cold woman who immures her secrets and feelings will succumb, both literally and figuratively, to exposure.

MYSTERIES WITHIN MYSTERIES

*L*ady Dedlock's gesture switches on the plot machinery, setting the narrative action into high gear. With each chapter the novel gains in richness and complexity, surprises and secrets unfolding at every turn. Mr. Tulkinghorn traces the document in question back to Mr. Snagsby, the law stationer, who reveals that it was written by a destitute law writer, Nemo (Latin for "no one"), the alias for Captain Hawdon, Lady Dedlock's former lover and Esther Summerson's father. Nemo commits suicide before Mr. Tulkinghorn reaches him, and it becomes the lawyer's mission to find documentary evidence linking the law writer to the lady. Beginning with Nemo's recent past, he hunts up Jo, the homeless boy the dead man had befriended, and moves all the way back to Honoria Barbary (now Lady Dedlock), meanwhile drawing more and more people into his web. And an enigmatic web it is, creating unlikely pairings and bringing about tragedies, misdemeanors, and sins. Disguised as her maid, the sinister Hortense, Lady Dedlock of Chesney Wold secretly meets Jo of Tom-All-Alone's at the burial yard of her former lover; while there, Jo becomes infected with smallpox; when he begins to talk about his encounter with "the Lady," Mr. Tulkinghorn forces him to leave London. The sick boy ends up in Hertfordshire, where he infects and disfigures Esther, Lady Dedlock's lost daughter. From Lady Dedlock to Hortense to Jo to Mr. Tulkinghorn to Esther, everyone is mysteriously interconnected.

In his introduction to the Penguin edition of the novel, J. Hillis Miller notes, "Many characters find themselves surrounded by mysterious indications, sinister, threatening or soliciting." And he quotes the bedeviled Mr. Snagsby: "I find myself wrapped round with secrecy and mystery, till my life is a burden to me." As the omniscient narrator observes, Mr. Snagsby believes he is "a party to some dangerous secret, without knowing what it is. And the fearful peculiarity of this condition is that, at any hour of his daily life . . . the secret may take air and fire, and explode, and blow up." To the characters as well as to the reader, the events of *Bleak House* are fragmented and confusing, requiring interpretation. Almost everything and everyone in this novel seems to possess secret significance. Esther sees herself mirrored in a "confused way" in Lady Dedlock's face; Mr. Guppy tries to make sense of the physical resemblance between Esther and Lady Dedlock (Esther's features, a crucial element in the novel, are damning evidence, a "document" that is destroyed so it can't be "read"); the illiterate Krook rummages through his detritus, searching for a document containing the few letters of the alphabet (G.A.R.N.) that mean something to his vaporous brain; Mr. Weevle (alias Tony Jobling) tails Krook and tries to acquire his discovery; lost in a maze of suspicions, Mrs. Snagsby shadows her husband, convinced he is Jo's father. Even the law is a conspiracy among lawyers. Enthralled by the lawsuit, Richard Carstone convinces himself that he "had got at the core of the mystery now." The horrible thing is that when he gets to the "core," he finds there's nothing there. Finally, to Jo, the entire world is an indecipherable mystery:

It must be a strange state to be like Jo! To shuffle through the streets, unfamiliar with the shapes and in utter darkness as to the meaning, of those mysterious symbols, so abundant over the shops, and the corner of streets, and on the doors, and in the windows! . . . It must be very puzzling to see the good company going to the churches on Sundays, with their books in their hands and to think (for perhaps Jo *does* think, at odd times) what does it all mean, and if it means anything to anybody, how comes it that it means nothing to me?

It is fitting that Nemo and Jo, both lost souls, should befriend one another; the former is "no one," and the latter "knows nothink."

ESTHER

*L*ady Dedlock was falsely told that her infant daughter was born dead—and in a sense Esther *is* dead. To compensate for the shame of her illegitimate birth and her mother's sin, Esther has buried her deepest feelings, replacing them with a compulsion toward duty. Critics carp at the way Esther coyly smuggles in compliments to herself: "I have mentioned that, unless my vanity should deceive me (as I know it may, for I may be very vain, without suspecting it)." This is not a coy girl, but a faltering obsessive-compulsive, troubled by overscrupulousness. Esther's only childhood friend was a doll to whom she confessed all her feelings. When she leaves her aunt's, she buries her sole confidant, and with it her secrets and desires. From that point, whenever she begins to feel emotional, she reminds herself of her allegiance to duty (" 'Once more, duty, duty, Esther,' said I"). Generations of readers, repelled by such remarks, have seen Esther as a prig rather than a woman terrified by emotional intensity. As a woman, she is "deadlocked." She denies her passion and buries her desires in order to satisfy the needs of others.

But there are depths beneath Esther's placidity. After rejecting Mr. Guppy's proposal, she continues her household tasks as if nothing has happened, yet later, closeted in her bedroom, she gives way to choked-up laughter and tears. In spite of himself, the foolish clerk strikes a nerve of repressed longing. With Freudian perspicacity, Dickens has his heroine at this moment recall the doll she buried in the garden.

Despite her outward serenity, Esther's quest for identity is threatened by negation, illness, physical changes, and people who, though loving, impose their own needs and ideals on her. Always sensitive to the relationship between name and identity, Dickens pointedly tells us that Esther is called everything but her own name. Nicknames such as "Mrs. Shipton," "Little Old Woman," and "Mother Hubbard"—no matter how endearing—depersonalize her, transforming a lovely young woman into a "methodical old-maidish sort of foolish sort of little person." With all these nicknames, her own name "soon became quite lost among them." Mr. Jarndyce's house may be a kindly refuge, but like so many havens in Dickens's novels, it threatens individuality and autonomy.

Esther's fever dreams during her illness symbolically express her inner sadness and a longing to be rid of the heavy weight of duty that binds her to others:

I am almost afraid to hint at that time in my disorder—it seemed one long night . . . when I laboured up colossal staircases, ever striving to reach the top, and ever turned, as I have seen a worm in a garden path, by some obstruction, and labouring again.

Dare I hint at that worse time when, strung together somewhere in great black space, there was a flaming necklace, or ring, or starry circle of some kind, of which *I* was one of the beads! And when my only prayer was to be taken off from the rest, and when it was such inexplicable agony and misery to be a part of the dreadful thing?

The endless stair-climbing reflects the acts of goodness she feels compelled to perform in expiation of her mother's sin. Strung taut against the sky, Esther yearns for individuation, freedom from her past and from the expectations and conventions of society. In fact, every important character in *Bleak House,* without knowing it, is part of some "dreadful thing" they can never shake off.

Just before the onset of her illness, Esther finds herself the object of male admiration for the first time in her life. During her convalescence, she burns her potential suitor's flowers, thus symbolically destroying any possibility of romantic love. With calm resignation she accepts Mr. Jarndyce's proposal and prepares to enter a sexless union with a man old enough to be her grandfather. It looks as if Esther is following in her mother's footsteps: a childless marriage to an older man and a half-life of remembered passion. This sterile dead end *is* a potential conclusion for *Bleak House*—if the novel were to end on the same note it began: the end of the world, the end of the Dedlocks, the end of Esther, the immolated mistress of Bleak House. Yet despite everything, Esther refuses to bury herself.

In Dickens's novels, illness can be a catalyst to self-awareness. The healing process is a transformation, either morally or spiritually. Esther changes physically, of course, but she also undergoes emotional changes so subtle that they are not apparent until the novel's end.

Like everyone else in the story, Esther must grope through obscurity before finding clarity of vision. Her blindness ultimately deepens her insight, and her flawed face, paradoxically, becomes a mask that frees her to be herself. Esther's stern rebuke to Mr. Skimpole indicates how much she has changed since her illness. From the beginning, she sensed that his childish pose hid a man with the cunning of a shark. She never confronted him, however, because she mistrusted her instincts and relied on others to tell her how to feel. But by the end, she no longer doubts herself, and the anxious, hedging tone disappears from her narrative.

Moreover, since she no longer fears her sexual allure, she has no fear at all. Speaking to Mr. Guppy, she says, "[A]ny little delicacy I might have had in making a request to you is removed." She emerges from her illness stronger, more decisive, less apologetic; she is ready to meet her mother, confront her past, and, as she lifts her veil increasingly higher, show her flawed face to the world.

The culminating moment occurs when she sets off with Inspector Bucket in pursuit of her mother, Lady Dedlock. After a hallucinatory night journey in which they seem to ride forever in circles, Esther is reunited with her mother at the graveyard where her father is buried. The snow, her mother's corpse, the iron gates, the pauper's grave—a bleak family reunion indeed. Yet it *is* a reunion—and a "recognition scene" with a twist. Stripped of her grand persona, Lady Dedlock first appears to Esther as the brickmaker's wife, "the mother of the dead child." Esther is both mistaken and correct: Lady Dedlock *is* the mother of a dead baby named Esther Hawdon. In recognizing her mother, Esther, like so many of Dickens's abandoned children, ultimately finds herself: she is the baby, once presumed dead but now restored to life.

THINGS FALL APART

*T*he threat (or promise) of social revolution reverberates throughout the novel, echoing even in the most minor vignettes and details. The Dedlocks personify an enervated and decaying order, yet it isn't until chapter 27 that the narrator offers a vital replacement for their values.

The specter of Wat Tyler, the twelfth-century leader of a peasant rebellion, is never far from Sir Leicester's mind; he is thus astonished and disturbed to learn that his housekeeper's son, grown rich in the iron trade, is being considered for Parliament. The housekeeper's grandson, whose name happens to be Wat, stirs up his own rebellion when he decides to marry Lady Dedlock's maid and take her away from Chesney Wold. Sir Leicester can't understand why anyone would leave the shelter of Chesney Wold; the ironmaster can't understand why his son would marry someone from the class he left behind. But, like Dickens, Wat is the grandson of a servant, and as the first generation born to a self-made man, he represents the spirit of the age. The Watt/Rosa subplot chronicles in miniature the rise of a new class in England—and a fruitful merger between the feudal south and the industrial north.

The rumblings of revolution are even heard in the leitmotiv of the spectral footsteps of Ghost Walk. The footsteps are those of a former Lady Dedlock, a Cromwellian married to a Royalist during the Civil War. Their marriage became a domestic war that ended with Lady Dedlock's death. But before dying, she vowed that her steps would echo on the parapet until the family suffers dishonor or ruination.

The present Lady Dedlock's shame brings about the fall of the house, and, it would seem, the triumph of the common people over modern "Royalists" like Sir Leicester. But Dickens's view of the aristocracy is elegiac, an acknowledgment that there is part of the nobility worth preserving. In the final hour the old codes enable Sir Leicester to stand up to tragedy and shame. When informed of his wife's flight and the circumstances behind it, Sir Leicester rises to the occasion with the dignity and gallantry of an ancient race. Unable to speak, he manages to scrawl "Full forgiveness" on a note intended for his fallen wife. Our last glimpse of Chesney Wold is one of desolate stagnation: paralyzed, Sir Leicester lives on, and the old estate, darkened and partly abandoned, has "yielded to a dull repose."

BLEAK HOUSE, "NATIONAL AND DOMESTIC"

B leak House is filled with families. Almost everyone in the novel is defined by his familial role, and adults are judge by how they care for children. Mrs. Jellyby (a personification of England), Mr. Turveydrop, Mrs. Paradiggle, and Mr. Skimpole (especially) are all examples of neglectful parents and/or bad homemakers. In contrast, Charley is a young girl who acts as a mother to her orphaned siblings, and Caddy Jellyby undoes the wrongs of her mother and studies domestic economy with a vengeance. More than just cleaning, Dickensian homemaking is a sweeping away of metaphorical debris and fog. Krook (pointedly dubbed "the Chancellor"), the sinister and parodic embodiment of the legal system, remarks: "I have a liking for rust and must and cobwebs." As her nickname, "Little Old Woman," implies, Esther will clean the country and "sweep the cobwebs out of the sky" and, with her totemic keys, unlock musty secrets of the past. (Only two people in the novel clear away fog and filth: Esther with her broom, and the Inspector, the felicitously named Bucket.) Oddly enough, this quiet "little woman" is the mouthpiece for Dickensian reform. As editor of *Household Words,* Dickens cozily writes, "Supposing we were all of us to come off our pedestals and mix a little more with those below us, would it do any harm or would it be productive of lasting good?" His tone, chatty, even girlish, has a decidedly Summersonish ring. Practical deeds of loving kindness—washing

IF YOU LIKED THE O. J. SIMPSON TRIAL, YOU'LL LOVE *BLEAK HOUSE*

*I*n a *Time* essay entitled "Our Mutual Houseguest," Bruce Handy compares the "Trial of the Century" to the "overstuffed nineteenth-century novel, one of those ripping 800-page doorstops from college, a real cinderblock of a narrative. We got cliffhanger after cliffhanger, and more subplots than a contemporary storyteller might deem prudent." There were also the usual characters from every stratum of society: "earthy Salvadoran housemaids, beadle-like cops, bumbling civil servants, stalwart limo drivers, beaten-down screenwriters, and, of course, comically obsequious houseguests." Handy reminds us what teachers don't very often tell us: seamy drama is the stuff of great literature. What devotees of nineteenth-century fiction keep secret is that they read them not for the uplifting moral content but for the lurid plots—and with much the same intensity that others read the tabloids or watch Court TV.

Peepy Jellyby, teaching Charley, caring for Jo—will do more than windy bombast and reams of parchment.

Dickens obviously conceived his heroine with her role as savior in mind: Esther alludes to her biblical counterpart, another outsider who saves her people from destruction, whereas her surname implies her power to clean brumal fog. Although many contemporaries mocked his naïveté, Dickens believed that spiritual homemaking would become England's salvation.

The chapter detailing the end of the suit is fittingly entitled "Beginning the World." Richard Carstone dies with the case's final judgment and is judged in another, better world. He leaves behind a child who, raised by Ada and John Jarndyce, will become part of a potential new dispensation. The novel ends with a vision of reparation—even Esther's scars have disappeared! Does this mean that *Bleak House* is optimistic about the fate of England? Partly. One can't foget the echoing excoriations of the narrator, who like Blake sees in London's children "marks of misery and woe." Nevertheless, *Bleak House* moves from the threat of apocalypse to a qualified promise of rebirth.

CHANCERY

*M*ost American readers of *Bleak House* are understandably perplexed by Dickens's repeated references to "Chancery" or the "Court of Chancery." Several types of courts existed in Dickens's England, but they fall roughly into two categories: the Courts of Common Law and the Court of Chancery. The former dealt with criminal cases such as murder or theft, in which a suspect was examined, tried, and sentenced by a judge and jury. Such cases were decided by the principles of common law.

The Court of Chancery dealt with disputes about mortgages, legacies, and trusts, cases that were resolved by Equity rather than Law. The principles of Equity are unwritten, and each suit is considered singular. Equity arose to protect the individual from the inflexible Law, but by the nineteenth century it had become as corrupt and rigid as the system it originally sought to remedy. Chancery suits were notoriously protracted, expensive, and mired in paperwork. All this Dickens learned in 1844, when he appealed to Chancery to restrain infringements of his copyright to *A Christmas Carol*. He won the suit, but when he found that he could not recover the substantial costs, he declared in a letter, "I was really treated as if I were the robber instead of the robbed."

In 1873, three years after Dickens's death, the Court of Chancery was merged with other British courts to form the Supreme Court of Justice for England and Wales.

❖ Devotees of detective mysteries owe a great debt to Sir Robert Peel, whose act of 1829 founded the Metropolitan Police (who were called "Bobbies" in honor of their patron), and to the creation of the Criminal Investigation Department in 1842. Ever alert to the possibilities of anything new, Dickens was the first writer to use a detective as a pivotal character in a novel. Based on Inspector Field of the Metropolitan Police, the inscrutable "Inspector Bucket" ushered in a new genre, the novel of detection.

✤ In *Dickens and Crime,* Philip Collins notes that "the apotheosis of the Bobbie occurs . . . in *Bleak House.*" Nemo's body is found; a professional policeman immediately enters the suicide's room and puts the beadle, an outmoded, ridiculous "institution," to shame. Unlike most of his contemporaries, Dickens had nothing but admiration for the Metropolitan Police.

DICKENSIAN LISTS

One of the most memorable moments in Miriam Margolyes's show *Dickens's Women* is her haunting portrayal of Miss Flite:

It is an amazing imaginative feat! How did he think of a character like Miss Flite? The pathos of those words: "Their lives, poor things, are so short in comparison with Chancery." I can't believe how Dickens encapsulated in such a brief way these two gigantic ideas: the length of a Chancery suit and the brevity of the lives of pet birds. . . . When I did the show in America originally, my producer, Norman Lear, the television man, said, "Oh, the end is terribly depressing. You should move it around." You don't understand, I cried, it has to end on a dying fall."

—MIRIAM MARGOLYES

As enchanting as a prose poem, as jokey as a nonsense lyric by Edward Lear, the literary list is a (very) minor poetic genre in itself. There's something uncommonly satisfying about a long list of objects that only a devotee of lists appreciates. Few writers enjoyed assembling words, images, and sounds as much as Dickens. Some Dickensian lists are homages to order and harmony, such as the pleasing inventory of the contents of Mrs. Crisparkle's pantry in *Edwin Drood.* But in *Bleak House* lists generally suggest chaos and confusion, such as the jumble of detri-tus in Krook's rag-and-bottle shop:

In all parts of the window, were quantities of dirty bottles: blacking bottles, medicine bottles, ginger-beer and soda-water bottles, pickle bottles, wind bottles, ink bottles. . . . A little way within the shop-door, lay heaps of old crackled parchment scrolls, and discoloured and dog's-eared law-papers.

And the hodgepodge that spills from Mrs. Jellyby's closet sounds dadaesque in its startling juxtaposition of unlikely objects:

> Bits of mouldy pie, sour bottles, Mrs. Jellyby's caps, letters, tea, forks, odd boots and shoes of children, firewood, wafers, saucepan-lids, damp sugar in odds and ends of paper bags, footstools, blacklead brushes, bread, Mrs. Jellyby's bonnets, books with butter sticking to the binding, guttered candle-ends put out by being turned upside down in broken candle-sticks, nutshells, heads and tails of shrimps, dinner-mats, gloves, coffee-grounds, umbrellas . . .

But of all Dickensian lists, the most powerful and moving is Miss Flite's revelation at the end of the novel. Her refusal to divulge the names of her caged birds until a "Judgement" has been reached lends her recitation when it finally comes an incantatory power that is both startling and awful: "Hope, Joy, Youth, Peace, Rest, Life, Dust, Ashes, Waste, Want, Ruin, Despair, Madness, Death, Cunning, Folly, Words, Wigs, Rags, Sheepskin, Plunder, Precedent, Jargon, Gammon and Spinach."

With accumulating intensity, Miss Flite's roll call corresponds to the forces that blight Hope, Joy, Youth, and Beauty—it is a litany of the evils of Chancery itself. The final name, "Spinach," is the surprise; its very unexpectedness evokes the absurdity of existence in the *Bleak House* world.

THE HORROR, THE HORROR

*A*nyone who wants to write horror fiction should study the scene that leads up to Krook's fantastic end. It has all the creeping terror of a Wes Craven film, with the added dimension of metaphysical dread.

Mr. Guppy and Tony Weevle wait in the room where Nemo died "for the appointed time," i.e., when they can acquire the compromising letters about Lady Dedlock from Krook. Suddenly soot like "black fat" falls from the ceiling onto the floor; a thick odor, like that of rancid pork, permeates the air. The atmosphere grows increasingly putrid: "a thick yellow liquor" collects in a "nauseous pool" in the corner of the room. Finding the stuff on his finger, Mr. Guppy cries, "Give me some water, or I shall cut my arm off." At midnight, the clerks peer into the rag-and-bottle man's room and see nothing but a "burnt patch of flooring." "Is—is it the cinder of a small charred and broken log of wood sprinkled with white ashes, or is it coal? O Horror, he *is* here! . . ." It is death "inborn, inbred, engendered in the corrupted humours of the vicious body itself. . . ." The chapter ends with the pronouncement: "Spontaneous Combustion, and none other of all the deaths that can be died."

The notion that organic matter—in this case, a human being—could suddenly and inexplicably explode into flames had been widely accepted until it was disproved by Antoine-Laurent Lavoisier around the time of the French Revolution. Nonetheless the subject continued to spark debate, and some still believed in the phenomenon. In 1850 the *Times* reported the findings of an investigation into the mysterious death of one Countess Görlitz, who appeared to have been a victim of Krook's fate. Among the educated, the phenomenon was the equivalent of the pseudoscience that makes the front pages of the *National Enquirer*—lurid "facts" for the uneducated or the gullible.

It's easy to see why spontaneous combustion attracted Dickens—it is dramatic and freakish, with a suggestion of the unholy. Poof! and the sinner is vaporized, carried off into who knows where. Krook's death also makes poetic sense—how else should the alcoholic sinner die but by his own noxious fumes? In one of the most sensational ends in literature, Krook reverts to his primal elements, becoming just another greasy smell in the atmosphere.

It seems petty to quibble, but reviewers such as George Henry Lewes, the critic and consort of George Eliot, took Dickens to task for his scientific license. Lewes was right, of course, but Dickens could never be wrong. In the preface to the novel's first edition Dickens defends himself, noting that there are at least thirty such cases on record.

❖Lovers of Dickens make strange bedfellows. The poet Algernon Swinburne, for one, was a great admirer of Dickens. While *Bleak House* was being serialized, he terrified a friend he met on the street by hurriedly asking him, "Have you heard about the murder?" He was, it turned out, referring to the murder of Mr. Tulkinghorn in the novel's latest installment.

A LONDON FOG

It helps to be reminded that the fog that opens *Bleak House* is more than just a literary conceit:

Such of our country readers as have never been in town about this season of the year, can scarcely imagine what it is to grope their way through a downright thorough London Fog. It is something like being imbedded in a dilution of yellow pease-pudding, just thick enough to get through it without being wholly choked or completely suffocated. You can just see through the yard of it which, at the next stride, you are doomed to swallow, and that is all.

—THOMAS MILLER, 1849

Jo

*J*o, the street sweeper, is one of the most abject characters in all Dickens. He is not a winsome waif but a carrier of infection and death. He is the individualized counterpart to the allegorical children, Ignorance and Want, shown cowering beneath the robe of the Ghost of Christmas Present. There were hundreds of originals for Jo—one could find them on almost any city street, sweeping dung and dirt for pennies. But one boy in particular, George Ruby, stands out among the anonymous hordes. In January 1850, George was examined as a witness in an assault on a policeman:

Alderman Humphrey: Well, do you know what you are about? Do you know what an oath is?

Boy: No.

Alderman: Do you know what a Testament is?

Boy: No.

Alderman: Can you read?

Boy: No.

Alderman: Can you ever say your prayers?

Boy: No; never.

Alderman: Do you know what prayers are?

Boy: No.

Alderman: Do you know what God is?

Boy: No.

Alderman: Do you know what the Devil is?

Boy: No. I've heard of the Devil, but I don't know him.

Alderman: What do you know, my poor fellow?

Boy: I knows how to sweep the crossing.

Alderman: And that's all?

Boy: That's all. I sweeps the crossing.

A street waif—this is how the homeless street sweeper Jo in *Bleak House* might have looked.

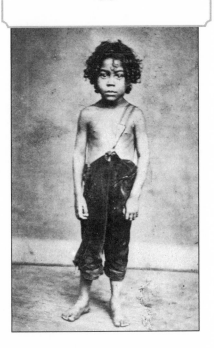

Like Jo at the "inkwitch," George was found ignorant of all knowledge of the outside world. Dickens was appalled by the moral and intellectual darkness in which these children lived. The stark honesty of the sweep's answers mocks the law's circumlocutions.

Dickens's London

※

"So you were never in London before?" said Mr. Wemmick to me.
"No," said I.
"I was new here once," said Mr. Wemmick. "Rum to think of it now!"
"You are well acquainted with it now?"
"Why, yes," said Mr. Wemmick. "I know the moves of it."
—Great Expectations

B alzac's Paris, Dostoyevsky's St. Petersburg, Joyce's Dublin, Dickens's London—these are the great cities of the novel. Part fictional, part real, they are topographical renderings of the writer's imagination. The myth of Dickensian London is so pervasive that even today, in an age of space probes and cyberchat, we are not wholly free of it: tourists still marvel at the city's "Dickensian" aspect. But is that because he described it so accurately, or because we have come to see it through his eyes?

"THE MOVES OF IT"

From the used clothing stores on Monmouth Street in *Sketches by Boz* to an opium den in Limehouse in *Drood,* Dickens's affinity for London appears in all his major works. Like Mr. Wemmick, he knew "the moves of it." The novelist George Augustus Sala marveled at Dickens's familiarity with all the "back streets behind Holborn, the courts and alleys of the Borough, the shabby sidling streets of the remoter suburbs, the crooked little alleys of the City, the dark and oozy whays of the waterside."

Unlike his richly particularized London, with its diverse neighborhoods, arterial streets, mews, and shops, Dickens's rural settings, like the nameless village where Oliver Twist was born or the countryside through which Nell and Grandfather wander, are generic. His imagination only gets as far as bright sunshine, green grass, and colorful, unnamed flowers—a paint-by-number narrative. His cityscapes, however, are so meticulously realized that readers can still follow the route the Artful Dodger and Oliver take into the city (from Clerkenwell to Saffron Hill) or stand on the exact spot where Mr. Pickwick first met Sam Weller. Specific landmarks such as Chancery Lane, Lincoln's Inn Fields, Holborn Hill, Covent Garden, and the Strand are recurring "characters" in the novels, imparting a continuity of place in which character and action are subservient to setting. Chancery Lane, the site of the coffeehouse where Tom Jarndyce of *Bleak House* blows his brains out, is also where Mr. Boffin meets John Rokesmith in *Our Mutual Friend*. Like Thomas Hardy's Egdon Heath, the metropolis endures, impervious to human tragedies and triumphs.

After Dickens's death, almost any site mentioned in the novels assumed the sanctity of a shrine. Readers scanned the novels for "clues," trying to correlate a fictitious place to an actual location. In its palmy days, Dickens studies were more topographical than literary. Early issues of *The Dickensian* were filled with painstaking accounts of excursions or "rambles" through what was known as "Dickensland," a virtual theme park filled with law offices, coaching inns, and curiosity shops. Even today, the stereotypical old-school Dickens scholar is a doddering codger in quest of a certain pub mentioned in one of the novelist's obscure works.

THE MAGIC LANTERN

*T*he city was to Dickens what the Lake District was to William Wordsworth. It was, as he famously put it, his "magic lantern." While the name conjures exotic images from *The Arabian Nights,* Dickens was referring to a device that enlarges pictures and projects them on the wall. A metropolitan muse, Dickens's London projected enhanced images onto the writer's imagination. Before he began writing, he had to pace about the city, unconsciously absorbing its scenes and sounds. Dickens would probably have agreed with the woman in a *New Yorker* cartoon who complained that nature has no plot.

Conditions that would drive most writers mad—noise, dirt, smoke, crowds—Dickens found invigorating. The hubbub of the city greased the wheels of his invention. While writing *Dombey and Son* and "The Chimes" in Lausanne, he wrote home, complaining:

> You can hardly imagine what infinite pains I take or what extraordinary difficulty I find in getting on FAST. . . . I suppose this is partly . . . the effect of the absence of streets and numbers of figures. I can't express how much I want these. It seems as if they supplied something to my brain, which it cannot bear, when busy, to lose. For a week or a fortnight I can write prodigiously in a retired place . . . and a day in London sets me up again and starts me.

For Dickens, inspiration is reflected in fictional style: like the city itself, his narrative canvas is crammed with people and objects, and his plots are tortuous and intricate, filled with abrupt detours into strange domains.

URBAN PASTORAL AND URBAN GOTHIC

Turn on the magic lantern, and Dickens's London is transformed into an industrialized version of the Forest of Arden from *As You Like It*. Dazed by love, Ruth Pinch and Tom Westlake in *Martin Chuzzlewit* wander among the sparkling fountains of Lincoln's Inn, and for a brief moment we have entered an urban pastoral. With centripetal force the city, like Shakespeare's forests, draws everyone in: it is where characters end up, where they discover themselves, fall in love, make their fortunes; it is an open sesame to adventure, coincidences, and unexpected encounters, where anything can and does happen.

At such times the visitor experiences a sense of unease, and in Dickens's London unease can quickly turn to terror. This dark metropolis is where Krook, the rag-and-bottle man, explodes into greasy ashes, and where Mr. Venus, the taxidermist, collects dismembered parts of the human body. This London is a paranoiac's worst nightmare, filled with hiding places and secret lookouts. Its houses are irregular and threatening, more animate and knowing than their inhabitants. In Dickens's London, even buildings are estranged from their surroundings.

This city is usually populated by grotesques, creatures that threaten our sense of normality. Dickens creates what is now known as the "urban gothic." Neither as obvious as magical realism nor as flashy and supernatural as gothic romance, the urban gothic takes the trappings of mystery and horror and transplants them into a perfectly realistic setting. One *should* feel safe among throngs of people, butcher shops, and tobacconists, yet there's an unmistakable sense of menace.

NOVEL NOIR

Dickens's vision of London is nothing like the choreographed bustle in Hollywood's version of Victorian life. Less Disney than film noir, it is a place of corruption and secrets, a nocturnal underworld populated by petty crooks and "respectable" citizens on the make. The pavement is damp, the air thick with mist, smoke, and fog. (Dickens's skies are rarely clear.) A poet of the crepuscular, his London exists in perpetual shadow, in the dim interval between day and night, in the gloom of Sunday evening or a fog-bitten November night.

DIRT AND DUNG

O ur vision of Dickens's England, perpetuated by Hollywood, theme parks, and murder mysteries, is either that of a gloomy, gaslit cityscape, or a quaint village with cheery chimney sweeps and moral, upright citizens. Those who praise Victorian values need a strong dose of reality. If you could somehow uncork a bottle of London air, vintage 1840, you'd inhale a mix of ordure, dirty rainwater, acrid smog, and rancid food. This was the smell of London during the first half of the nineteenth century. The measure of a society's civility is not in its art, politics, or conquests, but in the way it handles its dirt. Hence London, according to Dickens, was barbaric.

The rise and fall of civilizations depend on the conditions of their sewage systems, potential conduits of bacteria carrying the combined effluvia of millions of bodies. The rise in London's population from 1800 to 1850 created the stench of mass humanity and sanitary conditions that were the shame of Europe. In his exhaustive six-volume account of England's working class, *London Labour and the London Poor,* Henry Mayhew calculates with typical Victorian earnestness the total animal droppings voided on London thoroughfares, according to species:

Gross weight of the horse-dung and cattle-droppings annually deposited in the streets of London:—

	TONS
Horse-dung	36,662
Droppings of horned cattle	1,125
Droppings of pigs, calves, and sheep	1,805
TOTAL:	39,592

Hence we perceive that the gross weight of animal excretions dropped in the public thoroughfares of the metropolis is about 40,000 tons per annum, or, in round numbers, 770 tons every week—say 100 tons a day.

What the numbers don't reveal is the ordure that filled the crevices of cobblestones, forcing Victorian ladies and gentlemen to tread upon excrement whenever they left their houses. Animal dung was carried into houses as dust, staining carpets, furniture, and clothing.

By the Victorian age, it was common knowledge that such diseases as typhoid fever, cholera, and smallpox were the result of contaminated air, water, and food. Dickens, almost phobic about dirt, was convinced that disease was airborne. (Mr. Jarndyce's metaphorical East Wind, his "code word" for anything foul or unpleasant, is based on what Dickens knew to be scientific fact.)

In 1848 a cholera outbreak caused by tainted water raged for fifteen months, infecting 30,000 and killing 15,000. At last people were ready to act.

In response to the epidemic, a sanitation movement arose that eventually led to closed drains and a general cleanup of streets and gutters. During the second year of the epidemic, in an overcrowded orphanage at Tooting, 180 children had succumbed to the disease, the result of poor ventilation, inadequate nourishment, and filthy conditions. The incident, alluded to in chapter 10 of *Bleak House,* led to Dickens's involvement with sanitation reform. In a speech to the Metropolitan Sanitation Association in 1851 (the year he was writing *Bleak House*), Dickens declared that dirt was the root of all evil:

> That no one can estimate the amount of mischief which is grown in dirt; that no one can say, here it stops, or there it stops, either in its physical or its moral results, when both begin in the cradle and are not at rest in the obscene grave is now as certain as it is that the air from Gin Lane will be carried, where the wind is Easterly, into May Fair, and that if you once have a vigorous pestilence raging furiously in Saint Giles's, no mortal list of Lady Patronesses can keep it out of Almack's.

An astonishing statement, summing up both metaphorically and literally the essence of the novel he was working on. Infection, as *Bleak House* reveals, has little respect for class distinctions.

Power Walking

Restlessness, you will say. Whatever it is, it is always driving me, and I cannot help it. I have rested nine or ten weeks, and sometimes feel as if it had been a year—though I had the strangest nervous miseries before I stopped. If I couldn't walk fast and far, I should just explode and perish.
—Dickens to John Forster, 1854

F or Dickens, walking was a way of stoking the engines of creativity and working off the infernal restlessness that plagued him all his life. He had an insatiable need to walk—and not a leisurely amble through the countryside, but furious strides through crowded city streets. According to Peter Ackroyd, Dickens could cover twelve miles in two and a half hours—a remarkable rate of twelve and a half minutes per mile.

Restiveness, particularly in the later years, preceded the act of creation. Before he could write, Dickens needed to walk. Writing to Angela Burdett-Coutts, he anatomized his condition:

During a fight with Catherine, not content to leave the room or even hire a cab, Dickens leaped out of bed at two the morning and trudged the entire thirty-three miles from Kent to London. The next day, writing to Forster, he gloated over his triumph, seeing it as just one more anecdote for posterity.

In the wandering-unsettled-restless uncontrollable state of being about to begin a new book. At such a time I am as infirm of purpose as Macbeth, as errant as Mad Tom, and as ragged as Timon. I sit down to work, do nothing get up [sic] and walk a dozen miles, come back and sit down again next day, again do nothing and get up, go down a railroad, find a place where I resolve to stay for a month, come home next morning, go strolling about for hours and hours, reject all engagements to have time to myself, get tired of myself and yet can't come out of myself to be pleasant to anybody else, and go on turning upon the same wheel round and round and over and over again until it may begin to roll me toward my end.

How to explain this lifelong compulsion? Perhaps he was simply working off nervous energy, but it also seems that Dickens had a dread of inertia, a belief that if he ever stopped moving or working, he would "rust and die."

INTERVIEW WITH FRED KAPLAN

Professor of English at City College of New York, Fred Kaplan is the author of the acclaimed biography *Carlyle* (winner of the National Book Award) and, of course, his *Dickens: A Life* (1988).

NE: *One quality that strikes the reader of your biography of Dickens is the tremendous amount of energy Dickens brought to everything he did. Just where did he find the time to accomplish everything?*

FK: Dickens did have a lot of energy. But what interests me is how effectively he disciplined it so that he increased its power by square root factors. Henry James met Dickens only once, in November 1867, in Cambridge, Massachusetts, where as a young man he was invited to meet the visiting celebrity. Young Henry wanders from room to room, and suddenly in the doorway he sees Dickens. Their encounter doesn't take more than a few seconds. But it was an epiphany for James. When he looked at Dickens, he saw in his eyes an extraordinary aura of authority and discipline even though it was a tired Dickens at the end of his life, looking prematurely old. James described Dickens's look as a "merciless, military gaze," and he says that this was a moment of growth for him as an artist. What he says (in Jamesian periphrasis) is that when he looked at Dickens looking around the room, he realized that Dickens could get the maximum amount of life out of the smallest experience. That, combined with his talent, was conducive to the creation of great art. So the lesson James learned from Dickens is that the great artist has to use his energy in the most disciplined and ruthless way. Although Dickens was old and tired, James saw him as bursting with creative juices.

*D*ickensian London was not at all the cozy "village" depicted in movies. Noisy and filthy, it was Dickens's "magic lantern." Before he could begin a novel he would take to the city's streets and walk as fast as he could for hours.

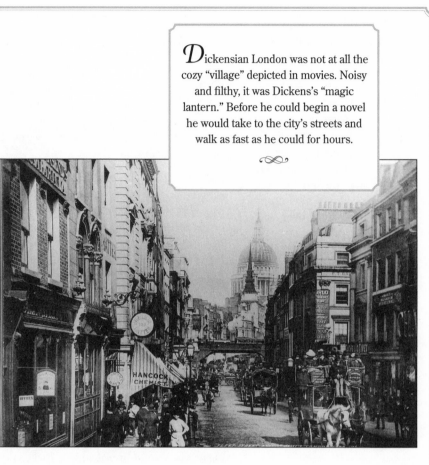

Midlife Yearnings

⚓

*This is what I call my Wandering days, before I fall to work. I seem to
be always looking at such times for something I have not found
in life, but may possibly come to, a few thousands of years hence,
in some other part of some other system, God knows.*

—DICKENS, 1852

y 1853, Dickens, now 41, had become increasingly unhappy in
his marriage. With ten pregnancies behind her, Catherine had
grown middle-aged before her husband—or before he thought
he had. By 40, Catherine was stout, plain and prone to chronic in-
validism. But his conjugal misery probably had less to do with Catherine than
with a yearning for his youth. His disastrous attempt at a dalliance with the
now middle-aged Maria Beadnell Winter in 1855 (see page 272) and his growing friendships with younger men suggest a longing to be free of his domestic
prison.

He began to complain about Catherine's family, projecting his disaffection
with her onto them. During one of their many extended visits, he told Wilkie
Collins, "I am dead sick of the Scottish tongue in all its moods and tenses."
While he was away, the Hogarths would often descend upon Tavistock
House, leaving it, much to his consternation, a mess. After receiving a letter
from Mrs. Hogarth, Dickens baldly wrote, "I never beheld anything like your
mother's letter, for the desperation of its imbecility."

Dickens's misery took the form of restlessness in which bouts of manic exertion alternated with periods of deep gloom. In 1852, he drove himself so
hard that he practically suffered a nervous collapse. His childhood kidney ail-
ment returned, a reminder of his old pain and loneliness. As he confessed to
Forster, "Hypochondriacal whisperings tell me I am rather overworked." Relentless activity distracted him from the empty feeling of middle age—that period, as John Irving put it, when one feels that the best of life is over, and the
worst is yet to come. Hard work was his way of fighting against despair and

This Ary Scheffer portrait shows Dickens in middle age. He hated sitting for it and called it the "nightmare portrait." When it was finally completed, he looked at it and declared that he would never have recognized himself. "It is always possible that I may know other people's faces pretty well, without knowing my own." When others praised the picture, he declared, "So I come to the conclusion that I never *do* see myself." There is nothing in the portrait to suggest its subject's inner demons.

stagnation. Thus he immersed himself in acting, philanthropy, official dinners, novel-writing, and the latest fad from the Spiritualist cult, table rapping.

His physical exhaustion, coupled with his psychic pain, slowly drained him of his health, and even youth itself. At forty he looked fifty. But Dickens did everything fast: he grew up too fast and looked old before his time. The young actor Edmund Yates had never seen Dickens and had always imagined him as he appeared in the "Nicholas Nickleby" portrait. Expecting to find a beardless youth with flowing auburn hair, he instead saw an "aggressive"-looking older man with sparse hair, a heavily lined face and a "door knocker" beard flecked with gray. His mother, who hadn't seen Dickens in fifteen years, observed, "Save his eyes there is not a trace of the original Dickens about him."

THE DICKENS DOCKET CIRCA 1847–1855

*H*is calendar is a dizzying round of events, both official and personal. In one week he can be overseeing Urania Cottage, his home for fallen women; visiting slums in Bethnal Green with Miss Burdett-Coutts; dictating *A Child's History of England* to Georgina; speechifying for charities or the Literary Guild; rehearsing until after midnight for amateur theatricals and then traveling with a troupe of friends from London to Liverpool or Birmingham for sold-out performances.

He takes several trips with male friends: Norwich Cathedral, site of a double murder; a riverside tavern that features performing dogs; Yarmouth, a potential site for a new novel which will be called *David Copperfield*. He also spends several weeks traveling throughout Italy and France. Most important, in 1855, he buys Gad's Hill Place, his first and only permanent home—although he would always have lodgings in London.

The years from 1847 to 1855 are marked by recurring events: the births of three children his annual Twelfth Night parties; the anniversaries of Mary Hogarth's death (page 96); the family's summer pilgrimages to the sea; the monthly installments of each novel, first *David Copperfield* (1850–51), followed by *Bleak House* (1852–53), *Hard Times* (1854), and *Little Dorrit* (1855–56). There are also deaths, two instances of art predicting life: In 1848, his sister, Fanny, dies of consumption; in *A Christmas Carol,* written in 1843, Scrooge's delicate sister, also named Fanny, dies of the same disease. Then, in 1851, his infant daughter Dora dies, just eight months after her namesake, the fictional Dora Spenlow. Less than a week after Dora, Dickens's father died, perhaps the most difficult loss of all.

He also begins a new venture: while writing *David Copperfield* he designs and edits *Household Words,* a weekly journal of informative essays, fiction, and investigative reporting (on sanitation, sewage, and factory conditions). In the midst of all this, he manages to write some of his greatest novels. Out of pain, irritation, and anxiety emerge enduring works. The novels of these middle years, especially *Bleak House* and *Little Dorrit,* are markedly different, both in tone and style, from their predecessors. The novels' heroes are less heroic, and their tone is decidedly cheerless. Life for Dickens, as for Stephen Blackpool in *Hard Times,* is an irresolvable "muddle."

Hard Times

⚕

*T*he devil hath established his cities in the north.
—SAINT AUGUSTINE

H *ard Times* is a portrait of a soulless industrial city and its deadened inhabitants. With its allegorical characters and simple plot,
it reads like a futuristic parable, but Dickens makes it clear that
the story is set in the reader's present and that the conditions he
depicts are all too real. Modern readers forget that the novel's complete title
is *Hard Times: For These Times.* The emphatic "these" conveys a sense of immediacy and moral imperative.

The setting, Coketown, is a "red brick city," located in the industrial north,
a region known for its dreary ugliness, coal smoke, and relentless drizzle.
The blank uniformity of the town's buildings and streets reflects the leaden
existence of its citizens, who live without joy or hope. Smoke has turned the
once green landscape a dull gray, and the workers, blackened by smoke, are
indistinguishable from one another. Known as "Hands," they are automatons
whose lives consist of going to work and returning home. The synecdoche
suggests that these human beings have been reduced to just that,
grotesquely disembodied appendages, severed from hearts and minds.

Dickens uses bizarre imagery in his description of the monotonous landscape. Glimpsed fleetingly through a railway window, the factories look like
"fairy palaces that illuminate the sky," an ironic simile given that fairy tales
are suppressed in Coketown. But Dickens also suggests, whether he means
to or not, that Coketown contains its own form of poetry, although those who
live there are too numb to appreciate it. A surreal vision in red and black, the
factories resemble "the painted face of a savage"; the piston of the steam en-
gine pounds "monotonously up and down, like the head of an elephant in a

state of melancholy madness." The satanic factories are the sole image of passion and energy in the novel. When Louisa Gradgrind, herself a victim of a repressed libido, describes the factories at night, she might as well be speaking of herself: "There seems to be nothing there, but languid and monotonous smoke. Yet when night comes, fire bursts out, Father!" Even today, despite what we know about pollution and toxic waste, the sight of powerworks illuminating a night sky possesses an unnatural beauty.

This demonic landscape, with its eternal fires, is a modern version of Milton's Pandemonium, the capital of hell built by the fallen angels after their exile from heaven in *Paradise Lost*. Built on a hill that "belches fire and smoke," Pandemonium is the devil's Coketown, mechanistic and perverse; and both exist, in Milton's memorable phrase, in "darkness visible."

What is truly hellish about Coketown is its enforced uniformity: every resident is governed by the doctrine of utilitarianism—Dickens's main target in the novel. As he interprets it, utilitarianism professes function over feelings, facts over fancy. All behavior is motivated by self-interest, every question can be answered by a statistic. (Dickens considered calling the novel *Prove It.*) Mr. Gradgrind, the main proponent of utilitarianism, rejects all imaginative adornments: "You are not to have, in any object of use or ornament, what would be a contradiction of fact. You don't walk upon flowers in fact; you cannot be allowed to walk upon flowers in carpets." Altogether, utilitarianism is a no-nonsense doctrine, but in these hard times, such "nonsense" is necessary.

Raised according to utilitarian principles, the children of Coketown die at an early age. Their creativity, synonymous for Dickens with individuality and vitality, is stunted, turning them into fact-spouting drones. They are products, manufactured in a factory called "school," where the necessary facts are ground into their heads by their teacher, Mr. McChoakumchild. In the novel's second chapter—entitled "Murdering the Innocents"—a new student, "girl number twenty," is asked to define a horse. Although "girl number twenty," a circus child named Cissy Jupe, has lived among horses, she is unable to precisely state just what a horse is. The odious Bitzer steps in with the correct answer:

> Quadruped. Graminivorous. Forty teeth, namely twenty-four grinders, four eye-teeth, and twelve incisive. Sheds coat in the spring; in marshy countries, sheds hoofs, too. Hoofs hard, but requiring to be shod with iron. Age known by marks in mouth.

Has Bitzer indeed described a horse? Can a horse be reduced to the sum of its parts? What about the essence of "horseness"? Or, for that matter, of humanity? Are we simply two hands, two feet, thirty-two teeth, and so on? The individual spirit that transcends physical traits cannot exist within the soul-killing utilitarian framework.

The novel's main plot concerns the fates of Louisa and Tom Gradgrind. Theirs is a childhood devoid of circuses, fairy tales, and childish games, in which wonder is a punishable offense. Louisa is the more tragic of the two, since she knows her soul is being violated, but like an abused child, she is powerless to stop it.

Trained that the heart is only a circulatory organ, she enters a loveless but statistically advantageous marriage with the middle-aged boor Mr. Bounderby, but her composure gives way when she meets a seductive playboy and nearly succumbs to his advances. Though taught to ignore natural impulses, she is defenseless against the sudden rush of desire. She leaves her husband, and although he soon dies, she never marries again. Though chastened and gentle, Louisa does not completely recover from her childhood.

Tom, deprived of a normal boyhood, grows up eager to take revenge on the society that ill-used him and greedy for the pleasure he's been denied so long. Dickens shows keen insight into the psychological effects of denial:

> It was very remarkable that a young gentleman who had been brought up under one continuous system of unnatural restraint, should be a hypocrite; but it was certainly the case with Tom. It was very strange that a young gentleman who had never been left to his own guidance for five consecutive minutes, should be incapable at last of governing himself; but so it was with Tom. It was altogether unaccountable that a young gentleman whose imagination had been strangled in the cradle, should be still inconvenienced by its ghost in the form of grovelling sensualities; but such a monster, beyond all doubt, was Tom.

In contrast to Mr. Bounderby, who believes that if the Hands are permitted one liberty, they'll soon be demanding "venison and turtle soup with a gold spoon," Dickens asserts that restraint leads to uncontrollable desires. Tom robs a bank to pay his debts, frames one of the Hands for the crime, and flees—ironically disguised as a clown—to escape imprisonment. He dies in a strange country, penitent and alone. *Hard Times,* as Russell Baker has noted, is the only Dickens novel with an unhappy ending.

One of the most poignant scenes in the novel is the death of Mrs. Gradgrind, until now a whimpering nonentity, confused by all the "Ologies" that surround her. When asked if she's suffering, the invalid replies, "I think there's a pain somewhere in the room, but I couldn't positively say I have got it." A remarkable statement. For Coketowners, both pain and pleasure exist "somewhere," but they can never connect their feelings to their selves.

The tender ministrations of Cissy, the circus child, have given Mrs. Gradgrind a novel idea that she struggles to express before dying: "But there is something—not an Ology at all—that your father has missed, or forgotten, Louisa. I don't know what it is. . . . I shall never get its name now." But there is no dictionary that can help Mrs. Gradgrind, and she dies without ever having lived.

Two people in the novel stand out, each with a distinct moral character that cannot be smothered beneath the weight of facts or conformity. Stephen Blackpool's story seems more characteristic of the tragic vision of Thomas Hardy than of Dickens—even the "dark Dickens." Unable to obtain a divorce to marry the woman he loves, he is trapped in his marriage to a "drunken creature." (In an earlier Dickens novel, such a situation would have been unthinkable.) When he refuses to agree with the bloated rhetoric of the union delegate, Mr. Slackbridge, he is ostracized by his fellow workers and then fired as a troublemaker. Stephen courageously stands up for his beliefs rather than submit to a collective idea, but the penalty for individuality is death. Saint Stephen was the first Christian martyr; Stephen Blackpool is the first saint of the industrial age. Life, as he puts it, is a "muddle"—a muddle that will not be resolved until people recover their lost feelings and their capacity for joy.

If the novel offers any hope, it is through the circus "philosophy" of Cissy Jupe, the daughter of a clown. Hopeless at multiplication and division, Cissy brings vitality and joy to the deadened Gradgrind household, showing them that not everything can be summed up in an -ism or an -ology. At the end of the novel, the narrator peers into "futurity," and sees Cissy surrounded by children, teaching them the "childish lore" that will "beautify their lives of machinery . . . with imaginative delights" and, happily, ensure that laughter and "nonsense" will survive into the next generation.

In the end, it is Mr. Sleary, the circus owner (only Dickens would name a lisper "Sleary"), who sums up the novel's moral: "People mutht be amuthed. They can't be alwayth a-learning, nor yet they can't be alwayth a-working, they an't made for it. You *mutht* have uth."

Readers who agree with Mr. Sleary may well wonder why Dickens wrote this charmless novel. With some exceptions, there is little here to amuse us. Instead of comedic digressions, the novel possesses a grim power, a concentration of vision, and a simplicity rare for Dickens. This is fiction as manifesto, stripped of anything that might detract from its moral agenda. In *Hard Times,* Dickens's purpose is uncompromised by his characteristic sentimentality and humor.

✱The great English critic F. R. Leavis places Dickens in the "Great Tradition" of English novelists solely on the basis of this one novel. *Hard Times,* Leavis wrote, is Dickens's "masterpiece," his "only completely serious work of art."

Maria Redux

anuary 1855: Dickens is forty-three years old, and as he confesses to Forster, in a "disheveled" state of mind: "motes of new books in the dirty air, miseries of older growth threatening to close upon me. Why is it, that as with poor David [Copperfield], a sense comes always crushing on me now, when I fall into low spirits, as of one happiness I have missed in life, and one friend and companion I have never made?" His state of mind accounts for his susceptibility to what happened next.

Unexpectedly, one month later, like a missive from a ghost, a letter arrives from Maria Winter, née Beadnell, the woman he was infatuated with for four years from 1829 through 1833.

Having rejected the young Dickens, she is now married to Henry Winter, a poor sawmill manager. ("Did *she* make a mistake!" quips the actress Miriam Margolyes.) Stunned by the unexpected sight of the familiar hand, he never stops to consider that Maria, two years older than himself, is no longer an adorable coquette of twenty but a forty-six-year-old matron.

Thus begins a flurry of correspondence in which they relive their courtship, which seems even more momentous and romantic in retrospect.

His prompt reply to Maria's first letter vibrates with suppressed emotion:

You so belong to the days when the qualities that have done me most good since, were growing in my boyish heart that I cannot end my answer to you lightly. The associations my memory has with you, make your letter more—I want a word—invest it with a more immediate address to me—than such a letter could have from anybody else.

Filled with references to their past, his letter was not written to a Mrs. Winter, a person who scarcely seems to exist for him, but to Maria Beadnell. She wrote that she had two little girls; he replied that her daughters must be a "delusion of yours." The years, full ones for Dickens in which he had married, become famous, written ten novels, and fathered nine children, "vanished like a dream."

In one letter Maria apparently asks Dickens to buy her a velvet ribbon while he is in Paris, and her request in turn brought back the memory of a certain pair of blue gloves. Dickens sounds just like one of his own spoony lovers, an Augustus Moddle or a Mr. Toots: "There are things," he solemnly informs her, "I have locked up in my own breast, and that I never thought to bring out anymore." At some point Maria must have confessed that he had been her only love; for his part, he avows that he had read her letter "with great emotion," adding, "Remember, I accept all with my whole soul, and reciprocate all."

The editors of the Pilgrim edition of Dickens's letters surmise that Maria next proposed a tryst, which probably occurred a few weeks after the first letter. She warned him that she had changed, but he brushed the caution aside: "When you say you are 'toothless, fat, old and ugly' (which I don't believe), I fly away to the house in Lombard Street which is pulled down, as if it were necessary that the very bricks and mortar should go the way of my airy castles, and see you in a sort of raspberry colored dress with a little black trimming on the top." He's off and running through the alleys of the past.

Because he is "a dangerous man to be seen with," they make elaborate plans for the rendezvous. When Mrs. Winter calls at the Dickens's residence, she is to ask for Catherine ("It is almost a positive certainty that there will be no one here but I"); upon being told that the mistress is not home, she is then to ask for Mr. Dickens. After these instructions, he ends the letter with professions of hope for a "fresh beginning."

Then the fateful meeting. The sight of the overweight, middle-aged matron—who, ironically, resembled his wife—at his doorstep was shattering: "Clennam's eyes no sooner fell upon the subject of his old passion, than it shivered and broke to pieces." This is Dickens's account of a similar episode in *Little Dorrit,* and it's the closest he comes to revealing his feelings. One can only imagine Mrs. Winter's feelings when she read this cruel description months later. In fact, the passage is so brutal that it seems vindictive, as if Dickens were unconsciously punishing Maria for having grown old.

Twenty years had transformed the enchanting coquette into a raddled matron. As Georgina (Dickens's sharp-tongued sister-in-law) happily reported, "She had become *very* fat! and quite commonplace." Further adding to her distinct lack of physical charms, Mrs. Winter was suffering from a head cold, which, much to Dickens's annoyance, he caught. The young Maria had giggled girlishly, a habit that, unfortunately, the old Maria retained. Allusions to their shared past now sickened him. What once delighted now repelled.

We don't know what strain or embarrassment each endured at that meeting, but by the next letter Dickens's tone has altered drastically. Gone are the rhapsodic re-creations of the past; distant politeness has replaced ardor. In another letter he tries to arrange a suitable occasion for her to call, this time with Catherine firmly present. His remaining three letters to her are a string of evasions and excuses for not meeting her again.

As preposterous as it may seem, it apparently never occurred to Dickens that unlike his fictional women, Maria was subject to age and decay. His rational side, which must have been aware of Maria's age, had split from that part of him that yearned to recapture his old love. (Psychologists would say he suffered from cognitive dissonance.) For Dickens, the real, very much alive Maria Beadnell Winter was a walking memento mori, a chilling reminder of the passage of time. Seeing her, he could no longer delude himself that he was still young.

In *David Copperfield* the young Maria was the inspiration for Dora, David's fetching child bride. In *Little Dorrit,* Mrs. Winter was cold-bloodedly put to good use as the middle-aged hero's first love, Flora Finching, now a garrulous, florid widow who makes alarming advances toward her old sweetheart. That Dora and Flora are the same person is a hideous revelation—and surely Mrs. Winter, who was no fool, must have recognized herself in the portrait. In creating this devastating portrait of Maria, Dickens finally exacted revenge for the humiliations she made him suffer so many years before. Maria Beadnell Winter is buried in an unmarked pauper's grave in Kensal Green, the same cemetery where Ellen Ternan was buried in 1914.

Little Dorrit

⁜

[Little Dorrit] was amazing, it was so crammed and chaotic, and yet so touching, a kind of miracle, a strangely naked display of feeling, and full of profound ideas, yet one felt it was all true!
—IRIS MURDOCH, *Nuns and Soldiers*

$\diamond\bullet\bullet\diamond\diamond$

*L*ittle Dorrit *is a more seditious book than* Das Kapital.
—GEORGE BERNARD SHAW

$\diamond\bullet\bullet\diamond\diamond$

 ittle Dorrit is the most claustrophobic of novels. Dead ends, enclosed spaces, stifling rooms, and prison cells recur throughout the book. Dickens rings countless changes on the multiple meanings of imprisonment, entrapment, paralysis, suffocation, repression—in society, politics, and within the psyche. Readers may be forced to put the book down, gasping for air.

THE OVERTURE

*T*he novel opens on a blazing afternoon in Marseilles. Nothing moves or breathes in the stillness of the heat, and the monotonous repetition evokes a sense of restriction, as if the narrator himself were pacing up and down a narrow linguistic path:

> Everything in Marseilles, and about Marseilles, had stared at the fervid sky, and been stared at in return, until a staring habit had become universal there. Strangers were stared out of countenance by staring white houses, staring white walls, staring white streets, staring tracts of arid road, staring hills from which verdure was burnt away.

From the parched landscape, the narrative eye pans to a dank prison cell, where Rigaud and John Baptist await sentencing. Each man's role is left unexplained, but for now it is sufficient that the prison theme has been sounded. The next chapter moves abruptly to a more civilized setting, although still a prison of sorts: a group of English travelers is waiting to be released from quarantine before entering England. Just before they depart, kindly Mr. Meagles declares that any man can forgive his prison after he's freed, whereupon the embittered Miss Wade replies, "If I had been shut up in any place to pine and suffer, I should always hate that place and wish to burn it down, or raze it to the ground." Morbidly dwelling on past wrongs is itself a form of captivity ("I should always hate . . ."), while only forgiveness can bring about true release. The English travelers disperse, but their lives, and those of the two convicts, will become fatefully entwined.

ARTHUR CLENNAM

Little Dorrit also follows the path of one of the voyagers, the forty-year-old Arthur Clennam. After twenty years in the East, Arthur returns to London, his childhood home. In two decades the city, at least in Arthur's eyes, has remained virtually unchanged, as though it had been embalmed and entombed. He arrives on the Sabbath—giving Dickens a chance to attack the grim English Sundays, with their strict prohibitions against pleasure. Gloom is diffused through the city: "Melancholy streets, in a penitential garb of soot, steeped the souls of the people who were condemned to look at them out of windows, in dire despondency." Sitting in the twilight, Arthur recalls his austere childhood, which has haunted and oppressed him, and his future seems as closed and desolate as his past. Those who condemn Dickens for his lack of psychological insight need only look to the character of Arthur Clennam. Through Arthur, one of his finest creations, Dickens anatomizes that form of anguish and frustration particular to the unfulfilled and middle-aged.

The Clennam house, which stands in an enclosed courtyard on a narrow street, is one of Dickens's most impressively gothic manses, representing the pent-up emotions and closely guarded secrets of its inhabitants:

> Its close air was secret. The gloom and must, and dust, of the whole tenement, were secret. At the heart of it his mother presided, inflexible of face, indomitable of will, firmly holding all the secrets of her own and his father's life, and austerely opposing herself, front to front, to the great final secret of life.

The house is a bell jar that has preserved everything within it; time seems to have stopped, and indeed, to Mrs. Clennam, all seasons are alike.

The guardian of the mysteries is a forbidding Sabbatarian who raised her only son on wrathful pieties and sulfurous sermons in an atmosphere of joyless self-denial. For the past twelve years she has remained in her room, confined to a wheelchair, her limbs as rigid as her moral outlook—while enjoying a "grim luxuriousness" in her martyrdom.

As a result of his upbringing, Arthur is a meticulous, overly scrupulous man who seems to have been born middle-aged. Grave and reserved, he is oddly subdued, as though something vital within him had been quashed and buried.

Upon returning home, Arthur presents his mother with his father's watch with the enigmatic monogram "D.N.F.," standing for "Do Not Forget." He instinctively knows that the engraved command refers to an old injury that the dying Mr. Clennam wished to set right. After questioning his mother, Arthur senses that in some way she *has* wronged someone, and that her paralysis is a hysterical symptom, a self-inflicted form of justice. As Arthur's interest in the little seamstress (now known as Little Dorrit) deepens, he begins to speculate on how she might be involved in the affair. Arthur's precocious conscience and his hatred of injustice impel him to uncover the mystery and repair the sins of his elders. Only then will he be free of the past.

LITTLE DORRIT

Our first glimpse of the titular heroine is scarcely a glimpse at all: she possesses a "diminutive figure and small features, and is little and light . . . noiseless and shy. . . . She had all the manner of and much of the appearance of a subdued child." Little Dorrit's face is "transparent," a detail that sharply contrasts with the impenetrable expressions and pretenses of those around her. At twenty-two, she could pass for a girl half her age, and although Arthur couldn't possibly know it, her juvenile appearance displeases her. Certainly it prevents him from recognizing her capacity for passion and his love for her.

Inexplicably drawn to the girl, Arthur initially sees Little Dorrit as a child, thereby desexing her and depriving himself of her mature love. Her singular name, which she prefers to the conventional "Amy," and her calm determina-tion suggest a woman who is clearly herself. In her typical parenthetical patter, Arthur's old sweetheart Flora Finching plays on the curious nickname, groping toward what it could possibly mean: "and of all the strangest names I ever heard the strangest, like a place down in the country with a turnpike, or a favourite pony or a puppy or a bird or something from a seed-shop to be put in a garden

or a flower pot and come up speckled." But there are no similes for Little Dorrit, either the girl or the name—she is simply herself. It is precisely this quality that attracts Arthur: "She had interested him out of her own individuality."

One night Arthur secretly follows her home and discovers that she lives with her father in the same debtor's prison where Dickens's father was incarcerated, the famous Marshalsea.

THE MARSHALSEA

The fly-infested, stifling Marshalsea is the centerpiece of the novel, the frame of reference against which Dickens compares "outer" society with its strictures and rules. Dickens describes prison life, literally and figuratively, both from the outside in and—considering his past intimacy with it—from the inside out.

In the Marshalsea, standard definitions of liberty and captivity are obscured. For many inmates, imprisonment means freedom from bankruptcy, bill collectors, and family trouble. Indeed, for some the Marshalsea is a haven from the press and fever of the restless crowd.

Crushed with shame when he was first incarcerated, Mr. Dorrit "languidly slipped into this smooth descent, and never more took one step upward." Now, more than twenty years later, his long tenure at the Marshalsea has become a source of jealous pride. As the "Father of the Marshalsea," he presides over a miniature kingdom with its own observances and rituals:

All new-comers were presented to him. He was punctilious in the exaction of this ceremony. The wits would perform the office of introduction with overcharged pomp and politeness, but they could not easily overstep his sense of gravity. He received them in his poor room (he disliked an introduction in the mere yard, as informal—a thing that might happen to anybody) with a kind of bowed-down beneficence.

Visitors and departing collegians are expected to present "the Father" with a half-crown or two, not as degrading tips or handouts but as "testimonials" or tributes from admirers. Not only is he behind bars, he is also captive to the idea of gentility at all cost. After learning that his daughter was seen in public with a workhouse inmate, he upbraids her: "I have done what I could to give you a position here," he tells her, forgetting that "here" is a debtor's prison. Society (with a capital *S*), Dickens witheringly notes, holds such sway over the hearts and minds of men that its flourishes and minutiae are diligently observed, even in prison.

THE STATE OF ENGLAND

*A*rthur's inquiry into Mr. Dorrit's affairs necessitates a visit to what Dickens darkly calls the Circumlocution Office, the governmental department known as the Civil Service. The department, whose administrators belong to the aptly named Barnacle family, operates according to the principle of "How not to do it" or how not to get anything done. This non-goal is accomplished through reams of forms, appointments with functionaries, lengthy and pointless delays, official memoranda, and other bureaucratic absurdities. The purpose of the Civil Service is to maintain the governmental gridlock by impeding progress and social change. The Circumlocution Office, as its name implies, represents futility and stagnation on a national scale.

After numerous rebuffs, Arthur goes to the home of the eminent administrator, Mr. Tite Barnacle. As is usually the case with Dickens, the house is a metaphor for its inhabitants. Tite Barnacle lives on Mews Street (a pun: "mew" means to confine), an alley with "dead walls" and "a few airless houses." Tite's house is "squeezed" and has dingy windows and a stifling pantry; and its owner, Tite Barnacle himself, is bound in a white cravat, his gouty foot swathed in bandages. This chair-bound bureaucrat, chief of England's Civil Service, is the personification of bondage and immobility.

Of course, Tite Barnacle can't help Clennam, since "one of the principles of the Circumlocution Office [is] never, on any account whatever, to give a straightforward answer." Arthur persists: "I want to know," he begins each query, until Barnacle junior, sounding like a creature from Alice's Wonderland, balks: "Look here! Upon my SOUL you mustn't come into the place saying you want to know, you know!"

When the brilliant engineer Daniel Doyce tries to patent an invention that will benefit society, he is treated like a felon who should be locked up. Doyce's "crime" is that he wants to move England into the future; he represents imaginative practicality. But his splendid Victorian energy is squelched at every turn. England, Dickens angrily insists, is a country that rewards stagnation and punishes initiative. As Lionel Trilling points out, the "Circumlocution Office is the prison of the creative mind of England."

IN SOCIETY

*T*he novel's two parts, Poverty and Wealth, show the Dorrits first in prison and then out in the world. The difference is not as stark as one might expect. Through a fairy-tale coincidence, Mr. Pancks discovers that Mr. Dorrit is not only free of debt but immensely wealthy from a mysterious inheritance. This turn of fate—common in Dickens's novels—allows the writer to explore the nature of these two extremes. Although he travels throughout the continent, Mr. Dorrit is no more free than he was back in the Marshalsea. With a cinematic eye, Dickens makes this point abundantly clear by a quick transition of scenes. The first time we see the freed Mr. Dorrit, he is visiting the monastery of Saint Bernard. Despite his new affluence and status, Mr. Dorrit has only exchanged one cell for another.

The family's new wealth initiates Dickens's savage attack on being "in Society"—in custody is more like it. In fact, the mastermind of the age, the illustrious Mr. Merdle, habitually clasps his own arm as if he were taking himself into custody. The Merdles, along with the Barnacles, the Dorrit girls' chaperon, Mrs. General, and Mrs. Gowan, the voices of received opinion, lack independence and authenticity, following a code that disguises genuine emotion. As that arbiter of good taste, Mrs. General, puts it, "When touring Europe, all persons of polite cultivation should see with other people's eyes, and never with their own."

> Nothing disagreeable should ever be looked at. Apart from such a habit standing in the way of that graceful equanimity of surface which is so expressive of good breeding, it hardly seems compatible with refinement of mind. A truly refined mind will seem to be ignorant of the existence of anything that is not perfectly proper, placid and pleasant.

Much like the Circumlocution Office, Mrs. General operates according to a "circular set of mental grooves or rails on which she started little trains of other people's opinions, which never overtook one another, and never got anywhere."

But the more Mr. Dorrit tries to deny his past, the more the shadow of the Marshalsea's black walls looms over him. Living in perpetual dread of detection, he imagines whispered innuendos, secret looks, veiled allusions to his former self:

> He had a sense of his dignity, which was of the most exquisite nature. He could detect a design upon it when nobody else had any perception of the fact. His life was made an agony by the number of fine scalpels that he felt to be incessantly engaged in dissecting his dignity.

The prison in *Little Dorrit* is a metaphor for the inescapability of the self.

Little Dorrit is everything this shabbily false world is not. Although technically "in Society," she's unable to play by its rules. Most tellingly, she's afraid that those who love her will think of her differently now that she is rich. Whereas her father and sister, Fanny, are eager to change, Little Dorrit clings to her real self as she clings to her shabby clothes. With an eloquence that barely hides deep longing, she writes Arthur: "I have been afraid that you may think of me in a new light, or a new character. Don't do that, I could not bear that—it would make me more unhappy than you would suppose. It would break my heart to believe that you thought of me in any way that would make me stranger to you than I was when you were so good to me." Though he doesn't realize it, Arthur has received a love letter.

TIME AND LOVE

Of course, no good Victorian novel is without its love story. But what is rare and poignant about this one—aside from its retiring lovers—is the way Dickens portrays love as liberation from the tyranny of the past. For the past twenty years, while in the East, Arthur has clung to the memory of his former sweetheart as "the one bright thing, that soared out of his gloomy life into the bright glories of fancy." Upon returning home he is informed that Flora, now Mrs. Finching, is widowed and "available." His visit to her, an episode that parallels Dickens's own experience with his own sweetheart (see page 272), is shattering, revealing that time is the most brutal captor of all. As airtight and silent as a pharaoh's tomb, Flora's house has remained untouched by time. Only the loud ticking of a "grave" clock breaks the sepulchral silence. Even Flora's father, Mr. Casby, looks exactly the same as when Arthur left him.

While waiting for Flora, Arthur breathes the familiar scent of dried lavender and rose, which retain their fragrance long after the flowers have died. Lost in a Proustian moment, he is transported to the past. Time stands still. Then Flora appears. Fat, florid, and garrulous, she is time's grotesque joke, proof that the past is dead to the present—and that the body is the ultimate prison. This flora is no dried flower but an overripe peony, way past her prime. Yet, like dried roses, she is a reminder not only of the passage of time and mortality but of something lovely that once bloomed. She is the embodiment of the universal fear of aging. Later that evening Arthur gloomily sits before the dying fire, struck by the blank sterility of his life, which now seems like a one-way passage to the grave. At that moment, the door opens and Little Dorrit walks in.

But Arthur can't see that she's his savior—he's too distracted by another romantic folly. If Flora represents the past, Pet Meagles, the young daughter of his traveling companion, is the unrealized present— and an attempt to recreate the past. When Pet, who resembles the young Flora, chooses the callow Henry Gowan, Arthur tosses the roses she gave him into the river and, watching them float away, feels suddenly old and "done with the tender part of life." Longing for things that never were and yearning for things that can never be, Arthur reaches an emotional stasis.

Finally completing the cycle of women—and flower imagery—is Little Dorrit herself. Imprisoned in the Marshalsea after investing in Mr. Merdle's fraudulent scheme, Arthur awakens from the feverish dreams of illness to a sensation of freshness in the air. Home from Europe, her father dead, Little Dorrit brings a bouquet of flowers, an emblem of love and renewal. For the first time he sees her as a woman: "She looked something more womanly than she had when she had gone away, and the ripening touch of the Italian sun was visible upon her face." The allusions to Italy, sun, and ripeness have a delicate eroticism. Arthur doesn't feel old anymore.

RELEASE

*I*n his introduction to the Penguin edition, John Holloway notes that as the novel nears its climax, characters let their rigid masks and defenses fall, revealing themselves and others for what they are. When his financial bubble bursts, the great Merdle kills himself and is exposed as a crook and a forger, "a man that had sprung from nothing"; after years of collecting rents for the the benevolent-looking slumlord "Patriarch" Mr. Casby, Mr. Pancks explodes with rage and publicly humiliates his employer, exposing him as a greedy sham; at a formal dinner party Mr. Dorrit lapses into his former self and, imagining he's back at the Marshalsea, calls for the turnkey, oblivious to the dumbstruck guests. Affery, Mrs. Clennam's maid, long terrified into silence by her husband's threats, throws away all fear and speaks the truth. Finally, in a confession that will tie up all loose ends, Mrs. Clennam reveals the past to Rigaud, her blackmailer, and her servants, Flintwinch and Affery: before his marriage Arthur's father had gone though a form of marriage with a struggling young singer; upon learning of her husband's sin, Mrs. Clennam forced the girl to give up her son, Arthur, and hounded her into an early death in an insane asylum. Seeing herself as an instrument of divine vengeance, she suppressed the codicil in her husband's will that would have bequeathed a thousand guineas to Little Dorrit (as the youngest niece of the man who helped Arthur's mother). With this admission, Mrs. Clennam's rigid arms and legs begin to move; liberated from her chair, she rushes as if possessed to Little Dorrit and kneels before her, imploring forgiveness. After her confession, the two women walk home through a London transfigured by redemption. For the first time in the novel, the city is joyous, radiant with tranquillity and light, its grime, both literal and metaphysical, having been miraculously swept away:

> People stood and sat at their doors, playing with children and enjoying the evening; numbers were walking for air; . . . As they crossed the bridge, the clear steeples of the many churches looked as if they had advanced out of the murk that usually enshrouded them, and come much nearer. The smoke that rose into the sky had lost its dingy hue and taken

a brightness upon it. . . . From a radiant centre, over the whole length and breadth of the tranquil firmament great shoots of light streamed among the early stars, like signs of the blessed later covenant of peace and hope that changed the crown of thorns into a glory.

There are other miracles: the rotting house, the repository of old secrets, spontaneously heaves and, with a thundering noise, collapses, burying the wicked Rigaud and leaving behind nothing but dirty heaps of rubbish. All the tightly held energies have erupted. The deceptions and sins of two generations have been played out. The next generation will start anew.

FINALE

*I*f the novel opens on a closed world, its conclusion is open-ended. The ending marriage is very different from Dickens's usual wildly happy nuptials. Two modest people marry and slip unobtrusively into the "roaring streets":

> Little Dorrit and her husband walked out of the church alone. They paused for a moment on the steps of the portico, looking at the fresh perspective of the street in the autumn morning sun's bright rays, and then went down. . . .
>   They went quietly down into the roaring streets, inseparable and blessed; and as they passed along in sunshine and shade, the noisy and the eager, and the arrogant and the froward and the vain, fretted and chafed, and made their usual uproar.

Dickens usually presents the concluding marriage as vitiating the social horrors portrayed throughout the novel. But in *Little Dorrit* nothing has changed; the Circumlocution Office, the falsity of society, bankruptcy schemes, all continue. Perhaps modest happiness is all that good people can achieve. But the moving conclusion, with its echoes of Adam and Eve's departure from Eden in *Paradise Lost,* suggests that although the city may be fallen, it is still possible for a man and woman to create an inner sanctuary that will neither confine nor suppress them.

SHADES OF THE PRISON HOUSE

While the original Marshalsea dates back to the reigns of Charles I and II, the building that Dickens and his father would have known was built in 1811, about eleven years before Mr. Dickens was incarcerated there. According to Trey Phillpots who wrote about the "real Marshalsea" in *The Dickensian,* Dickens's portrait of the prison in *Little Dorrit*—the courtyard, barracks, and famed snuggery—might have been lifted from a blueprint of the prison itself.

What Dickens seemed to remember most vividly about the Marshalsea was its intensely claustrophobic atmosphere. While this might seem generic detail, in fact Dickens was recalling an accurate detail, especially particular to the Marshalsea. Apparently, the Marshalsea's oppressiveness was legendary. The lawyer Mr. Rugg warns Arthur against going there: "Now you know what the Marshalsea is. Very close. Excessively confined. Whereas the King's Bench. . . ." New arrivals, like Mr. Dorrit and Arthur Clennam, feel as if they were slowly choking to death. One contemporary pamphleteer, indignant over prison conditions, wrote: "I'll leave the reader to imagine what the situations of men, thus confined, particularly in the summer months must be." The courtyard, where the prisoners took their exercise, was five feet wide, the water filthy, the drains choked with waste, and, according to one account, strangers were forced to live together in rooms that were less than four feet square. Indeed, just reading about Arthur's feverish first days in the Marshalsea, and its hot, fetid, fly-ridden air, is apt to induce an attack of claustrophobia in the reader.

In 1842 the Marshalsea shut its doors for good, twenty-two years after John Dickens first entered its doors. The site, however, is still called Little Dorrit's Court.

❧ TATTYCORAM ❧

The Tattycoram subplot of *Little Dorrit* is as close as Dickens ever came to writing a tale of psychological terror. Although it ends with a clear and typically Victorian moral, the story of Tattycoram is filled with disturbing contradictions. Indeed, a half century later Henry James would use a similar idea to create his masterpiece of ambiguity, *The Turn of the Screw.*

Years before the narrative begins, the Meagleses had adopted an orphan named Harriet Beadle. The girl's name undergoes various transmutations: Harriet becomes Hattey, which leads to Tatty, because, as Mr. Meagles explains, "even a playful name might prove a novelty to the girl and have an affectionate and softening effect." The unpleasant associations evoked by the word "beadle" prompts Mr. Meagles to change the girl's surname to Coram, in honor of the "blessed personage" who founded the charity hospital. Soon Christian name and surname merge, creating the odd yet engaging "Tattycoram."

But when we first see Tattycoram, she's anything but endearing. In the throes of what she calls her "madness," she keens with grief and rage over what she perceives as her low status in the Meagleses' household, biting her arm and pinching her neck until welts appear: "It was wonderful to see the fury of the contest in the girl, and the bodily struggle she made as if she were rent with the Demons of old." All her turbulent emotions—self-hatred, pride, resentment, remorse—seize her like mysterious forces over which she has no control.

The confused adolescent is ripe for Miss Wade's sinister tutelage. Watching Tattycoram with a "strange attentive smile," she is a spiritual vampire, intent on her prey. But she is also an emanation of the girl's own dark desires. Whenever Tattycoram is gripped by one of her fits, the figure of Miss Wade suddenly materializes. In a moment of clarity, Tattycoram tells the older woman: "You seem to come like my own anger, my own malice, my own—whatever it is—I don't know what it is."

The older woman battles to possess Tattycoram and woo her from the good-hearted Meagleses. The singular name "Tattycoram" becomes her rallying cry. Dickens probably knew better than anyone that naming is serious business, fraught with implications of power and control. To change someone's name without their consent is to appropriate and deny their identity. To Miss Wade, the vile "Tattycoram" depersonalizes the girl, turning her into a pet. Dumbfounded, Mr. Meagles recounts the girl's accusation:

> There was Mrs. Tickit, only yesterday, when her grandchild was with her, had been amused by the child's trying to call . . . [Tattycoram] by the wretched name we gave her; and laughed at the name. Why, who didn't; and who were we that we should have a right to name her like a dog or a cat?

Little Dorrit embraces her "nonperson" nickname (which to Flora sounds like something speckled) as a badge of her true identity.

While the Meagleses teach Tattycoram to repress her anger ("Count to twenty-five, Tatty!"), Miss Wade whips the girl into a frenzy of revolt until she finally turns on the Meagleses. Miss Wade's seduction ends in triumph, and the pair flee.

But Harriet's emotional bondage to the older woman poses a bigger threat to the girl's autonomy than her tie to the Meagleses. In leaving them, she sheds the name of her bondage, and as Harriet Beadle tries to assert her individuality. But there is an irony underlying her dramatic gesture: as it turns out, Harriet Beadle is an "arbitrary," generic name given to her by the Institution. True freedom, then, has little to do with names or social position, but with integrity of the self, as embodied by Little Dorrit's quiet self-containment. And with Miss Wade, Harriet's identity is ill-defined, her position and future uncertain. Turning to the older woman, Mr. Meagles asks, "What can you two be together? What can come of it?" Their relationship, while homoerotic, is neither romantic nor tender. In an oblique reference to her lesbianism, he says:

"I don't know what you are, but you don't hide, can't hide, what a dark spirit you have within you. If it should happen that you are a woman, who, from whatever cause, has a perverted delight in making a sister-woman as wretched as she is (I am old enough to have heard of such), I warn her against you and I warn you against yourself."

Desperately ignoring Mr. Meagles's pleas, Harriet allows herself to be lead away by Miss Wade, who had "watched her under this final appeal with that strange attentive smile, and that repressing hand upon her own bosom. [She] put her arm about her [Harriet's] waist as if she took possession of her for evermore."

In one of the many variations on the theme of imprisonment, Dickens shows how love can be as confining as iron bars. The claustrophobic curtained lodgings suggest an unhealthy solitude where nothing young can flourish and where everything is static and dead. Grasping and voracious, Miss Wade tries to subdue the girl's budding independence, which she sees as a threat. Upon learning that the girl has visited the Meagleses' home, Miss Wade turns on her, crying, "Is that your fidelity to me?"

Miss Wade's intense gaze suggests she possesses mesmeric powers, yet in this novel, mesmerism is not a parlor trick but a metaphor for a pathology of the soul. Her magnetism reflects a will to power. Her love—if it can be called such—is omnivorous. Yet Harriet proves a worthy opponent and enmeshed in the destructive relationship, she struggles to maintain her individuality. Clennam watches the couple, and in an acutely modern insight, "felt how each of the two natures must be constantly tearing the other to pieces." The symbiotic bond between the two women is perhaps Dickens's most modern relationship, anticipating the soul-crushing unions in D. H. Lawrence's novels.

Of course, the Meagleses are on the right side; they reflect the hero's, and hence the novelist's, values. And yet it's clear that Miss Wade, perverse as she is, does have a point. Dickens, like Blake before and Conrad after him, knew that what often passes for charity is rooted in the need to control and subdue. Viewed in the worst light, the Meagleses change Harriet's name with the same casual assumption of superiority with which Robinson Crusoe enslaves a primitive man and calls him "Man Friday." Mr. Meagles is like a kindly missionary, gently imposing his faith on the rest of the world. (Although he travels widely, he can't understand why everyone doesn't speak English and sees no reason to learn another language.)

But this is a Victorian, not a modern novel. Tattycoram learns to accept her lowly origin and to try, like Little Dorrit, to transcend it through a sense of duty and selfless love. In the end, Tattycoram, once in danger of becoming like Miss Wade, stands before the Meagleses, weeping with gratitude and remorse: "I hope I shall never be so bad again, and that I shall get better by very slow degrees. I'll try very hard. I won't stop at five-and-twenty, sir, I'll count five-and-twenty-hundred, five-and-twenty-thousand!"

Modern readers are uncomfortable with such lessons. We can only rejoice when the girl, Tattycoram once more, returns to the Meagleses; in the moral context of the novel, she belongs with Little Dorrit, Clennam, and Doyce. By endorsing social over individual values, Dickens is not guilty of bad faith. All the good people in the novel are misfits and each is quietly subversive. Tatty-coram doesn't surrender to the social values, but rather learns to maintain her integrity and live in a society that worships sham and "polish." And she must also learn, like Little Dorrit, Clennam, and Doyce, to cope in a world in which they are threatened by dehumanization.

Dickens's Women

✧

INTERVIEW WITH MIRIAM MARGOLYES

iriam Margolyes is obsessed with Dickens, and after seeing her show, Dickens's Women, *one might well think she is possessed by his characters. Commissioned by the Edinburgh Festival in 1989 (and sold out before it opened),* Dickens's Women *is a one-woman show that seems to have a cast of hundreds. Miss Margolyes changes her voice the way other actors change costumes, and as an old-fashioned piano tinkles in accompaniment, she re-creates some of Dickens's most famous females: Mrs. Gamp, Mrs. Jarley, Miss Mowcher, Miss Havisham, Miss Wade, Miss Flite.*

NE: *Why are Dickens's women important?*

MM: Dickens's relations with women definitely affected how he wrote about them. The fact that he had unhappy relationships is reflected in the kind of women he depicted. I don't think he had an adult sexual relationship with any woman. Miss Coutts [Angela Burdett-Coutts] was his friend, but it wasn't a man/woman relationship. He was a wonderful friend to men, and it's as a friend that people can celebrate Dickens. As a husband, as a father, he was much less successful.

NE: *What influence did his mother have?*

MM: I think his feelings about her are absolutely crucial to understanding him. There are certainly very strong elements of her in his women. He felt that his mother had betrayed him, and he never forgave her for it. He felt she was a bit silly and a social climber, which of course *he* was. But he also understood that she was battling against poverty. My interpretation of Mrs. Micawber is influenced by that.

NE: *Your interpretation of Mrs. Micawber is unusual. She's normally portrayed as a comedic sidekick.*

MM: I see her both comically and sympathetically, but that duality is apparent in many Dickens characters. You relish someone like Quilp or Uriah Heep, but at the same time you are disgusted by them. Someone like Fagin is one of those gigantic comic characters—you know he's a pederast, don't you?

NE: *When I recently read* Oliver Twist, *it seemed very obvious, but I don't remember anyone talking about it before. Or Miss Wade, whom you call a lesbian in your show. Are we reinterpreting Dickens's characters in terms of our modern sensibilities, or were Dickens's readers aware of these things?*

MM: I don't think they were, no. I am sure the lesbianism has never been picked up before. That's the first thing I thought. How would you describe Miss Wade, "The Portrait of a Self-Tormentor"? Dickens shows us someone who's twisted and perverted, and he tries to explain why. He was very much aware of all kinds of sexual peculiarities, because he saw it all as a child as he walked the streets to work in the early morning through the toughest part of London.

NE: *So you think Dickens understood more than we think he does?*

MM: Dickens could not have written after Freud. I really believe that Freud damaged everybody. We see Dickens as naive, because he didn't delve into things the way we do. But he perceived what was going on. In several of his essays about the theater, he draws very gay young men strolling about, and he obviously loved all the jejune campiness of the theater. He was perfectly aware of this kind of thing, but not in the psychological way we are. He would have known that Miss Wade was a lesbian; he would have daringly put it in the novel, but not in a way that would "bring a blush to a young person's cheek." So with Fagin: you can read *Oliver Twist* and never think he was a pederast. But think about the way he says, "My dears." It's quite clear, a very accurate portrayal because those kind of pederasts actually love little boys and love to entertain them.

NE: *Did Dickens have trouble creating sexually responsive female characters?*

MM: That's one of his major faults as a writer, and it stems from his problem as a man. I think he was cut into pieces, first by his mother, then by Maria Beadnell. I don't think he ever recovered. So he could only deal with women as prepubescent, giggly things, because they had no power over him that way. When they grew up to be fully formed people, he was unable to deal with them. But he enjoyed women when they became old and garrulous and were funny. He was fond of his grandmother. He depicts a lot of kindness in this

$\mathcal{M}$iriam Margolyes as the
irrepressible Flora Finching in
the 1987 film *Little Dorrit*.

sort of woman, like Peggotty and Betsey Trotwood, who, by the way, is another interesting character. You think she must be a lesbian because he always describes her as being mannish.

NE: *How is the famed Dickensian energy manifested in his characters?*

MM: He has these garrulous women who go off into endless parentheses, like Flora Finching and Mrs. Gamp . . . who go on and on . . . those spirals of imagination—that's what I think of as Dickensian energy. He takes ordinary life and somehow heightens it till it's almost off the edge, but not quite. The tension of sustaining that is the glory of Dickens.

NE: *Which characters do you enjoy most?*

MM: Those on the extremes—the so-called grotesques and caricatures that are enormous fun to act because you are allowed to go further than you normally do with most characters. I love that he takes us to the edge of possibility. That's his comic genius.

NE: *Which is your favorite novel?*

MM: *Little Dorrit*. It has that wonderful mixture of dark and light. It's fundamentally a very serious book, but it's relieved by extraordinary characters like Mr. F's aunt and Pancks. It has a dimension, a sureness that just sweeps you in and encloses you. I've always found it extremely moving and very funny. Dickens was familiar with the Marshalsea Prison, and it's an extraordinary account—almost journalistic in its accuracy—about debtor's prison and the effect it had. Dickens wrote about poverty so brilliantly because he had been through it.

NE: *Dickens makes Flora into a ridiculous creature, but in the end she becomes sympathetic and real.*

MM: Dickens's compassion, which was considerable, allows him to portray someone who is a sad creature. I think he also does it with Miss Mowcher, that funny little dwarf lady in *David Copperfield.* He sees duality in people; sometimes it's evil and comic, sometimes it's tender and comic. Of course, I very much identified with her. She's aware of her own absurdity, and that is what makes her heartrending.

NE: *You sound as if you feel for Dickens. When you read biographies about him, do you get a sense of his personality?*

MM: [Long pause] I wonder. . . . I probably do. . . . Or maybe I delude myself that I do. I have no doubt that he would have found *me* personally quite ghastly! He would have enjoyed my sycophancy because I think he's the greatest, and I think he would have enjoyed my being an actress because he loved theater people. But he hated fat women. And he would not have liked me delving into his life, because I think he was withdrawn in a funny sort of way.

NE: *Most of the Dickens biographies have been written by men. As a woman, how do you feel about Dickens's treatment of his wife?*

MM: I hate him for what he did to Catherine, and I've made the story of his marriage the focal point of my show. Most people are unaware of his domestic life.

NE: *Why do you think he made Catherine into a villain?*

MM: I think he felt guilty about something. He made Catherine into the villain to get rid of her. She was an encumbrance. Anything she said or did was vile. He couldn't stand her Scottish accent, though when he married her he found it rather charming. His behavior was born out of an absolute physical loathing for her.

Kate, his daughter, once said, "My father is a very wicked man," yet she loved him dearly. That's the paradox of Dickens. He was wicked, yet along with Shakespeare, he's our greatest writer. So that's the way life is, that's what makes art interesting.

NE: *When Claire Tomalin's biography of Ellen Ternan came out, people were disturbed by her claim that Dickens had slept with Ellen. What do you think?*

MM: Well, I think they're nutty if they don't think he did. Michael Slater is the quintessential Dickens scholar, and he didn't think Dickens had slept with Nelly. Neither does Dickens's biographer Peter Ackroyd. Claire Tomalin and I, both women, think he did sleep with her. Maybe it's a gender interpretation. No woman could believe for one *second* that he didn't sleep with her.

NE: *How would you sum up Dickens's attitude toward women?*

MM: I just don't think he was operating at his full potential with women, both personally and in his writing. His most successful female characters are the grotesques. But I exempt from that characters like Lady Dedlock and Edith Dombey, who are powerful creations. They are both tormented women. He could see that women could be tormented. Yet they are also heavily blamed. Whereas the people he approved of, like Esther Summerson, you just want to smack!

The Inimitable
Dickensian

For years I have been using in my lectures a headline from the local newspaper, "CITY TYPISTS WORK IN DICKENSIAN CONDITIONS." Readers of the Leicester Mercury *need not have read any Dickens to know that those typists are to be pitied, and that the headline testifies to Dickens's own special status quo (no need to have read him, to understand references to him) and specifically to his representing a period—being as Walter Bagehot foretold in 1858, a "special correspondent for posterity," to a degree that none of his contemporaries can match. Typists cannot work in Thackerayean or Brontean or Eliotan or Tennysonian conditions.*
—PHILIP COLLINS

n amazing word, *Dickensian*. It's extraordinary how one man could inspire an adjective with dozens of meanings, many of which are contradictory. Only a few authorial names have entered the nonliterary, everyday lexicon. Three of the most popular—Rabelaisian, Machiavellian, and Kafkaesque—have precise meanings: *Rabelaisian* refers to a robust bawdiness, usually of a gustatory or scatological kind; *Machiavellian* denotes cunning or corruption, usually political; *Kafkaesque* connotes a nightmarish absurdity, suggesting the meaninglessness of life.

Dickensian, however, is a word for all seasons. It can refer to a person, a humor, a social condition, a name. And it can assume contradictory meanings. Applied to a person, it suggests a strange being that could only have emerged from Dickens's imagination—a mystical dwarf with luxuriant hair who makes clothes for dolls, a gnarled clerk perched on a high stool. As it evokes a mood or atmosphere, it can run the gamut from the coziness of home to the desolation of an orphanage. The Dickensian experience can be a stint in a prison

⫻

camp, a ten-course banquet, a vermin-infested slum, a bout of chilblains, bureaucracy, and of course, Christmas. (Of his last one with Mia Farrow, Woody Allen said, "It was not exactly a Dickensian Christmas.") Relied on by journalists and political analysts as an all-purpose adjective, *Dickensian* can be adapted to describe any legal or political situation that the writer finds absurd. The civil service, renamed the Circumlocution Office in *Little Dorrit,* is always Dickensian. The term may now safely be applied to anything sentimental, squalid, homey, quaint, absurd, extravagant, or nightmarish. (What do Harold Ross, urbane editor and founder of the *New Yorker,* and Tonya Harding, the low-rent Olympic skater/bottle cap collector who ordered her rival's knees clobbered, have in common? Both have been called Dickensian.)

In fact, the word is so pervasive, one could say that it means everything and nothing. Dickens's landscape and tone are so varied and yet so thoroughly stamped with the man's character and style that everything he wrote about, and the manner in which he did so, is called Dickensian. No wonder he thought of himself as "The Inimitable." *Dickensian* now has a life independent from its association with Charles Dickens, author, and is freely used even by those who have never read him.

THE DICKENSIAN ORPHANAGE

Some words, like *orphanage* or *childhood* (if miserable) beg to be coupled with *Dickensian.* When House Speaker Newt Gingrich spoke approvingly of orphanages in December 1994, one's thoughts turned naturally to Charles Dickens. Allusions to the novelist, to *Oliver Twist* and to *David Copperfield,* appeared in newspapers and magazines across the country. Yet neither David nor Oliver was ever in an orphanage—we just feel they should have been. Oliver spent his early years in the Union Workhouse, whereas David worked in a warehouse. In fact, not one major Dickensian hero or heroine was ever in an orphanage. The association between Dickens and orphanages arose simply because so many of his characters are neglected children.

INTERVIEW WITH ROGER ROSENBLATT

Although many readers can easily identify a name, a character, a moment, or an ambiance that's Dickensian, they have a harder time defining what exactly the word means. Here a writer is called to account for his use of the term: in a March 1993 essay in the New Republic *lamenting the demise of the old-fashioned family-owned bookstore, Roger Rosenblatt writes, "There was always some old Dickensian man parked in the front behind some old Dickensian desk, talking to some other old man in disgruntled, conspiratorial tones—about Stalin, most likely."*

NE: *What did you mean by your use of the word* Dickensian *in this context?*

RR: I used the word *Dickensian* to describe the old, curious, mystery-laden, eccentric, obsessive, cramped bookstores of the past, and their political, eccentric, cranky, and obsessive proprietors. I was thinking of the old guys who populated Dickens's world, like Jaggers the lawyer or Jaggers's assistant, Wemmick. Or Cratchit—the old clerk who worked when Scrooge was just starting out. In other words, all the old people who sit in shops and are content—more than content—with being planted in their station of life. They don't move—they show no inclination to move. Dickens develops their characters in one place, and they seem to stick to it.

Dickens is very interesting in that you find yourself using him as a reference or an adjective when you want to describe all that you love about reading. When I used it in my essay, I wasn't merely making an association with downtown bookstores. I was making an association with books in the curious way the mind makes its leaps. To see a Dickensian character in real life is a reflection of how Dickens, more than any other author, invites you into the lives of his books so that his people become people you never want to leave—and you don't leave. One or another of Dickens's characters, quirky or heroic or wicked, stays with you all your life.

Years

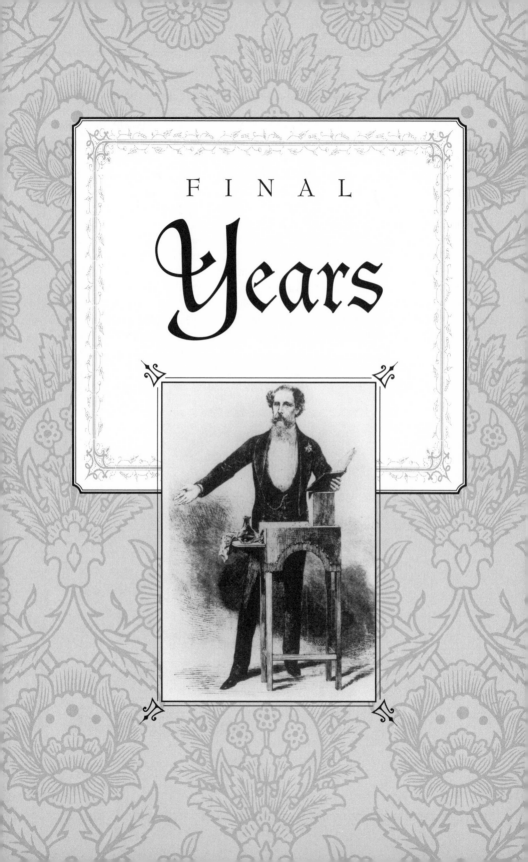

The Frozen Heart

✵

In August 1856, Dickens and Wilkie Collins began collaborating on *The Frozen Deep*, a second-rate melodrama that, if authored by anyone else, would have been quickly forgotten. Written during a period of unhappiness, the play became a lodestone for all of Dickens's restless desires. Like a dream that has import only for the dreamer, it tapped into a reservoir of unexpressed, inchoate feelings, giving him access to an intensity of experience he craved from ordinary life: "I derive a strange feeling out of it . . . a satisfaction of a most singular kind, which has no exact parallel in my life; a something . . . which has for me a conviction of its being actual truth without its pain that I never could adequately state if I were to try never so hard."

The following June, Dickens learned that his old friend Douglas Jerrold had suddenly died, leaving a widow and several children. (The night before he had dreamed of Jerrold; the next morning he overheard two men discussing his death in a railway compartment.) With his usual

impetuous generosity, he at once revived *The Frozen Deep* and arranged for a series of performances to benefit the Jerrold family. He presented the play several times in London at the Gallery of Pictures to great success. Then, in late July, he received an invitation to perform the play on a much grander scale in Manchester's enormous Free Trade Hall. He was delighted, and resolved to hire professional actresses so the female voices would carry throughout the house. On the advice of a friend, he hired a family of actresses, a Mrs. Fanny Ternan and her two daughters, Maria and Ellen, the latter called Nelly. (The eldest daughter, Fanny, was engaged elsewhere.)

According to Collins, Dickens (playing the hero, Richard Wardour) "electrified" the audience. Apparently he had a similar effect on Nelly Ternan: when it came time for Wardour to die in her arms, she lost all self-control. As Dickens described the incident to Miss Burdett-Coutts,

> Her tears fell down my face, down my beard . . . down my ragged dress—poured all over me; like rain, so that it was much as I could do to speak for them. I whispered to her, "My dear child, it will be all over in two minutes. Pray, compose yourself." "It is of no comfort to me that it will be soon over," she answered.

But then it *was* over, and Dickens's depression returned, this time worse than ever. Nelly left for her next acting engagement, and Dickens once again turned to Collins for relief: "My blankness is inconceivable," he wrote, "indescribable—my misery amazing." He was, he confessed, "horribly used up." But before Nelly left Manchester, Dickens learned that her next stop was Doncaster, where she would be appearing at the Theatre Royal. Dickens thus proposed a walking tour to Collins through Cumberland; their destination, Doncaster. Sometime during the preceding weeks, he had fallen deeply in love with Nelly Ternan.

*E*llen (Nelly) Lawless Ternan, the "one spirit" that haunted Dickens's final years, as she appeared when Dickens first met her in 1857.

The Marriage Ends

In the fall of 1857 Wilkie Collins and Dickens set out on a walking tour, ostensibly to write a series of sketches entitled *The Lazy Tour of Two Idle Apprentices* in which Collins and Dickens appear as two young men on holiday. But the truth was that Dickens wanted to see Ellen Ternan, who would be appearing at the Theatre Royal in Doncaster.

We'll never know what happened that week. The only "evidence" we have are two cryptic messages Dickens wrote to his manager, W. H. Wills. The first reads, "The strongest parts of your present correspondent's heart are made up of weaknesses. And he just came to be here at all (if you knew it) along of his Richard Wardour! Guess *that* riddle, Mr. Wills!" The tone is exultant, as if assured of a conquest. Obviously Nelly was with him, but Dickens refuses to reveal any more. She was his "little riddle," an enigma, tantalizing yet maddening.

Two days later a perplexed Wills received another note. "I am going to take the little—riddle—into the country this morning. . . . I *think* I shall leave here on Tuesday, but I cannot positively say. . . . I did intend to return home tomorrow, but have no idea now of doing that. So let the riddle and the riddler go their own wild way, and no harm come of it!" Obviously, Dickens was unwilling to commit himself to a return date as long as he was with Nelly. The two rode in the country, visited the local ruins, and took in the view—all of which was reported in the *Doncaster Gazette.*

Dickens was, of course, deluding himself that someone as famous as he was could simply go "his own way." And as for "no harm," the effects of his infatuation would be far-reaching and damaging to all concerned. He *did* do harm—to his reputation, to his friendships, to his children, and of course to his wife, Catherine. By the time he left Doncaster, whether consciously or not, he was already planning her removal.

The *Lazy Tour* includes a sketch that indicates Dickens's state of mind. It's about a man who murders his wife by simply willing her death.

HE CONFESSES

*I*t's impossible to pinpoint the moment Dickens became aware of his connubial misery, but we do know the first time he expressed it. In September 1857, just before he left for Doncaster to see Nelly, Dickens wrote to John Forster and confessed the truth about his marriage. He sounds sad and resigned, and his sympathy, for once, extends not only to himself but to Catherine:

> Poor Catherine and I are not made for each other, and there is no help for it. It is not only that she makes me uneasy and unhappy, but that I make her so too—and much more so. She is exactly what you know, in the way of being amiable and complying; but we are strangely ill-assorted for the bond there is between us. God knows she would have been a thousand times happier if she had married another kind of man.

Forster counseled him to be tolerant and to bridle his pain, adding that couples who marry young often experience difficulties later, to which Dickens responds with a confession he would never make again: "I claim no immunity from blame. There is plenty of fault on my side, I dare say, in the way of a thousand uncertainties, caprices, and difficulties of disposition but only one thing will alter all that, and that is, the end which alters everything." Never again would Dickens sympathize with Catherine or admit his own culpability. Within a month of writing this letter, he would decide to make his impossible "wish" a reality; but to do so, he had to turn Catherine into an enemy.

Faced with public criticism, Dickens did the only thing possible: he blamed Catherine. He magnified her shortcomings into serious character flaws, which he then used to justify his desire to leave her. He couldn't simply admit that he hated her; he had to invent reasons. And he couldn't risk his reputation by simply deserting her, so he engineered it so that they would part "by mutual consent."

In October 1857, just two months after Dickens met Ellen Ternan, Catherine came home to find workmen in the bedroom she had always shared with her husband. She quickly discovered that Dickens had moved into the adjoining dressing room, and was now sealing off the door between the two rooms, his way of informing her that their conjugal relations had ended. It was the

*T*he forty-three-year-old Catherine Dickens at the time of her separation from Dickens in May 1858.

first step toward a more permanent estrangement. From then on, his feelings and thoughts would also be sealed off from her. The unthinking cruelty of his action corroborates Kate Dickens Perugini's later assertion that during this time Dickens behaved like a "madman, a very wicked man."

Then there was the famous jewelry episode. In April Dickens had ordered a brooch for Nelly; the jeweler, seeing Dickens's signature, assumed it was meant for Mrs. Dickens and sent it to Tavistock House, where Catherine received it and confronted him. Whenever accused of anything (and at this point he was still technically innocent in his relations with Nelly), Dickens would fly into righteous rage. Catherine, he claimed, had gone mad with her infernal jealousy. He always, he insisted, sent his actresses gifts after a performance. But this time it was different, and Catherine knew it. He then compounded the injury by ordering Catherine to pay a social call on Nelly. Perhaps he hoped that a visit from Mrs. Charles Dickens would dispel some of the gossip that was already starting to surface. Or perhaps he was just being cruel.

Kate recounted that she found her mother sobbing as she put on her bonnet: "Your father has asked me to go and see Ellen Ternan."

"You shall not go!" screamed Kate. But the daughter was overruled by her father, and Catherine, ever submissive, dutifully paid her call. What agonies she must have endured: the soon-to-be-discarded, middle-aged wife confronting her lovely eighteen-year-old rival. One can only imagine the awkward conversation, the strained avoidance of unpleasant subjects, the stilted remarks about the weather and the tea.

CATHERINE LEAVES

*L*ife in the Dickens ménage became impossible, taut with unexpressed rage and stifled tears. Catherine's mother, the domineering Mrs. Hogarth, brought events to a crisis. Upon discovering her daughter's anguish, all her latent antagonism toward Dickens surfaced (i.e., the resentment of a dependent toward a benefactor). Catherine, she claimed, could only save the Hogarth family honor by leaving Dickens first. In the 1850s, when few women abandoned their families, this would be a desperate remedy indeed. Catherine had nine children, the youngest now six. Torn between a dominating husband and an overbearing mother, Catherine succumbed to the latter.

Negotiations for the separation began in May 1858, with John Forster—who disliked the whole business—acting on behalf of Dickens, and Mark Lemon, Dickens's old friend from *Punch,* representing Catherine. In the early stages of the negotiations, Dickens hoped for a compromise and offered several "solutions": Catherine would remain in London while Dickens resided at Gad's Hill; Catherine would continue to act as wife and hostess, but they would occupy separate apartments; Catherine would live in London while he was in Kent, and when he came to London she would move to Kent; and finally, as if she were the mad wife in a gothic novel, he proposed that Catherine should restrict her movements to the top floor of the house. Catherine rejected them all, realizing that she could not live with a man who loathed her.

It was eventually settled that Catherine should receive 600 pounds a year and a carriage. Charley, their eldest child, now twenty-one, would be permitted to live with her while the dependent children would stay with Dickens at Gad's Hill. The youngest, Edward Bulwer-Lytton, known as Plorn, would be raised by his aunt "Georgy." The children were forbidden to be in the same room as Catherine's mother or sister, but they were allowed free access to their mother. Nevertheless, they rarely visited her. Years after her mother's death, Kate would write, "We were all very wicked not to take her part."

With reticence and dignity, Catherine Dickens left her married home. She would never see her husband again. She lived another twenty-two years, dying in 1879, nine years after Dickens.

THE QUESTION OF GEORGINA

Complicating matters was the presence of Georgina, Dickens's sister-in-law, who had lived with the couple since she was fifteen. Now thirty-two, she had devoted her entire adult life to Dickens, reveling in his affection and trust. Through the years she had gradually assumed Catherine's role in the household (possibly without Catherine's awareness), fulfilling all the duties of a wife except conjugal. As Catherine sank in Dickens's estimation, Georgina rose.

No doubt she was reluctant to give up her status as helpmeet to the Great Man. Although Mary, Dickens's eldest daughter, would now be mistress of Gad's Hill, Georgina was the real force in the house. Frequently cited as the model for the saintly Agnes Wickfield and Esther Summerson, Georgina may have been more spiteful than her reputation suggests. Dickens always maintained that it was Georgina who pressed him toward a reconciliation, but it is arguable that she did so only when it seemed that Catherine's departure would necessitate her own.

Georgina may have regarded Dickens's home and children as her own, but society did not view it that way. Public opinion—or "Mrs. Grundy," as it was called then—whispered that a decent woman would have sided with her sister. And naturally there was the impropriety of an unmarried woman, particularly a sister-in-law, living with a single man. Legally, marriage to or sexual relations with a sister-in-law constituted incest. Without Catherine, Georgina's presence in the Dickens household was anomalous. It is a testament to her steely will (and perhaps her desperation) that she chose to ride out the ugly gossip.

Georgina never saw her sister again during Dickens's lifetime, but, remarkably, after his death they resumed their relationship virtually as if nothing had ever happened. But one wonders if Catherine ever truly forgave her. In her will, she bequeathed only one item to Georgina: a ring in the shape of a snake.

It Comes Out

Who then could have conceived or prophesied that in the year of grace 1858, the whole fabric would have begun to totter, and that a strange, sudden change should have come about. This literally— I remember it well—took away all our breaths.

—PERCY FITZGERALD

As rumors began to circulate about his marital difficulties, Dickens was subjected to public condemnation for the first time in his long career. Some may not have liked his politics or his novels, but practically everyone had trusted that he was a good man. When the news first came out, it was the scandal du jour, and most of the literary world sided with "Poor Catherine," as she would henceforth be known. His colleagues were no different. From Rome, Elizabeth Barrett Browning, secure in her own connubial joy, could barely contain her anger at Dickens and her sorrow for Catherine:

> What is this sad story about Dickens & his wife? Incompatibility of temper after twenty-three years of married life? What a plea!—Worse than irregularity of the passions, it seems to me. Thinking of my own peace & selfish pleasure, too, I would rather be beaten by my husband once a day than lose my child out of the house—yes indeed. . . . Poor woman! She must suffer bitterly—that is sure.

Many women—and not a few men—agreed with Mrs. Browning.

People might have accepted anything from Dickens, but he violated a primary taboo of his age, one that he had helped create and upon which he had built his own reputation: domestic harmony. Now that Dickens's fans saw him in a less than sanctified light, they were forced to question and revise their own literary and moral judgments. Was Dickens, as one of his own characters might have said, a humbug?

THE ADDRESS TO THE READER

*T*hree days after Catherine received her deed of separation, Dickens sat down to write an "Address to the Reader," to be printed in *Household Words*. His friends warned him against it. Finally, he asked John Delane of the *Times* for his opinion, and Delane inexplicably urged him to go ahead. That was all Dickens needed. He wrote to Catherine explaining his intentions, and Catherine, either too cowed or too stunned, did not stop him.

Ironically, few outside London's literary circle would have known about Dickens's marital difficulties had he not informed them himself through his "Address." It's a remarkable document, a strange mix of self-pity, defensiveness, and cruelty. It is also typical of a man with a compulsive need to justify his behavior. Dickens was unable to simply ride out the scandal; he had to act. As his intimate friend John Forster once observed, Dickens was the sort of man who, if he wanted air, would rather punch his fist through the wall than struggle to open a window. Judging by the intensity of its effect, the "Address" was indeed a fist through a wall.

On June 5, 1858, readers of the London *Times* must have been shocked to find the following statement printed under a heading marked PERSONAL:

> Three-and-twenty years have passed since I entered on my present relations with the Public. They began when I was so young, that I find them to have existed for nearly a quarter of a century.
>
> Through all that time I have tried to be as faithful to the Public as they have been to me. It was my duty never to trifle with them, or deceive them, or presume upon their favour, or do anything with it but work hard to justify it. I have always endeavoured to discharge that duty.
>
> My conspicuous position has often made me the subject of fabulous stories and unaccountable statements. Occasionally, such things have chafed me, or even wounded me; but, I have always accepted them as the shadows inseparable from the light of my notoriety and success. I have never obtruded any such personal uneasiness of mine, upon the generous aggregate of my audience.
>
> For the first time in my life, and I believe for the last, I now deviate from the principle I have so long observed. . . .

With this dramatic opening, Dickens sets forth his side of the story:

> Some domestic troubles of mine, of long-standing, on which I will make no further remark than that it claims to be respected, as being of a sacredly private nature, has lately been brought to an arrangement, which involves no anger or ill-will of any kind, and the whole origin, progress, and surrounding circumstances of which have been, throughout, within

the knowledge of my children. It is amicably composed, and its details have now but to be forgotten by those concerned in it.

By some means, arising out of wickedness, or out of folly, or out of inconceivable wild chance, or out of all three, this trouble has been made the occasion of misrepresentations, most grossly false, most monstrous and most cruel—involving, not only me, but innocent persons dear to my heart, and innocent persons of whom I have no knowledge, if, indeed, they have any existence. [These innocent persons were probably Nelly and Georgina.]

Four days later the statement appeared in his own journal, *Household Words.* But Dickens misjudged his audience. His vague allusions to "grossly false misrepresentations" only piqued their curiosity as to the exact nature of the charges. He did what he would never do if he were writing a novel: raise the specter of a secret without explaining it. Readers, left wanting more, believed the worst. Why else would he take the trouble to explain himself? Thus, far from placating readers, the "Address" turned them against him. For the first time in his life, Dickens found himself attacked not by critics but by his own readers.

THE LETTER

A s if this weren't enough, Dickens wrote another, even more detailed letter and gave it to his manager, Arthur Smith, with permission to show it to anyone who asked to see it. In mid-August it appeared in the *New York Tribune* and for the rest of the summer it was reprinted in almost every newspaper in England. The letter has since become known as the "Violated Letter" because Dickens—rather disingenuously—always maintained that it was stolen from Smith and printed without his permission.

As Phyllis Rose points out in *Parallel Lives,* the letter begins like a grotesque parody of a fairy tale:

Mrs. Dickens and I have lived unhappily together for many years. Hardly anyone who has known us intimately can fail to have known that we are in all respects of character and temperament wonderfully unsuited to each other. I suppose that no two people, not vicious in themselves, ever

were joined together who had a greater difficulty in understanding one another, or who had less in common.

The letter is typically Dickensian in its use of hyperbole: no other couple is as ill-matched "in all respects" as he and Catherine; "no two people . . . ever were joined together who had a greater difficulty in understanding one another." He needed to overstate his case to a public who didn't understand why he couldn't either endure the marriage or quietly live apart. Disastrously, he alludes to other parties, hinting at the existence of another woman:

> Two wicked persons [Mrs. Hogarth and Helen] who should have spoken differently of me, in consideration of respect and gratitude, have accused me of relations with a young lady for whom I have a great attachment and regard. Upon my soul and honor, there is not on this earth a more virtuous and spotless creature than the young lady. I know her to be innocent and pure, and as good as my own dear daughters.

After informing readers that his wife was a bad mother, that she suffered from a "mental disorder," and that she had neglected her children, Dickens continues:

> In the manly consideration toward Mrs Dickens which I owe to my wife, I will merely remark of her that some peculiarity of her character has thrown all the children on someone else. I do not know—I cannot by any stretch of fancy imagine—what would have become of them but for this aunt, who has grown up with them, to whom they are devoted, and who has sacrificed the best part of her youth and life to them.

This was all the press needed. The *Liverpool Mercury*'s response was typical: "If this is 'manly consideration,' we should like to be favoured with a definition of unmanly selfishness and heartlessness."

The "Violated Letter" opens a window on Dickens's psyche under duress; it reveals his compulsive need to be right, his inability to keep silent, and his compulsion to explain his actions until he is assured of victory. At no time does it seem to occur to him to discreetly separate from his wife, nor does he ever publicly assume responsibility for his part in the marital breakup. As odd as it seems, this powerful, famous, and admired man presents himself as the helpless victim. More than thirty years after the fact, he reverts to the lost boy in the warehouse, vulnerable to maternal abandonment—although this time Catherine is the bad mother who ignores her children and her husband. In the "Violated Letter," as Phyllis Rose points out, Dickens portrays himself as one of his own waifs.

Bradbury and Evans had been publishing Dickens's journal *Household Words* since 1850, but when they refused to print Dickens's original letter, he abruptly broke off all relations with them, even though they had been close friends as well as business partners. Imperiously, he proposed to start a new weekly journal that, with laughable blindness, he intended to call *Household Harmony*. (Typically, Dickens became annoyed when Forster delicately hinted that, given Dickens's domestic trials, the name might not be appropriate at the moment.) The inoffensive *All the Year Round* was the result.

Trophy Wives

🌿

INTERVIEW WITH PHYLLIS ROSE

professor of English at Wesleyan University, Phyllis Rose is the author of Parallel Lives: Five Victorian Marriages, *a lively study of five couples who illustrate the variety of ways the Victorians arranged their domestic and romantic affairs. For many readers the* book was a revelation, not only for its depiction of the intimate lives of eminent Victorians but also for its devastating portrait of Dickens, the family man.

NE: *You write a lot about Catherine Dickens in* Parallel Lives.

PR: Writing about Catherine was the most fun in the book in some ways. Hers was the untold story. There's so little information about her, I had to use banal passages in letters that you wouldn't think would be useful. For instance, Dickens writes a note thanking someone for sending him a book. Okay, perfectly routine—but Dickens says, "I enjoyed it, and Mrs. Dickens is now reading it and she is enjoying it too." Suddenly you realize that he actually talked to her and gave her books to read. He respected her opinion enough to mention it in a letter to someone. I felt I was bringing her into existence out of virtually nothing. Nobody had written about her. Even her own daughter didn't think she was worthy of attention. That's incredible to me!

NE: *What was Catherine like?*

PR: When Dickens was a young man in his early twenties, he was proud of having captured her. She was pretty—when she was young, which was very important. I think she appeared as what they now call a "trophy wife." She was not exactly his boss's daughter, but the daughter of a man who was successful in journalism, the field that he wanted to succeed in. The Hogarths represented a life he very much desired. She was fun-loving when she was young, she was pleasant and serviceable in many ways. I wouldn't underestimate her at all. She must have been a charming young woman.

NE: *You are kinder to her and harder on Dickens than most critics.*

PR: Well, poor Catherine. She didn't have anything going for her except her qualities as a human being. Dickens can be the biggest shit in the world, but he's still the greatest novelist who ever lived. It doesn't really matter. I get impatient, I feel horrible when people say to me, "Oh, I read your book, and I can't read Dickens now that I know what a terrible person he was." That's so stupid. One thing has nothing to do with another. I wrote about Dickens's marriage because it offered a lot of material for me to work with, not because I think that writers are models of human behavior. In many cases they are more ruthless about satisfying their needs than other people. Without being romantic about it, I believe that they have the right to be. It's too bad, but yes, if Dickens has to be terrible to his wife in order to write his last few novels, that's okay. But the least I can do is be charitable to Catherine and to try and give her due as a human being. Bernard Shaw said that the only thing she did wrong was not to be a female Charles Dickens. Which is just brilliant! Exactly to the point.

NE: *He wanted someone who was docile and girlish, and yet at the same time he wanted her to be like himself, energetic and determined. She couldn't win.*

PR: That's absolutely true. But I think that what you're saying is that she wasn't an adequate wife in the early years, whereas I think she was perfectly adequate. He *was* happy with her. But Dickens's self-justifying mechanism was so strong that when he wanted to leave her he convinced himself that she was objectively hateful, horrible. Maybe he rebuked her, but that doesn't mean that she deserved to be rebuked. The only objective thing you can say is that she got very, very fat.

NE: *Obviously something happened to their relationship. You attribute it to a midlife crisis.*

PR: A term receding into the distance! But always serviceable!

NE: *What does it mean?*

PR: It's a certain point in one's life when the structures that enabled you to live earlier are no longer helpful. It may be your job, it may be your marriage, but in many cases it's easier to get out of a marriage than to get out of a job, and that's certainly true for Dickens. Although I do think he changed in subtler ways. He changed his writing style at about the same point, after 1857. But I think that at midlife the feeling suddenly that life is unlivable, that you are suffocating, that you can't stand all the things that used to nourish you, is a common feeling.

NE: *Were women allowed to have a midlife crisis?*

PR: In the Victorian age? Absolutely not. It was just not possible, for too many reasons to be listed. There was no such thing as divorce, for instance.

NE: *Why couldn't Dickens simply live with Nelly openly, as George Eliot did with her lover?*

PR: He had created a role for himself that was a terrible burden. He was the bard of the hearth, so he couldn't suddenly cast off that role and appear publicly as the louche bohemian with a mistress. His friend Wilkie Collins could keep a mistress because he had no status to maintain. But Dickens had created a unique position for himself. His reputation became like a medieval contraption of torture that encaged him. Remember, too, he was English, not French. He was not Balzac. He lived in a country where Mrs. Grundy was powerful, and public morality was very different from that in France. On the Continent a man could live more openly with a woman who was not his wife. England has always been much more Puritan than the Catholic European countries.

NE: *What about the controversy surrounding his affair with Nelly? Peter Ackroyd says he didn't sleep with her; others say he did.*

PR: These things are such Rorschach tests—they say more about the speculator's view of human nature than they do about Dickens. I cannot believe they didn't have sex. But I have no evidence one way or another. I cannot believe that he would leave a wife who physically revolted him to turn to an obsessive ideal that he didn't touch.

NE: *Why did Dickens feel he had to placate his public after his separation?*

PR: He had a compulsion for self-explanation. He seemed to believe that if he only explained enough, eventually the public would accept his version, which was that his wife was uniquely horrible and worthy of being cast off in this terrible fashion. He needed his own version of the breakup to be accepted by the public. He casts himself as the victim when he was patently *not* the victim but the one with power. I don't blame Dickens for casting her off—I blame him for the self-righteousness with which he did it.

Also, he had enormous success very early in life. He was loved, lionized, and trusted from the age of twenty-three. He had to have that in every aspect of his life; and he particularly had to have it from the public. For him, the public was one entity, and his relationship with it was as intense as his relationship with a woman. He couldn't accept a truth that most other people manage to live with: you can't please everybody. He never felt you can't please everybody! He thought he could.

NE: *Did he create the scenario with himself as the hero who rescues the children from this horrible woman?*

PR: I don't think his children come into it that much. Yes, he feels he is the rescuer. But the person he is rescuing is also himself. He is both the hero and the victim. And in the late novels you see over and over the story of men who are two people coexisting in the same body. Bradley Headstone is not a case of schizophrenia but a tormented man divided between two selves. Dickens is more and more attracted to writing about that kind of character because that's how he felt in his later years. There was the public persona, and then there was this victim.

NE: *So you think Dickens actually rewrote his life to give it a hero and a moral?*

PR: I'm fascinated by the way fiction works as a template for action. In *Parallel Lives* I wanted to find examples of fiction actually influencing behavior. And Dickens's late behavior, in his marriage, is a perfect example of the structures of melodrama actually serving as a paradigm for his actions.

NE: *In what way?*

PR: Well, this business we were talking about, that of the rescuer and the rescuee. These polarized, simplified roles are melodramatic. A man as smart as Dickens shouldn't have been thinking that way! I think it was acting in too many second-rate dramas that pounded these paradigms into his head.

NE: *What is the source of his genius?*

PR: His depth comes from his breadth; because his canvas is so enormous, it becomes finally a profound picture of society and of human possibility. I don't think there is anything analytical about his genius.

NE: *Do you think his women are flat characters? Everyone complains about Esther Summerson, for instance.*

PR: You know, when I taught *Bleak House* I used to bring in some of Queen Victoria's letters and diaries. And they sounded just like Esther. Esther Summerson is a perfect image of the genteel Victorian lady. That's the brilliance of that portrait. It's not a model of feminine behavior, it's the feminine voice of public behavior that he has captured.

NE: *What about the complaint that his characters are flat, his world unrealistic?*

PR: Dickens is not a psychological realist. He is writing in a completely different tradition. I don't think you can ask Dickens's characters to be deep and complicated. They are one-dimensional, and I don't use that word in a pejorative sense. If you are working on a broad enough canvas and you have enough one-dimensional characters, you get a different kind of depth.

NE: *What about the sentimentality? Some critics say that when Dickens gets gushy, it's because he's being inauthentic. But you wrote that it's because he believes in it so much. What did you mean by that?*

PR: Call me simplemindedly Freudian, but I think it's because he came from a bad family where he was put to work, and he hated it. Hated it! He was always very ambitious. Even as a child he had hopes for himself, and he saw his parents systematically undermining them. He saw himself going nowhere, and then he was put to work in a shoe polish factory! Can you imagine what it was like for a kid who had hopes and dreams to be put in a situation of virtual slave labor? You would *hate* the parents who did it to you. And Dickens did. He hated his mother more than his father, because his father was willing to let him off. His father was in such bad shape he didn't care what Dickens did, but his mother hoped that the family could be gotten out of the hole it was in, and she pinned her hopes on this twelve-year-old kid! So he was in a situation where the parents depended on the child. It isn't surprising that he would idealize a family in which parents are parents and the children really are children and had the luxury of being dependent on their parents. That's why he believed it sincerely. It's because he wanted it so much.

A Double Life

I am here, there, everywhere, nowhere.
—DICKENS

o fully understand Dickens's final years, one must see Nelly Ternan standing in the shadows. His relationship with her forced him to become an escape artist, and it's because of her that the last thirteen years of his life are filled with periods in which they both seem to disappear—not even their letters survive.

In 1860 Nelly "retired" from the theater and figuratively (unless she lived in the cellar) went underground. After Dickens's death in 1870 she reemerged, and her life assumed a traceable, normal course. Yet thirteen years had been completely erased. Her biographer Claire Tomalin declares that Nelly was "someone who—almost—wasn't there; who vanished into thin air. Her names, dates, family and experiences very nearly disappeared from the record for good." Through the work of scholars and literary detectives, Nelly Ternan has been partially rescued from obscurity.

After his marital separation in 1858, Dickens's life branches into three divergent paths: the public, the private, and the secret. His relationship with Nelly was conducted through codes, aliases, and trusted third parties. The rate book for her cottage in Slough reveals that the rent was variously paid by Frances Turnham, Thomas Turnham, Thomas Tringham, and Charles Tringham. (Dickens never kept an alias for long.) During this time, he was putting money into what he elliptically referred to as the "N Trust."

Given his taste for the dramatic, one suspects that Dickens enjoyed such sub-rosa activities. Before leaving for America in 1868, he devised a code to indicate whether Nelly should join him. Upon his arrival, he would send his manager a telegram that would "have a special meaning for Nelly." That "special meaning" remained hidden until scholar-sleuth Ada Nisbet cracked a cryptic memo in the pocket diary Dickens lost: "Hidden away in some blank pages," Nisbet wrote, were "what seemed to be a code for that message to Nelly":

Tel: all well means
  you come

Tel: safe and well, means
  you don't come

Upon arriving in America, Dickens wired, "Safe and well expect letter full of good hope." Nelly remained with her sister in Italy.

When Dickens returned, he did not, as reported, immediately rush to Gad's Hill for a festive homecoming, but returned discreetly to Nelly's cottage, where they had two days of undisturbed calm. Two days later, he "officially" returned home with no one the wiser.

THE LOST DIARY: 1867

*B*ecause of a rare act of negligence on Dickens's part, we know more about his secret life than he would have liked. While in New York during the winter of 1868, he lost the small leather pocket diary that he used to jot down the day's events and appointments. Years later it turned up at an auction, where it was bought by the Berg brothers. It is now part of the Berg Collection at the New York Public Library. It was ignored until the late 1950s, when the code was cracked by the actor and Dickensian sleuth Sir Felix Aylmer, who discovered that the diary is a record of Dickens's daily journeys and that the initialed entries represent different rail lines. Using nineteenth-century timetables, Aylmer traced the circuitous routes Dickens took to avoid being recognized. Since then the diary has been mined to the last letter.

In his biography of Dickens, Peter Ackroyd cites January 7, 1867, an ordinary day, as an example: "The diary reads: 'at G.H. All go. To Sl at 2.'" which, translated, means "that he was at Gad's Hill Place, that the Christmas Party finally disassembled, and that he went on to Slough, no doubt to his own 'secret' cottage there before visiting the Ternans' just a short walk away."

According to Claire Tomalin, the diary reveals "a man intent on a split life; a man almost demented in his determined pursuit of it." It also displays Dickens's extraordinary knowledge of the rail system, and shows that he was almost continually migrating from one house and one way of life to another. His office and apartment on Wellington Street in London, Nelly in Slough and later in Peckham, and his official residence in Gad's Hill, Kent, all represent different facets of his personality, never to be brought together.

A page from the pocket diary Dickens lost in New York during the winter of 1868; more than eighty years later it was decoded by scholars.

❧ BONFIRE OF THE VANITIES ❧

As the most famous—and popular—writer of the age, Dickens knew that practically every chance word he uttered and every scrap of paper he wrote upon would be scrutinized posthumously, and that death alone would be victorious over his "love of control and order." But not completely: he could apply in advance some measure of damage control. To that end he took an irrevocable step that makes every Dickensian wince. On a crisp fall day in 1860, three years after beginning his liaison with Nelly Ternan and ten years before his death, Dickens went to his backyard in Gad's Hill, built an enormous bonfire, and tossed every personal letter he had ever received into the flames. As his sons Henry and Plorn carted out one stuffed basket after another, he cast "the accumulated letters and papers of twenty years" into his epistolary pyre. His daughter Mamie begged him to salvage the letters from the more eminent correspondents, but Dickens, according to biographer Fred Kaplan, was "mercilessly indiscriminate, absolutely insistent." Letters, Dickens informed Mamie, were "written in the heat of the moment"; and it is fitting that these unguarded, heated moments should be destroyed by fire. Fire—the Victorian paper shredder—was the only way Dickens had of mitigating history's judgment.

While the letters burned, the father and three children sat down and with Neronian indifference "roasted onions on the ashes of the great." Suddenly, the sky darkened and a heavy rain soon doused the fire, turning the letters into sodden pulp. With wry solemnity, Dickens remarked, "I suspect my correspondence of having overcast the face of the Heavens."

He never regretted the action: "Would to God every letter I had ever written was on that pile." His bonfire of vanity would become an annual rite of fall.

❋After Dickens's death, Georgina went through Dickens's letters, obliterating. Dickens's references to Nelly or "N" with black ink (an ironic touch: all his life Dickens had tried to cover up his experiences with blacking, and now it was being used to cover up *him*). Scholars have used infrared photography to read through the ink and find detailed evidence of Dickens's involvement with Nelly.

THE QUESTION OF A CHILD

—☙—

Since Nelly eventually had two healthy children, and because Dickens had fathered ten, it seems odd—given the precarious state of birth control—that Nelly and Dickens did not have a child. Dickens's two most outspoken children, Henry and Kate—and there's no reason to doubt them—told their friend Gladys Storey (author of the controversial *Dickens and Daughter*) that Nelly had a son who was born and died in France. If Nelly had a "confinement," it was one in the literal sense of the word. Whether the infant was stillborn or lived several months is unknown. Tomalin cites three cryptic entries in Dickens's pocket diary: in April 1867 he writes, "N. ill latter part of the month"; a few days later he notes, "Arrival"; and a week later, a single word, "Loss." There is no documentary evidence of a pregnancy, but as Fred Kaplan and others have suggested, there is nothing to disprove it either. Nineteenth-century archives are notoriously unreliable; illegitimate births often went unrecorded, and false names were easily assumed. Thus in the first decades of the twentieth century, various pretenders to the Dickens line have stepped forward to claim their heritage. And in 1902 one even claimed to be the son of Dickens and Georgina.

❋Ada Nisbet's *Charles Dickens and Ellen Ternan* appeared in 1952. The *Times* of London expressed outrage at such unsporting behavior, calling the American scholar unladylike for probing into mysteries not meant for mortal eyes.

The Readings

A Photography likeness sells a book; how much more likely that it would sell when the living author stands before you.
—*Saunders News-letter*, 1857

ntil Dickens's readings, no author had ever appeared on a public stage for profit. The notion of a public appearance as a marketing strategy was completely unknown at the time—the age of public relations was still in its infancy. One might say that Dickens's readings constituted the first author's book tour. (Other writers such as Mark Twain and Thackeray were quick to follow his example.) After one of his first appearances, the *London Illustrated News* announced, "Mr. Dickens has invented a new medium for amusing an English audience, and merits the gratitude of an intelligent public." They were his most lucrative venture, netting him about £45,000, more than all his books combined and made him the richest, most famous author in the world. And his performances sold books. Dickens's friends had warned him that few people would want to buy a book after they had already "heard" it; yet after a performance, sales of the novels increased significantly.

It's perfectly clear from everything you read about him that when he got up to read he was a man on fire! He literally consumed himself. As an actor, he is a real case of a man who can't separate himself. Dickens was emotionally part of everything he wrote and every time he got on stage, he practically killed himself. We don't encourage the idea that you become the character.

—TONY CHURCH, founding member of
The Royal Shakespeare Company, actor, and teacher

A contemporary artist's sketch of an
audience mesmerized by Dickens.

"THE MURDER"

Charles Dickens Jr. never forgot the first time he heard "The Murder."
While working in the solitude of Gad's Hill, he suddenly heard "a noise as
if two people were engaged in a violent altercation or quarrel which threatened serious results to somebody." He looked out the window and saw his father "striding up and down, gesticulating wildly, and, in the character of Mr.
Sikes, murdering Nancy with every circumstance of the most aggravated bru-
tality." Later, at dinner, Charley told his father what he had seen, and Dickens,
curious, asked his opinion. Charley replied, "The finest thing I have ever
heard, but don't do it." From then on, "The Murder" was regarded as though
it wielded an unholy power.

A novelty designed for the farewell tour, "The Murder," or as it is sometimes called, "Sikes and Nancy," was a terrifying enactment of Nancy's grisly
murder by Sikes in *Oliver Twist*. Dickens took more than his usual care with
this reading, annotating his acting text with stage directions such as "mystery" and "terror to the end!" Sikes's beating was to be "continually done with
great passion and fury." Typically, he tested it on friends, solicited their advice, and then did exactly as he liked.

Predictably, John Forster found the subject too unpleasant for a family audience; the tour's producers feared that terrified audiences would cause ticket
sales to drop, and a doctor specializing in female complaints warned Dickens,
"If only one woman cries out when you murder the girl, there will be a conta-

gion of hysteria all over the place." Few said what they thought, that Dickens's precarious health could not sustain such a strenuous performance.

Opposition made him more determined. But first he subjected it to his usual practice and read it to a trial audience. Their response was more than satisfactory—in fact, it was everything he had hoped for and more. The critic of the *Times* exulted, "He has always trembled on the boundary line that separates the reader from the actor, now he clears it by a leap." More accolades were to come. The Shakespearean scholar William Harness confessed that hearing "The Murder" made him feel like "screaming, and that, if anyone had cried out, I am certain I should have followed."

To an audience unaccustomed to violence, it was heady fare; no one who heard it ever forgot it. Dickens wanted to entertain, but even more he wanted to excite wonderment over the performance and his own daring. "I don't think a hand moved while I was doing ['Sikes and Nancy'] last night," Dickens wrote in April 1869. "And there was a fixed expression of horror of me, all over the theatre, which could not have been surpassed if I had been going to be hanged." When Dickens shrieked, "Bill! Dear Bill! for God's sake!" some listeners felt as if they were witnessing a real murder. After reading in Clifton, he boasted to Forster, "We had a contagion of fainting; and yet the place was not hot. I should think we had from a dozen to twenty ladies taken out stiff and rigid, at various times!"

The reading took a gruesome toll on Dickens, psychologically and physically. He was now in the strange position of scaring himself. Identifying with the guilty and the hunted, he told a friend, "It is horribly like, I am afraid. I have a vague sensation of being 'wanted' as I walk the streets." Those given to psychological interpretations have claimed that Charles Dickens was obsessed by Bill Sikes, that Nancy is the scapegoat for all the women Dickens wanted to kill, starting with his mother and ending with Ellen Ternan.

"For God's sake! Bill!"

*A*rtist's rendering of Dickens performing "The Murder" in 1869.

But Dickens was more victim than murderer. No doubt he knew it was killing him, but gripped by its power, he either felt invincible or else determined to go out in a blaze of glory. He *needed* to read "The Murder." When his stage manager, George Dolby, a loyal and conscientious man who worshiped "the Chief," advised him to save it for the larger towns, Dickens, according to Dolby, listened quietly and then coldly asked, "Are you finished?" Dolby replied, "I have said all I feel on the matter."

Insomnia, chronic pain, and nerves had taken a toll: Dickens leapt from his chair and smashed his plate with his knife and fork, breaking it "to atoms." "Dolby!" he yelled, "your infernal caution will be your ruin one of these days." "Perhaps so, sir," replied Dolby. "In this case, though, I hope you will do me the justice to say it is exercised in your interest." Dolby turned and through his own tears saw Dickens weeping. "Forgive me, Dolby! I really didn't mean it; and I know you are right." But he continued to perform "The Murder."

THE FINAL NIGHT

Two thousand people filled St. James's Hall the night Dickens gave his final performance. When he finished *Carol* and *Pickwick,* the audience burst into cheers. Motioning for silence, he said, "I have enjoyed an amount of artistic delight and instruction which perhaps it is given few men to know; from these garish lights I vanish now for evermore, with a heartfelt, grateful, respectful, and affectionate farewell."

He might have been reciting his own epitaph.

As the audience once again broke into deafening applause, Dickens walked off the stage with tears in his eyes. It was both moving and theatrical—rehearsed, yet deeply felt. He was Prospero abjuring magic. Dickens's first grandchild, "Mekitty," never forgot the terrifying sight of "Venebles" crying.

MR. CHARLES DICKENS'S LAST READING

*D*ickens takes his last bow. All the props are neatly in place: the famed reading desk, which he devised himself, the carafe of water, and the scarlet geranium as his boutonnière.

A Tale of Two Cities

A Tale of Two Cities *is Dickens's best advertisement.*
—P. CLAXTON WILLIAMS, the *Dickensian*, Summer 1938

The least admired and least discussed of the later novels.
—PHILIP COLLINS

Most of us have studied it (or the Cliffs Notes) in school, read it for pleasure, or seen at least one of the many film or television adaptations, and just about everyone knows its famous opening and closing lines. If there were a popularity contest for Dickens novels, *A Tale of Two Cities* would probably win. And no wonder: the action is well paced; it's set during one of the most colorful periods in history; and its antihero, Sydney Carton, is the sexiest male character Dickens ever created. (For many readers, *A Tale of Two Cities* is really a tale of two Sydneys, the drunken profligate and the noble friend.) In short, it has all the makings of a terrific miniseries.

But for all its popularity, *A Tale* somehow seems like ersatz Dickens. First, it's his least "Dickensian" book, both in spirit and style. If *A Tale* were the only Dickens novel you ever read, you'd have little idea of his skill with language and character, or how funny he can be. In *A Tale,* Dickens abandons almost everything he does best. There's no cozy Englishness (much of the novel is set in France), no quirky characters with memorable tag phrases or gestures, and little or no comedy. And since he was writing for weekly publication, which required fewer pages, the novel is short by Dickensian standards. The populous landscape is absent, the action being strictly confined to a triangle of principal characters. Finally, for a novelist known for his portraits of cities, the London and Paris of *A Tale* are remarkably flat, more like theatrical backdrops than dynamic centers of political and social upheaval.

In *A Tale,* Dickens attempted what he called a "novel of incident," by which he meant he would create characters "whom the story would express, more

*D*irk Bogarde as Sydney Carton, Dickens's most romantic hero, poised for his big moment at the guillotine.

than they should express themselves by dialogue." Usually Dickens's plots showcase his extraordinary creations, but here characters are diminished by the grand sweep of historical events that bears them helplessly along.

Thus, while *A Tale* can be exhilarating and suspenseful (which makes the novel so adaptable to stage and screen), its characters are like wooden actors rehearsing how to be spontaneous. This is especially so with Lucie (whom Carton rightly describes as a "golden-haired doll") and the insufferably fault-less Charles Darnay. With Jerry Cruncher, the novel's only "clown," Dickens tries so hard to be Dickensian that Cruncher sounds like a Dickens imitation by a minor novelist. Even the unforgettable Madame Defarge is less a person-ality than a personification of revolutionary force, inexorable and heartless.

Sydney Carton, however, is a departure for Dickens. As the novelist's first antihero, he is more reminiscent of the self-destructive Steerforth in *David Copperfield* or the languid Harthouse in *Hard Times* than the earnest David Copperfield, the typical Dickensian protagonist. The Cartonesque figure, moody, antisocial, and self-destructive, suggests the darker strain of mas-culinity that emerges in Dickens's last period.

But the most vivid character of all is the swarming mob. Dickens had al-ways been fascinated by the psychology of the crowd, in which the individual sheds his identity and inhibitions and merges with a larger entity. The collec-tive force, a monstrosity containing all the suppressed energy of its members, secretly attracts even the most civilized creature. As Dickens noted, "And all of us have like wonders hidden in our breast, only needing circumstances to evoke them." Events in such places as Nazi Germany and Bosnia have proven him right.

Dickens detested and feared revolution, not only because it threatened the social order but also because in chaos the individuality of the self ceases to matter. The rebels are haters and destroyers, not only of nobility and wealth but also of learning, beauty, grace, and justice. Personal integrity is replaced by a collective will, and people are executed not for who they are, or even for what they do, but for what they represent.

❈ ❈ ❈

But is *A Tale of Two Cities* anything more than a riveting adventure story? Well, yes, otherwise untold legions of teachers would be in trouble. In fact, one reason *A Tale* is so teachable is that its themes, images, and design are so understandable and distinct. From the title and the parallelism of its famous opening sentence to its final words, *A Tale* plays with paired contrasts that finally unite in the novel's moving conclusion. Montagelike, the novel moves from one extreme to another: London to Paris, British stolidity (as represented by Teson's bank) to French turbulence, Miss Pross's sturdy love to Madame Defarge's tigerish hatred, and most important of all, death to renewal. Such oppositions are so schematically balanced that the novel seems to run along parallel tracks. So too our emotions, as Dickens nimbly manipulates our sympathies, first showing us the effeteness of the aristocrats, then the suffering of the common people, and then turning everything around. The novel even has two different types of heroes in the doppelgangers earnest Charles Darnay and cynical Sydney Carton, two halves of one being who end up exchanging identities and roles.

As critics and students have noted, the novel opens with Dr. Manette being "recalled to life" after being "buried" alive in the Bastille for eighteen years. Carton's life is a living death, while his valiant death becomes his salvation. Darnay is rescued from three different death sentences. The bloodshed of the revolution is the birth of the republic. This theme is even sounded in a blackly comic mode through the grisly activities of Cruncher, a "resurrection man" who digs up fresh corpses to sell to physicians. And, in a minor key, there are two faux resurrections—the French aristocrat Foulon and the English spy Cly feign their own deaths to escape mob violence. Thus in Carton's final scene, when he utters the words from the Anglican burial service, "I am the Resurrection and the Life saith the Lord," his words assume the weight of accumulated meanings, resonating with significance that transcends religious sentiment.

But Carton's self-sacrifice is more than just a neat tying up of the novel's themes. Dickens idealized love, and his imagination was fired by the supreme romantic gesture. In *The Frozen Deep*, the melodrama Dickens had written and performed three years earlier, the hero, Richard Wardour, sacrifices his life to save his beloved's fiancé. Dickens didn't just play the role of Wardour—he was haunted by him, seeing in the character the lover in extremis, experiencing all the intensity of love his creator yearned for. As he moved into middle age, Dickens longed to be a romantic hero occupying a realm outside the workaday world of duty and responsibility. Both Richard Wardour and Sydney Carton act out their creator's fantasy.

Carton is Dickens's alter ego, a projection of the author's inchoate yearnings, and, like Dickens, an idealist living in an iron age, as personified by the philistine Stryver. An aristocrat by nature and a secret romantic, Carton belongs to another, more idealistic age. Because he can't channel his energies into an action worthy of his ideals, he does nothing; but in his magnificent death, he fulfills his true destiny. (He never seems so alive as when he's bustling about Paris planning his death.)

Some readers take a more pragmatic view of Carton, interpreting his final gesture as suicidal rather than heroic. According to the critic George Woodcock, "When he chooses death, it is not as heroes do in the prime of life, but when he has already abandoned all hope of a meaningful existence." Perhaps Carton isn't a hero but a man who simply wants out. It's in keeping with the dualities of the novel that Carton's gesture should evoke two such contradictory interpretations. Admittedly, *A Tale*'s conclusion is stagy and overwrought. But Dickens's theatrical sense didn't fail him. The scene works—and there are still some readers who can't read Carton's final words without tears in their eyes.

MADAME DEFARGE

*T*he lurid figure of Madame Defarge knitting implacably as Paris burns must be etched on the collective memory of generations of high school graduates. No matter how much of the novel is forgotten, Madame Defarge remains—an icon of female menace, the personification of revolutionary ardor, an image of unspeakable cruelty and vengeance.

For media mogul Ted Turner, she is a cautionary image: extolling the virtues of charity, Mr. Turner (sounding a bit like the reformed Scrooge) predicts that unless the rich tend to the poor, there will be "another French Revolution and . . . another Madame Defarge knitting and watching them come in little oxcarts down to the town square and BOOM! Off with their heads" (mem. to Mr. Turner: the "little oxcarts" are called tumbrels).

And for U.S. Congresswoman Grace Mary Stern, she embodies the spirit of revolution—any revolution: "I feel like Madame Defarge at the guillotine—knit one, purl one. It's the Boston Tea Party all over again."

❖ *A Tale of Two Cities,* Dickens's sprawling, populous novel, has been turned into a one-man show by Everett Quinton, artistic director of New York's Ridiculous Theater Company. The show's premise is neo-Dickensian in its outrageousness: Jerry, a middle-aged drag queen, is preparing for his big number at a neighborhood club when he discovers a foundling on his doorstep. Simultaneously trying to soothe the squalling infant and prepare for the show, Jerry tries various children's stories. When Little Red Riding Hood and Rapunzel are dismissed with screams, he desperately tries another: "It was the best of times, it was the worst of times." Blessed silence ensues. The kid is hooked on Dickens's tale. In the two hours it takes Jerry to bathe, dress, and bewig himself, he recites—in French and English accents—and acts out the entire novel, playing everyone from Madame Defarge (with turkey basters as knitting needles) to Sydney Carton. For the most part, Dickens's text is left intact. But everything else is maniacally unpredictable. Jerry's Lucie emerges from the closet in a hastily improvised getup consisting of stiletto heels, a hoop skirt made of coat hangers, and a hair-dryer cap. The play concludes with Jerry, dressed to kill and his *Tale* told, performing a momentous lip-sync number. Shakespearean actor Floyd King, who plays Jerry, prefers this "uplifting" end over Dickens's. "After all," he says, "the end of the story is something of a downer."

Surely this is the only time in the history of the novel and its numerous stage and film adaptations that Sydney Carton utters "It is a far, far better thing" in a blue lamé gown.

✣ In creating Jerry Cruncher, the "resurrection man," Dickens was counting on his readers' familiarity with the sensational murderers Burke and Hare. Knowledge of these real-life criminals added an extra *frisson* to Jerry's dubious profession. The two purveyors of cadavers steadily supplied Dr. Knox's Anatomical Rooms in Edinburgh—but unlike Jerry, Burke and Hare didn't have to dig for their wares. Although the murders occurred twenty-seven years before *Tale* was published, at the end of 1828 the two men still exercised a shiveringly horrific appeal over the populace. Their images, looking suitably corpselike, were a prime attraction at Madame Tussaud's newly opened waxworks museum, then called the "Chamber of Horrors."

✣ As Sydney Carton heads toward the guillotine, its hard to imagine him uttering the jocular catchphrase "23 skidoo." The phrase, however, may derive from Carton's plight. The enigmatic twenty-three may well refer to the ominous number in *Tale*: Carton is the twenty-third man guillotined on the twenty-third day of the month.

Great Expectations

✿

Droll thing life is—that mysterious arrangement of merciless logic for a futile purpose. The most you can hope from it is some knowledge of yourself—that comes too late—a crop of inextinguishable regrets.
—JOSEPH CONRAD, *Heart of Darkness*

reat Expectations is a brutally honest novel. Like *David Copperfield,* it is autobiographical, a first-person account of a young man's rise, his fall, and his reintegration with society.

Before writing it, Dickens reread *Copperfield* to make sure he wouldn't repeat himself. But whereas David discovers that he is the hero of his own life, Pip realizes that he is *not.* Pip is Dickens's most rounded character, and the novel his most mature and moving work. Despite its title, *Great Expectations* is not the traditional Victorian novel in which marriage, money, and progeny are the summum bonum of existence. In his last unequivocally great novel, Dickens even questions the possibility of human happiness.

The novel's opening, one of the most famous in literature, is what Dickens's friend John Forster admiringly called a "clincher": a raw December evening in a church graveyard. Behind the gravestones lies a long stretch of flatland, and beyond, the dark marshes, mysterious and distant. Dickens is not just portraying a winter's day. The desolate scene suggests the insignificance of human life in a dark, cold world. The emphatic black gash that divides earth and sea creates a stark landscape where neither beauty nor romance can flourish—survival is the best one can hope for. In this austere, ungiving land, Pip's siblings lived and died, having "given up in the universal struggle to survive." Finally, there's the ubiquitous marsh mist, a dank veil that distorts everything, turning familiar objects into unrecognizable shadows. Like Hardy's Egdon Heath, the marshes existed long before civilization began and will endure long after human beings are extinct.

One of the most famous openings in fiction and film: Magwitch seizes Pip in the graveyard at dusk.

⌦

A BUNDLE OF SHIVERS

*I*t is against this backdrop that seven-year-old Pip has his first moment of self-awareness:

My first most vivid and broad impression of the identity of things, seems to me to have been gained on a memorable raw afternoon towards evening. At such a time I found out for certain, that this bleak place overgrown with nettles was the churchyard; and that Phillip Pirrip, late of this parish, and also Georgiana, wife of the above, were dead and buried; and that Alexander, Bartholomew, Abraham, Tobias, and Roger, infant children of the aforesaid, were also dead and buried; and that the dark flat wilderness beyond the churchyard, intersected with dykes and mounds and gates, with scattered cattle feeding on it, was the marshes; and that the low leaden line beyond, was the river; and that the distant savage lair from which the wind was rushing, was the sea; and that the small bundle of shivers growing afraid of it all and beginning to cry was Pip.

This cinematic passage takes in the graves, the flatlands, the marshes, and the sea, until finally it zooms in on a shivering bundle that Pip recognizes as himself.

Neither Pip nor Dickens dwells on this insight: in a flash a figure leaps from the tombs, seizes the child, and turns him upside down. This vertiginous moment shakes Pip's newly acquired sense of self and forever alters it. The man, an escaped convict, demands that the child return the next day with "wittles" and a file. Out of this command springs the novel's action.

The convict, Magwitch, instigates the boy's first crime—he will steal from his own family—and awakens his conscience. In one chapter, Dickens shows how the birth of consciousness is accompanied by an awareness of sin.

CRIME AND PUNISHMENT

*A*fter leaving the convict on the marshes, Pip's guilt transforms the once-familiar landscape into a lurid vision in red and black: "The marshes were just a long black horizontal line then, as I stopped to look after him; and the river was just another horizontal line, not nearly so broad nor yet so black; and the sky was just a row of long angry red lines and dense black lines inter-mixed."

The next day—which happens to be Christmas—as he runs to "his convict" with the "wittles" and a file, the marsh mist thickens, causing him to feel that instead of running toward something, everything is running toward *him:*

The gates and dykes and banks came bursting at me through the mist, as if they cried as plainly as could be, "A boy with Somebody-else's pork pie! Stop him!" The cattle came upon me with like suddenness, staring out of their eyes and steaming out of their nostrils, "Holloa, young thief!": One black ox, with a white cravat on—who even had to my awakened con-science something of a clerical air.

To some readers, Pip's guilt must seem excessive—after all, he's only a child, and Magwitch has threatened his life. But how Pip's theft should be re-garded is irrelevant. What matters is that he believes he has committed a crime almost akin to murder: he has stolen from his sister, and worse, he has abetted a criminal to whom he is now bound as if they shared leg irons.

Pip's is one of the most dismal Christmases in all of Dickens: at dinner, his sister, a virago named Mrs. Joe, continually reminds him that he's a burden, unwanted and unloved:

"Trouble?" echoed my sister; "trouble?" And then entered on a fearful catalogue of all the illnesses I had been guilty of, and all the acts of sleep-lessness I had committed, and all the high places I had tumbled from, and all the low places I had tumbled into, and all the injuries I had done myself, and all the times she had wished me in my grave, and I had con-tumaciously refused to go there.

Instilling in Pip what Holocaust scholars have called "the guilt of the sur-vivor," she treats him as if he remained alive out of some act of stealth or malice. The dinner guests concur: all boys are bad, they insist; in fact, they are like "swine." If any reader wonders why Pip feels like a felon, he need look no further.

THE MORAL COMPASS

*P*ip's feelings toward his sister correspond to the earliest stage in a child's moral development. Mrs. Joe is a punitive deity to be feared and obeyed. Pip writes, "I do not recall any tenderness of conscience in reference to Mrs. Joe, when the fear of being found out was lifted off me." But his feelings toward her husband, the blacksmith Joe Gargery, are deeper, more mature. "But I loved Joe . . . and, as to him, my inner self was not so easily composed." A crime against Joe awakens true remorse in Pip, because the former embodies values the boy admires and has internalized: throughout his life, sin will mean a betrayal of Joe, Pip's better self.

One of Dickens's most endearing characters, Joe is a moral touchstone, the foil against whom every character is tacitly compared. As far as Pip can remember, Joe has always been his protector, and despite the difference in age, his best friend. The two have another bond as well: when Pip comes of age, he is to be apprenticed to Joe, an event both happily anticipate.

That Christmas night Joe, with Pip on his shoulders, accompanies the police as they search for Magwitch. The two watch as the convict, clasped in irons, is hauled back to the Hulks, the prison ship. Just before he is taken away, he confesses to his theft of a pie and a file from the Gargerys, thus letting Pip off the hook. Joe replies, "We don't know what you've done, but we wouldn't have you starved for it poor miserable fellow-creatur." The blacksmith's words indict Pip, who has hidden his encounter with the criminal; Joe openly acknowledges him as a fellow being.

But wherever Pip strays, whatever he does, Joe's constant, reassuring presence at the forge will be waiting for him: "When I neared home the light on the spit of sand off the point on the marshes was gleaming against a black night-sky, and Joe's furnace was flinging a path of fire across the road."

SATIS HOUSE

*T*ime passes, the event is forgotten. One cold night, Pip lies on the ground, stares up at the heavens, and muses: "I looked at the stars, and considered how awful it would be for a man to turn his face up to them as he froze to death, and see no help or pity in all the glittering multitude." That terrible image, which will prove prophetic, introduces the next phase of Pip's life.

The sequence of seemingly casual events in this novel is part of a design that is only fully revealed at the end. Within seconds, his sister and the toadying Pumblechook arrive, flushed with excitement, to inform Pip that an eccentric recluse named Miss Havisham has invited Pip to her house "to play."

Upon his arrival there, Pip is greeted by Estella, Miss Havisham's adopted daughter. As her name suggests, Estella is associated with the stars: remote, dazzling, and indifferent. The old house, she informs Pip, is called Satis: "Greek, or Latin, or Hebrew or all three—or all one to me—for enough." The name means "that whoever had this house, could want nothing else." Her words are a curse: Pip will never own Satis House, yet after one afternoon he will never want anything else. Like Keats's knight, Pip is ensnared by *la belle dame sans merci* and left forever hungering, never satisfied.

MISS HAVISHAM

*T*he character of Miss Havisham takes the novel out of the province of realism and into the fantastic. Her shadowy room, a monument to stagnation and decay, is filled with relics of a wedding that never took place. Everything remains exactly as it stood at the moment she learned of her lover's betrayal. Clocks are stopped at twenty minutes to nine, the wedding cake has turned to mold, and the yellowed bridal dress, which she still wears, hangs on her withered frame. Miss Havisham is a creature of operatic proportions, tortured and mad. In her attempt to freeze time, she has ceased to be a living human being. Her name is apt: she *is* a sham.

True to the novel's fairy-tale motif, Miss Havisham is a witch who turns her victims into stone. Under her tutelage, Estella becomes a heartless beauty, as cold and hard as the jewels that adorn her. Defeating readers' expectations, she's not a sleeping beauty who can be awakened with a kiss. There's nothing romantic or magical about her; she is Miss Havisham's creature, not a princess but a monster.

Like most haunted houses, Satis House works transformations, and the boy who enters that first day leaves a very different person. Feverishly egged on by Miss Havisham, who also urges Pip to love Estella, the girl scornfully calls attention to his rough hands, his clumsy boots, and his lack of sophistication.

For the first time in his life, Pip knows shame, an emotion that leads to concealment. Joe and home are now objects that Pip seeks to keep from Estella, whose judging eyes seem to follow him everywhere.

But the power of the house and its inhabitants to hold Pip spellbound is not uncanny.

He returns there, again and again, because he has woven a fantasy about it that satisfies his own inchoate dreams. Even before Miss Havisham's summons, Pip had wanted to be a scholar and to "rise." Entering Satis House, with its aura of gothic mystery (and where time stands still), he is transported from the workaday world into a romance.

APPRENTICESHIP

Pip's visits to Satis House continue until he is fourteen. Then, after presenting Joe—to Pip's mortification and Estella's delight—with a handsome sum for the boy's "services," Miss Havisham exiles Pip from Satis House. But the prospect of working with Joe at the forge, once so delightful, has turned repugnant. Recalling those years, an older Pip writes,

> I remember that at a later period of my "time," I used to stand about the churchyard on Sunday evenings when night was falling, comparing my own perspective with the windy marsh view, and making out how flat and low both were, and how on both there came an unknown way and the dark sea . . . any good that came out my apprenticeship came of plain contented Joe, and not of restlessly aspiring discontented me. What I wanted, who can say? How can *I* say?

Estella's disdain makes Pip want to become a gentleman. To a Victorian, "gentleman" referred to a man of independent means, or at least one who doesn't work. But to Pip it means much more. What he craves is as old as civilization itself: to transcend earthly limitations—which in class-bound Victorian England translate into social aspirations. It would be hypocritical of Dickens to fault Pip's desire to make something of himself; what he condemns is Pip's idle yearning, his failure to have any real goal or vocation. For obvious reasons, the image of an idealistic boy toiling under lowly conditions is dear to Dickens's heart. But while we sympathize with Oliver Twist's and David Copperfield's distaste for their working-class environments, we condemn Pip for his pretensions and brand him a snob.

ORLICK—THE CREATURE FROM THE MARSHES

Looking back on his time at the forge, Pip recalls it as devoid of adventure and delight:

> There have been occasions in my later life . . . when I have felt for a time as if a thick curtain had fallen on all its interest and romance, to shut me out from everything save dull endurance any more. Never has that

curtain dropped so heavy and blank, as when my way in life stretched out straight before me through the newly-entered road of apprenticeship to Joe.

He yearns for the extraordinary, even hallucinatory atmosphere of Satis House as a release from his blank existence. Ignoring Miss Havisham's injunction, Pip cannot resist one more visit.

His fellow laborer, Orlick, sullenly observes Joe give Pip a holiday and then demands one for himself. When Mrs. Joe sharply intervenes, the laborer turns on her, spewing the invective that Pip must have wanted to say for years. A hulking creature who seems to have risen from the marsh's slimy ooze, Orlick is pure impulse—the id made flesh. Magwitch, we later learn, was turned into a criminal by society's ills, while his fellow convict, Compeyson, is a depraved specimen of his class. But "old Orlick" is pre-social man.

Returning from Miss Havisham's, Pip meets Mr. Wopsle, the cleric turned tragedian, who treats him and Pumblechook to a recitation of the tragedy of George Barnwell, a melodrama about an unusually depraved murderer. Pip's sympathetic identification with the villain threatens to overwhelm him:

> What stung me, was the identification with my unoffending self. When Barnwell began to go wrong, I declare that I felt positively apologetic, Pumblechook's indignant stare so taxed me with it. Wopsle, too, took pains to present me in the worst possible light. At once ferocious and maudlin, I was made to murder my uncle with no extenuating circumstances whatever; . . . Even after I was happily hanged and Wopsle had closed the book, Pumblechook sat staring at me, and shaking his head, and saying, "Take warning, boy, take warning!" as if it were a well-known fact that I contemplated murdering a near relation.

Pip's empathy sets the stage for what happens next. When he arrives home, he finds that someone *has* attempted murder on a near relation—and it's the one Pip would most enjoy seeing dead: Mrs. Joe. Pip's unconscious desire to kill his sister is reflected in his readiness to assume guilt: "With my head full of George Barnwell, I was first disposed to believe that *I* must have had some hand in the attack upon my sister." Mrs. Joe's fate is a classic case of wish fulfillment. She survives but, deprived of speech and understanding, is reduced to an infantile state. Pip now has power over her—an abused child's dream come true.

And although it is Orlick who has assaulted her, it is Pip who indirectly supplies the weapon—the leg iron that Magwitch had sawed off with the stolen file nine years earlier. Orlick is Pip's evil brother, the Cain to his Abel. Assault becomes murder as Mrs. Joe eventually dies, a direct result of Orlick's attack. And just as Mrs. Joe is felled, another secret wish is unexpectedly granted: Pip is to be a gentleman after all.

THE GREAT EXPECTATIONS

*A*gain, violent death presages the unexpected fulfillment of a wish: now eighteen, Pip sits in the local tavern listening to Mr. Wopsle's account of a "highly popular murder." Just as the listeners are "imbrued in blood up to the eyebrows," Mr. Jaggers, Miss Havisham's lawyer, appears and dryly informs Pip of his "great expectations": he is to be "removed from his present sphere of life and from this place, and be brought up as a gentleman."

"Great expectations" is a particularly Victorian expression, a delicate means of indicating anticipations of an impending inheritance. But in *Great Expectations* the term assumes larger, almost mythic significance. His benefactor, who is to remain secret, will reveal himself and his purpose at some vague future time. Naturally Pip assumes that Miss Havisham has recognized his noble nature and decided to reward him. As one who "expects," Pip must live in a state of suspended animation, always waiting and never becoming. His patron's sole condition—that he retain the name Pip—suggests that while Pip waits for his inheritance, he can only be a pip, a seedling that will never blossom or bear fruit.

THE GENTLEMAN

*P*ip's "great expectations" allow Dickens to explore various meanings of this term. Pip becomes a vulgar embodiment of that ambiguous term *gentleman*. He adopts the accoutrements of the gentlemanly class but none of its finer values. That he is a caricature of a gentleman is a fact hilariously recognized by Trabb's boy (just about everyone's favorite minor character), who mimes the newly made man as he struts down the main street in his new attire. Fencing, punting, clubs, clothes, drinking, and, Dickens hints, debauchery become a necessary part of life, and Pip, as Mr. Jaggers predicted, runs up enormous debts, which increase in proportion to his "needs." What once seemed a fortune now barely covers necessary expenses. Need, like desire, expands the more it is fulfilled.

Is being a gentleman, as Pip believes, merely a matter of manners, clothes, and clubs? By snubbing others, Pip believes he elevates himself. In the strict sense of the word, the crass Bentley Drummle is the only gentleman in the novel. But Dickens removes the term from the context of wealth, breeding, and class and restores its original meaning. According to Dickens's standards, only the lowborn Joe and Magwitch are men of honor, true gentle men.

DESIRE

*P*ip is not a materialist. Objects are just surrogates for the "real" object of his desire, and one can argue that even Estella is a surrogate for some larger, nameless object. But is he telling the truth when he says, "I did not invest her with any attributes save those she possessed"? The reader can only wonder.

Pip arrogantly assumes that Estella is a condition of his inheritance and creates a drama in which he casts himself as the chivalric hero in an old romance:

> Miss Havisham had adopted Estella, she had as good as adopted me, and it could not fail to be her intention to bring us together. She reserved it for me to restore the desolate house, admit the sunshine into the dark rooms, set the clocks a-going and the cold hearths a-blazing, tear down the cobwebs, destroy the vermin—in short, do all the shining deeds of the young Knights of romance, and marry the Princess.

But Estella and Pip are Miss Havisham's pawns and must act in accord with her whims: after relaying Miss Havisham's orders and conditions, Estella tells Pip, "We have no choice. It is part of Miss Havisham's plans for me." Throughout his life, Pip has been at the mercy of others, their whims, demands, and expectations. His actions—with the exception of his private act of kindness toward his friend, the worthy Herbert Pocket—are rarely self-generated and never reflect the dictates of his own heart. He's been whirled about, beaten, forced to steal and play. He is compelled against his will to become a blacksmith, then abruptly removed from the forge and turned into a London gentleman. Even his love for Estella has been engineered by Miss Havisham. While he has, as promised, retained the name "Pip," he has forgotten his origins and who he is. He will soon be reminded.

THE RETURN OF THE REPRESSED

*A*n atmosphere of suspense more fitting to a gothic tale of terror surrounds the appearance of Pip's benefactor. Darkness, tempests, winds, and other ominous portents arouse a creeping sense of horror—as though a spectral rather than a human visitor were about to appear. Uneasy and anxious, Pip tries to read but can't settle down. As the wind picks up, unfamiliar footsteps are heard on the stairs and grow steadily louder as they make their way toward Pip's rooms. A stranger enters and looks about with a proprietary air, "as if he had some part in the things he admired." At first condescending, Pip turns sententious when the man identifies himself as his old partner in crime, Magwitch. But his assumption of moral and social superiority make his discovery all the more terrible. That the lowborn convict "made" him is a deep narcissistic wound, punishment for his snobbery.

Magwitch's reappearance corresponds to what Freud calls the "return of the repressed," a memory or event, long buried, that has now come to light. Pip's image of Magwitch has remained unchanged since childhood. The man (ironically, as it turns out) represents all that is "un-Estella"—vulgar, mean, and ugly—everything from which he has tried to escape. "The abhorrence in which I held the man, the dread I had of him, the repugnance with which I shrank from him, could not have been exceeded if he had been some terrible beast." When he proudly clasps Pip to his breast and calls him "my boy," he claims what seems to Pip an unholy alliance.

The evocative name "Magwitch" emphasizes the novel's magical, fairy-tale elements: the convict, who has risked his life to return to England, is a magus figure whose rough appearance disguises his inner wisdom.

But the felon's reappearance is much more than a social embarrassment for Pip. The knowledge that everything he owns is a gift from a criminal shatters his identity, his dreams and expectations. Estella is not his intended bride, nor is Miss Havisham his fairy godmother.

> Miss Havisham's intentions towards me, all a mere dream; Estella not designed for me; I only suffered in Satis House as a convenience, a sting for the greedy relations, a model with a mechanical heart to practise on when no other practice was at hand; those were the first smarts I had. But, sharpest and deepest pain of all—it was for the convict, guilty of I knew not what crimes, and liable to be taken out of those rooms where I sat thinking, and hanged at the Old Bailey door, that I had deserted Joe.

In a flash Pip sees through his vanity; everything that gave his life meaning has vanished.

THE FINAL TESTS

*A*t this point the novel turns into something of an adventure tale, as Pip and his friends struggle to get Magwitch safely out of England, where his status as a returned exile is like that of an escaped convict. Like a hero in a medieval romance, Pip must undergo a series of ordeals, each with its own moral lesson, before he can find forgiveness for his misguided life. The first test is Magwitch himself: although disgusted by the old man, Pip does not desert him. Hearing Magwitch's story, he sees a wronged human being behind the criminal's face, and his growing love for the bogeyman of his youth is a moral and psychological turning point. Pip now accepts in himself what he hoped to escape by becoming a gentleman.

The second test is a trial by fire: Pip returns to Miss Havisham's, where he learns of Estella's betrothal to the odious Drummle. Without any of the rancor that consumed Miss Havisham, Pip accepts the loss of Estella without ceasing to love her. He learns to love without expectations.

For the first time since her aborted wedding, Miss Havisham feels the weight of another's pain. Falling at Pip's feet, she begs his forgiveness. Pip could, as he has before, succumb to self-righteousness or false magnanimity. But he realizes his unworthiness to stand in judgment on others: " 'O Miss Havisham,' said I, 'I can't do it now. There have been sore mistakes; and my life has been a blind and thankless one; and I want forgiveness and direction far too much, to be bitter with you.' " Miss Havisham is no longer a creature of romance but a woman crazed by grief. He sees in her all the dangers that rejected love is heir to: isolation, paralysis, self-pity, and greed that feeds on its own misery.

When her bridal dress goes up in flames, Pip struggles to save her, and the two, bound in his greatcoat, struggle "like desperate enemies." Pip is symbolically battling his own unchecked passions, his tendency to give way, as Miss Havisham did, to the "vanity of sorrow." Consequently, all that is rotten in Satis House bursts into flames, breaking the curse of Miss Havisham. In nobly risking his life to save the woman who wronged him, Pip endures the archetypal trial by fire.

His confrontation with Orlick is far more terrifying—for, to paraphrase Marlow on Kurtz in *Heart of Darkness,* he "could not appeal [to him] in the name of anything high or low." Miss Havisham can seek forgiveness, but Orlick is scarcely human, let alone humane. In facing Orlick, Pip confronts and conquers his own unconscious murderous instincts.

"Old Orlick's a-going to tell you somethink. It was you as did for your shrew sister."

" ' 'Twas you, villain," said I.

"I tell you it was your doing—I tell you it was done through you," he retorted catching up the gun. . . . "I come upon her from behind, as I come upon you to-night. *I* giv' it to her! I left her for dead, and if there had been a limekiln as nigh here as there is now nigh you, she shouldn't have come to life again. But it warn't old Orlick as did it; it was you. . . . Now you pays for it. You done it; now you pays for it."

Facing what seems certain death, Pip looks into the emptiness of his past and thinks not of himself but of those he has wronged. Like Scrooge, he sees his dead self, unloved and unmourned: "The death close before me was terrible, but far more terrible than death was the dread of being misremembered after death. And so quick were my thoughts, that I saw myself despised by unborn generations. . . ." But Pip is handily rescued, and Orlick vanishes into the marsh mist like an amphibious creature. As the embodiment of unconscious drives, Orlick can never die, but he can be confronted, exorcised, and banished.

Pip attempts to steal away with Magwitch and live with him in exile, but the two are caught by the police. In the struggle, Pip almost drowns, and Magwitch suffers fatal injuries. After the convict's death (one of Dickens's most moving deathbed scenes), Pip returns to his old rooms, already sick with brain fever, the stock Victorian metaphor for spiritual rebirth. Unconscious for over a month, he awakens in springtime to find Joe tenderly bending over him. Weakened by illness, Pip regresses to the early days when Joe was everything to him, but as he regains his strength and loses his childish helplessness, the blacksmith grows politely distant—a reminder that adulthood and independence mean the reassertion of artificial social barriers. When Pip recovers, Joe quietly leaves. Only then does he learn that Joe has paid his debts. The term "Christ figure" should be used sparingly, but in "redeeming" Pip, Joe certainly earns the title.

Having passed through the crucible of self-doubt, Pip achieves self-knowledge, one of the central themes of the book. Alone, poor, and without his old dream to sustain him, he must learn how to live and work like an ordinary man. His decision to propose to Biddy—the village girl he would have married before his "great expectations"—shows his willingness to return to his humble origins. His discovery that she is already married to Joe painfully reveals that the past is sealed off and that, like an existential antihero, he must move into an uncertain future. Unlike any other Dickensian hero, Pip goes abroad to work in the Eastern Branch of Clariker and Co. with Herbert Pocket (Dickens is characteristically vague as to the precise nature of Pip's business). In the Victorian novel, "abroad" is the symbolic destination of self-discovery.

The rest of Pip's story can be told in a few pages. Thirty-something and a bachelor, he has lived frugally, paid his debts, and has methodically risen in the firm. The boy with the unruly heart has grown into a man who has learned to sublimate desire into duty. The question is, having done so, should Pip then be rewarded with the object of his desire?

THE TWO ENDINGS

When Dickens showed the novel's conclusion to his friend, the writer Edward Bulwer-Lytton, the latter disapproved, arguing that readers would want to see Pip and Estella united. In this original ending, Pip recounts his final meeting with Estella. Having been beaten by Bentley Drummle (is he too one of Pip's sadistic doubles?), she is greatly altered in appearance. Now married to a country doctor—Drummle having been killed in a riding accident—Estella is a Victorian matron with nothing about her to suggest her fantastic upbringing. The two old friends shake hands and part, and the novel ends on a note of quiet satisfaction:

> I was very glad afterwards to have had the interview; for, in her face and in her voice, and in her touch, she gave me the assurance, that suffering had been stronger than Miss Havisham's teaching, and had given her a heart to understand what my heart *used to be*. [italics mine]

"Used to be" is a sad phrase—one suspects that Pip, damaged by his past, will never marry. In this version Dickens departs from every novel he ever wrote: this hero does not get the girl, the inheritance, and the wonderful life. In fact, *Great Expectations* is a Dickens novel in reverse.

Surprisingly, Dickens agreed with Lytton and wrote a new conclusion. Of the second ending, Dickens, with rare understatement, wrote, "It is a pretty . . . little piece of writing." Actually, it is achingly beautiful. As George Bernard Shaw wrote, "though psychologically wrong, it is artistically much more congruous than the original. The scene, the hour, the atmosphere, are beautifully touching and exactly right." Restraining his sentimental tendencies, Dickens made the ending as sad as a happy ending could be. In the published chapter, Pip and Estella marry, but their reunion is so restrained and ambiguous that readers might well wonder what exactly took place. If it is read one way, Pip and Estella will never part; read another, they will never really see each other again:

> I took her hand in mine, and we went out of the ruined place; and, as the morning mists had risen long ago when I first left the forge, so the evening mists were rising now, and in all the broad expanse of tranquil light they showed to me, I saw no shadow of another parting from her.

Dickens has ingeniously created the requisite happy ending without compromising the novel's meaning. Yet for some reason he continued to tinker with the final phrase. By the 1868 edition, it has grown more ominous: "At this happy moment, I did not see the shadow of our subsequent parting looming over us." Clearly, Dickens wanted to end on a note of uncertainty, or perhaps he wasn't sure what he wanted.

Modern readers tend to find the original conclusion more in keeping with the narrative's introspective, brooding tone. Angus Calder voices the majority opinion:

> [It] is moving in its very sobriety, and commends itself above the present conclusion when we consider that the remorseful, probing, brooding tone of disillusionment which pervades the first person narrative of the novel, most notably in the passages dealing with Estella, is rendered more than slightly nonsensical if the supposed author is both successful and happily married. It is, besides, merely more *probable* than its successor.

(The ornery Shaw also noted that the original ending "was in fact the truly happy ending.")

But ultimately it does not matter: married to her or not, Pip can never possess the rare Estella he once worshiped—because that woman never existed. Estella was lovable precisely because she was unobtainable. The old Estella's origins were tantalizingly mysterious; the "real" one is the daughter of a felon and a murderess. She is no more a princess than he a gentleman. Both have adoptive parents who exploit them to serve their own ends. With the best of intentions, Magwitch turned Pip into a gentleman to avenge himself on society; Miss Havisham used Estella to avenge herself on the male sex. Pip's symbolic father is Estella's real one, and the two are not only husband and wife but spiritual siblings. Thus the dream girl is not the inaccessible Other, but Pip's other half, from whom he is cut off forever.

To give Pip what had been portrayed all along as an impossibility—i.e., romantic fulfillment—subverts the meaning of the novel. Great expectations by their very nature can never be fulfilled—which is why the euphoric conclusion to David Lean's film rings so false. In the published ending, Pip tells Estella, "I work pretty hard for a sufficient living, and therefore—Yes, I do well." In this beautiful and moral work, sufficiency is all.

🐝 ON GREAT EXPECTATIONS 🐝

✱Just how rich is Pip? According to Julia Prewitt Brown in *A Reader's Guide to Nineteenth-Century Fiction,* the 20 guineas that Jaggers gives him to buy clothes worthy of a gentleman would be $4,000 today. The scope of Pip's transformation hits us in a flash. It also explains why Joe almost falls over when Jaggers hands the money over to Pip.

✱There have been several contenders for the real-life model for Miss Havisham, thus proving once again that truth is stranger than Dickens's fiction. In fact, the scholar Richard Altick notes that "more 'originals' have been proposed for her than for any other character in Dickens." She is the stuff of urban legends, ballads, melodramas, and real-life eccentrics. One of the more verifiable accounts concerns a Miss Eliza Emily Donnithorne of Newtown, New South Wales. According to contemporary accounts, one morning in 1856—five years before Dickens wrote *Great Expectations*—Miss Donnithorne carefully prepared for her wedding. The wedding feast, including the cake, was laid out, the bride was dressed, the

MISS HAVISHAM, C'EST MOI!

Miss Havisham is Dickens. Do you recall the speech where Miss Havisham talks about the self-humiliation of love? Who else would describe love like that? One could say that love is uplifting, thrilling, paralyzing. It takes your breath away; it lifts your soul. But self-humiliating? . . . When I read that, I couldn't believe anybody would describe love like that. And I suddenly thought, that's him, that's the way Dickens loves. With Maria, with Nelly Ternan . . . always battering against a wall. Bitter. Love for him was a painful experience. Very little of the good stuff thrown in, I suspect.

—MIRIAM MARGOLYES

guests had gathered; only the groom was absent. Until her death thirty years later, Miss Donnithorne remained immured among her nuptial relics, impervious to the outside world. Even the famous cake, which seemed like such a fantastic detail in Dickens's novel, remained untouched. It is said that Miss Donnithorne found solace in fiction; it would be nice to think that perhaps she found solace in finding a companion soul in Miss Havisham. Ironically, the woman who lived apart from the world came to be one of literature's most famous characters and the inspiration for the composer Peter Maxwell Davies's monodrama, *Miss Donnithorne's Maggot.*

❈ William A. Cohen's study of sex in Dickens's novels is the most controversial book on Dickens to appear since the Nelly Ternan crisis in the 1930s, even making the front page of the *London Observer.*

Most readers think *Great Expectatons* is about snobbery or desire, but in *Manual Conduct in Great Expectations,* Professor Cohen reveals that the novel is really about masturbation. He cites, for example, the scene in which young Pip hides the bread and butter in his trouser leg to give to the convict Magwitch. Pip goes to his bedroom, where he relieves himself of the bread, his "secret burden." Cohen continues his fantasia on the novel by imagining—which Dickens does not—the butter dribbling down the boy's leg. At the time, however, Pip is only seven, rather young to be indulging in "the solitary vice."

Great Expectations, according to Cohen, is a homosexual novel. Pip's fights with Drummle, Orlick, and of course Herbert Pocket—whose surname in this light is certainly intriguing—are all homosexual. Cohen also attributes pedophiliac impulses to Magwitch, and dismisses Pip's professions of revulsion toward the felon as evidence of his secret attraction. So much for Estella—it's Magwitch Pip desires.

Miss Havisham's Fire

Tales were told. Songs sung.
Letters purloined. Diamonds lost.
Faces came and went and no one knew.
Too late. She remained alone.
Clocks were broken. (Oh, tales were told!)
The gate was shut.
—Prologue to *Miss Havisham's Fire*

INTERVIEW WITH DOMINICK ARGENTO

hen Beverly Sills commissioned Dominick Argento to compose an *opera for her valedictory performances at the New York City Opera, she requested a piece that, in her words, would leave her feeling like "a wrung-out rag." The composer complied with* Miss Havisham's Fire, *one of the few operas based on a full-length Dickens novel. In it, Miss Havisham is a heroine of grandiose proportions, victimized and vindictive. Even by the standards of the opera—a genre famous for putting its characters under severe duress—*Miss Havisham's Fire *is extreme, containing what is, at thirty minutes, the longest mad scene in the operatic repertoire.*

NE: *Why is Miss Havisham a fitting subject for an opera?*

DA: Beverly Sills said she thought Miss Havisham was very much like all those nineteenth-century mad heroines. Her situation is the *fou d' amour,* as in *Lucia di Lammermoor;* the difference of course is that extra dimension Dickens gives his story. Out of vengeance and spite, Miss Havisham wreaks havoc on other people's lives—that gives the story a quasi-modern touch.

NE: *Dickens's novels didn't initially strike me as particularly operatic in their subject matter.*

Miss Havisham among the decay: a Dickensian character of operatic proportions. (From David Lean's 1946 *Great Expectations;* Martita Hunt as Miss Havisham; Anthony Wager as Pip.)

DA: Dickens is not fertile ground for an opera composer because the one thing that an operatic source needs is the ability to be condensed to death. The big lesson about that is *Othello* and *Otello,* in which Verdi jettisoned the whole of Shakespeare's first act. Well, you can't do that with Dickens. His are gigantic stories. You start jettisoning, and you end up with nothing.

NE: *Are there any other Dickens works in music?*

DA: Actually there's another piece about Miss Havisham, a monodrama for soprano called *Miss Donnithorne's Maggot,* which is based on the real Australian woman, the model for Miss Havisham. But the character is nothing but creepy, and she uses a lot of four-letter words beginning with *F,* which has more to do with the composer, Peter Maxwell Davies, than with Dickens.

There are at least three operas based on *A Christmas Carol,* but they are all short. And then, believe it or not, an Italian composer did *The Cricket on the Hearth,* but that's as short as *A Christmas Carol.* I can't imagine anyone tackling *Hard Times* or *Dombey and Son.* There have been a couple of attempts to do the big novels—an English composer tried to do *A Tale of Two Cities*—but they don't work, not because the characters are wrong, but because to tell the story, the opera has to go on forever, and it's too long and boring.

NE: *How did you translate Dickens's elaborate settings into a opera set?*

DA: When I envision Miss Havisham's room where her wedding cake is, I see something almost hermetic, tiny, claustrophobic. She's stuck in there with her trunks and her jewelry and her mirrors. But the designer created a set about five stories tall; when Miss Havisham sat on the stage, she was this tiny little character. The walls were meant to look like they were oozing, which is okay but it had nothing to do with the opera. And the worst part was that the only way we could do the inquest scene was to put everyone on a trolley and push them in from the wings. Every time you heard this squeak backstage, you would think, Oh, oh, my God, here we go again. And out would come these twelve characters sitting on this thing, floating as it were, and then they'd be pulled off. It was a nightmare.

NE: *How did you deal with the text?*

DA: We used Dickens's prose where we could. For example, the long aria that Pip sings at the end of the first act, "One Memorable Day," is straight from the book. There's a reference in the novel to the blacksmith song, "Old Clem," and I tried to find out if there was such a song, but it turns out there isn't. So I had to make up a folk song.

NE: *What about Dickens attracts a composer?*

DA: Under all of the grotesquerie—and we are talking about Uriah Heep and all those other characters—there's a real heart beating underneath the toga. You read about such characters in other novelists, and they are unbelievable, but when you read Dickens, you think, That could be somebody I know! There's a real quality to his works that makes sense in music. I hate cardboard figures in opera, those heroes who walk in and do stupid feats. A character as eccentric as Miss Havisham is still understandable. You know how she got to be that way, and that's true right down the line: you know Estella's background, and even Pip's. In that sense Dickens is operatic—his characters are larger than life. I don't know of another writer in English who has such a gargantuan array of characters—both pathetic and beautiful—who can be expressed through music. Characters like Miss Hav-

Miss Havisham would probably be diagnosed as agoraphobic today. I understand it because just before I played her I had been through an agoraphobic period, and funnily enough, when they asked me to do it, I said, "You must be crazy!" But Miss Havisham is not completely crazy: she's still able to raise a daughter, she knows what's what with her parasitic relatives, she knows enough to send Estella to school.

She was trying to prevent Estella from being as hurt as she had been, but in the meantime, she became hard. The Miss Havisham I discovered was a heartbreak. That's how I saw her. Which is totally different from other versions. But the only thing I can't explain is that fabulous dress that she wore! My God! Can you imagine the smell?

—JEAN SIMMONS, Estella in David Lean's film version of *Great Expectations* (1946) and Miss Havisham in the Disney production (1988)

isham need more than normal speech, so when they break into song, there's nothing odd about it. She is one of those characters who live on the edge of where speech can go.

Jean Simmons in her screen debut as Estella in David Lean's *Great Expectations* (1946).

America Redux

Another such star-shower is not to be expected in one's lifetime.
—John Greenleaf Whittier, on Dickens's second visit to America

n November 1867, twenty-five years after his first trip, a very different Dickens returned to America. Prematurely old and ailing, he was barely recognizable to those who remembered him as Boz. The long auburn hair that the press once mocked was now sparse and gray. This time the reason for his journey was uncomplicated and pragmatic. Quite simply, Dickens feared he was losing his creative energy. Told that a series of readings in the United States would be extremely lucrative, he wanted to amass as much money as possible while he was still healthy enough to read. Dickens's need for money was not just Scroogean greed; during this time he was maintaining at least four establishments and had numerous dependents. In fact, James Fields, publisher of the *Atlantic Monthly,* promised him £10,000, which would be banked in advance in England. It would take a lot of money to induce the ailing Dickens to travel 3,000 miles from a home he loved to a country he hated.

Although it had been twenty-five years since his "American novel," *Martin Chuzzlewit,* had been burned in New York, Dickens still worried about how he would be received. Before agreeing to go, he sent George Dolby, his devoted manager, to the States to see if "The Inimitable" could still command large crowds. The answer was affirmative.

His friends begged him not to go, but once Dickens made up his mind about anything, he was intractable. (One observer noted, "I think myself that his lust for money made him unconsciously a suicide.") Although the grueling six-month tour nearly killed him (and perhaps hastened his death),

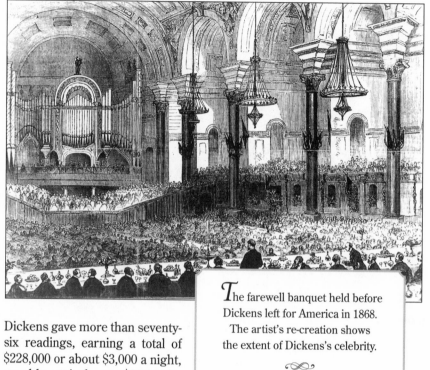

The farewell banquet held before Dickens left for America in 1868. The artist's re-creation shows the extent of Dickens's celebrity.

Dickens gave more than seventy-six readings, earning a total of $228,000 or about $3,000 a night, roughly equivalent to $50,000 by today's standards. Two years later he died, a rich man.

The country Dickens had toured in 1842 had changed as much as he had. The Civil War was over, slavery abolished, and the nation was in the throes of Reconstruction. Although Dickens abhorred slavery on principle, he had, like many British, sided with the Confederacy during the war. During his first trip he was repelled by slavery, but now he was disgusted by the behavior of freed slaves under Reconstruction. This is a side of Dickens few care to acknowledge: "The mechanical absurdity of giving these people votes, at any rate at present, would glare out of every roll of their eyes, chuckle in their mouths, and bump in their heads, if one did not see . . . that their enfranchisement is a mere trick to get votes." This time, however, Dickens wisely kept such opinions to himself.

As soon as he arrived, he saw that a new generation had grown up on his works and that the past had been forgiven. Americans flocked to his readings like adolescents to a rock concert. In New York, 5,000 people waited for tickets in a queue half a mile long. In the frigid night air, fans slept on blankets just to secure their place in line. More than 40,000 people heard Dickens read in New York alone.

The tour was an unequivocal triumph. Dickens, now regarded as a grand old man of letters, was provided with every comfort. Gratified by the ardent

*D*ickens as he appeared during his American tour of 1867–68. At 55 he looked so old that his American friends barely recognized him. This formal shot was taken by Ben Gurney, the American photographer who held a monopoly to photograph Dickens during the tour. Dickens despised being photographed, calling it "an unremunerative investment of time and temper."

response—and the remuneration—Dickens found little to complain about. It was, he decided, time to make amends, and he did so in a typically theatrical manner. On April 18, 1868, the American press held a banquet in his honor in New York. In his after-dinner speech Dickens acknowledged the "amazing changes" in America since his last visit and, more important, the changes in himself. He concluded with a resolution:

[O]n my return to England, in my own person, in my own Journal [*All the Year Round*], to bear, for the behoof of my countrymen, such testimony to the gigantic changes in this country as I have hinted at tonight. Also, to record that wherever I have been, in the smallest places equally with the largest, I have been received with unsurpassable politeness, delicacy, sweet temper, hospitality, consideration, and with unsurpassable respect for the privacy daily enforced upon me by the nature of my avocation here and the state of my health. This testimony, so long as I live, and so long as my descendants have any legal right in my books, I shall cause to be republished, as an appendix to every copy of those two books of mine in which I have referred to America. And this I will do and cause to be done, not in mere love and thankfulness, but because I regard it as an act of plain justice and honour.

His vow is both a moving apology and a virtuoso act of public relations.

Like Scrooge, Dickens was as good as his word. Although his descendants have long ceased to have any legal claim upon his works, his speech before two hundred American journalists is still reprinted in every copy of "those two books," *Martin Chuzzlewit* and *American Notes.*

*A*n American cartoonist lampoons Dickens's lucrative trip to America. He left $228,000 richer—and without paying a cent in taxes.

Our Mutual Friend

⁜

*There are changes which often make the final period
of a writer's career the most interesting of all.*
—Virginia Woolf

ur Mutual Friend is the entire Dickens canon redux, and reading it can be a daunting, exhausting, not to say fascinating, experience. It is doubtless his most convoluted and challenging novel, a narrative labyrinth in which numerous stories radiate from a common center. What's more, the novel has various, sometimes conflicting, styles: the critic Stephen Gill isolates five, but there are probably more. Treacly sentiment collides with sharp-eyed realism, which gives way to barbed satire, broad comedy, and a baroque weirdness, all uniquely Dickensian. There are also two main plots and numerous subplots, which present various and often conflicting visions of life. But Dickens's finer insights tend to pass unnoticed, because frankly, one would need the literary equivalent of a Weed Whacker to cut through the novel's dense landscape.

Dickens manages to transcend what in any other novel would be fatal flaws. Today *Our Mutual Friend* is regarded as one of the most intriguing works in the oeuvre—which says as much about the modern sensibility as it does about Dickens, for it is his darkest, most sardonic, and hence most modern novel.

As usual, Dickens deals with traditional Victorian themes: marriage, money, morals, and class. But for the first time he probes beneath the veneer of civilization to express something much deeper and older in human nature. Although he lacks the vocabulary to describe the workings of the unconscious, Dickens conveys through imagery and recurring symbols the age-old tension between anarchy and order, convention and desire, society and self, ego and id.

Among its many themes, *Our Mutual Friend* is about the duality of identity. Just about every character in the novel has a sidekick, double, accomplice, or "front" who mirrors, masks, or reverses a secret self. Isolated figures, like Charlie Hexam, are presented as conflicted creatures at war with their own impulses. This divided-self theme haunts the late Victorians, culminating in two novellas, Robert Louis Stevenson's *Dr. Jekyll and Mr. Hyde* and, in the last year of Dickens's century, Joseph Conrad's *Heart of Darkness.*

Our Mutual Friend opens with a scene that is both a surreal nightscape and an incident that might have come straight out of Henry Mayhew's sociological study *London Labour and the London Poor.* A young woman named Lizzie Hexam rows her father, Gaffer, in a small boat on the Thames, searching for something unnamed. It gradually transpires that father and daughter are fishing for the bodies of the drowned. Dredging the Thames for corpses was lucrative, for rewards were often posted for information about the missing, and the dead sometimes still had cash in their pockets.

Throughout the novel documentary realism vies with the mythic and the alien. Dickens's haunting riverscape suggests the ghostly moonlit seas in a painting by Albert Pinkham Ryder. And the Thames is both a topographical and a symbolic landscape. In *Our Mutual Friend,* as in countless other works, water symbolizes the elemental realm of birth, death, dissolution, and regeneration. Dickens suggests that the river's currents and its varying depths correspond to the unconscious processes of his characters, as if the natural world and the human were organically united. The poet Algernon Swinburne, that master of decadence (and a perceptive reader of Dickens), called the Thames the "real protagonist in the novel."

DINNER AT THE VENEERINGS

Suddenly the dark, watery scene shifts to one of startling brilliance, the "brand-new" house of a nouveau riche couple fittingly named Veneering. Their dinner parties punctuate this thickly plotted novel, providing structure and continuity as well as choric commentary. In these sections Dickens's social satire reaches toxic levels. Everything in the Veneering establishment, from their baby to the pianoforte, is "in a state of varnish and polish."

The stark juxtaposition with the ancient river sets the modish and artificial Veneerings in high relief, making society seem all the more sterile and garish. The Veneerings' "set," who remain constant throughout the story, are grotesquely reduced to body parts or ornaments: Lady Veneering is "aquiline nosed and fingered"; Mrs. Podsnap has a "quantity of bone, neck and nostrils like a rocking horse"; Lady Tippins is the owner of a "drab, oblong face, like a face in a tablespoon and a dyed Long Walk up the top of her head." Viewed as a whole, the guests resemble the display of body parts or "human miscellanies" in the taxidermy shop of another character, Mr. Venus.

To emphasize their illusiveness, Dickens introduces not their actual bodies but their reflections as they appear one by one in the large mirror above the Veneerings' sideboard. For example, Lady Tippins, who clings to her youth with grisly tenacity, is a skeleton adorned with rags, wigs and powder. Nevertheless she resolutely maintains the fiction that the young gentlemen around her are attentive swains. Nearby, a heavily powdered "mature young woman" flirts with a "mature young gentleman—the proud owner of a great quantity of gingery whiskers and teeth." Flirtatious gaiety hides their predatory instincts. And it is at the Veneerings' that the reader is introduced to the legendary Podsnap, whose name has become synonymous with the prudery we mistakenly attribute to his creator. "Will it bring a blush to the cheek of a young person?" is Podsnap's famous catchphrase, and by "it" he means anything unpleasant, unconventional, or un-English. In the world according to Podsnap, such "ugly" truths as old age, poverty, and passion are unmentionable.

Two young gentlemen at the party pique our interest. Bored, flippant, and indolent, Mortimer Lightwood and Eugene Wrayburn can't see anything worth living for in their desiccated world—and, after dinner at the Veneerings', who can blame them? Lawyers without clients, they lack the muchprized Victorian virtues, earnestness and energy. Normally, such idle dogs would be objects of the author's scorn. But in *Our Mutual Friend* they surprisingly turn out to be heroes.

THE MAN FROM SOMEWHERE

*A*ctually, Lightwood has one client, a former dustman named Nicodemus ("Noddy") Boffin, and through him he learns the tale of the "man from Somewhere": "The man, named [John] Harmon," begins Mortimer, "was the son of a tremendous old rascal who made his money by Dust. By which means, or by others, he grew rich as a Dust Contractor, and lived in a hollow in a hilly country entirely composed of Dust." After violently disowning his wife and daughter (who die prematurely) and his young son (who does not), "the old rascal" prospers, and, in the natural course of time dies, leaving the inevitable whimsical legacy of an eccentric old man. He bequeaths one lucrative dust mound to his servant, Noddy Boffin, and the rest of his fortune to the son he had disinherited fourteen years earlier. Now living abroad "Somewhere," the legatee, John Harmon, has been notified and is eagerly expected. The old man has added one condition to his son's inheritance: John Harmon must marry one Bella Wilfer, who was four years old when his father made his will. If he is dead or refuses to marry the designated girl, the entire fortune falls to Boffin, popularly known as the "Golden Dustman."

A Note about Dust—and Money

To modern ears, dealing in dust sounds as fantastical as fishing for corpses. Yet it too is based in fact. The Victorians, as one critic noted, must have been among the first recyclers, turning everything, including human waste, into a profitable commodity. Rubbish was collected all over London, conveyed to yards owned by private contractors, sifted according to its components, and sold to various tradesmen. Bones, for instance, were used to make soap; rags, paper; and ashes, brick.

The critic Humphrey House maintains that the mounds also yielded a profitable stock of human feces, but others insist, no doubt correctly, that dung was collected in cesspools and then sold by "nightwatchers," who used it to make fertilizer. Dickens didn't need Freud to link money with excrement.

Money—which makes society spin, buys Lady Tippins's powder, Podsnap's plate, and Mrs. Veneering's rings—originates in dust, rags, bones, and dead bodies. Yet Dickens, who was almost as fond of cash as Scrooge himself, is not, as most readers assert, denigrating money as excremental filth. What he *is* saying is that the real crime is a denial of our fundamental connection to such "ugly" truths.

Bradley Headstone

Bradley Headstone, the Norman Bates of the Dickens canon, is the most disturbing character Dickens ever created:

> In his decent black coat and waistcoat, and decent white shirt, and decent formal black tie, and decent pantaloons of pepper and salt, with his decent silver watch in his pocket and its decent hair-guard round his neck, looked a thoroughly decent young man of six and twenty.

Just by reiterating the word *decent,* Dickens conveys its very opposite. A whiff of something unsavory emanates from this portrait of the desperately respectable schoolmaster. Bradley's middle-class attire conceals the true self he has repressed through years of unnatural toil:

> Suppression of so much to make room for so much, had given him a constrained manner, over and above. Yet there was enough of what was animal, and of what was fiery (though smouldering), still visible in him, to suggest that if young Bradley Headstone, when a pauper lad, had chanced to be told off for the sea, he would not have been the last man in the ship's crew.

This is a portrait of a psychopath as the man next door.

INTERVIEW WITH FRED KAPLAN

———m———

NE: *In your biography you refer to Dickens as "cannibalistic," and there are lots of voracious oral images in the novels. How does all that relate to Dickens's life?*

FK: The dark side of living off people, in a sense ingesting others. First, there's the social aspect: Dickens sees society as devouring people and exploiting them. Recent critics have also commented on the notion that cannibalism is a metaphor for describing Dickens as artist. He ingests experiences and people into himself. Dickens is the great devourer, a man of huge appetites. I don't mean it in a bad way, but he had a powerful, domineering, manipulative hunger that damaged the people in his life. At the same time, it is this creative voraciousness that enables him to both ingest and eject his great novels. It's horrible, but there's an aspect of cannibalism that is attractive to him. Not only in terms of his fear of being exploited, but in his interest in exploiting others.

NE: *But Dickens's heroes and heroines are usually extremely passive. Why is that?*

FK: Dickens creates intransigent, bad characters out of his awareness of his own nature. This willfulness allows him to create his own extraordinary personality, but it also goes against the way he saw himself. Dickens was consciously and purposely committed to being good and doing good deeds. For Dickens—and his culture—to be a man means to assert one's will in ways that are compatible with the needs of others and to avoid tension—and certainly explosive conflict. Dickens always comes down on the side of restraint, of keeping the wild beast of desire in control. But in the novels it's the desirous male figures, like Bradley Headstone in *Our Mutual Friend,* or Quilp in *The Old Curiosity Shop* who are the most vivid and exciting for modern readers. Bradley Headstone is a horrible human being, but he is striking. He's always hugging himself closely, trying to keep himself in control until finally he can't. When he falls in love with Lizzie Hexam, he simply explodes.

DEATH BY DROWNING

Lightwood's postprandial account flows into Dickens's story as it introduces the novel's two main plots. John Harmon is the "mutual friend" of the novel's title, and as the chapter draws to its dramatic end, we learn his fate: Lightwood receives a message, reads it three times, and, looking around at the expectant party, exclaims, "Man's Drowned!"

In literature, myth, and dream, submersion in water, like having sex, being in love or in utero, often involves a "sea change," a dissolution of ego boundaries, loss of self, and rebirth. Samuel Taylor Coleridge's Ancient Mariner only finds redemption after he is shipwrecked and has almost drowned. In Shakespeare's magical last play, *The Tempest,* drowning attains mythic significance. And in the *The Waste Land,* T. S. Eliot's poem about a sterile society, it is "death by water" that holds the promise of renewal. Few novels have as many drownings or near-drownings as *Our Mutual Friend,* which has seven. Dickens, no less than Eliot, was aware that to survive in the arid "upper world" of cash, commerce, and class, one must stifle genuine emotion and compartmentalize experience.

After nearly drowning, the gentleman Eugene Wrayburn marries Lizzie Hexam, the waterman's daughter. For the first time, a Dickensian hero marries a woman who is his social inferior. Having "touched bottom," he can perceive the shallowness of his former existence. Eugene may have mocked the Veneerings, the Podsnaps, and Lady Tippins, but he was still one of them, his cynicism a mask that shielded him from emotion. In marrying Lizzie, he renounces the old self who took everything lightly and embraces an existence where things matter. And, thankfully, Dickens does not succumb to the clichéd ending in which Lizzie's long-lost parents suddenly turn up, titled and rich.

True to the ancient metaphor, Eugene undergoes a sea change of moral reformation. Spiritual ontology recapitulates phylogeny: first, the oblivion of the womb, then the helplessness and dependence of childhood, and finally, in a triumph for the ego, maturity and marriage. Eugene vows to direct his energies toward fruitful labor. The ideals of work, earnestness, and energy are, in this case, more than Victorian platitudes. After experiencing Eros's danger, Eugene resolves to channel their energies into work and love—the secret, Freud maintained, of human happiness.

Daddy Dearest

I am certain that the children of my father's brain
were much more real to him than we were.
—CHARLES DICKENS JR.

I have no energy whatsoever—I am very miserable. I loathe
domestic hearths. I yearn to be a vagabond. . . . Why
have I seven Children? [There would be three more.]
—DICKENS

---

ickens always claimed *David Copperfield* was his "favorite child"—by which he meant that he preferred it over all his other novels. But his statement implies something more: he preferred his imaginary creatures to his own flesh and blood. He literally liked David more than Alfred, Walter, Frank, or Sydney Dickens, in part because, unlike his real sons, David would never grow up to disappoint him.

After the arrival of his fourth child, Dickens began to react to each birth with mock surprise, as if he'd had nothing to do with it. As usual, he used humor to convey an unpleasant, unacknowledgeable truth. Two days after Francis Jeffrey Dickens was born, Dickens eagerly accepted a dinner invitation while professing reluctance to leave "such delights of private life as nurses, wet and dry; apothecaries, mothers-in-law; babbies [sic]." A month later, he's still complaining: "I decline (on principle) to look at the latter object" [i.e., his son].

When Edward Bulwer-Lytton Dickens, his last child, made his appearance, the irritated father wrote: "My wife has presented me with No. 10. I think I could have dispensed with the compliment." And he milked his Malthusian gag: "I have some idea—with only one wife and nothing particular in any

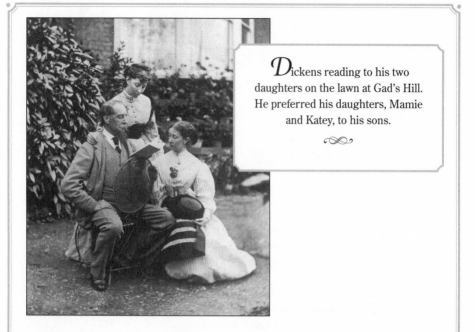

*D*ickens reading to his two daughters on the lawn at Gad's Hill. He preferred his daughters, Mamie and Katey, to his sons.

other direction—of interceding with the Bishop of London to have a little service in Saint Paul's beseeching that I may be considered to have done enough toward my country's population."

Catherine Dickens reportedly observed that her husband liked his children "new"—that is, when they were malleable like his fictional creatures and could be named and fitted to a personality. Only when they grew beyond his control did he find them burdensome and unappealing.

Little children brought out the best in Dickens—perhaps his own lonely childhood had sharpened his sense of what children want. Through them, he gave himself the childhood he never had: birthday parties, Yuletide revels, magic shows, seaside holidays, late bedtimes, ingenious nicknames. He brought home numerous pets, endowing each one with a comical name and a personality to match. Annie Thackeray, the novelist's daughter, recalled that the Dickens children were the envy of their circle.

But he was also a disciplinarian. Each day he routinely inspected their rooms for any sign of disorder. According to his oldest daughter, Mamie, "He was strict, in the way of

*M*idshipman Sydney Dickens, the boy his father dubbed the Ocean Spectre.

insisting upon everything being done perfectly and exactly as he desired. . . .
He made a point of visiting every room in the house once each morning, and
if a chair was out of place, or a blind not quite straight, or a crumb left on the
floor, woe betide the offender!" And he struggled relentlessly to cure Francis
(called Frank) of his stammer, drilling the boy over and over, and probably
making it worse.

Dickens found his sons "disappointing," claiming that they lacked persever-
ance and industry, the qualities he valued most. He ruefully boasted that he
had "brought up the largest family ever known with the smallest disposition to
do anything for themselves." Exasperated to the breaking point, he once exclaimed, "Why was I ever a father? Why was my father ever a father?" Not
knowing what to do with them, he sent them away at the earliest possible age.
"I have always purposed to send him abroad," he wrote of the eleven-year-old
Alfred. At sixteen Walter was banished to India, and at seventeen the "baby,"
Plorn, was packed off to Australia to join Fred. Neither was successful. With an
eloquence that would have surprised his father, Plorn summed up the tragedy
of the Dickens boys: "Sons of great men," he wrote, "are not usually as great as
their fathers. You cannot get two Charles Dickens in one generation."

But no Dickens child would have ever written a "Daddy Dearest" biography. They accepted everything he did, whether it was deserting their mother
or exiling them to a foreign country. They adored him, and would have unhesitatingly gone to the North Pole if he demanded it. They believed that
whatever they received in
life would be due to him.
Dickens biographer Una
Pope Hennessey notes
that it was drummed into
the children that "their
father's name was their
best asset." For most of
them, it was their only
asset.

*F*rank, the son with the incurable
stammer, already looks like the
disappointment his father feared he
would become. Henry became Sir
Henry Dickens, an eminent barrister.

❧

The Mystery of Edwin Drood

The Mystery of Edwin Drood is Dickens's shortest novel both by design and by accident. Weary, melancholy, and in declining health, he tried to husband his energy by writing a serial that would last only twelve months instead of his usual nineteen. As it turned out, he was writing against time: his death on June 9, 1870, midway through the serial, turned a mystery that was to have lasted a year into one that has haunted and challenged readers ever since his death. Dickens created the perfect unsolvable crime.

One approaches an unfinished novel differently than a finished one. The last words of chapter 23 evoke a chilling finality. We almost feel the void left by the novelist's death, as if we were his contemporaries reading the terminal sixth number. The lack of closure is disconcerting: Dickens, the novelist we depend upon to tie up narrative loose ends, has abandoned us. Yet such open-endedness is also liberating, allowing limitless interpretations and endings. In leaving *Drood* incomplete, Dickens in effect gives readers permission to finish it for themselves, a liberty many have found difficult to resist.

Four and a half years had passed since Dickens wrote *Our Mutual Friend*, the longest he had ever gone without writing a novel. By the end of that period, he had become prematurely old at fifty-seven. Just as *Pickwick* is clearly the work of a young man, *Drood* bears all the signs of age. Gone is the acrobatic prose, the spontaneous flow of words that sounds as if Dickens were talking directly to readers. What little comedy there is seems forced. Not surprisingly, the novel is filled with memento mori: tombs and crypts and bones and the damp, earthy smell of final things. Dickens's "opulence and great, careless prodigality," to use Franz Kafka's phrase, is replaced by an unprecedented terseness that suggests that the novelist has lost his appetite for language—and for plot-making. A rarity among Dickens's novels, *Drood* has a single plot. (It also lacks those delightful supernumeraries, irrelevant characters who exist solely to amuse us.)

Just about everything in *Drood* subverts the "cozy Dickens." We've come a long way from the Pickwickians' Christmas festivities at Dingley Dell: Edwin Drood's Christmas Eve, a night of furious gales and grim portents, is his last night on earth. The few nuggets of comfort and joy that Dickens provides dissolve in an atmosphere of gloom.

Drood is not a bittersweet elegy, "the great man bidding farewell to his readers." Rather it is a grim reckoning, as if Dickens is now exposing the artifice of his pleasant fictions and saying, "This, my friends, is how life really is."

But this is not how most readers like their Dickens. After his mentor's death, Wilkie Collins cruelly commented that *Drood* is "the melancholy product of a worn-out brain." And George Bernard Shaw, who only appreciated the subversive Dickens, declared it "a gesture by a man who was already three-quarters dead." Shaw and Collins are mistaken. *Drood* may lack the ebullience, the righteous fury, and the scorching satire of earlier works, but there is much about it to admire—not the least of which is the author himself, who, though "three-quarters dead," was still prepared to view the world from a new perspective.

You can read *Drood* as an unsolved mystery and search for clues and blind leads, or as an artistic fragment, rich in imagery, motifs, and character. Those armchair detectives, the Droodians (see page 364), comb the novel, training a magnifying glass on every word, hoping to discover how Dickens might have ended the novel had he lived. The literary critic also examines it carefully, trying to make sense of the novel and its place in the Dickens canon. And of course there are those who simply enjoy *Drood* as a well-told—if only half-told—tale. *Drood* is at once a parlor game and a work of art.

Murder, He Wrote

The novel may be confusing, but its plot—as we have it—is the simplest and most straightforward of any Dickens novel. John Jasper, choirmaster in the cathedral town of Cloisterham, is the prime suspect in the murder of his nephew and ward, Edwin Drood. His motive seems to be his "mad love" for Edwin's fiancée, the succulent Rosa Bud (known as "Rosebud"), and his envy of Edwin's charmed, easygoing life. But Jasper is more complex than the usual Dickens villain (if he is indeed the killer). Fagin, Quilp, Jonas Chuzzlewit, and Bill Sikes, Dickens's greatest villains, are caricatures of wickedness, more like Vice figures in medieval drama than fully realized criminals. In *Drood,* Dickens creates a killer who could be one of us. John Jasper, a middle-class paragon of respectability, reflects Dickens's first attempt to create a tortured man who happens to be a murderer. Edmund Wilson saw him as a Dickensian Raskolnikov, a claim that would strike most readers of Dostoyevsky as somewhat of an overstatement. What makes Jasper intriguing is that he loves the nephew he allegedly murders.

If *Drood* were a classic whodunit with Jasper as the murderer, then Shaw and Collins are right in their assessment. But if, as Dickens's friend John Forster maintains, the novel centers on the manner in which the crime was committed, confessed, and detected, then *Drood* is a mystery of character, Dickens's final attempt to probe into the heart of human darkness and the culmination of his fascination with evil.

A DISORIENTING DAWN

*T*he novel's opening is what John Forster called a "clincher." Instead of the usual "I am born" preliminaries that orient readers, supplying background, time, setting, and context, Dickens deliberately disorients his readers by plunging them into an unfamiliar dreamscape filled with fantastic, contradictory images. This enigmatic novel aptly begins with a question:

> An ancient English Cathedral town? How can the ancient English Cathedral town be here! The well-known massive gray square tower of its old Cathedral? How can that be here! There is no spike of rusty iron in the air, between the eye and it, from any point of the real prospect. What is the spike that intervenes, and who has set it up? Maybe, it was set up by the Sultan's orders for the impaling of a horde of Turkish robbers, one by one. It is so, for cymbals clash, and the Sultan goes by to his palace in long procession. Ten thousand scimitars flash in the sunlight, and thrice ten thousand dancing-girls strew flowers. . . .

We are certainly not in Dickens's England anymore. We are in fact inside the drugged brain of John Jasper, opium addict and creature of the night.

Suddenly, without any transition, the narrative leaps to the real Cloisterham, where we see Jasper again, this time in a completely different light, as the choirmaster at the cathedral. We are given two contradictory impressions of the man: the crazed and violent addict lounging among unsavory companions in an opium den, and the loving uncle and respected member of the cathedral community. At this point the reader is confused—which one is the "real" John Jasper? Will he be the novel's villain or its hero?

In chapter 2, during Edwin's visit, Jasper appears as a solicitous, if nervous, uncle. And yet even here, Jasper's transformation begins: for a brief moment he seems to succumb to the influence of some unholy truth serum, revealing his anguish behind the smiling public man. A strange film clouds his eyes, and he cryptically alludes to a "skeleton in [his] closet." Edwin lamely catalogues his uncle's public achievements—as much for our benefit as for

Jasper's. Dickens clearly wants to establish Jasper's credentials as a pillar of the community: "Your being so much respected as Lay Precentor . . . of this Cathedral; your enjoying the reputation of having done such wonders with the choir; your choosing your society, and holding such an independent position . . . your gift of teaching." Jasper blurts out that he hates Cloisterham's "repressive respectability." To his ears, the celestial music of the choir sounds "devilish." One can't resist the horror-movie image: Jasper, cloaked in black and vampirish, hunched over the keyboard, playing demonic trills in a minor key. (Indeed, the diabolical musician plays upon his victims as though they were instruments, making them harmonize to his own tune.) His confessional trance passes, and Jasper reverts to devoted guardian. But as the novel progresses, his civilized self recedes, only to be replaced by a sociopath who methodically carries out his plan to murder his nephew. At times one feels as if *Drood* were a horror movie, and we, the audience, watch in terror as man turns into monster.

BUILDING THE CASE

*D*rood is filled with meaningful gestures and suggestive statements that no doubt would have been amply explained at the novel's end. Readers must piece together discrete bits of information to form a picture of what might have happened had Dickens continued in the same vein. Although they would not convict him in a court of law, Jasper's actions are damning, or at the very least prove that Dickens wants us to think he is guilty. The major evidence in the case against him: Jasper accompanies the local stonemason, Durdles, on a nocturnal expedition among the cathedral's crypts and discovers a vacancy in the Sapsea vault. Along the way, Durdles points out the corrosive properties of quicklime: "quick enough to eat your boots: with a little handy stirring, quick enough to eat your bones." Jasper perks up with interest. Plying Durdles with drink laced with drugs, he steals the key to the crypt when the stonemason passes out.

Later, when Rosa and Edwin break off their betrothal, Dickens repeatedly and ominously alludes to a ring of diamonds and rubies that Edwin was to present to her. Since they are no longer engaged, he still has the ring inside his coat pocket when he disappears—a fact that only three people know. Although Jasper is familiar with every piece of Edwin's jewelry, he is unaware that his nephew has this ring in his possession. The significance of the ring and the role it might have played in the novel's denouement have occupied many a Droodian.

According to orthodox interpretation, Edwin's murder might have happened this way: Jasper strangles Edwin with his long black scarf, throws him down the steps of the cathedral tower, drags the body into the crypt, removes what he believes to be all the dead man's jewelry, and covers the corpse with quicklime. Only the ring, impervious to the corrosive effects of the chemical, remains—evidence that will be used to identify the body and indict Jasper.

The unexpected arrival of Neville and Helena Landless, the orphaned twins from Ceylon, turns out to be crucial to Jasper's—and Dickens's—plot. Quickly sensing Neville's and Edwin's instantaneous aversion to one another, Jasper waits for them to quarrel and then in an apparent effort at peacemaking invites them home for a drink. There he prepares a potent concoction, which may or may not be drugged—and, turning his mesmeric eye upon them, foments a quarrel that almost ends in violence. Seemingly jovial, Jasper calculatingly points out everything that will rouse Neville's rage:

> "Look at him," cries Jasper, stretching out his hand admiringly and tenderly though rallyingly too. "See where he lounges so easily, Mr. Neville! The world is all before him where to choose. A life of stirring work and interest, a life of change and excitement, a life of domestic ease and love! Look at him."
>
> "See how little he heeds it all," Jasper proceeds in a bantering vein. "It hardly is worth his while to pluck the golden fruit that hangs ripe on the tree for him. And yet consider the contrast, Mr. Neville. You and I have no prospect of stirring work and interest, or of change and excitement, or of domestic ease and love. You and I have no prospect (unless you are more fortunate than I am, which may easily be), but the tedious, unchanging round of this dull place."

Immediately following the quarrel, Jasper needlessly rushes to Mr. Crisparkle and reports the event, exaggerating its danger. He confesses his fear for his nephew's life and thus shrewdly plants the idea of Neville's homicidal tendencies in the canon's mind. Thus when Edwin disappears, suspicion naturally falls on Neville, the foreigner with dark skin.

WHEN SHALL WE THREE MEET AGAIN?

*C*hapter 14, "When Shall We Three Meet Again?" opens with allusions to *Macbeth* and is filled with portents. Cawing rooks, a preternaturally windy night, a dire prediction by an old crone, all create an atmosphere of impending evil. Suspense mounts. But after building to Christmas dinner with the principal characters—one of whom is presumably the killer—we never see the climax, much less the crime. Indeed, we don't even know if a crime has been committed—all we know is that the next morning Jasper is frantically searching for his nephew, and Neville is hunted down and accused of murder.

One more enigma: the appearance of the mysterious, white-haired stranger, Dick Datchery, in Cloisterham. We can assume three things about Datchery: he is in disguise, he is someone we already know and whose identity would have been revealed near the end, and he is a detective figure determined to hunt down Jasper. What he finds, and who he is, we'll leave to the Droodians.

Drood is Dickens's *Macbeth,* his most perverse and sinister novel, the one that comes closest to touching pure evil. Animal magnetism, voyeurism, uncanny predictions, Eastern exoticism, deviant sexuality, and opium addiction contribute to its darkly unsettling ambience. As Dickens wrote in his last installment, "The Power of Evil is abroad."

❧ DROODIANA ❧

❧ At one point while Dickens was writing *Drood,* his sister-in-law, Georgina, said to him, "I hope you haven't really killed poor Edwin Drood." Dickens replied: "I call my book the *Mystery,* not the History, of Edwin Drood."

❧ During a private interview with Queen Victoria, Dickens gallantly offered to divulge the contents of each number of *Drood* to Her Majesty before it appeared in public, thus giving her the imperial honor of learning what happened before her subjects. Unfortunately for us, the royal curiosity was insufficiently piqued, and the queen never took him up on his offer.

❧ In 1873, three years after Dickens's death, a new version of *Drood* appeared, written by none other than the author himself. Apparently Dickens, now in spirit form, chose an obscure medium in Brattleboro, Vermont, to transcribe and publish his new edition of *Drood.* The two-volume work, modestly titled *The Mystery of Edwin Drood Complete,* includes a surprising title-page line: "By

> *S*urely *Drood* must contain the most hair-raising dialogue Dickens ever wrote: Mr. Grewgius, Rosa's guardian, has just finished talking to Jasper about their two wards. As he leaves the choirmaster, Grewgius exclaims:
>
> "God bless them both!"
> "God save them both!" cried Jasper.
> "I said, bless them," remarked the former, looking back over his shoulder.
> "I said, save them," returned the latter. "Is there any difference?"

the spirit-pen of Charles Dickens, through a Medium." Once raised, the ghost of Charles Dickens had no intention of being laid to rest. Volume 2 promises readers another work by the dead author: *The Life and Adventures of Bockley Wickleheep.*

❧ On January 14, 1914, the trial of John Jasper for the murder of Edwin Drood was held in King's Hall, Covent Garden. With G. K. Chesterton presiding as judge and George Bernard Shaw as foreman of the jury, the five-hour trial included testimony from the novel's various characters, and ended in a verdict of manslaughter.

❋In 1878 *A Great Mystery Solved* appeared under the Dickensian pseudonym Gillan Vase. The author, who claimed to be a lady of literary distinction, initially viewed her project as an "idle" diversion for friends; she soon discovered, however, that she had embarked "upon a road from which there was no turning back." The three-volume result is a dreary and rambling road indeed.

❋As facts about Dickens's "dark" side emerged, people began to see *Drood* as an anguished autobiography, a tale of blighted desire. Thus, *Drood,* like the sonnets of Shakespeare, is the key to Dickens's heart. Dickens's double, once the practical David Copperfield, is now the tormented John Jasper. Both men are expert mesmerists who are also artists, both are obsessed with younger women, and both appear to act in conformance with society, while they are secretly isolated by their guilt and nervous cravings. Few, however, can satisfactorily explain the significance of Helena Landless's name and that of Ellen Lawless Ternan. The novel's setting, Rochester, is a poignant giveaway. In his final work, Dickens returns in memory and imagination to the ancient cathedral city, the site of his keenest joy, his home when his life was still unclouded.

❋The most celebrated *Drood* spin-off, of course, is the 1985 musical *Drood.* To those familiar with the novel's dark themes, the idea of turning it into a musical must have seemed strange indeed.

But *Drood* also has a winning gimmick: whereas Dickens's novel is without an ending, the play has a dozen of them. The audience participates in the drama by voting on "whodunit," and there's a different culprit every night. Now standard fare on the dinner theater circuit, the play won five Tony Awards, including Best Musical.

He essayed a detective story, he who could never keep a secret; and he has kept it to this day.
—G. K. CHESTERTON

🍂 DROODIANS AFOOT! 🍂

In Jorge Luis Borges's enigmatic story "The Garden of the Forking Paths," the narrator stumbles upon a novel of infinite possibilities and permutations. Droodian scholars must know the feeling. After reading a fraction of the hundreds of Droodian theories, revisions, interpretations, spin-offs, and "authentic" conclusions, one feels as if *Drood* is a novel of "forking paths" in which almost every sentence—and sometimes every word—leads into another story.

Dickens was scarcely in the grave when fantasies on the theme of *Drood* began to appear, each declaring itself complete and authentic. In fact solutions, continuations, and "what might have happened" tales are so abundant that they have become a subgenre in themselves. In 1951, Dickens critic George Ford wrote: "The number of books and articles provoked by that tantalizing fragment is breathtaking. One collection of Droodiana, assembled over a period of fifty years, is said to have filled every shelf on all four sides of a great exhibition hall used by the Grolier Club in New York."

The palmy days of Droodiana coincided with the golden age of mysteries and detective fiction, which began after Dickens's death in 1870 and continued through the 1930s. During this period *The Dickensian,* a fanzine published by the Dickens Fellowship, was filled with essays and queries concerning the all-consuming question: did John Jasper murder his nephew Edwin Drood?

Those obsessed by that question are known as Droodians—dubbed "the Druids" by G. K. Chesterton. Not all Droodians are Dickensians—some are amateur sleuths challenged by an unsolved mystery, particularly one by England's greatest novelist. Not content to speculate on how Dickens might have completed *Drood,* they revise and reinterpret everything in the novel in light of pet theories. The results have ranged from the ingenious to the ludicrous. In their own zany ways, a few neo-*Drood*s are almost as diverting as the original.

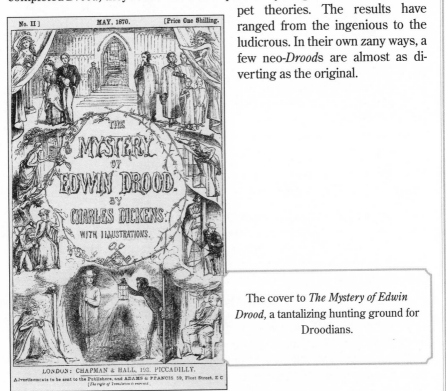

The cover to *The Mystery of Edwin Drood,* a tantalizing hunting ground for Droodians.

A Modern Critic
Reviews Dickens

INTERVIEW WITH JONATHAN YARDLEY

onathan Yardley is the chief book critic and columnist at the Washington Post *and the author of three books. Although he is one of the most important critics writing today, his name is rarely seen on the back of dust jackets; not for him the usual blurbese for the latest trendy experimental novel. Mr. Yardley is known for his high standards, his opinionated views, and an absolutist sense of what literature should and should not be.*

NE: *As a reader and book reviewer, how would you describe Dickens, especially in regard to modern fiction?*

JY: What is most Dickensian about him is his extraordinary combination of inwardness and expansiveness. The modern novel, which in some ways begins with Dickens, is, to my great regret, more and more an exploration of the individual writer's psyche. It's an inner-directed exercise that I think is increasingly narcissistic and disconnected from the world at large. Dickens, in many important respects, is an autobiographical writer. His presence is almost always felt in his work in one way or another—sometimes very centrally, as in *David Copperfield* and *Oliver Twist,* in other books less so. But he is always there. Yet he always, always, *always* reached out beyond himself. He was ultimately more interested in other people than he was in himself. And that, it seems to me, is where he is completely separate from the great run of twentieth-century novelists.

NE: *But modern readers don't seem to want the old-style plot-driven novel that Dickens wrote.*

JY: I have a standard talk that I give about contemporary American literature, and one of the things I talk about is the startling popularity seven or eight years ago of Tom Wolfe's novel *Bonfire of the Vanities.* The reason why so many millions of readers seized that book with such avidity and gratitude was that at last there was a writer of serious fiction who is going into the world. Well, that's what Dickens did. A big, populous story covering a lot of time and space with a lot of characters can still tell us a lot about how we live. I feel an enormous sense of pleasure in all the minor characters, all the people who come onstage for a few pages and then disappear and then come back a few hundred pages later and are still alive in your mind. Dickens had a capacity to invest each character with life, sometimes in just a few sentences.

Of course, the world changes, and fiction changes with it. We can't keep rewriting *Bleak House* any more than we can keep recomposing Beethoven's Fifth Symphony. We change—but we don't necessarily improve. I think that the Dickensian novel could be written now, can be written now, because Tom Wolfe and Vikram Seth have proved it. But I don't think it's going to happen as a general rule.

NE: *Are there any vestiges of the Victorian novel alive today?*

JY: What we get now in the worst sort of reductive way are these big, fat pop novels. The Arthur Hailey, James Michener sort of thing in which there's a lot thrown in; but there's no art, no real craft. Just an accumulation of stuff. But you know, I think the fact that people buy books by Hailey, Grisham, and Michener suggests that they long for what Dickens satisfied. They want stories. They want stories about their own world that can help them understand it. They want stories about worlds they don't know. There is some interest in tiny, airless stories about people's interior lives, but even the great psychological novelists—Henry James, for instance—wrote about society! He wrote about the individual, but it was the individual *in the world.* The age of autobiography was not upon him yet, so it must not have occurred to him that he, Chuck Dickens, was supposed to be the hero of his own book.

NE: *What would happen if Dickens came back today and enrolled in a creative writing program at a university? What would they make of him? Would they hail him as a star?*

JY: They would think he was a clown. The highbrows pretty much turn up their noses at Dickens; he is much too melodramatic for them. Essentially they don't like him.

NE: *They wouldn't see the humor, the energy? What about his genius, his gift for character? Aren't those timeless?*

JY: Those people? Bah! Don't get me going. No. No. No. Although Dickens had a view of society that I suppose you could call political in the received understanding of the word, he wasn't a political novelist. But there's a lot of politics in writing-school fiction—a lot of retrograde sixties left-wing American politics, a smug anti–middle class, and Dickens wasn't that at all. Despite all the criticism he directed against England, Dickens was English to the core. In the eyes of the literate world, Dickens *is* England.

Incidentally, I should say that *American Notes* is spectacularly good! There are parts of it that still have me roaring with laughter. It's a really, really hilarious book.

NE: *What about the people who condemn Dickens for his lack of depth or his cartoonish characters?*

JY: I've believed in his characters all my life. Uriah Heep is not just a person but a "concept," as we say these days. Uriah Heep is brilliant. Dickens liked broad strokes. Maybe it's a confession of a critical weakness, but I find myself very emotionally engaged when I read Dickens, and that doesn't happen unless I care about the characters. Sure, David Copperfield can seem too perfect and priggish and Oliver can seem a little too much the mournful waif, but melodrama was part of Dickens's arsenal. He wanted people to feel strongly. And the various fictive techniques and the characterizations he used were not idly chosen. I'm willing to accept Dickensian characters on their own terms.

NE: *Even his women? His critics say he can't create a convincing woman.*

JY: They will always say that. I suppose I indict myself for sentimentality here, but some of Dickens's women are quite wonderful. Miss Havisham is wonderful; Nancy is a fabulous character—a decent person caught in a bad world trying to be loyal to her world and her husband.

NE: *If you were reviewing Dickens, would you charge him with "wordiness"?*

JY: There are times when I want to take Tolstoy out to the woodshed and say, "Get rid of 15,000 words!" I never have had problems with Dickens in that regard. Perhaps some of the diction is dated, but when I was reading Dickens several years ago, what I noticed was how modern he is.

NE: *In what way?*

JY: The world changes, but people don't. Dickens's understanding of human character is as pertinent now as then; you can find in public and private life types who exactly fit the Dickensian mold. Shakespeare understood everything! Dickens isn't like that. There are lots of things Dickens doesn't understand. Dickens was not given the gift of subtlety; he was prolix. He probably oversimplified things; he was guilty of sentimentality and melodrama and so forth, but he did have that same visceral sense of *Homo sapiens*.

NE: *You've studied the reading habits of Americans. How and why have they changed since Dickens's day?*

JY: In Dickens's day, and this was really true up to World War II, serious popular fiction served a cultural role. That role is essentially now assumed by television and movies. It's a lot easier to sit down and flip a button and watch *The*

Horse's Mouth than read it. That's how we get our stories now. Dickens's were what people talked about. His readers would go to work the next morning, and they would talk about what they read the night before. Not many people today do that kind of book talk. And no one writing today has an audience even within sniffing distance of a Dickensian audience. Movies and videos have largely supplanted the old world of fiction, which in turn supplanted the old world of sitting around the fire and telling stories. Contemporary American writers and English departments scorn storytelling. They think it's for infants. But the need for story is as deep as almost any human need there is, because it's a way of understanding. The world changes, and the way our desires are fulfilled changes, but whether it's sex or food or understanding or compassion or a sense of dignity or whatever, the things that we want are basic to the human condition. I think we all have a desire for stories.

NE: *Will readers turn to Dickens on their own?*

JY: If kids don't get Dickens in school, they'll probably never read him at all.

Death Comes to
"The Inimitable"

ome claim that Charles Dickens killed himself. If so, it was not the calculated death of the suicide, but a slow process of self-destruction, perceptible only to family and friends. Dickens worked himself to death, driving his body beyond its natural limitations. He died because he lived too intensely.

In 1865 Dickens's left foot became seriously inflamed; it looked like gout, was diagnosed as gout, but Dickens insisted it was not gout. He attributed the swelling to frostbite: out walking on a winter's day, he "fell lame and had to limp home dead lame, through the snow for at least three miles—to the remarkable terror, by the bye, of two big dogs." It is typical of Dickens to note the reactions of others—whether animal and human—in the midst of extreme duress. In June that year he was involved in a train wreck. Throughout the ordeal he remained composed and courageous. Only later did emotional shock set in. The episode left him high-strung, overly sensitive to the precariousness of life. He, who had once exulted at the rail's speed and energy, now panicked whenever he boarded a train, thinking only of the carnage and the terror of that day. Perhaps it is not entirely coincidental that Dickens's death occurred on the fifth anniversary of the accident.

His reading schedule for 1866

was grueling: five performances a week for six weeks. That year, he was "seized in a most distressing manner—apparently in the heart." For some reason, he attributed the symptoms to his nervous system. But Dickens was suffering from coronary disease. A typical type A personality, he restlessly chain-smoked cigarettes at the office and puffed cigars at home.

Shortly after his return from his second American tour, he noted that his left leg felt fragile and strange, and on April 17, 1868, he became suddenly giddy, "with a tendency to go backwards, and to turn round." He also complained of a "strangeness of his left hand and arm." The "strange" feeling was probably paralysis resulting from a series of strokes that were affecting his motor skills. The actor Edmund Yates noted, "As he walks along the

*D*ickens during the last year of his life, a caricature by Spy (Leslie Ward).

street one day, he can read only the halves of letters over the shop-doors that were on his right as he looked." Friends who hadn't seen him for a while were stunned by the change in his appearance. Yates saw a man who looked "desperately aged and worn; the lines in his cheeks and round the eyes, always noticeable, were now deep furrows; there was a weariness in his gaze and a general air of fatigue and depression about him."

In 1869, Dickens began his Farewell Tour, a series of seventy-five readings. Forster remonstrated with him, calling the arrangement a "fatal mistake." During one of his last appearances, in January 1870, Dickens found himself unable to say "Pickwick," a name he knew almost as well as his own: "Picksnick," "Picnic," "Peckswicks" came out—everything but "Pickwick." He looked toward his family with an expression of comical bewilderment. He later dismissed the episode as a side-effect of medication.

That spring, the last performance behind him, he resumed his busy London schedule: He was writing *Drood,* dining out regularly, and speaking on behalf of charitable organizations.

In May, when he attended a formal dinner for the Prince of Wales, the guests saw an apparition who had to be helped into the dining room and practically carried upstairs to the reception. He was barely fifty-eight years old.

Despite ill health and depression, he continued to work on *Drood.* To a young friend who asked what would happen if he died in the middle of the mystery, he replied sadly, "One can only work on, you know—work while it is

The last page of *Edwin Drood,* written on June 8, 1870, the day of Dickens's fatal stroke. The writing is crabbed with many deletions and interlinear additions. In his early years, his copy was meticulous, with few blots or cross outs.

day." Yet when his publishers had drawn up his contract for *Drood,* Dickens insisted they insert a clause about what to do in case of his death, the only time he ever did so. Meanwhile, he was gratified that sales of the novel had soared into record numbers. The first installment, which appeared in March, sold 50,000 copies. That spring he was industrious, writing each day in the Swiss chalet, his office set among the treetops in back of his home in Gad's Hill.

On Saturday, June 4, he stayed up until 3:00 a.m. talking in the garden. Brooding and regretful, Dickens confided his fear that he might not live to finish *Drood.* That night, before his daughter Katey left, Dickens abruptly told her that he "wished he had been a better father, and a better man."

The next morning, she interrupted him at work to say good-bye before leaving for London. Usually, when Dickens was writing, he would just hold up a cheek to be kissed, but this time he folded Katey his arms, saying, "God bless you, Katey!" Halfway back to the house, she returned:

Something said to me, "go back," and I immediately ran up the steps, through the shrubbery, into the Chalet and tapped on the door. My father—who was seated with his back to it—called out, "Come in"; turning and seeing me he held out his arms into which I ran, when he embraced me again and kissed me very affectionately.

This was a rare gesture, as Dickens was by no means a demonstrative man.

On June 8, after walking to the village to post some letters, he had a quiet dinner with Georgina, who noticed he looked peculiar and that his eyes were filled with tears. Refusing to let her send for a doctor, he asked to finish his dinner, hoping perhaps that this spell would soon pass like the others. She urged him to lie down. "Yes, on the ground," he said. Those were his last words. He rose from the table and collapsed into unconsciousness.

He lived through the night, the sound of his labored breathing filling the house. The London specialist who arrived the next day declared that Dickens had suffered a cerebral hemorrhage. At 6:10 p.m. on June 9, a tear trickled down his cheek, he gave a deep final sigh, and "The Inimitable" was no more.

❖ ❖ ❖

Dickens's death was as momentous as those of Prince Albert and the Duke of Wellington. He hated the ostentation their passing had occasioned and had written his will to protect himself from funereal fanfare. In keeping with his wish that his obsequies be "inexpensive, unostentatious and strictly private," the family arranged for a burial in the graveyard at Rochester Cathedral. Yet the *Times* recommended that England's greatest novelist be buried in Westminster Abbey, and the dean seconded the proposition.

He lay in state for three days as thousands filed past the bier, weeping and tossing bouquets into the coffin. The day of his funeral was declared a national day of mourning—shops were closed, bells tolled, and ministers eulogized him from their pulpits. Despite the grand surroundings of Westminster, the funeral was remarkably simple. As was his wish, there were no ostentatious displays

*O*ne day after Dickens's death, the painter Sir John Everett Millais rushed to Gad's Hill to quickly sketch him on his deathbed. Dickens, like Marley's ghost, has his jaw wrapped to prevent it from suddenly dropping open.

of mourning, the coffin was plain, the service simple, short and private. Catherine Dickens, his wife of thirty-three years and the mother of his ten children, was not present. Some believe that Nelly Ternan was somewhere in the Abbey, watching the proceedings from a hiding place. To his survivors, the world seemed diminished: As his friend lay in his coffin, John Forster bent to kiss his cheek. "The duties of life remain," he wrote, "while life remains, but for me, the joy of it is gone for ever more."

Life after Dickens

Dickens never ended a novel without informing the reader about each character's fate and fortune. In that spirit, here's a brief account of the major figures in Dickens's life and how they fared after his death.

Ellen Ternan

Dickens's death cut Ellen adrift. In 1871 she met a Cambridge undergraduate at a party. They flirted and exchanged verses, and by 1874 he was writing ardent Latin poetry in her commonplace book. Six years after Dickens's death, Ellen, now thirty-six, married the the Reverend George Wharton Robinson, age twenty-eight. The new Mrs. George Wharton Robinson, however, had shaved a decade off her age. Without income taxes, driver's licenses, passports, and social security, it was easy to adopt a new identity. In 1881, when she was forty-two, Ellen gave her age as twenty-eight to the census bureau.

Persuading her new husband to give up the church, she decided that together they would run a private boy's school. They settled in Margate, beginning what Claire Tomalin calls the happiest years in Ellen's life. To her great delight, she gave birth to two children, Geoffrey and Gladys, the latter when she was forty-four.

As a reaction against her unorthodox past, Ellen had developed a rage for respectability. She sent her children to strict boarding schools, where they received conventional educations. Socially and politically conservative, she would never have seen herself as a feminist heroine. Indeed, in 1911 she joined the Anti-Suffrage League.

In 1907, when she was nearly seventy (officially sixty), she was operated on for breast cancer. She recovered rapidly, but George became ill and died. Ellen moved in with her older sister, Fanny. Despite their fragility and age, they turned to playwriting. Then, after Fanny's death, Ellen and Geoffrey moved to London, where she died on April 25, 1914, having outlived Dickens by forty-four years. Geoffrey duly entered her age as sixty-five on the death certificate. Her tombstone, next to her husband's, reads "Ellen Wharton Robinson, His Loving Wife."

In 1920 Geoffrey returned home, ready to go through his mother's belongings. He found playbills with his mother's name, theatrical mementos, and documents containing her true age. He hadn't even known that he was descended from a long line of professional actors. Sensing that something was amiss, but needing facts, he wrote to Sir Henry Dickens requesting a meeting. What Sir Henry told him can only be surmised by what happened next: Geoffrey returned home and destroyed everything that had belonged to his mother.

His entire past, all his memories of his mother, had to be reassessed in light of this devastating discovery. For the rest of his life Geoffrey remained silent on the subject. What Ellen had been spared was inflicted on him.

In the twentieth century Ellen Ternan Robinson would be variously labeled an adventuress, a victim, a vamp, or a feminist heroine. One anecdote captures the enigma of a woman who at once was conventional and broke all the rules: the summer before Dickens's death, Ellen played cricket for the first time. Later Katey Dickens, exactly Ellen's age and a keen observer of human behavior, dryly remarked, "I'm afraid she did not play the game."

CATHERINE DICKENS

*F*rom May 1857, when she left the house she shared with Dickens, to her death in November 1879, Catherine Dickens lived quietly on Gloucester Crescent. Katey, remorseful over their neglect, visited her mother often. Just before her death, Catherine handed her daughter a packet of her husband's letters, saying, "Give these to the British Museum so they'll know he loved me once."

JOHN FORSTER

*J*ohn Forster died in February 1876, his task as Dickens's official biographer complete. He began working on his friend's life immediately after his death, pasting together old letters and memoranda Dickens had sent him through the years. The biography is more an account of John Forster, friend to Charles Dickens, than a detailed study of the novelist's life. For more than thirty years Forster had jealously guarded Dickens's reputation; it is therefore all the more ironic that the *Life* actually harmed Dickens's reputation—Victorian readers were displeased to discover that Dickens was not always kind to his mother.

BARONESS ANGELA BURDETT-COUTTS

The image of Victorian rectitude, the sixty-seven-year-old philanthropist surprised everyone by marrying her twenty-seven-year-old secretary, who possessed the Dickensian name of Ashmead Bartlett. One wishes Dickens could have lived to have seen—and written about—the event.

GEORGINA HOGARTH

The redoubtable Georgina remained at Gad's Hill as keeper of the flame. Soon after Dickens's death she carefully combed his bachelor flat in Wellington Square and destroyed any potentially incendiary information. She published a sanitized collection of Dickens's letters and made sure that his letters to Maria Beadnell were banned in England.

KATE DICKENS PERUGINI

Outspoken when her siblings were reticent, unorthodox when they huddled into conformity, Katey knew the worst about her father and still loved him. She was a feminist and insisted, *pace* Georgina, that her father admired working women. Her marriage to a successful painter was a happy one. She died in 1929, at the age of ninety.

The Master

⁂

*He did too much for us surely ever to leave us free—free of judgment,
free of reaction, even should we care to be, which heaven
forbid: he laid his hand on us in a way to undermine as in
no other case of the power of detached appraisement.*
—HENRY JAMES

hether one approved or disapproved of his writings or his morals, one couldn't ignore him: "Dickens was," George Orwell wrote, "there." The master's influence cast a shadow over later writers as the Monument did over London. In *Decline and Fall,* Evelyn Waugh depicts the collapse of English culture by having his hero, Tony Last, end his days reading the complete works of Dickens aloud to a lunatic in the outposts of Africa. Dickens, the very model of Englishness, ends civilization, not with a bang or a whimper, but with a roar of laughter. Virginia Woolf may have complained about Dickens's heavy-fisted, "materialist" meat-and-potato style, but she never stopped reading him: her diary records that she read *David Copperfield* "at least six times." Dickens belonged to her father's generation, and for young, experimental novelists, he was the archetypal father one seeks to appease, escape, and eventually surpass.

Upon his death in 1870, Dickens was hailed as the Shakespeare of the novel. *The Complete Works of Charles Dickens* could be found in every home library next to the Bible, and some regarded the two as morally equal. Thousands lined up to view his body and toss bouquets into his coffin; preachers extolled his virtues from the pulpit. Dickens was not only a great writer, but also a great man.

In 1906 G. K. Chesterton published the landmark *Charles Dickens: A Critical Study,* the first important survey of the author. It championed the manly, robust Dickens:

Whatever the word "great" means, Dickens was what it means. Even the fastidious and unhappy who cannot read his books without a continuous critical exasperation, would use the word of him without stopping to think. They feel that Dickens is a great writer even if he is not a good writer.

According to Chesterton, those who don't appreciate Dickens tend to be fastidious, rigid, effeminate, and humorless.

After the Great War, some readers found the very Englishness of Dickens consoling, but to a generation that had witnessed the collapse of its most revered traditions, Dickens's world, with its Honor and Virtue, seemed diminished and simplistic. Suffering was not ennobling, and goodness did not guarantee happiness. The Bloomsbury circle, which ridiculed the pieties of its elders, made Dickens the literary scapegoat for the age. His characters lacked soul and moral complexity and, worst of all, were sexually unenlightened. In 1925 Bloomsbury's high priestess, Virginia Woolf, haughtily declared that she wouldn't cross the street to meet Dickens, while D. H. Lawrence deplored the Dickensian habit of rewarding the virtuous with marriage and money. In the preface to *My Life and Loves,* the autobiography of a prodigious sex life, Frank Harris disparages Dickens's portrayal of the relations between men and women: "Under Victoria, English prose literally be-

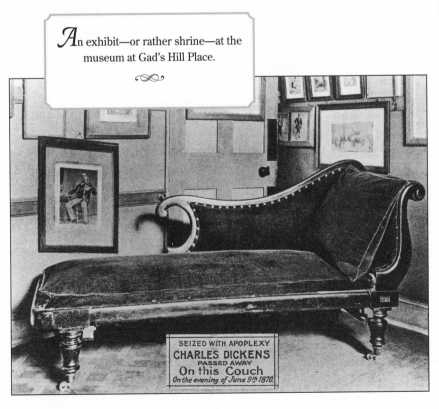

*A*n exhibit—or rather shrine—at the museum at Gad's Hill Place.

SEIZED WITH APOPLEXY
CHARLES DICKENS
PASSED AWAY
On this Couch
On the evening of June 9th 1870.

came half-childish, as in stories of 'Little Mary,' or at best provincial, as any-one may see who cares to compare the influence of Dickens, Thackeray and Reade in the world with the masterpieces of Balzac, Flaubert and Zola."

Not until World War II were Dickens's novels again classified as "real" liter-ature, serious classics that could take their place in the literary pantheon. Up to then the typical Dickensian was an amateur "scholar," who "rambled" through what *The Dickensian* called "Dickensland," trying to find the exact tavern where Tony Weller ate lunch. In the *Dickensian,* topographical studies ("Dickens in Birmingham") overwhelmingly outnumbered critical analyses of the novels. In 1939 Edmund Wilson psychoanalyzed Dickens in a landmark essay, "The Two Scrooges," and almost overnight Dickens studies underwent a revolution. Declaring that the author was "the victim of a manic-depressive cycle, and a very uncomfortable person," Wilson gave Dickens his creden-tials as a serious artist. George Ford wrote, "Had Mrs. Woolf lived to read Ed-mund Wilson's analysis of Dickens' character, it is possible that she might have found the novelist a more interesting and sympathetic figure."

Dickens's life and works were not so much read as diagnosed. No longer the sunny creator of Mr. Pickwick but the lonely genius of *Bleak House, Great Expectations,* and *Drood,* Dickens was ripe for the 1950s mania for psycho-analysis. No longer disparaged, the later novels were regarded as the high point of Dickens's career, while the early ones were dismissed as juvenilia. The neo-Dickens was "modern," even Kafkaesque, in his appreciation of cosmic absur-dities. To such readers, the Nelly Ternan affair could only enhance his reputation.

In a literary canon that has been shaken up, revised, decon-structed, and repackaged, in which perennials have been up-rooted up to make way for weeds, Dickens's stature re-mains secure. In perhaps the modern acid test, his works were among the first to be made avail-able on CD-ROM. And critics are now paying more attention to the minor short stories and essays. He's been subjected to every critical theory, from deconstruc-tionism to French feminist: for years women have complained about Dickens's female charac-ters, but now it turns out that his

*T*he reverential painting by J. R. Brown, *Dickens Surrounded By His Characters.*

pallid creatures are made of sterner stuff. We are now told, for example, that Miss Wade is gay.

Outside the academy, Dickens continues to thrive on *Masterpiece Theatre* and in Dickens Fellowships that host jaunts and "rambles" in "Dickensland" and—to use his own phrase—"keep his memory green" with annual wreath ceremonies at Westminster Abbey. But the membership is aging. Eliot Engel of the North Carolina Dickens Fellowship points out that those who grew up with Dickens are now almost always older than fifty.

A Select Filmography

※

SILENT ERA

*I*t has been said that the Victorian novel was just waiting to burst into film. With their melodramatic plots, sentimentality, villains, heroes, and maidens, the silents were Victorian novels in pictures. And more than any other writer of his time, Dickens wrote with a cinematic eye. The Russian director Sergei Eisenstein notes that Dickens is a link "between the future, unforeseen art of the cinema, and the not so distant (for Dickens) past—the traditions of the 'good murderous melodramas.'" Cinematographers and directors developed the technology to express what had always been embedded in the artist's psyche.

But Dickens not only inspired the content of early film. Within the Victorian novel lie the seeds of such cinematic techniques as the dissolve, the close-up, and most important, the montage, a device for showing parallel action.

When D. W. Griffith was editing *Enoch Arden,* he first showed a man on a desert island, then cut to a woman pining at home. When an assistant protested that viewers would be unable to follow the action without some transitional image, Griffith said, "Well, doesn't Dickens write that way?"

Indeed, all Dickens's novels follow a montage progression, moving from one vivid picture to another. In short, they are movies in words.

1897: *Death of Nancy Sikes,* US; scenes of *Oliver Twist.*

1901: *Scrooge; Or, Marley's Ghost,* GB; dir. W. R. Booth.

1902: *Nicholas Nickleby,* US.

1903: *What Are the Wild Winds Saying, Sister?,* US. *Dombey and Son's* nine-hundred-plus pages are packed into three evocative images of childhood, time, and death. The scene is an isolated seashore: a boy and girl hold hands and carry pails. Their backs to the camera, they stare out to the blank ocean. In the last scene, they turn and walk slowly past a stationary camera. This is the minimalist *Dombey.*

1904: *Mr. Pecksniff Fetches the Doctor,* based on *Martin Chuzzlewit,* GB; 1 reel. Dickens's influence pervades early movie-making—even when the film is only marginally related to Dickens's novel, as it is here. The plot is simple: Mr. Pecksniff fetches the doctor for his wife and faints when he sees him with three babies in his arms.

1909: *The Cricket on the Hearth,* US; dir. D. W. Griffith; with Herbert Pryor, Mack Sennett, Linda Arvidson Griffith, Violet Mersereau, Owen Moore. It is not surprising that D. W. Griffith turned to Dickens early in his career. Dickens, the director claimed, was the inspiration for his most innovative cinematic techniques. The film opens with what the Russian director Sergei Eisenstein called a "typical Griffith-esque close-up," a shot "saturated with Dickensian atmosphere." A kettle is boiling on the hearth; the text reads, "The kettle began it." Dickens's kettle opened an era in cinematic history. In *Dickens, D. W. Griffith and the Film Today,* Eisenstein wrote, "Movies were also boiling in that kettle."

1909: *Edwin Drood,* GB; dir. Arthur Gilbert; with Copper Willis, Nancy Bevington.

1910: *Oliver Twist,* Denmark; dir. August Blom; with Agnes Norlund.

1910: *To the Crossing Sweeper,* based on *Bleak House,* GB.

1911: *Oliver Twist,* Italy.

1911: *How Bella Was Won,* based on *Our Mutual Friend,* US.

1912: *The Pickwick Papers,* US.

1912: *The Old Curiosity Shop,* France.

1912: *The Old Curiosity Shop,* GB; dir. Frank Powell.

1913: *Scrooge,* GB; dir. Leedham Bantock; Seymour Hicks as Scrooge; William Lugg. The beginning of Hicks's obsession with the character. He would go on to play the role more than a thousand times on stage, in music halls, and in film.

1913: *David Copperfield,* GB; dir. Cecil Hepworth and Thomas Bentley; Master Eric Desmond as David.

1914: *The Old Curiosity Shop,* GB; 6 reels; dir. Thomas Bentley; Mai Deacon as Nell; Warwick Buckland as Grandfather; E. Felton as Quilp; Willie West as Dick Swiveller.

1915: *Barnaby Rudge,* GB; dir. Thomas Bentley; with Tom Powers, Violet Hopson. This was the biggest film undertaking of the day. More than one thousand extras were needed for all the mob scenes.

1915: *Hard Times,* GB; dir. Bransby Williams.

1915: *Drood,* GB; dir. Herbert Blache; Tom Terriss as John Jasper; Rodney Hickok as Edwin Drood; Vinnie Burns as Rosa Bud. Writing in *The Dickensian,* Willoughby Matchett complained that Jasper had a bad case of the "jumps": "Poor Jasper can't get a quiet five minutes at his organ but there is murdered Drood standing at his elbow saying he's alive. Naturally the thing gets on a man's nerves. Develops concertina legs, he does."

1916: *The Right to Be Happy,* based on *A Christmas Carol,* US; dir. Rupert Julian.

1916: *Oliver Twist,* US; dir. James Young; Marie Doro as Oliver; Hobart Bosworth as Bill Sikes; Tully Marshall as Fagin; Raymond Hatton as the Artful Dodger. Famous for her portrayal of Oliver on the stage, Doro is probably the only woman to play him in film. Her presence is a relic of the days when Oliver was a celebrated "breeches role."

1917: *A Tale of Two Cities,* US; dir. Frank Lloyd; William Farnum as Darnay/Carton; Jewel Carmen as Lucie; Josef Swikard as Dr. Manette. Farnum plays both Darnay and Carton, and the double-exposure shots showing the two "together" were at the time considered a highlight of cinematic achievement.

1917: *Great Expectations,* US; 5 reels; dir. Robert G. Vignola and Joseph Kaufman; Jack Pickford as Pip; Louise Huff as Estella; Frank Losee as Magwitch; W. W. Black as Joe; Grace Barton as Miss Havisham.

1919: *Our Mutual Friend,* Denmark; dir. A. W. Sandberg and Peter Malberg; with Aage Fonss.

1920: *Oliver Twist,* Hungary; dir. Peter Lubinsky.

1920: *Bleak House,* GB; dir. Constance Collier.

1921: *Barnaby Rudge,* GB; dir. Thomas Bentley.

1921: *Oliver Twist, Jr.,* US; 5 reels; dir. Millard Webb; Harold Goodwin as Oliver; Lilian Hall as Ruth Norris; G. Raymond Nye as Bill Sikes. Or perhaps *Son of Oliver?* This is *Oliver Twist* set in modern America—orphan is taken up by hoods, shot in a robbery attempt, found by a young woman, and discovers his true identity—all in five reels.

1922: *Oliver Twist,* US; dir. Frank Lloyd; Jackie Coogan as Oliver; Lon Chaney as Fagin. This is one of the great classics of the silent era—and with its range of actors and extraordinary acting, it manages to capture all the vitality of the original. Casting Chaney was a masterstroke—his Fagin is one of his own monsters made human. British censors objected to the film on the grounds that "it would encourage juvenile crime" and that it didn't depict the novel in a manner appropriate to its status as a classic.

1922: *Fagin,* GB; dir. H. B. Parkinson; with Ivan Berlyn.

1922: *David Copperfield,* Denmark; dir. A. W. Sandberg; with Martin Hertzberg.

1923: *A Dickensian Fantasy,* based on *A Christmas Carol,* GB; dir. Aveling Ginever; with Lawrence Manray.

I think Dickens would be in his element if he lived and wrote now. . . . He would surely have made films and done things for television. . . . But there is one way I think he would have been different. He would never have wanted to seduce people as we do now by diluting his message for the benefit of the wider public. He would have gone straight for the jugular. . . .
—CHRISTINE EDZARD, director, *Little Dorrit,* 1989

*O*ne of the greatest—and least seen—Olivers of them all: Jackie Coogan as the orphan and Lon Chaney as Fagin in the 1922 silent film. One of the few instances when Oliver is not a fair-haired angel.

SOUND ERA

*D*avid Edgar's play *Nicholas Nickleby* and David Lean's Dickens films forcefully illustrate that the best Dickens adaptations are those inspired (in the strict meaning of the word) by Dickens, not confined by him. *Nickleby* is not bookish but theatrical, and in filming *Oliver,* Lean exploited what the camera, not words, could do.

Television ushered in a new age in Dickens adaptations. As several critics have pointed out, TV comes closest to reproducing Dickens's format, since it often serializes stories, drawing them out over a period of weeks. *Masterpiece Theatre* productions, spanning five or six episodes, allow us to feel like Victorian readers, eagerly waiting for the next installment.

1931: *Rich Man's Folly,* based on *Dombey and Son,* US; dir. John Cromwell; with George Bancroft, Robert Ames. This updated version of Dickens's novel is set in 1931 America. Brock Trumbull is a shipping magnate who ignores his daughter, Dee, in favor of his heir, Durand. During the 1930s the studios turned to Dickens and other "classic" authors as a way of relieving the sufferings of the Great Depression. Such adaptations emphasized the sentimental and the heroic.

1933: *Oliver Twist,* US; dir. William J. Cowran; Dickie Moore as Oliver; Irving Pichel as Fagin; William "Stage" Boyd as Sikes; Doris Lloyd as Nancy Sikes; Barbara Kent as Rose Maylie; Sonny Ray as the Artful Dodger. In this chaste version Nancy and Bill are "Mr. and Mrs. Sikes." This alone should warn viewers away from the film. Surprisingly, the first talkie *Oliver* is moribund affair. The eight-year-old Moore is too young for the part. While it seems churlish to criticize a child, his lack of range seems to inhibit the other actors. Despite its flaws, this film inspired a brief Dickens mania in Hollywood.

1934: *Great Expectations,* US; dir. Stuart Walker; Henry Hull as Magwitch; Phillips Holmes as Pip; Jane Wyatt as Estella; Florence Reed as Miss Havisham; Alan Hale as Joe; Douglas Wood as Compeyson; Rafaela Ottiano as Mrs. Joe; Walter Armitage as Herbert; Francis L. Sullivan as Jaggers. This adaptation, which received poor reviews when it came out, sank into obscurity after Lean's film. It also suffered from comparison with the acclaimed *Old Curiosity Shop* of the same year.

1934: *The Old Curiosity Shop,* GB; dir. Thomas Bentley; with Elaine Benson, Hay Petrie. The novelist Margaret Kennedy collaborated on the screenplay.

1934: *Little Dorrit (Klein Dorrit),* German; dir. Carl Lamac; Anny Ondra as Amy Dorrit. *The Dickensian* expressed bemusement when *Klein Dorrit* premiered in London. Its plot and mood evoke prewar Germany, more *Cabaret* than *Little Dorrit.*

1935: *A Tale of Two Cities,* GB; dir. Jack Conway; Ronald Colman as Sydney Carton; Elizabeth Allan as Lucie; Reginald Owen as Stryver; Isabel Jewell as Seamstress; Edna May Oliver as Miss Pross; Blanche Yurka as Madame Defarge; Donald Woods as Charles Darnay; Basil Rathbone as the Marquis St. Evremond. For most of us, this is the definitive *Tale*—a Selznick extravaganza featuring the great MGM contract players. There have been eight productions of Dickens's epic, and this still ranks as the best. The intelligent script, written by W. P. Lipscomb and S. N. Behrman, includes all the minor characters and subplots. The producers spared no expense: 17,000 extras stormed the Bastille.

Although it's hard to imagine anyone but Colman uttering, "It's a far, far better thing," Leslie Howard, England's other Gentleman, was originally slated for the role. Colman took the role seriously, immersing himself in the part and in Dickens's novel. He has become synonymous with the character: in parodies and send-ups, actors ape his nasal dignity. (Incidentally, before she could play Madame Defarge, Yurka had to learn how to knit.)

1935: *The Mystery of Edwin Drood,* US; dir. Stuart Walker; Claude Rains as John Jasper; David Manners as Edwin Drood; Valerie Hobson as Helena Landless; Francis L. Sullivan as Mr. Crisparkle. Dickens's unfinished novel gets a new twist. Rains is superb as the tormented, and slightly demented, choirmaster. The set was pure gothic: the mossy crypt where Jasper buries his nephew was originally built for the 1931 *Dracula.*

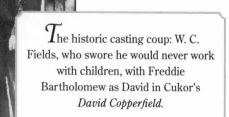

The historic casting coup: W. C. Fields, who swore he would never work with children, with Freddie Bartholomew as David in Cukor's *David Copperfield.*

*B*asil Rathbone as Mr. Murdstone appears with a frightened Freddie Bartholomew. Rathbone dreaded having to whip the boy and although he was equipped with foam rubber padding, Bartholomew wept out of real terror.

1935: *Scrooge,* GB; dir. Henry Edwards; Sir Seymour Hicks as Scrooge; Donald Calthrop as Bob Cratchit; Robert Cochran as Fred; Mary Glynne as Bella; Oscar Asche as Christmas Present; Athene Seyler as a charwoman; Maurice Evans as a Poor Man; Philip Frost as Tiny Tim. That the film is *Scrooge* and not *A Christmas Carol* indicates its focus. *Scrooge* is a showcase for the sixty-four-year-old Sir Seymour Hicks, who made a career playing the role on stage and in music halls. His Scrooge is adapted from his staged dramatizations rather than from Dickens's book. As critics have noted, the theatrical quality of Hicks's acting style is more suited to the stage than films. Much of the story is pared away, leaving us mostly with Hicks, who also cowrote the screenplay. Gone are the delightful Fezziwig Ball episode and the scenes from Scrooge's lonely boyhood. We see little of his moral transformation, the Cratchits, or Fred. And in this version, it's Scrooge who utters Tiny Tim's signature line, "God bless us, every one." The film's only value—it was the first talkie *Carol*—is historical.

1935: *David Copperfield,* US; dir. George Cukor; W. C. Fields as Mr. Micawber; Lionel Barrymore as Dan Peggotty; Freddie Bartholomew as Young David; Edna May Oliver as Aunt Betsey Trotwood; Elizabeth Allan as Mrs. Copperfield; Lennox Pawle as Mr. Dick; Maureen O' Sullivan as Dora; Basil Rathbone as Mr. Murdstone; Roland Young as Uriah Heep; Frank Lawton as the adult David; Madge Evans as the adult Agnes. Those expecting a stuffy English classic with stiff-necked actors will be delightfully surprised by Cukor's high-spirited treatment of Dickens's favorite novel. Neither reverent nor adoring, Cukor and Selznick take a refreshingly offbeat approach to the novel. The casting is against type. The idea of W. C. Fields as

Mr. Micawber was a bit of inspired lunacy. Freddie Bartholomew got the role of David, beating out 10,000 boys—including Jackie Cooper, the early favorite. Cukor brought Bartholomew over from England and led him into Selznick's office, where, costumed as David, he tipped his hat, bowed, and said, "I am David Copperfield." "Right you are," returned Selznick. It was the first and only time Fields played someone other than himself, and the first and only time Roland Young played a villain. It was also Basil Rathbone's first villainous role, and his success as Mr. Murdstone launched a career playing cold-eyed sadists.

1938: *A Christmas Carol,* US; dir. Edwin L. Marin; Reginald Owen as Scrooge; Gene Lockhart as Bob Cratchit; Kathleen Lockhart as Mrs. Cratchit; Leo G. Carroll as Marley's Ghost; Terry Kilburn as Tiny Tim; Barry Mackay as Fred; Lionel Braham as Ghost of Christmas Present; Ann Rutherford as Ghost of Christmas Past; D'Arcy Corrigan as Ghost of Christmas Yet to Come.

There were more *Carol*s produced during the Depression than in any other period. The public wanted to be soothed by familiar classics, particularly ones that paralleled their own situation. Since so many in the audience identified with Bob Cratchit, the sight of a well-fed, robust Gene Lockhart must have been subliminally reassuring. There's nothing harrowing in this *Carol*—reality is kept firmly at bay.

This Hollywood *Carol* gave the characters romance and a touch of glamour. Fred's love for Bess, his young bride, plays a larger part than ever before. The newlyweds even indulge in a flirtatious snowball fight outside the church after services. This is a distinctly American touch—young love and high spirits triumph over the holiday's religious meanings. And finally, there's the unsettling apparition of the Ghost of Christmas Present, an MGM Technicolor blonde with scarlet lips and blue eyeshadow.

1946: *Great Expectations,* GB; dir. David Lean; Anthony Wager as Young Pip; John Mills as Older Pip; Jean Simmons as Young Estella; Valerie Hobson as Estella and Mollie; Finlay Currie as Magwitch; Martita Hunt as Miss Havisham; Francis L. Sullivan as Jaggers; Alec Guinness as Herbert Pocket; Ivor Barnard as Wemmick; Hay Petrie as Uncle Pumblechook.

Considered one of the finest film adaptations of a novel, Lean's interpretation captures the moody atmosphere of deep longing and emptiness that pervades the novel. The opening view of the marshes at twilight, with its streaks of black and white, and the loneliness of the church burial yard burn in the memory. Like that of the novel, the movie's opening is celebrated: Curry's Magwitch, one of filmdom's most underrated performances, leaps out at Pip like a mad dog.

As the man-hating recluse Miss Havisham, Hunt evokes an emotional intensity that's almost palpable. Despite the cobwebbed decay that surrounds her, Miss Havisham possesses her own mad beauty, which makes it easy to see why Pip would be bewitched by her as well as by the lovely Estella—fifteen-year-old Jean Simmons in her first screen role.

Even masterworks have flaws: Lean ignores the novel's two fine endings and writes a third that turns angst into Hollywood marsh mist. Dickens's tale about the sadness of desire suddenly changes course, and in the final minutes, ends on a jarringly happy note.

1947: *Nicholas Nickleby,* GB; dir. Alberto Cavalcanti; Derek Bond as Nicholas; Sir Cedric Hardwicke as Ralph Nickleby; Stanley Holloway as Vincent Crummles; Bernard Miles as Newman Noggs; Cyril Fletcher as Mr. Mantalini; Sally Ann Howes as Kate Nickleby; Sybil Thorndike as Mrs. Squeers; Cathleen Nesbitt as Miss Knagg; Fay Compton as Mrs. Mantalini; Alfred Drayton as Squeers; Jill Balcon as Madeline Bray; Roddy Hughes as Tim Linkinwater.

Take a dozen of England's finest actors, cast them in a film version of Dickens's classic *Nicholas Nickleby*—and then hire a French-trained, avant-garde Brazilian to direct them. This scenario could be the basis of another movie, but in this case, the collision between two cultures has produced a muted *Nickleby,* dutiful yet original. Known for introducing documentary realism into his fictional films, Cavalcanti treats the Dotheboys Hall section like an exposé. Drayton doesn't play Squeers for laughs. The actors, like Dickens's characters, reveal themselves through appearance, mannerisms, and speech patterns. Fanny's simpering lisp, and her unfortunate tendency to let her jaw go slack convey more than any speech. Sybil Thorndike, waving her ladle like a shillelagh, has the grotesque outlines of a drawing by Phiz. Among all these luminaries is Aubrey Woods, an obscure drama student chosen to play Smike. We look down from above the courtyard and see just his head as he runs in circles in the snow: a brief scene, but it captures all that the boy can't articulate: his desperation to escape, his solitude, his longing for a home. Miles's Newman Noggs cuts a curious figure: his mysterious smile implies worlds of meaning. The Crummles episode is the lifeblood of the story—Holloway's declamations are just right for an itinerant Shakespearean with great expectations. Then, of course, there's the perennial problem of the Dickensian hero. Bond isn't bad, but his emotional range is limited and he seems like a bore. Mantalini is amusing, but unfortunately, U.S. censors cut his favorite epithet, "Demmit."

Cavalcanti keeps the action going at a brisk pace: in two hours he compresses the entire *Nickleby,* and his canvas is suitably populous (there are more than forty speaking parts).

Finally, the director's use of light and dark is impressive; indeed, he subordinates a character's face to the visual effect of the film. The shadowy world suggests an undercurrent of menace, and his image of England, while true to period details, is that of a grotesque, melodramatic world where strange and wonderful creatures live.

1948: *Oliver Twist,* GB; dir. David Lean; Alec Guinness as Fagin; John Howard Davies as Oliver; Kay Walsh as Nancy; Anthony Newley as the Artful Dodger; Robert Newton as Bill Sikes; Francis L. Sullivan as Bumble; Henry Stephenson as Mr. Brownlow.

*I*n David Lean's postwar *Oliver Twist* workhouses resemble concentration camps. Indeed, unlike other versions, Lean's makes no attempt to humanize the authorities who run such places.

Lean's *Oliver* is about the anxiety and desolation of childhood. The film opens as Oliver's mother, hardly more than a child herself, struggles against the storm to the workhouse where her son is born and she dies. The infant's first screams express the desolation of the world he's born into. Right away, the atmosphere evokes a crushing sense of early loss and despair.

Lean's postwar *Oliver* conveys a horror and a loneliness that has never been captured in any other version. British audiences could draw parallels between Dickens's hero and the plight of their own children during wartime. The workhouse resembles a concentration camp, and Davies's Oliver has the pinched, haunted face that one sees looking out from a newsreel.

Those in authority—the beadle, wardens and matrons—are so odious, that one can see why Oliver is so easily seduced by a Fagin who lavishes protection, love—and, of course, glorious food. But for all his charm, Guinness's Fagin is among the damned. Modern viewers can sense his pedophiliac tendencies, his need to corrupt the innocent. And Guinness's is the last Fagin who is undeniably evil *and* Jewish. The war had sensitized American Jews to the slightest hint of anti-Semitism. (Although based on Cruikshank's original drawings, Guinness's false nose was terrifyingly reminiscent of Nazi caricatures.) It took three years before U.S. censors permitted the movie's release in the States, and only after Lean cut seven minutes of close-ups and profiles. It is a tribute to the complexity of the film that the "respectable citizens" who chase Fagin at the end are no better than the criminal they hunt. This is a world much like the one that existed in Germany under the Nazis, where ordinary citizens suddenly turn into animals.

Most horrible of all is Sikes's murder of Nancy. It seems to last forever. Lean's vision is pitiless. Eschewing melodrama and explicit violence, he, like Shakespeare, concentrates on small, almost homely details that convey an undercurrent of evil. The camera turns away from the murder as if the scene were too grisly to contemplate and focuses instead on Bill's dog scratching at the door.

1951: *A Christmas Carol,* GB; dir. Brian Desmond Hurst; Alastair Sim as Scrooge; Michael Hordern as Jacob Marley; Mervyn Johns as Bob Cratchit; Hermione Baddeley as Mrs. Cratchit; Glyn Dearman as Tiny Tim; Michael Dolan as the Spirit of Christmas Past; Francis de Wolff as the Spirit of the Present; C. Konarski as Spirit of Christmas Yet to Come. For many, this is the definitive *Carol,* as traditional as holly and mistletoe. And yet it differs from every other *Carol.* As Paul Davis points out, this version is a product of the fifties, a time when people believed that fifty minutes on the couch could cure all ills. Thus Sim's Scrooge is not so much haunted by actual spirits as tormented by inner demons; the ghosts are "analysts" who force him to confront the traumas of his past. Sim's performance makes the movie a classic. As each ghost appears and departs he descends into various stages of hell, his face a Kabuki mask of terror. His delirium of joy upon awakening is cathartic for the viewer as well.

1952: *The Pickwick Papers,* GB; dir. Noel Langley; James Hayter as Mr. Pickwick; Lionel Murton as Mr. Snodgrass; James Donald as Mr. Winkle; Alex Gauge as Mr. Tupman; Nigel Patrick as Mr. Jingle; Hermione Gingold as Miss Tomkins; Joyce Grenfell as Mrs. Leo Hunter; Donald Wolfit as Serjeant Buzfuz; Harry Fowler as Sam Weller; Hermione Baddeley as Mrs. Bardell; Mary Merrall as Grandmother Wardle. This is one of those black-and-white British films of the 1950s where the actors are homely and hilarious. Simple and unpretentious, it's one of the drollest Dickens movies ever made. Like the novel, it defies a linear plot as the Pickwickians bumble into one misadventure after another. There is nothing understated about this film. At first one might mistake *Pickwick* for a children's movie—the actors seem more like cartoons than real people—yet it is completely Pickwickian, evoking a spirit that transcends age. The cast, a true delight, consists of England's finest comic actors.

1958: *A Tale of Two Cities,* GB; dir. Ralph Thomas; Dirk Bogarde as Sydney Carton; Dorothy Tutin as Lucie; Paul Guers as Charles Darnay; Athene Seyler as Miss Pross; Christopher Lee as the Marquis St. Evremond; Alfie Bass as Jerry Cruncher; Stephen Murray as Dr. Manetter; Cecil Parker as Jarvis Lorrie; Rosalie Crutchley as Madame Defarge. This is the sixth attempt to bring Dickens's tale of the French Revolution to the screen.

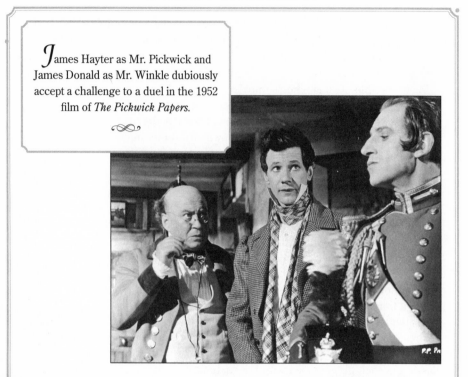

*J*ames Hayter as Mr. Pickwick and James Donald as Mr. Winkle dubiously accept a challenge to a duel in the 1952 film of *The Pickwick Papers.*

Considering the 1935 competition, this version manages to hold up fairly well—it's exciting, the cast is strong, and some may prefer Bogarde's understated heroism to Colman's theatrics.

1962: *Mister Magoo's Christmas Carol,* US; animated film for television. Jim Backus as the voice of Mr. Magoo/Scrooge; Jack Cassidy as Bob Cratchit; Joan Gardner as Tiny Tim and Christmas Past; Jane Kean as Belle Fezziwig; Morey Amsterdam as Brandy/James; Laura Olsher as Mrs. Cratchit. Music by Jule Styne and Bob Merrill. This is not Mr. Magoo playing Scrooge, but Scrooge as Mr. Magoo, a myopic miser. While the idea of an animated musical doesn't bode well, this *Carol* is an unexpected delight. The music ("The Lord's Bright Blessing," "Alone in the World," and "It's Great to Be Back on Broadway"), recalls a time when scores for children's movies were quirky and memorable. This *Carol* should become an annual ritual. For many baby boomers Mr. Magoo's *Carol* remains the definitive version of Charles Dickens's classic.

1968: *Oliver!,* musical based on *Oliver Twist,* GB; dir. Sir Carol Reed. Music and lyrics by Lionel Bart; Mark Lester as Oliver; Jack Wild as the Artful Dodger; Oliver Reed as Sikes; Ron Moody as Fagin; Harry Secombe as Bumble; Shani Wallis as Nancy.
    The exclamation point captures the film's mood of trumped-up enthusiasm. This is about Oliver!, a plucky lad, not Oliver Twist, Dickens's workhouse orphan. *Oliver!* is an upbeat musical about orphanages, teen-age

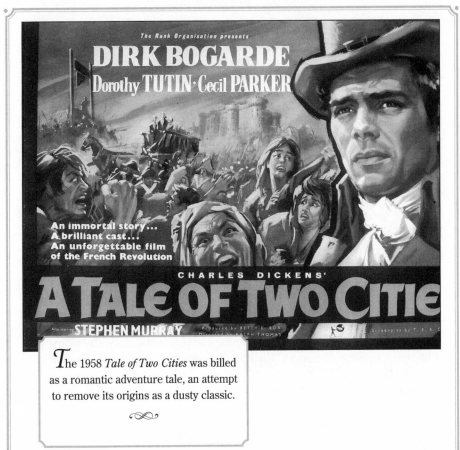

The Rank Organisation presents

DIRK BOGARDE
Dorothy **TUTIN** · Cecil **PARKER**

An immortal story...
A brilliant cast...
An unforgettable film
of the French Revolution

CHARLES DICKENS'
A TALE OF TWO CITIE

Also starring **STEPHEN MURRAY**   Produced by BETTY E. BOX   Screenplay by T. E. B. C

*T*he 1958 *Tale of Two Cities* was billed
as a romantic adventure tale, an attempt
to remove its origins as a dusty classic.

pregnancy, indifferent bureaucrats, child abuse, workhouses, and domestic
violence.

Compared to David Lean's concentration camp, Reed's workhouse is
summer camp with singalongs. Watching starving children do a big dance
number about food in a workhouse is a bit like seeing inmates high step in
Auschwitz. And, given our sensitivity to domestic violence, one can only
cringe when Nancy launches into the lovely ballad, "As Long As He Needs
Me" just after Sikes threatens her. A small shift of perspective is all that
would be needed to make *Oliver!* as fatuous as Mel Brook's parady musical
Springtime for Hitler.

That said, we can now enjoy the movie in good conscience. For instance,
the scene in which Beadle Bumble parades the orphan through the streets
crying "Boy for Sale," a lament in a minor key, is truly affecting. The camera
looks down on the two human forms, black dots in an expanse of snow, and
for a moment a sense of terrible desolation is caught.

Of course, every cockney is winsome, and every prostitute a jolly sort.
Nancy is the whore with the "'eart of gold," kicking up her heels in pubs,
and, perhaps to avoid the charges of anti-Semitism that dogged Alec

Guinness's Fagin, Moody's is a comical bloke, a basically good sort who simply has to "to pick a pocket or two."

But it's Sikes, not Fagin, who is the real villain—and Oliver Reed is a stunner, the motionless eye in a movie that seems in perpetual cheery motion. He's the only character who never sings or dances, and the contrast and noise make him seem all the more wicked.

1970: *Scrooge,* musical based on *A Christmas Carol,* GB; dir. Ronald Neame; Albert Finney as Scrooge; Alec Guinness as Marley's Ghost; Edith Evans as Ghost of Christmas Past; Kenneth More as Ghost of Christmas Present; Laurence Naismith as Fezziwig; Michael Medwin as Fred; David Collings as Bob Cratchit; Richard Beaumont as Tiny Tim. This *Scrooge* is *A Christmas Carol* for the swinging youth culture. Even in makeup, Finney is the best-looking Scrooge ever, more middle-aged than elderly. (Of course, no one wanted a Scrooge who was actually *old*.) During the scenes of Christmas Pasts Finney, now divested of makeup, reverts to his handsome self, thus reassuring us that the "real" Scrooge is the young one.

This is a feel-good *Carol.* The preconverted Scrooge walks the streets singing a song called "I Hate People," a reflection of the 1960s imperative to love one another. The visitations of the ghosts are more like consciousness-raising sessions. In a complete departure from Dickens's text, the Ghost of Christmas Present dispenses "the milk of human kindness," a drink that has the effect of a mind-altering drug. As soon as he drinks the stuff, the grasping miser loosens up; he's like the drunk who embraces a stranger on the streetcar. The hard-won conversions of earlier *Carol*s are quickly dismissed; underlying this Carol is the belief that moral change is easy. The extravagant musical finale resembles, if such a thing were possible, a Victorian love-in.

1970: *David Copperfield,* US/GB; dir. Delbert Mann; Laurence Olivier as Mr. Creakle; Richard Attenborough as Mr. Tungay; Cyril Cusack as Barkis; Dame Edith Evans as Aunt Betsey; Ron Moody as Uriah Heep; Robin Philips as David; Sir Ralph Richardson as Micawber; Wendy Hiller as Mrs. Micawber; Pamela Franklin as Dora; Susan Hampshire as Agnes; Emlyn Williams as Mr. Dick; Sinead Cusack as Emily; Anna Massey as Jane Murdstone; James Donald as Mr. Murdstone; Michael Redgrave as Mr. Peggotty.

With a sterling cast and screenwriter (Jack Pulman of *I Claudius*), one might expect better. This can't even begin to compete with Cukor's rollicking version. But all the venerable actors—even Ralph Richardson as Micawber—only make brief appearances, while most of the film consists of a Byronic David walking up and down the Yarmouth shore, brooding on the past and "hearing voices." The film opens with the twenty-eight-year-old David in the throes in a Hamletesque identify crisis; Agnes—Susan Hampshire in false eyelashes—sent by Aunt Betsey, arrives to soothe him, and then they walk the shore together, as she anxiously watches his face. At the end, he runs into her arms, the sea roaring behind them.

Through brief flashbacks—which don't follow any apparent logic—the story of David Copperfield is told. A snippet of his mother's funeral, a very brief stint at the warehouse, and then suddenly he's on the road to Dover. Little Emily's seduction takes place before he meets Dora. The young principles, Hampshire, Franklin, and Philips play their parts with generic blandness. Ralph Richardson, however, is splendid as Micawber, a role he was born to play.

1973: *Smike!,* GB; adapted for television by John Morley. Ian Sharrock as Smike. This sounds like a sick joke or an Andrew Lloyd Webber parody. The retarded and dying boy in *Nicholas Nickleby* is an unlikely subject for a rock musical.

1973: *Marcel Marceau's Christmas Carol.* US. Well, at least it's not Marcel Marceau's *Bleak House.* Marcel Marceau mimes the story to Michael Hordern's narration.

1974: *Great Expectations,* GB; dir. Joseph Hardy; Michael York as Pip; Margaret Leighton as Miss Havisham; Sarah Miles as Estella; Robert Morley as Pumblechook; James Mason as Magwitch; Anthony Quayle as Jaggers; Joss Ackland as Joe; Simon Gipps-Kent as Young Pip.

Most productions have two actors playing younger versions of Pip and Estella. But whereas York has a youthful stand-in as Younger Pip, Miles plays Estella throughout. The effect of the mature Miles in pigtails playing a sixteen-year-old girl is disconcerting in itself, but the sight of her paired with an adolescent boy is even more jarring. Miles is suitably unlikable for the role, and York looks like a blacksmith who could pass for a gentleman. For the first time, Joe is presented as a real man, not an endearing yokel. Joss Ackland is attractive, strong, and believably good; indeed, at times he seems to find it hard to play the fool, even a wise one. But this interpretation works because it means that Pip rejects a real person, not a cartoon figure, and we are all the more moved and outraged by his behavior. Mason is superb as the convict, but even he can't match the great Finlay Currie.

This version transforms Dickens's most nuanced novel into a conventional love story in which the meaning of desire is taken at face value. The pièce de résistance is Estella's confession that she's always been in love with Pip—a statement tantamount to all those endings in which the alarm clock goes off and the hero discovers that it's all been a dream. The viewer—and Pip—should feel cheated and if they know the novel they'll probably feel angry as well. This is *Great Expectations* as Harlequin romance.

1975: *Mister Quilp,* GB; dir. Michael Tuchner; Anthony Newley as Quilp; Sarah-Jane Varley as Nell; Michael Hordern as Grandfather; David Hemmings as Dick Swiveller; David Warner as Samson Brass; Paul Rogers as the Single Gentleman; Mona Washbourne as Mrs. Jarley. Financed by the Reader's Digest Group, this a dismal attempt to make *The Old Curiosity Shop* palatable to the masses. Thus it focuses on the "intriguing" villain instead of the limpid heroine. Quilp is now a hunchback instead of a dwarf, and the

*A*nthony Newley plays Quilp in the
unsuccessful musical of *The Old
Curiosity Shop,* retitled *Mister Quilp.*

curiosity shop, cleared of debris and clutter, now resembles an upmarket
antique store in Sloan Square. Newley is responsible for the score, which
includes such forgettable numbers as "Happiness Pie," love Has the Longest
Memory," and "When a Felon Needs a Friend."

1982: *Oliver Twist,* GB; dir. Clive Donner; George C. Scott as Fagin; Tim
Curry as Sikes; Michael Hordern as Mr. Brownlow; Cherie Lunghi as Nancy;
Eileen Atkins as Mrs. Mann; Richard Charles as Oliver.

1984: *Dombey and Son* (TV film).

1984: *The Life and Adventures of Nicholas Nickleby;* dir. John Caird; Roger
Rees as Nicholas; David Threlfall as Smike; and members of the Royal
Shakespeare Company. This is the nine-video set of the landmark play (see
page 106). It is also one of those interpretations that are as great as the work
that inspired it. To get the true *Nickleby* experience, try watching the entire
set in one or two days. That way, you can grasp just how revelatory the play
was. Seeing *Nickleby* was a never-to-be-forgotten experience; the nine-tape

version is about the closest we'll ever get to seeing the original. Without being self-consciously actorish, Rees plays an adolescent without reminding the audience that he is a grown man playing an adolescent. He interprets the character rather than accepting him at Dickens's word. He lets us know that his Nicholas is a good guy, with a tendency toward self-righteous impetuosity. But the play's the thing, and it's everything the adoring critics said it was and more. After ten minutes you'll forget you're watching television and feel you've become a member of a dazzled audience.

1984: *A Christmas Carol,* GB; dir. Clive Donner; George C. Scott as Scrooge; Frank Finlay as Marley's Ghost; Roger Rees as Fred; Angela Pleasance as the Ghost Christmas Past; Edward Woodward as the Ghost of Christmas Present; Michael Carter as the Ghost of Christmas Yet to Come; David Warner as Bob Cratchit; Susannah York as Mrs. Cratchit. Donner, who had edited Alastair Sim's *Carol,* returned to the story thirty-three years later to film it with Scott. The two films are the best. The part of Scrooge is a little like Hamlet. They're so familiar that they've become stock figures instead of individuals. Indeed, Scrooge seems to require little thought; the character comes to the actor ready-made, a mouthpiece for greeting-card sentiments rather than a person with desires, regrets, and impulses. Scott, like Sim, invigorates the character. His Scrooge is not a caricature but a real businessman. One of the more realistic touches is his unwillingness to relinquish his old life and submit to ghostly ministrations. His gradual transformation is thus all the more credible. With his mutton-chop whiskers and wintry smile, Scott makes a superbly sardonic Scrooge. Filmed on location in Shrewsbury, the film is strikingly beautiful.

1985: *Oliver Twist,* GB; dir. Gareth Davies; Scott Funnell as Young Oliver; Eric Porter as Fagin; Lysette Anthony as Agnes Fleming; Godfrey James as Mr. Bumble; Ben Rodska as the older Oliver; Julian Firth as Noah Claypole; Michael Attwell as Sikes; Frank Middlemass as Mr. Brownlow; Pip Donaghy as Monks; Miriam Margolyes as Mrs. Corney. Whenever classics are turned into film, critics and viewers usually complain of the numerous cuts and omissions. Here, for the first time, is *Oliver Twist,* complete in 332 minutes. Characters are developed at a leisurely pace, events unfold with a Dickensian eye for detail.

The casting is brilliant. With his greasy locks and broken teeth, Eric Porter's Fagin is so loathsome you feel like recoiling. Miriam Margolyes, as Mrs. Corney, is the personification of female rage. The evil Monks is unintentionally hilarious; clad like Count Dracula, he hisses, gnashes his teeth, and falls into fits. This production is noteworthy in having two actors, of different ages, play the role of Oliver as he grows up in the course of the novel. Attwell's Sikes is a thuggish punk, impervious to human emotion.

1985: *Bleak House,* GB; dir. Ross Devenish; Diana Rigg as Lady Dedlock; Denholm Elliot as Mr. Jarndyce; Suzanne Burden as Esther Summerson; Lucy Hornak as Ada Clare; Philip Franks as Richard Carstone; Peter Vaughn as Mr. Tulkinghorn. This acclaimed production—the first in thirty-five years—is nothing short of miraculous. No one likes a sensible heroine, but this Esther, moral perfection and all, is endearing. Instead of softening her disfigurement, the makeup department gives her the full treatment: Her face scarred and her smile crooked, her appearance is at first shocking, then oddly beautiful and compelling. The romantic tension between Esther and the elderly Mr. Jarndyce is delicately handled. Casting Diana Rigg as Lady Dedlock was a stroke of genius.

1988: *Little Dorrit,* GB; 2 three-hour videos; dir. Christine Edzard; Derek Jacobi as Arthur Clennam; Sarah Pickering as Little Dorrit; Alec Guinness as Mr. Dorrit; Joan Greenwood as Mrs. Clenam; Miriam Margolyes as Flora Finching; Michael Elphick as Mr. Merdle.

Edzard's *Little Dorrit* focuses more on the psychological than on the politically subversive, and as such she separates her film, Roshomon-like, into two three-hour segments; the first, *Nobody's Fault,* presents the story from Arthur Clennam's point of view; the second, *Little Dorrit's Story,* is from Amy Dorrit's. This *Little Dorrit* is mainly a love story about an unlikely pair of lovers, the pale and unprepossessing Amy Dorrit and the haggard middle-aged Arthur Clennam. One would be hard-pressed to find a more improbable couple; but the movie is surprisingly erotic, more for what it doesn't say than what it shows, about frustrated dreams and erotic rejuvenation.

Verdi's voluptuous music seems an odd choice for a film set in gritty nineteenth-century London. But its emotional richness says everything the repressed characters cannot. At times, music replaces dialogue. A bustling, dashing rhythm accompanies Clennam rushing back and forth from the Circumlocution Office, frustrated yet determined.

There are 242 speaking parts, from shopkeepers to street sweepers, each with a face that can only be described as Dickensian, every one of which tells a story.

The heart of the film is Alec Guinness's self-pitying and fretful Mr. Dorrit. Guinness captures the character's nervous mannerisms, his querulous tone, his moodiness, even the way he fastidiously plucks at a flounce on a shirt sleeve. Few will forget Miriam Margolyes's performance as the widowed Flora Finching, Arthur's forty-something ex-sweetheart, a figure both ludicrous and poignant. Margolyes inhabits the role, speaking in the Floraesque stream—or torrent—of consciousness, discovering a sadness and an innocence where less subtle performers would find only comedy. Jacobi's unheroic Clennam is a portrait of a modest man experiencing a quiet revolution. He resigns himself to a joyless existence, only to discover, miraculously, that his life has been transformed by love. His awakening in the Marshalsea Prison, his bewilderment and then joyous awareness of Amy's presence, is as magical as a recognition scene in Shakespeare's last plays. These unworldly misfits come together, and their opposing cinematic points of view dissolve into one. By the end of the movie, the young heroine and the forty-five-year-old hero seem made for each other.

1988: *David Copperfield,* GB; Colin Hurley as David; Simon Callow as Mr. Micawber; Jenny McCracken as Peggotty; Paul Brightwell as Uriah Heep; Oliver Cotton as Mr. Murdstone; Brenda Bruce as Aunt Betsey; John Savident as Mr. Creakle; Thorley Walters as Mr. Dick; Francesca Hall as Dora; Natalie Cole as Agnes; Valerie Pogan as Emily. Like *Hamlet, David Copperfield* tends to suffer from staleness—everyone is terribly serious and very, very British, particularly the American actors. Still, this version is the most original since Cukor's. For the first time since 1935, we get a fresh Micawber: breaking with tradition, Callow turns to Dickens's novel, not W. C. Fields, for his interpretation of Mr. Micawber. Oliver Cotton's Murdstone is stunningly cruel; as one British critic put it, "His eyes disappear under his brows like stones down a well."

1988: *Blackadder's Christmas Carol,* GB; dir. Richard Boden; Rowen Atkinson as Ebenezer Blackadder; Tony Robinson as Baldrick; Miranda Richardson as Queen Elizabeth; Hugh Laurie as Prince Regent, Stephen Fry as Lord Melchet; Miriam Margolyes as Queen Victoria; Jim Broadbent as Prince Albert; Robbie Coltrane as Spirit of Christmas. A hilarious send up; perfect for those who'd like some bile with their Christmas cheer.

1989: *Great Expectations,* GB; dir. Kevin Connor; Anthony Hopkins as Magwitch; John Rhys Davies as Joe Gargery; Jean Simmons as Miss Havisham; Anthony Calf as Pip; Ray McAnally as Jaggers; Kim Thomson as Estella. Sentimentalists and critics alike were drawn to the idea of Jean Simmons moving full cycle from the young Estella in David Lean's 1946 film to the wizened eccentric, Miss Havisham, in Disney's production forty-three years later. Determined to forget the daunting Martita Hunt, who had played Miss Havisham to her Estella, Simmons created a Miss Havisham unlike any other. Influenced by her own bout with agoraphobia, Simmons's Havisham is the most sympathetic to date, more sick than sadistic. Yet one can't help but wish that she had imbibed some of Hunt's spectral-toned majesty.

Most of the acting is splendid, the sets are lovely, and Simmons's presence is moving. But considering how much money Disney put into this bloated six-hour production, it is nowhere near as good as it should be. With four films of the novel available, this should be last on your list. To see Jean Simmons at her best, rent or buy David Lean's and see her as the young Estella.

1989: *A Tale of Two Cities,* France/GB; dir. Phillippe Monnier; James Wilby as Sydney Carton; Serena Gordon as Lucie; Jean-Pierre Aumont as Dr. Manette; Anna Massey as Miss Pross; John Mills as Stryver; Xavier Deluc as Charles Darnay; Kathie Kriegal as Madame Defarge; Jean-Marc Bory as Marquis St. Evremonde; Alfred Lynch as Jerry Cruncher. Filmed in celebration of the centennial of the French Revolution, this *Tale* is all sound and fury, guts and glory. And it was directed by a Frenchman. Can the French understand Dickens? Many critics thought not. This Anglo-French multimillion-dollar coproduction was in filmed on location in Manchester,

*M*ichael Caine as Scrooge and Kermit the Frog as Bob Cratchit in *The Muppet Christmas Carol*.

England, and Bordeaux with a French and English cast. For the first time, Charles Darnay is played by a real Frenchman, Jean-Pierre Aumont. Serena Gordon's Lucie is as lovely as Dickens's description suggests, all tumbling blond curls. This is a *Tale* that strives for verisimilitude as well as drama. As the *London Daily Mail* sensationally put it: ". . . the love is red-hot, and the guillotine works."

The production is stirring and beautiful—and politically correct. Madame Defarge for the first time is portrayed as young and sexy (Dickens never said she was an ugly crone) and while not sympathetic, one can see that she has a legitimate grievance against the Darnay clan.

1993: *The Muppet Christmas Carol,* US; dir. Brian Henson; Michael Caine as Scrooge; Kermit the Frog as Bob Cratchit; Miss Piggy as Mrs. Cratchit. In his laudatory review of the Muppet *Carol,* film critic Roger Ebert complains that Dickens's version was too depressing for him as a child. Even more depressing is the sight of Michael Caine acting with Kermit the Frog. (Apparently the press kit for the movie included a photo of Kermit the Frog playing Bob Cratchit and Michael Caine as Scrooge with the caption: "Academy Award–winning Michael Caine [right] stars as the legendary Ebenezer Scrooge.") Non-Muppet fans may wish to see Caine play Scrooge "straight" in a real *Carol,* with human actors.

1993: *The Mystery of Edwin Drood,* GB; dir. Timothy Forder; with Robert Powell, Jonathan Phillips, Finty Williams, Rupert Rainsford, Nanette

Newman, Freddie Jones, Rosemary Leach, Ronald Fraser. One anticipates this film with genuine pleasure; after all, so few *Droods* have been made that there's nothing else to compare it to. Unfortunately, the film is depressing; it's not just that it's bad, or thin, or poorly acted, or low-budget, although it is all of these. Lacking the pleasing gloom of a good murder mystery or the dark Dickensian quality of the novel, it has all damp tedium of a rainy Sunday in England.

1995: *Martin Chuzzlewit* (TV film, 5 parts), GB; dir. by Pedr James; screenplay by David Lodge; Paul Scofield as Anthony and Martin Chuzzlewit; Pete Postlethwaithe as Montague Tigg; Tom Wilkinson as Mr. Pecksniff; Philip Franks as Tom Pinch; Elizabeth Spriggs as Sairey Gamp; Keith Allen as Jonas; Sir John Mills as Old Chuffey. Dickens's underrated, underread comic masterpiece is an invigorating departure from all the *Oliver*s and *David*s—it's about time producers realized that Dickens wrote other novels.

The Masterpiece Theatre image of Victorian London is usually that of a clean, well-lighted place, so *Chuzzlewit* is all the more welcome for portraying a city of filth, both moral and physical. This naturalistic portrait, the complete absence of nostalgia, and the proverbial Victorian coziness give *Chuzzlewit* a very different feel from the usual renditions of nineteenth-century novels.

Most of Dickens's episodic plot is preserved. This is an extremely funny production. And it is filled with fascinating faces: Allen's is a monument to evil, while Franks's is goodness incarnate. One is only sorry that someone chose to skip over the American sequence in the novel.

1995: *The Old Curiosity Shop,* US; dir. Kevin Connor; Peter Ustinov as Grandfather; Tom Courtenay as Quilp; Sally Walsh as Nell; James Fox as Single Gentleman; William Mannering as Kit; Adam Blackwood as Dick Swiveller; Christopher Ettridge as Samson Brass. It's been a long time since the last production of Dickens's sentimental favorite—modern directors tend to shy away from pathos unless it concerns politically correct diseases. Produced by Disney—the masters of childhood sorrow—this film retains all the beauty of the classic while making it accessible to adults and children. Walsh is neither ethereal nor otherworldly; in fact, she looks so robust it's hard to believe she's really dying. But in the final scene, modern viewers should be able to understand why Victorian readers wept over the death of Little Nell.

Unfortunately, Tom Courtenay, as fine an actor as he is, isn't quite Quilpian enough. Although he possesses some of the dwarf's anarchic malignancy, he is too good-looking, too tall, and too comical. The stately James Fox as the mysterious Single Gentleman adds moral weight to the film. But the director's decision to omit the Marchioness is almost unforgivable.

This Nell is a real girl, and Grandfather, played by a querulous Peter Ustinov, is a real dysfunctional guardian: a narcissistic compulsive gambler. (Modern viewers should identify with the family problems in this production.) Filmed by cinematographer Doug Milsome (*Lonesome Dove*) on location in Ireland, the film's beauty complements its elegiac atmosphere, which is juxtaposed against the nightmarish grotesqueries of Mrs. Jarely's waxworks.

1995: *Hard Times,* GB; dir. Peter Barnes; Alan Bates as Josiah Bounderby; Bob Peck as Gradgrind; Beatie Edney as Louisa; Bill Paterson as Stephen Blackpool; Emma Lewis as Cissy Jupe; Christien Anholt as Tom; Dilys Laye as Mrs. Sparsit. Russell Baker, who introduced the film for *Masterpiece Theatre,* wisely noted that the piece contains the only sad ending in all of Dickens. This production conveys all the dead-endedness and failure of human existence. To his credit, director Barnes never tries to make the sorrow palatable for TV audiences nor does the film ever veer into sentimentality.

Louisa, played with frightening stillness by Beatie Edney, looks as though her passion were simmering just below the surface of her pale face. Bates is still a little too dashing to play the bullying humbug Josiah Bounderby, but his acting is superb. This production shows how prophetic Dickens was: Utilitarianism is today's corporate capitalism, with numbed employees resembling the walking dead from the Village of the Damned. Yet despite the strict Utilitarianism propounded by the Bounderby/Gradgrind contingent, the production itself is starkly beautiful, at times almost expressionistic. The violence of the factory fires is a vision straight from hell.

1997: *Oliver Twist,* US; dir. Tony Bill; Richard Dreyfuss as Fagin; David O'Hara and Alex Trench as Oliver Twist; Elijah Wood as the Artful Dodger; Antoine Byrne as Nancy; Olivia Caffrey as Rose; Anthony Finnegan as Mr. Brownlow. Dickens purists beware: this movie has been Disneyfied. Its opening, a homage to Lean's 1948 film, suggests that the movie will follow tradition, but as soon as Oliver is born, the plot takes off in a new direction.

Trench's Oliver is not the typical passive, skinny waif, but a sturdy, dark-haired boy who seems to belong more in a movie like *Home Alone.* He rides into London in the back of a carriage, exhilarated and fearless. Then, just as he's about to steal some fruit (something the "real" Oliver would never do), he meets the Artful Dodger, whose role, in deference to the popular Elijah Wood, has been greatly expanded.

All this leads to Fagin. With stringy hair, watery eyes, and a beaky nose, Dreyfuss makes a credible Fagin. But he's different from his predecessors: he's younger, he doesn't lisp or call the boys "my dears," he likes Nancy and has nothing to do with her murder. You'd never know he's Jewish.

As the movie nears the end, the action accelerates: the discovery of Oliver's parentage, a climactic moment in the novel, is handily solved in a few minutes; Nancy's murder is dispatched like any other event, and Sikes barely registers the deed—in Dickens's novel, he wanders about London, haunted by the image of her eyes.

By the end of the film we are firmly ensconced in "The Wonderful World of Disney." Even Dickens isn't this sentimental. After leaving Fagin, Oliver returns to hug and thank the man who exploited, victimized, and stole from him. Fagin's eyes well up as he waves the boy off to a better life.

1998: *Great Expectations;* US; dir. Alfonso Cuaron; Ethan Hawke as Finn ("Pip"); Robert DeNiro as Lustig (Magwitch); Gwyneth Paltrow as Estella; Anne Bancroft as Nora Dinsmoor (Miss Havisham); Chris Cooper as Uncle Joe. This is more Jackie Collins than Charles Dickens. It portrays the lives of the rich and famous, and is filled with the trendy names of designers, galleries, restaurants. At first it's amusing to see how the nineteenth-century novel translates into a late-twentieth-century movie. The Dickensian novel translates into a thoroughly modern movie. The bleak English marshlands where Pip grows up are now Florida's Gulf Coast. Finn's sister doesn't bring him up by hand, but by exposing him to the "Grateful Dead." Satis House is a decaying Palm Beach mansion, and Miss Havisham is now the eccentric Nora Dinsmoor. She's camp and flamboyant (at one point she croons "Besame Mucho" to a child) whereas Miss Havisham is strange and otherworldly.

Ms. Dinsmoor, like Miss Havisham, trains her beautiful, young protégé to destroy men's hearts. This idea works in the gothic, dreamlike setting of Dickens's novel; here it seems cheap and weird. The convict, Lustig, is a death-row fugitive, convicted of a mob killing. The "vittles" Finn brings Lustig aren't mincemeat, brandy, and pork pie, but a Fluffernutter sandwich. Just as Pip moves to London, Finn moves to Yonkers, then, with success, to a loft in TriBeCa. An anonymous patron, it seems, has been helping him out.

Dickens's tale is more daring, for his hero lacks talent and ability. Pip's aspiration to be an idle gentleman points up the emptiness of desire. Viewers who yearn for more Dickens will be disappointed: there is no room in this movie for the Pocket family, Jaggers, Pumblechook, Wemmick, The Aged P., Biddy, or Orlick. If the movie is still about a young man and the unobtainable object of his desire, it's only "Light Expectations."

Bibliography

〽

BOOKS

Ackroyd, Peter. *Dickens*. New York and London: HarperCollins, 1990.

Altick, Richard D. *The Presence of the Present: Topics of the Day in the Victorian Novel*. Columbus: Ohio State University Press, 1991.

Aylmer, Felix. *Dickens Incognito*. London: Hart-Davis, 1959.

———. *The Drood Case*. New York: Barnes & Noble, 1965.

Baker, Richard Merriam. *The Drood Murder Case; Five Studies in Dickens' Edwin Drood*. Berkeley: University of California Press, 1951.

Blooms, Harold, ed. *Charles Dickens's David Copperfield*. New York: Chelsea House, 1987.

Brown, Julia Prewitt. *The Reader's Guide to the Nineteenth-Century English Novel*. New York: Macmillan; London: Collier Macmillan, 1985.

Butt, John, and Kathleen Tillotson. *Dickens at Work*. Fairlawn, N.J.: Essential Books, 1958.

Carey, John. *The Violent Effigy: A Study in Dickens' Imagination*. London: Faber and Faber, 1973.

Chesterton, G. K. *Charles Dickens: A Critical Study*. New York: Dodd, Mead and Co., 1907.

Collins, Phillip. *Dickens and Crime*. 3d ed. London: St. Martin's Press, 1994.

———, ed. *Charles Dickens: The Public Readings*. Oxford: The Clarendon Press, 1975.

————, ed. *Dickens Interviews and Recollections,* 2 vols. London: Macmillan, reprinted 1983.

Davis, Paul. *The Lives and Times of Ebenezer Scrooge.* New Haven, Conn.: Yale University Press, 1990.

Dickens, Cedric. *Dining with Dickens.* Somerset, U.K.: Elvendon Press, 1984.

————. *Drinking with Dickens.* New York: New Amsterdam Books, 1980.

Dickens, Sir Henry Fielding. *Memories of My Father.* New York: Duffield and Co., 1929.

Dickens, Mamie. *My Father As I Recall Him.* New York: Dutton, n.d.

Forster, John. *The Life of Charles Dickens.* 3 vols. London: Chapman & Hall, 1874.

Ford, George H. *Dickens and His Readers: Aspects of Novel Criticism Since 1836.* Princeton, N.J.: Princeton University Press, 1961.

———— and Lauriat Lane Jr., eds. The *Dickens Critics.* Ithaca, N.Y.: Cornell University Press.

Garis, Robert. *The Dickens Theatre: A Reassessment of the Novels.* Oxford, U.K.: Oxford University Press, 1965.

Gissing, George. *Charles Dickens: A Critical Study.* London: Gresham, 1904.

Hardy, Barbara. *Charles Dickens: The Writer and His Work.* Windsor, Berkshire, U.K.: Profile Books, 1983.

Hewitt, Edward, and W. F. Axton. *The Convivial Dickens: The Drinks of Dickens And His Times.* Athens: Ohio University Press, 1983.

House, Humphrey. *The Dickens World.* 2nd ed. London: Oxford University Press, 1961.

House, Madeline, Graham Storey, Kathleen Tillotson, and K. J. Fielding, eds. *The Letters of Charles Dickens.* 9 vols. to date. The Pilgrim Edition. Oxford, U.K.: The Clarendon Press, 1955.

Johnson, Edgar. *Charles Dickens: His Tragedy and Triumph.* 2 vols. New York: Simon and Schuster, 1952.

————, ed. *The Heart of Charles Dickens, as Revealed in His Letters to Angela Burdett-Coutts.* Boston: Little, Brown, 1952.

Kaplan, Fred. *Dickens and Mesmerism; The Hidden Springs of Fiction.* Princeton, N.J.: Princeton University Press, 1975.

————. *Dickens: A Biography.* New York: William Morrow and Co., 1988.

————. *Sacred Tears: Sentimentality in Victorian Fiction.* Princeton, N.J. Princeton University Press, 1987.

Kincaid, James R. *Dickens and the Rhetoric of Laughter.* Oxford, U.K.: Oxford University Press, 1971.

————. *Child-Loving: The Erotic Child in Victorian Culture.* New York and London: Routledge, 1992.

Leavis, F. R., and Q. D. Leavis. *Dickens the Novelist.* London: Chatto and Windus, 1970.

Marcus, Stephen. *Dickens: From Pickwick to Dombey.* London: Chatto and Windus, 1965.

————. *The Other Victorians: A Study of Sexuality and Pornography in Mid-Nineteenth Century England*. New York: Basic Books, 1966. Reprinted New York: Bantam Books, 1969.

Mayhew, Henry. *London Labour and the London Poor*. 4 vols. London: Griffin, Bohn, and Co., 1861. Reprinted New York: Dover Publications, 1968.

Miller, J. Hillis. *Charles Dickens: The World of His Novels*. Cambridge, Mass.: Harvard University Press, 1958.

McKenzie, Norman, and Jeanne McKenzie. *Dickens: A Life*. New York and Oxford, U.K.: Oxford University Press, 1979.

Mason, Michael. *The Making of Victorian Sexuality*. Oxford, U.K.: Oxford University Press, 1994.

McMaster, Juliet. *Dickens the Designer*. Totowa, N.J.: Barnes & Noble Books, 1987.

Newlin, George. *Everyone in Dickens*. 3 vols. Westport, Conn.: Greenwood Press, 1995.

Nisbet, Ada. *Dickens and Ellen Ternan*. With a foreword by Edmund Wilson. Berkeley: University of California Press, 1952.

Orwell, George. "Charles Dickens." In *Dickens, Dali, and Others: Studies in Popular Culture*. New York: Reynal & Hitchcock, 1946; paperback, *A Collection of Essays*. New York: Harcourt Brace Jovanovich, 1953.

Patten, R. L. *Dickens and His Publishers*. Oxford, U.K.: The Clarendon Press, 1978.

Pointer, Michael. *Charles Dickens on the Screen: The Film, Television, and Video Adaptations*. Lanham, Md.: Scarecrow Press, 1996.

Pool, Daniel. *What Jane Austin Ate and Charles Dickens Knew*. New York: Simon and Schuster, 1993.

Pope-Hennesey, Una. *Charles Dickens*. London: Chatto and Windus, 1945. Reprinted London: The Reprint Society, 1947.

Rose, Phyllis. *Parallel Lives: Five Victorian Marriages*. New York: Alfred A. Knopf, Inc., 1983; reprinted Vintage Books, 1984.

Schlicke, Paul. *Dickens and Popular Entertainment*. London: Allen & Unwin, 1985.

Slater, Michael, ed. *Dickens 1970: Centenary Essays*. London: Chapman & Hall, 1970.

————. *Dickens and Women*. London: J. M. Dent, 1983.

Slater, Michael, Nicholas Bentley, and Nina Burgis. *The Dickens Index*. Oxford, U.K.: Oxford University Press, 1988.

Stewart, Garret. *Dickens and the Trials of Imagination*. Cambridge, Mass.: Harvard University Press, 1965.

Stone, Harry, ed. *Charles Dickens' Uncollected Writings from* Household Words. 2 vols. Bloomington: Indiana University Press, 1968.

————. *Dickens and the Invisible World: Fairy Tales, Fantasy, and Novel-Making*. Bloomington: Indiana University Press, 1979.

————, ed. *Dickens's Working Notes for His Novels*. Chicago: University of Chicago Press, 1987.

Storey, Gladys. *Dickens and Daughter.* New York: Haskell House, 1971; originally published in London, 1939.

Sutherland, J. A. *Victorian Novelists and Publishers.* Chicago: University of Chicago Press, 1976.

Tomalin, Claire. *The Invisible Woman: The Story of Nelly Ternan and Charles Dickens.* New York: Alfred A. Knopf, 1991; reprinted Vintage, 1992.

Welsh, Alexander. *The City of Dickens.* Oxford, U.K.: The Clarendon Press, 1971.

———. *From Copyright to Copperfield: The Identity of Dickens.* Cambridge, Mass.: Harvard University Press, 1987.

Watts, Alan S. *Dickens at Gad's Hill.* Reading, Berkshire, U.K.: Cedric Dickens and Elvendon Press, 1989.

Wilson, Angus. *The World of Charles Dickens.* New York: Viking Press, 1970.

Wilson, Edmund. "The Two Scrooges." In *The Wound and the Bow: Seven Studies in Literature.* Boston: Houghton Mifflin Company, 1941.

PERIODICALS

The Dickensian. London: The Dickens Fellowship. 1905–.

Dickens Studies Annual: Essays in Victorian Fiction. Vols. 1–7 (1970–1978). Carbondale: Southern Illinois Press. Vols. 8–13 (1980–1985). New York: AMS Press, Inc.

Dickens Studies Newsletter. 1970–1983. Changed to *Dickens Quarterly.* Louisville, Ky.: The Dickens Society, 1984–.

Index

Page numbers in *italics* refer to illustrations.

approval needed by, 18, 305, 309, 310
autobiographical fragment of, 16, 25, 26, 81, 96
Boz as pen name of, 34, 39-42, 57, 157, 199, 200, 203, 345
bureaucracies as viewed by, 27, 79, 209
childhood factory work of, 22-27, 64, 82, 91-92, 96, 311-12
childhood of, 13-15, 16-21, 32, 80, 89, 186, 229
children of, 206, 307, 310-11, 355-57
class background of, 14, 23-24, 27, 92, 208
as comic writer, 169, 200, 290, 358
death of, 358, 370, 373-74
diary lost by, 314, *315*
dramatic readings by, 116, 168, 170, 185, 186, 187, 189, 232, 317-20, *318,* 345-47, 370-71
education of, 26, 27
energy of, 53, 76, 147, 170, 262-63, 265-67, 290, 358, 370-72
England and, 108-9, 368, 379
as freelance court reporter, 31, 32
health of, 18, 46, 89, 265-66, 319, 320, 345, 358, 370-73
income of, 116, 151, 158, 184, 317, 345-46, *348,* 352
as journalist, 30-31, 32-34, 36, 43, 46, 57
as law firm office boy, 29-30, 32
letters of, 45-47, 273, 377
London walks of, 30, 262-63, *264*
lowbrow amusements and, 68, 119
marriage troubles of, 265, 299-303, 304-7
as observer, 18, 21, 41
opium used by, 189
portraits and caricatures of, *30, 44, 77, 101, 231,* 266, *266, 319, 320, 347, 348, 356, 371,* 373, *380*
racism of, 209, 346
reading by, 5-6, 7-10, 19, 30
responsibility felt by, 15, 16, 114, 116, 312
sexuality of, 288, 291-92, 310
shorthand learned by, 30-31, *31,* 60
sociability of, 18, *77,* 147, 265, 267
as social critic, 79, 112, 199-200, 207-9, 250-51, 262, 276, 367-68
theater loved by, 18, 30, 31-32, 110-11, 170, 266, 267, 291, 324
theatrical temperament of, 14, 18, 30, *77,* 96-99, 310-11, 323-24

urban sketches by, 34, 36, 39-42, 76
wealth of, 151
work ethic of, 15, 33, 76
Dickens, Charles, novels of:
autobiographical elements in, 15, 124, 225, 229-31, 326, 339, 364, 366
critical responses to, 152, 185, 188, 200, 378-81
detail in, 21, 73
dialect in, 147
domestic harmony in, 305, 310
drinks in, 75
duality in, 154-56, 311, 323, 350, 352, 360
flat characters in, 108, 112, 113, 234, 311
fog in, 51, 241-42, 243, 254
food in, 69, 72-74, 81
illustrations of, 170, 171-73
inheritance in, 86, 87, 279, 333
later vs. earlier, 5, 167-68, 199-200, 203, 228, 309
length of, 184
literary lists in, 252-53
men in, 87, 131, 202, 353
merchandising inspired by, 68, 137, 139, 230
names in, 155, 237-39
oral imagery in, 73, 74, 124, 353
passivity of heroes in, 87, 131, 353
sales of, 49, 52-53, 67, 158, 184, 185, 317
sexuality in, 56, 83, 131-32, 216, 353
social class in, 207-9, 350-51, 354
social criticism in, 79, 112, 199-200, 207-9, 250-51, 262, 276, 367-68
theatricality of, 78, 100-101, 102-5, 168
water imagery in, 350, 353-54
women in, 99, 106, 108, 113, 131-32, 202, 204, 223-24, 229, 241, 247-49, 288, 311, 368, 380-81
writing methods of, 33, 50, 200, 201
Dickens, Charles, Jr. "Charley," 74, 186, 302, 318, 355
Dickens, Dora, 267
Dickens, Edward Bulwer-Lytton "Plorn," 302, 315, 355, 357
Dickens, Elizabeth Barrow, 13-15, 16-18, 22, 26, 29, 115, 229, 288-89, 311-12, 319
Dickens, Fanny, 17, 24, 37, 267
Dickens, Francis Jeffrey, 355, 357, *357*
Dickens, Frederick William, 18, 357
Dickens, Henry Fielding, 22, 228, 315, 316, *357,* 376

Fagin in the Condemned Cell (Cruik-
shank), 89, *172,* 173
Family Shakespeare (Bowdler), 213
Faraday, Michael, 109
Feeny, Mark, 233
Fellini, Federico, 117, 120
Ferenczi, Sandor, 231
Fielding, Henry, 19, 68, 228
Fields, James, 345
Fields, W. C., 173, 188
"Fifty Works of English (and American)
    Authors We Could Do Without"
    (Brophy, Levey and Osborne), 63
Finney, Albert, 190, *191*
Fitzgerald, Percy, 304
Flaubert, Gustave, 380
food:
    characters and, 73-74
    in Dickens's works, 69, 72-74, 81
    workhouses and, 94
Foote, Shelby, 9
Ford, George, 67, 365, 380
Forster, E. M., 2, 234
Forster, John, 15, 18, 38, *77,* 98, 115,
    126, 127, 137, 187, 212, 216, 228,
    229, 230, 232, 262, 265, 271, 300,
    302, 305, 307, 318, 319, 326, 360,
    371, 374, 376-77
French novels, 53, 54
Freud, Sigmund, 74, 87, 124, 127, 204,
    212, 214, 217, 220, 231, 247, 289,
    311, 352
Frith, W. P., 137, 139
"From Dickens to *Dallas* and *Dynasty*"
    (Engel), 69
Frozen Deep, The (Dickens and Collins),
    297, 298, 323

Gad's Hill Place, 267, 302, 314, 315, 318,
    356, 372, *373, 379*
Ganz, Lowell, 157-58
"Garden of the Forking Paths, The"
    (Borges), 364
Gay, Peter, 224, 229
Gay, Walter, 205, 206
gentleman, concept of, 27, 75, 227, 278,
    280, 331, 332-33, 335, 339
Gide, André, 3
Gielgud, John, 9
Gingrich, Newt, 163, 191, 294
    compared to Scrooge, 191, *191*
Gissing, George, 55, 159, 164
Goldsmith, Oliver, 19, 39
Gone With the Wind (Mitchell), 70
GOP Christmas Carol, A, (Roger), *191*

Gordon, Isabella, 211
Gordon Riots, 136-37
Gorey, Edward, *208*
Görlitz, Countess, 254
Graves, Robert, 228
Gravity's Rainbow (Pynchon), 172
Great Expectations (Dickens), 6, 7, 8, 10,
    26, 50, 92, 107, 132, 167, 170, 187,
    190, 239, 257, 326-44, 380
    Abel Magwitch, 20, 73, 132, 239, *327,*
        328, 329, 332, 333-36, 339, 340
    Bentley Drummle, 333, 336, 337, 340
    Biddy, 337
    David Copperfield vs., 326
    Estella, 132, 235, 330-31, 334, 335,
        336, 337-39, 340, 343, 344, *344*
    fairy-tale elements in, 335
    Herbert Pocket, 132, 334, 337, 340
    homoeroticism in, 132
    inheritance in, 333
    Joe Gargery, 132, 329, 330-32, 333,
        335, 337
    maturity of, 326
    Miss Havisham, 10, 288, 330-31, 332,
        333, 334, 335-36, 337, 339-40, 341-
        43, *342,* 344, 368
    Mr. Jaggers, 295, 333, 339
    Mrs. Joe Gargery, 10, 328-29, 332
    Mr. Wemmick, 10, 149, 257, 295
    Mr. Wopsle, 10, 170, 332, 333
    Orlick, 10, 331-32, 336, 340
    Pip, *see separate entry under* Pip
    Pumblechook, 10, 332
    social class in, 331, 332, 333
    two endings of, 337-39
Great Expectations (film), *342, 344*
Greedy (film), 158
Greenspan, Sydney, 205
Grey, Earl, 33-34
Grimaldi, Joseph, 76, 100
Grub Street, 151
gruel, 72, 73-74, 81, 94
Grundy, Mrs., 214, 303, 310
Guerard, Albert, 152
Guinness, Alec, *177*
Gurney, Ben, *347*

Hall, John, 33
Hall, William, 65
Halliday, Andrew, 140
Hamlet (Shakespeare), 87, 125, 154,
    170, 183, 185, 194, 213, 228
Handy, Bruce, 255
Hard Times, 17, 50, 119, 170, 208, 238,
    267, 268-71, 322, 342

King, Floyd, 325
King Lear (Shakespeare), 183, 205, 213
Kite as the Symbol of Erection, The (Ferenczi), 231
Kolle, Henry, 35

Laing (magistrate), 89-90
Lamert, James, 18, 22, 23, 24, 25
Lamert, Matthew, 18
Landseer, Edwin, 138
Lane, Margaret, 69
Larkin, Philip, 16
Lavoisier, Antoine-Laurent, 253
law, 32-33, 61, 64, 88-89, 90-91
  in *Bleak House*, 242-44, 246
  Dickens's career in, 29-30, 31, 32
  equity vs., 251
  futility of, 9, 31
  married women's rights and, 88
  see also Chancery, Court of
Lawrence, D. H., 202, 286, 379
Lazy Tour of Two Idle Apprentices (Dickens and Collins), 299-300
Leacock, Stephen, 237
Lean, David, 131, 173, 339, *342,* 344, *344*
Lear, Edward, 237, 252
Lear, Norman, 252
Leaves of Grass (Whitman), 152
Leavis, F. R., 271
Leigh, Mary Anne, 37
Lemon, Mark, 302
Leno, Jay, 192
lesbianism, 216, 231, 285-86, 289, 290, 381
  see also homoeroticism
Lesser, Wendy, 8
Levendusky, Philip, 189
Lever, Charles, 53
Levey, Michael, 63
Lewes, George Henry, 19, 254
Lewis, Donald, 188
Life and Adventures of Nicholas Nickleby, The, 100, 106-13, *111*
Life of Charles Dickens (Forster), 228, 376-77
Literature and Psychoanalysis, 74
Little Dorrit (Dickens), 3, 7, *36,* 39, 167, 170, 199, 216, 235, 267, 273, 274, 275-87, 290-91, 294
  Affery, 282
  Amy "Little Dorrit" Dorrit, 17, 131, 238, 277-78, 280-81, 282, 286, 287
  Arthur Clennam, 273, 276-77, 280-81, 282, 283, 284, 287

Barnacle family, 279, 280
  Circumlocution Office in, 279, 280, 283, 294
  claustrophobia of, 275, 284
  Daniel Doyce, 279, 287
  Fanny Dorrit, 17, 280
  Flintwinch, 237, 282
  Flora Finching, *36,* 170, 273, 274, 277, 281, 290, *290,* 291
  imprisonment as metaphor in, 286
  integrity of the self in, 285
  Miss Wade, 216, 276, 285-86, 288, 289, 381
  Mr. Casby, 281, 282
  Mr. Dorrit, 278, 280, 282, 284
  Mr. F's aunt, 291
  Mr. Meagles, 276, 285, 286
  Mr. Merdle, 280, 282
  Mr. Pancks, 279, 282, 291
  Mr. Plornish, 208
  Mr. Rugg, 284
  Mrs. Clennam, 276-77, 282
  Mrs. General, 238, 280
  Mrs. Gowan, 280
  Mrs. Plornish, 235
  Pet Meagles, 99, 281
  prison as metaphor in, 279-80
  Rigaud, 276, 282, 283
  Tattycoram (Harriet Beadle), 284-87
  time in, 281
  Tite Barnacle, 279
Little Dorrit (film), *290*
Little House on the Prairie, 131
Little Nell, 52, 73, 113, 119, 120-28, 131, 133, 134, 135, 172, 203, 230, 236, 257
  death of, 125-28
  as dream child, 121
  isolation of, 122
  passivity lacking in, 131
  purity of, 120, 121-22
Little Red Riding Hood, 120, 121-22
Liverpool Mercury, 307
Lodge, David, 7, 167-70
London:
  Dickensian, myth of, 257, *264*
  Dickens in, 16, 18, 262-63, 314
  Dickens's portrayals of, 79, 82, 83, 84, 108-9, *121,* 154, 157, 216, 224-25, 251, 257-61, 282
  fog in, 51, 241-42, 243, 254, 259
  in *Sketches by Boz*, 34, 36, 39-42, 76
  transition to modern metropolis of, 42, 65
Londonderry, Lord, 88

Wolfe, Tom, 233, 367
women, 310, 311
  in Dickens's works, 99, 106, 108, 113,
    131-32, 202, 204, 223-24, 229, 241,
    247-49, 288, 311, 368, 380-81
  novels and, 53-54
  rights of, 88, 209
  social roles of, 211, 377
Woodcock, George, 324
Woolf, Virginia, 74, 229, 349, 378, 379,
  380

Woollcott, Alexander, 2
Wordsworth, William, 16, 258
workhouses, 80, 81, 95, 161, 176, 182,
  191, 208, 209, 222, 294
World War I, 379
World War II, 380

Yardley, Jonathan, 366-69
Yates, Edmund, 266, 371

Zola, Émile, 380